Refiguring Mass Communication

THE HISTORY OF COMMUNICATION

Robert W. McChesney
and John C. Nerone, editors

*A list of books in the series
appears at the end of this book.*

Refiguring Mass Communication

A History

PETER SIMONSON

UNIVERSITY OF ILLINOIS PRESS

Urbana, Chicago, and Springfield

Library of Congress Cataloging-in-Publication Data
Simonson, Peter, 1962–
Refiguring mass communication : a history / Peter Simonson.
p.   cm. — (The history of communication)
Includes bibliographical references and index.
ISBN 978-0-252-03517-3 (cloth : alk. paper)
ISBN 978-0-252-07705-0 (pbk. : alk. paper)
1. Communication--Philosophy.
I. Title.
P90.S52   2010
302.201—dc22   2009034556

For Mac and Will,
inventive characters and filial friends

Contents

Acknowledgments

This book emerged from a number of places. Across them, I've accumulated happy debts to a small crowd of generous individuals. I'd like to thank them here, beginning with my teachers.

As an undergraduate and Masters student in religious studies at Stanford in the 1980s, I was introduced to the pragmatists by Henry S. Levinson, drawn into comparative religious thought by Lee Yearley, and mentored further by Diana Yoshikawa Paul. I'm very grateful to the three of them for opening new worlds to a kid from the provinces. As a doctoral student at the University of Iowa a decade later, I was fortunate to study intellectual history with three masters of the art, Ken Cmiel, John Durham Peters, and David Depew. In the Communication Studies Department there, I learned about media from Peters and Eric Rothenbuhler and rhetoric from John Lyne, Michael McGee, Bruce Gronbeck, and Kathleen Farrell. In American studies, Rich Horwitz gave me a lay of the land and introduced me to interviewing and fieldwork. My debts to Peters and the late, multiply great, Cmiel are especially significant.

Since graduate school, I have been blessed to work in three departments led by generous and good-humored chairs who materially advanced parts of this project: Beth Watkins at Allegheny College, John Lyne at the University of Pittsburgh, and Michele Jackson at the University of Colorado at Boulder. Across those institutions, a number of colleagues and friends helped through conversations or expressions of their support: Mike Keeley, Marilyn Bordwell Delaure, Pat Moynagh, Neil Arditi, Pete Lebar, and, especially, Dan Crozier and Roberta Levine at Allegheny; John Poulakos, Larry Glasco, Greg Crowley, Jonathan Sterne, Carrie Rentschler, and Adam Shear in Pittsburgh; and

Jerry Hauser, Lisa Kĕranen, John Ackerman, and Dick Jessor in Colorado. Pat Hanna provided crucial help and encouragement as I moved across those places, keeping me sane and focused. Doug Mitchell's support for the project made a big difference during its early stages. Emily Chivers, Kyle Kopnitsky, Carey Brezler, and Ethan Stoneman were all great undergraduate research assistants, while Lori Britt did yeowoman's work in checking citations, tracking down sources, and proofing a mountain of footnotes.

Other people have generously commented on drafts of chapters. Glenn Holland was a huge help when I first got going on Paul, and Father John Amankwah kindly assisted at a later stage. Carolyn Marvin and John Peters both read early drafts of several of the essays and offered crucial encouragement at the germinal stage of an offbeat project. Stephen Hartnett gave me copious feedback on Whitman and a key insight for the book as a whole. John H. Summers, Vanessa Merton, Craig Calhoun, John P. Jackson, Isaac Reed, and Harriet Zuckerman all read drafts of the Merton chapter, making suggestions or reflecting it back to me in important ways. Rosa Eberly responded to an early version of the fair essay and helped me think about the project more generally, while Alex Magoun shared his expertise on David Sarnoff. Paddy Scannell read a baggy, early draft of the entire manuscript and kindly found wheat among the abundant chaff. Bob Craig read the penultimate draft of the book and pushed me to sharpen my argument. Adriane Stewart read multiple versions of the whole manuscript and offered a bunch of insightful suggestions that ranged from macro-level arguments to micro-stylistics. My brother, John Simonson, deftly copyedited at the very late stages, when I was running low on fuel. My wife, Pam Talley, did the same at several earlier points.

I owe a special debt to the late Robert K. Merton, who gave me a great gift in granting interviews, corresponding by email, and making his papers available to me. His widow, Harriet Zuckerman, has continued that generosity, even when I've written things she might disagree with. Other members of Merton's family have also been kind in granting interviews or corresponding with me: his children, Stephanie, Vanessa, and Robert C. Merton; his granddaughter Kerstin Arusha; and his former in-laws Elizabeth Spragg and Charlotte Mae Weiler. A number of people who worked with or knew Merton have also graciously shared their memories and insights, including Thelma Anderson, Bernard Barber, Lotte Bailyn, Daniel Bell, Craig Calhoun, Jonathan Cole, Joan Doris Goldhamer, Herbert Gans, Thomas Gieryn, David Hollinger, Morton Hunt, Charles Kadushin, Elihu Katz, Kurt and Gladys Lang, Thelma McCormack, Rolf Meyersohn, John Shelton Reed, Alice Rossi, Alan Sica, David and Yole Sills, and Charles Wright.

At the University of Illinois Press, Kendra Boilieu pushed me to trim a 425-page manuscript down to a more athletic size and skillfully saw the project through from start to finish. John Nerone supported the book even before its weight-reduction program and offered kind words during a particularly bleak stretch for me. Nancy Albright deftly copyedited. I'd like to extend my special thanks to them.

I appreciate the opportunity to have tried out sections of the book orally in a number of formal settings: Allegheny College's Humanities Lecture Series, the Communication Department Honors Lecture at Muhlenberg College, and the Hitchcock Lecture for the University of Iowa's Department of Communication Studies; colloquia for a trio of departments at the University of Pittsburgh (Communication, History, and Religious Studies); and various talks for the Department of Communication and to the Institute for Behavioral Science at the University of Colorado at Boulder, the Department of Communication Studies at Northwestern University, the Department of Communication Arts and Sciences at Penn State University, and the Department of Communication at Texas A&M University. Very early iterations of Chapters 2 and 3 appeared in the *Journal of Media and Religion* and *Philosophy and Rhetoric*, respectively.

I would also like to acknowledge kind assistance by archivists at Columbia University's Rare Book and Manuscript Library, the University of Michigan's Bentley Historical Library, the Rockefeller Archive Center, the David Sarnoff Library, and Special Collections at Tulane University's Howard-Tilton Memorial Library.

Finally, through the entire process, my wife, Pam, and two boys, Mac and Will, have cheerfully lived with a husband and father who has had to "go work on the book," and provided welcome diversions. Meanwhile, my parents have offered steady support from afar. Thanks to all of them.

Refiguring Mass Communication

Introduction

Mass communication was a term invented, circulated, and partially abandoned in the twentieth century. This book takes that abandonment as an opportunity to revisit its history and prehistory and to refigure it as an idea and social form. It's a contrarian rehabilitation project that I offer as a contribution to both the history of communication and ongoing thinking about it. To those ends, I have written a series of stories organized around individuals, the ideas they gave voice to, and the forms of communication they engaged with. Embodied figures drive a reconsideration of the history and theory of mass communication that, I argue, is an important means of living together with others, local and distant. Narrating the story through individuals can help us work out our own engagements with this rich communicative form.

Though "mass communication" might mean a lot of different things, since appearing in the 1920s, it has come to be associated with a specific array of media technologies—radio, television, newspapers, motion pictures, broad circulation magazines, and related forms that fit what I call the *broadcast paradigm*: communication emanating from a more or less centralized source, reaching vast and geographically scattered audiences, and tied to what the sociologist Louis Wirth in 1948 referred to as "giant enterprises, dependent upon and designed to reach a mass audience."[1] Since the 1970s, though, technologies like narrowcast cable television, niche marketing, and the internet have carved up the old mass audiences; it has became less fashionable to use the term *mass* to refer to people; and the newer fields of media and cultural studies have arisen and often symbolically distanced themselves from the tradition of mass communications research. As a result, though it lives on in the names of departments, schools, and professional organizations, mass communication doesn't organize intellectual energies like it once did.

Instead of tossing the term into history's linguistic trash heap—arguably one manifestation of our broader throwaway culture—I want to argue that we should recycle it and will try to bend some of the creativity unleashed by cultural studies to refigure a sign from which it has often distanced itself. I believe that mass communication is an important idea, not just historically, but also morally, politically, spiritually, and aesthetically. I also believe that engaging with and talking about mass communication are important activities, which all of us do in one form or another. To begin to grasp the significance of the idea, though, we need to expand our thinking beyond dominant ways of conceiving the subject. We need to refigure mass communication.

This book seeks to do some refiguring—of mass communication as a historical concept, a rhetorical utterance, and a heterogeneous family of social forms. It advances those projects across six essays, each proceeding through an individual—a geographically emplaced, speech-producing body, not unlike yours and mine in those regards. As I've argued elsewhere, individuals can function as thread ends into the communicative fabrics of an era. Their lives provide starting points and pathways toward places and practices of communication in their times. In the case of bodies who left behind written texts, individuals guide us not just to common patterns, but also to *logoi*, communicated accounts of worlds they inhabited or imagined.[2]

I work with individuals not to revive any "great person" theory of history, or to return to the philosophical days of the self-determining autonomous subject, but rather in recognition of their status as socially contingent loci of thinking, action, and moral worth. Biography here links up to social and intellectual history and also to a kind of reflexive theoretical project that calls us to ask ourselves what forms of mass communication we participate in, how we go about doing so, and what accounts we produce in response and reflection upon them. The stories of the historical figures here open analogically toward yours and mine, both through variations on what Kenneth Burke called "perspective by incongruity," and through finding points of commonality with distant others. I hope this blend might find place in what John Nerone has called the "interdisciplinary and eclectic" field of communication history.[3]

Five historical characters play main roles in my refiguring—David Sarnoff, Paul of Tarsus, Walt Whitman, Charles Horton Cooley, and Robert K. Merton. Each developed a kind of vision for mass communication, expressed rhetorically and calling attention to particular species of the communicative genus. Visions are, in a broad sense, theories, ways of seeing composed from some reflective distance and offering general outlines or normatively hued standards. Visions take shape against ethical horizons, felt senses of good and bad, better and worse, that, as the philosopher Charles Taylor has argued, situate human selves inescapably within moral space.[4] They are informed by what might generically be termed "faiths"—webs of belief, trust, and hope anchored, as John Dewey wrote, "by vows to a particular way of life."[5] Faiths are marked by pieties, or ongoing commitments to Deweyan ways of life, and to the supernatural or secular gods that are served by them. In sketching the communicative visions of these historical characters, I hope to open up conversations about the history and rhetorical possibilities of mass communication theory and draw attention to important but overlooked social forms it has lighted upon.

David Sarnoff (1891–1971) launches the longer tale in Chapter 1, which revisits the rhetorical invention of mass communication in the 1920s. Then vice president of the Radio Corporation of America (RCA), Sarnoff operated within one powerful institutional center of the unorganized terminological vanguard that introduced the compound *mass communication* into American public discourse. From his strategic position, Sarnoff contributed to dominant understandings and institutional manifestations of mass communication in the United States and, through its influence, the world. Occupationally serving the gods of big business and capitalism, Sarnoff envisioned a centralized radio broadcasting system supported by advertising and moving toward monopoly. *Mass communication* was a term that helped legitimate this controversial project, and it was subsequently incorporated in scholarly discourses in the 1930s and '40s. I sketch this early history and then commence my rehabilitation project by turning toward repressed understandings and social species of mass communication that were left behind in the process. Chapter 1 also lays out a concept, *medium of invention*, that helps guide the stories I tell in the following four studies, organizing and drawing attention to communicative contexts that gave birth to visions different than Sarnoff's and others that came to dominate U.S. mass communication systems. If we are going to generate alternative forms of thought and action, we do well to attend to the contexts through which we invent them—and perhaps reinvent ourselves in the process.

In Chapter 2, I turn back first to an ancient alternative to Sarnoff's thinking, the radical Jewish universalism of Paul of Tarsus (?–ca. 62/64), played out through his rhetorical conceptualization of one of the world's more significant enduring forms of mass communication, the ritually enacted Body of Christ. Through his letters, Paul models the role of theorist as grassroots activist, communicating with communities he identifies with and offering critical, normatively hued accounts of their customary practices. Instead of the aspiring-to-be-universal gods of capitalism, Paul's vision served the God of Israel. I unpack the vision and rhetorical pathways leading toward it as a way to expand the historical frame and establish a base from which to consider subsequent moral universalisms that informed different accounts of mass communication.

After Paul, I return to the American context for the rest of my essays. Chapter 3 features Walt Whitman (of Brooklyn), the printer-and-journalist-turned-poet (1819–92), whose *Leaves of Grass* is a kind of bible for a polytheistic democracy that would be partly constituted through forms of mass communication. In Whitman's writings we see several species of mass communication, variably tied to the heterogeneous crowds he enjoyed sauntering through, and to embodiments of that crowd by compositely formed democratic individuals and the geographical spaces they inhabited. Coming of age in the print-and-transportation revolution of the first half of the nineteenth century, Whitman offers a full-throated democratic vision that lovingly embraces "the masses," and points us toward ways that poetry can function as a powerfully reorienting sort of theory.

From the activist-theorist Paul and poet-theorist Whitman, we turn in Chapter 4 toward the contemplative humanist Charles Horton Cooley (of Ann Arbor). A late-nineteenth-century Emersonian working as a sociologist in an early research university, Cooley (1864–1929) advances the story through his quest to figure the idea of "communication" itself and to develop a social theory around it. Though John Dewey and George Herbert Mead are usually credited with writing the foundational American work on communication, I show that Cooley got there first, and he developed the fullest social account of "communication" of any American writing in the pre–World War II era. I trace the development of Cooley's vision from early oratorical dreams, through studies in the political economy of transportation, and finally to "communication"—an idea that came to serve as an object of secular faith and led him to a spiritualized vision of mass communication tied to a sense of belonging to a cosmopolitan totality he termed *the Great Life*. Beyond his historical significance, Cooley points us toward craft ideals in the composition of theoretical texts and to links among local communicative scenes, first-person experience, and more general visions of moral possibility.

Following Cooley, I turn to Robert K. Merton (of Philadelphia and suburban Hastings, New York), one of the pioneering figures of mass communication research so named, and a skeptical antidote to Cooley's borderline mystical communication hope. Born Meyer Schkolnick to Jewish immigrants from Russia, Merton (1910–2003) left the faith of his Jewish forebears behind and put his trust instead in skeptical inquiry and the scientific ethos, operationalized in a professionally oriented mid-century sociology. He brought his skepticism to bear in analyzing manifestations of the media system Sarnoff had helped construct, investigating wartime propaganda, news, and celebrity in addition to other, less-recognized species of mass communication—including citizen mail and interracial housing projects. Unlike his predecessors, Merton resisted identifying with the mass communication he conceptualized, thus taking up critical, analytic, and objectivist distance of sorts that are common in scholarly writings about mass communication today. Merton is also important as a key player and conduit to the founding decade of mass communication research, the 1940s, and helps us see possibilities not pursued in the decades following.

The historical studies lead into the book's Afterword, which brings the rehabilitation project into the present with an account I give of an alternative form of mass communication today—the popular ritual of an American county fair. Building upon a longer-term participant observation, I interpret the fair as a communion of the democratic crowd and a ritual assembly of the local public that does important civic work and provides a model for analogous gatherings elsewhere. My account of the fair is inflected by a Whitmanesque sensibility but also gathers elements from Paul, Cooley, and Merton, all of whom I draw together and discuss in the final pages of the book. Built upon first-person experience, the Afterword also extends the discussion of individuals and rhetorical visions through quasi-performative means. I hope it might serve as a rhetorical prompt toward you—the places you inhabit, the forms of mass communication to be found there, and the accounts you might give of them. As Whitman wrote, "The reader will always have his or her part to do, just as much as I have mine."[6] Yours is the next chapter in the story.

Overall, the book is intended to extend pragmatist and Emersonian traditions of thinking about communication and rhetoric. On the contemporary scene, it has affinities with Steven Mailloux's neo-pragmatist project of "rhetorical hermeneutics," which he describes as "the use of rhetoric to practice theory by doing history."[7] I lean regularly on Rortyean redescription[8] as an interpretive technique—calling attention to overlooked forms of mass communication in texts that don't use that term and using religious vocabularies to describe secular and spiritual figures alike. The latter move, in turn, draws sustenance from a long line of thinkers in the tradition—from Emerson and Whitman through William James, Kenneth Burke, James W. Carey, Cornell West, and John Durham Peters—all of whom utilized religious texts, understandings, and vocabularies to make sense of communication and social life.[9] Religion has sometimes functioned as a symbolic "other" avoided by the mainstream of communication and media studies, though there are signs that's changing.[10] I turn to it here not as a subterranean evangelist or observant believer, but rather out of the conviction that religious traditions house some of the oldest, deepest, and most significant ideas about and forms of mass communication today. Contrary to the hopes of some secularists, religion will always be with us, both enabling and constraining human potential. As both students of communication and inhabitants of the world, believers and unbelievers would do well to find ways to mutually engage one another and the intellectual traditions each embodies and trails.

William James once wrote, "Faiths and utopias are the noblest exercise of human reason, and no one with a spark of reason in him will sit down fatalistically before the croaker's picture."[11] The post-Sarnoff essays here follow in something of that Jamesian spirit, sketching a series of unorthodox faiths that, with the exception of Merton's, fueled visions of mass communication that sometimes bordered on the utopian. For the most part, I do not critically deconstruct those visions, or subject them to what Peter Sloterdijk calls "the enlightenment critique of ideology and critique-through-unmasking whose polemical modes of procedure have become paradigmatic."[12] Instead, I deploy a hermeneutic reflected in Cooley's early meditation on Emerson, where he wrote, "It is the affirmative, not the negative, that is in the end important," and in reading we should estimate an author "by what he is rather than by what he is not."[13] To be sure, I exercise criticism and judgment across these essays. But generally I refrain from critique-through-unmasking and operate instead with a generally charitable interpretive stance, imperfectly guided by an ethic of retrieval and hopes of finding true or useful things in flawed texts, ideas, and people.

This book itself falls into the category of flawed texts, for, among other reasons, the limited variety of emplaced bodies whose visions it charts. It does take up texts composed by members of different *ethnoi*—two unorthodox Jews and two unorthodox Christians, members of ethnic minorities and majorities—and by at least one figure who seems to have sexually desired both men and women. But, what Carolyn Marvin would call "the bodies behind the texts" discussed here were all male. The makeup is a reflection on how the book grew. I had originally intended to do relatively light revisions of earlier studies, which I planned to make quick work of before turning to a book I was researching on Merton, who was then still living. Quick turned slow as I turned back to the studies and found new topics and questions emerging. I returned to primary sources and archives, added to the empirical base, read more about the main characters, and developed new schemas for organizing the stories. I was well beyond simply revising and was also committed at that point to the four figures I'd started with. The book is thus a series of masculine visions of mass communication, each differently enabled by supporting labor and conversation with women around them—gendered ecologies of invention that I sketch aspects of in my essays on Cooley and Merton. In retrospect, I wish I had thought more systematically when I first set off, though I also believe the figures chosen cover significant ground.

Beyond contributing to the history and ongoing thinking about mass communication, I hope these essays might add to a couple of other collective projects, too. One is the effort to reestablish connections between communication and transportation, and between rhetoric and place, both of which have historic precedents and contemporary advocates.[14] We need to do more on these fronts, though, in order to fill out the material and geographically situated dimensions of communication matrices that often include ethereal and promiscuously circulating aspects. My contribution consists of tracing ways in which the figures featured here moved through transportation networks that sometimes served as inventional media for their communicative visions. I also draw attention to select compositional places—the cities, neighborhoods, and rooms where bodies dictated, wrote, or typed texts that have come down to us. The result is a kind of contextually focused, communicative history of ideas about mass communication.

In making connections among places, texts, and ideas, I sometimes extend concepts drawn from the rhetorical tradition, one of the deep intellectual taproots for communication and media study in the twentieth and twenty-first centuries. In drawing upon rhetoric, and working from the Emersonian-pragmatist tradition as well, I am hoping to contribute to a humanist "third way" of communication study, which might complement social scientific approaches on the one hand and critical-cultural studies on the other. My essays link up with these other two general approaches, taking two social scientific characters as objects of study but doing so with some of the inventional impulses of cultural studies.

As part of that humanist third way, I have tried to write a scholarly book in a relatively accessible narrative style. I did so partly because I find most academic journal articles a little dreary, and I wanted to try to do something with a bit more pleasure in it. I also wanted to keep the essays open to any students or general readers who might pick up or be subjected to them. But perhaps the leading motive was my desire to address academics and academics-in-training in their less specialized, human selves—by presenting a series of stories about people and places, made possible by scholarship and academic specialization, but aspiring to leave them in footnotes or as partly unstated foundations beyond the pages. Specialization, linguistic and otherwise, is a powerful strategy, but it carries its human costs. Stylistically, I haven't succeeded in the way I'd wish, but I think it's important to put forth the effort and not let communication study drift too far from its civic and generalist roots in the ancient and modern eras. I hope others might go further than I have here.

As for audience, I've written these essays primarily for students and scholars interested in the history, theory, and cultural study of communication, but I welcome others as well. The chapter on Merton draws from unpublished material not yet available in archives and so has particular value for those interested in the history of sociology or twentieth-century intellectual life. My reading of Paul is intended to throw the apostle into different light than most Christians see him, and I have tried to write the chapter so that both believers and outsiders might take something from it. Early readers seem to like the Whitman chapter best, though the Afterword on the fair is perhaps the most generally accessible and is of potential interest to students of ritual, civil society, and political culture. Across the book, I also welcome free-thinking scholars and general readers with interests in intellectual biography, American studies, religion, ethics, and moral communities.

1

The Rhetorical Invention
of "Mass Communication"

"We're not one-at-a-timin'. We're *mass* communicatin'."
—Governor Pappy O'Daniel, entering radio station WEZY,
in Joel and Ethan Coen's *O Brother Where Art Thou?*

In September of 1927, a short article appeared in the *New York Times*. Titled "Radio Progress Passes in Review" and attributed to David Sarnoff, vice president of the Radio Corporation of America (RCA), the article confidently declared, "The two greatest contributions to the progress of mass communication in 1927 were the record of the National Broadcasting Company in the field of nation-wide service, and the passage of the Federal Radio Act which made order out of chaos in broadcast transmission." The article had come to the *Times* by way of RCA's active Information Bureau or public relations department. It was the first time the new compound term *mass communication* appeared in the paper.[1]

Discerning readers might have wondered about both the meaning of the new term and the links asserted among its progress, NBC, and the Federal Radio Act. Though we do not know who first spoke the phrase "mass communication," Sarnoff was among its earliest high-profile adopters, and his use of it in the *Times* was probably the first many readers had seen or heard. They had certainly heard of radio, though, which in 1927 was still very much an unsettled media technology. Beyond the nascent NBC, there were no national radio networks, little commercial advertising, and a great deal of variety available to adventurous souls who tuned in their receivers to capture faraway sounds in a romance of the air known as "DXing." Men and boys still built their own sets, though companies like RCA had carved out a market share by selling prefabricated radios to markets aggressively cultivated in America's growing consumer society. The company faced obstacles, though—ongoing patent rights battles, charges that it was a monopoly in need of regulation, and a perceived sense that demand for receivers would not continue to grow unless the quality of radio programming improved. The formation of NBC in 1926 was presented as one solution to this last obstacle, while also providing another potential revenue stream for the parent company. It further added another vertical layer to what some were already calling a "monopoly of the air," while also setting into motion the kind of chain broadcasting that some Americans found undemocratic and distasteful.[2] It would ultimately be up to RCA's lawyers to solve the patent rights issues and those who lobbied Congress to fend off government regulation, but there was also a battle to be fought for public opinion. The 1927 *Times* press release was one small salvo on this larger, more diffuse front.

Thus opens the rhetorical history of mass communications, a story I will flesh out further in the next few pages through the figure of Sarnoff. "Mass communication" emerged during the battle for the airwaves in the late 1920s. Though it took on different meanings and inflections, it helped legitimize RCA's efforts to establish NBC in a form that was favorable to its commercial interests. I tease out the rhetorical origins and early uses of "mass communication" through Sarnoff's speeches, newspaper articles, and RCA press releases in the 1920s and early '30s, and show how it served as a democratic-sounding alternative to charges of monopoly and industrial overreaching. While Sarnoff's institutional role in the development of American broadcasting is well known, his rhetorical role in disseminating the new compound "mass communication" is not. From those beginnings, I sketch the rise and fall of a scholarly discourse of mass communication, the founding of a scholarly field, and the partial abandonment of the term—a story that begins in the 1930s, and that partially revolves around the dominance of the broadcast paradigm for understanding mass communication. I pivot from history to the rhetorical reinvention of mass communication, turning toward genealogy to parse out social forms of mass communication cast from view by dominant forces of definition and institutional growth. Redefinition then gives way to the individuals who people the rest of the book, and whose lives and writings can help us recognize alternative, non-paradigmatic forms of mass communication. I close the chapter by introducing a concept that partly guides my discussion of them, *media of invention,* which I use to pick out elements of their social worlds that enable them to find ideas and generate published discourse about communication worth our attention.

Sarnoff's Invention

In the mid-1920s, Sarnoff, who after World War II became known as "The General," was perhaps RCA's most valuable human weapon for public relations. The facts of his life are hard to disentangle from his embellishments of it since all details were subsequently amplified by an institutionalized apparatus of semiofficial hagiography that rivaled a great dictator's. In 1927, Sarnoff was thirty-six, and he had risen from humble roots as a Yiddish-speaking Russian immigrant boy on New York's Lower East Side to his position as vice president and general manager of RCA. Born in a Jewish shtetl in 1891, he was part of the great wave of Russian-Jewish emigration that changed the face of the world in the twentieth century.[3] In 1900, he had traveled with his family by train and boat from Minsk to Libau, Liverpool, Montreal, Albany, and down the Hudson River to New York. The first-born son of observant Jews, he had been schooled in the prophets and Talmud by his great uncle, a rabbi. He learned in the traditional ways, through reading, recitation, and repetition of digestible segments of the texts. In the United States, he was thrown into a new world. By the age of ten, he was helping support the family by selling Yiddish newspapers to fellow Eastern European Jews on the streets of Hell's Kitchen. He apparently had a lovely voice, dulcet soprano, which was heard not only on the streets but also in the local synagogue, where he sang for services and weddings, and at the Educational Alliance on East Broadway, where he attended English classes religiously and participated successfully in its debating society. Debate and public speaking remained pleasures throughout his life, and he practiced them regularly in speeches he gave on behalf of RCA from the 1920s on, including some mobilizing the new compound term, "mass communication."[4]

Sarnoff was a public-relations natural, as adept at creating favorable images for RCA as he was for himself. As he became the public face of the corporation in the mid-1920s, those two projects converged.[5] He had begun work for the American Marconi wireless telegraphy company in 1906 and had to fend off widespread and sometimes vicious anti-Semitism to rise within it, from office boy to telegrapher and beyond. After RCA bought out Marconi, Sarnoff faced ethnically coded complaints that he was overly aggressive, accusations of "stock jobbing," and harassment by peers and competitors, but he managed to succeed on the basis of knowledge, intelligence, hard work, and a knack for establishing relationships with superiors who could protect and advance his career. These behind-the-scenes facts did not appear, however, in the long 1926 *Saturday Evening Post* profile that introduced Sarnoff to a national audience and created some of the pseudo-facts of a public image he filled out over the next four decades.

One of the most enduring legends concerned his role as the central on-land telegrapher for the *Titanic* disaster, working from the Marconi station installed at Wanamaker's department store in New York. "It happened that I was on duty at the Wanamaker station in New York and got the first message from the *Olympic*, 1,400 miles out at sea, that the *Titanic* had gone down," Sarnoff told the *Saturday Evening Post*'s Mary Margaret McBride, in a profile whose title, "Radio," rhetorically merged Sarnoff and the technology. "I gave the information to the press associations at once, and it was as if bedlam had been let loose. Telephones were whirring, extras were being cried, crowds were gathering around newspaper bulletin boards. The air was as disturbed as the earth. Everybody was trying to get and send messages. Some who owned sets had relatives or friends aboard the *Titanic* and they made frantic efforts to get and send messages. Finally, President Taft ordered all stations in the vicinity except ours closed down so that we might have no interference in the reception of official news." Sarnoff remained at his post, he said, listening for names of survivors. "Much of the time I sat with the earphones on my head and nothing coming in. It seemed as if the whole anxious world was attached to those phones during the seventy-two hours I crouched tense in that station." Afterward ("my first long tryst with the sea," he called it), he "was whisked in a taxicab to the old Astor House on lower Broadway and given a Turkish rub" (perhaps he was misremembering his trysts), only to return for another shift, "heartbreaking in its finality—a death knell to hope." He "passed the information on to a sorrowing world" and only then "when messages ceased to come in, fell down like a log at my place and slept the clock round."[6]

Though not exactly true, the story functioned as an ideal public relations fable for Sarnoff and RCA in 1926 and after. As David Lewis has noted, Wanamaker's would have been closed on a Sunday night when the *Titanic* sank. Any signals Sarnoff received at the small station, installed as a publicity gimmick for Marconi and Wanamaker's, would have been relayed through stronger telegraph stations on the coast. President Taft did not clear the air-waves for the station to operate. It is unlikely Sarnoff remained at his desk for three days, much less crouched there.[7] Yet facts be damned, the story was a good one. Here was Sarnoff, physically inseparable from the communications technology with which he was associated, the radio telegraph, hyper-responsibly run by two private commercial enterprises, and manned by a dutiful employee intent on serving the public. The main obstacle they faced was bedlam in the ether ("the air was as disturbed as the earth"), which was solved by a federal government with enough sense to clear the airwaves so that Sarnoff's own station could do its essential work. As a result, Sarnoff sat at the center of the communications universe while "the whole anxious world" listened intently to his tryst with the sea. Thus the Titanic story presented Sarnoff's vision for RCA and its new broadcasting network, if only the government would step in and clear the airwaves of the chatter of small broadcasters and amateurs disturbing the ether and preventing them from providing the heroic national service Sarnoff believed possible.

As a supporting term in Sarnoff's rhetoric, "mass communication" did complementary public relations work. It was a relatively favorable alternative to some of the other terms for describing what RCA was up to. AT&T, one of RCA's competitors, had used the term *toll broadcasting*, which foregrounded the fact that airtime was put up for sale to advertisers and other potential sponsors. When AT&T stepped out of the broadcasting business in 1926 and RCA started up its new National Broadcasting Company, the term *toll* was "quietly dropped from the vocabulary of broadcasting."[8] "Mass communication" was one of the terms that replaced it. Critics charged that through NBC, RCA was creating a system of chain broadcasting that would result in standardization and elimination of local competition and add a new dimension to the monopoly of the air. In response, Sarnoff could say that in fact RCA was in the business of bringing about mass communication, a term that in his usage carried a sense of unprecedented potential that could be given a populist ring when it was strategically appropriate.

Although "mass communication" was a term used for radio broadcasting of the sort Sarnoff envisioned and by which he would profit, its meaning could shift to suit the particular audiences he addressed. To elite groups like the Boston Chamber of Commerce and the Army War College, he called radio the first and only "universal system of one-way mass communication," which enabled "thousands, and even millions of people, simultaneously to respond to the same thought or to the same appeal in the instant that it is communicated." RCA was helping create "the nerve center of the world's body politic"—with enormous implications. To these business elites, he emphasized that this medium of mass communication provided "a direct and effective channel to the home" that offered "not only a vast audience but a means of conveying to that audience a business or industrial message."[9] It offered the same audience to military elites, though they would want to reach the home with a different set of messages. Broadcasting would play a huge role in future wars, Sarnoff told the War College. It was an instrument that could "sow consternation" behind enemy lines, create "favorable attitudes" in neutral countries, and bring about "mass education" at home.[10] To a London audience interested in propagating Esperanto, the hybrid international language invented by another Russian-born Jew drawn to universalist rhetoric, Sarnoff declared that broadcasting faced "no barrier of time nor space" and thus could prove "a powerful influence in the adoption of a universal auxiliary language."[11] As it turned out, the system Sarnoff helped create was far more effective at providing a direct channel into the home for propaganda during wartime and advertising at all times than it was at spreading Esperanto around the globe. But as a medium for reaching the many through "one-way mass communication," radio stoked the imaginations of marketers, propagandists, and social engineers alike.

Given the right opportunity, Sarnoff could strike more populist chords with his rhetoric. In a 1923 speech, for instance, he addressed the topic of "broadcasting to the masses," briefly envisioning a medium in which the masses might be heard and not simply reached. "The time will come when we will hear in our homes, in our public places, in our offices, the protests of a multitude in some foreign or oppressed land, crying out against the tyranny of their rules, or the acclamations of the public toward some great and beneficent leader," he intoned. "When this comes to pass, we have literally, for the first time, the voice of the people, and what this will bring in its wake challenges the imagination of a Wells or the prophetic powers of an Isaiah."[12]

The image of hearing the crowd through broadcasting did not last through the decade, and H.G. Wells turned out to hate radio, but Sarnoff's early rhetoric resonated with the universal dreams of Isaiah, the Hebrew prophet who had also inspired an earlier visionary of mass communication, Paul of Tarsus. "In days to come," Isaiah had prophesied, "the mountain of the Lord's house shall be established as the highest of the mountains, and shall be raised above the hills; all the nations shall stream to it . . . [and] out of Zion shall go forth instruction, and the word of the Lord from Jerusalem" (Isaiah 2:1–2). In retrospect, one might say that Sarnoff envisioned a radio system that displaced the Lord's mountain as the centralized site from which the broadcast word emanated, controlled by the few and blanketing the many with its sacred commands.

Sarnoff did not describe the new technology in these ancient Hebrew terms (though as an observant Jew he may have thought through them), but instead he tapped into the nation's democratic core mythos to frame his broadcast system as a service to the many. In a 1927 address at Syracuse University, condensed and distributed by the enterprising workers in the RCA Information Bureau, Sarnoff defended radio against Wells's charges that it was of abysmal cultural quality. "The fundamental basis of broadcasting is service to the many, not to the few," Sarnoff intoned. "Broadcasting cannot hope to thrill the intellectually overfed or the spiritually jaded, but it can and does fulfill a splendid destiny in the field of mass entertainment and edification."[13] There was rhetorical strength in numbers for Sarnoff, whose chain broadcasting system faced opposition from multiple quarters, including those educational, religious, and labor groups who operated their own stations and fought to preserve space on the wavelength to serve their own publics. Sarnoff could boast in 1928 that "a conservative estimate places the total of those who 'attended' the recent National Political Conventions . . . at 50,000,000," and though he could produce no hard evidence for that number, it added to the sense that the networks were serving the needs of a mass audience.[14] The Radio Act of 1927 had stipulated that broadcast licenses be allocated on the basis of who could best serve the "public interest, convenience, or necessity," which the newly established Federal Radio Commission clarified in 1929 by introducing the distinction between "general public service" and "propaganda" stations—the former being those that served the "entire listening public within the listening area of the station" and the latter those aligned with a particular group or point of view. As Robert McChesney writes, "ownership by any group not primarily motivated by profit automatically earmarked a station to the FRC as one with propaganda inclinations," which placed it in a disfavored category and conveniently bracketed the ways that advertising on commercial stations was a more obvious form of propaganda.[15] Sarnoff piggybacked on this ruling by asserting that, while "the instrumentalities of radio reception include some of the facilities necessary for selective entertainment and educational programs," broadcasting was, in fact, "essentially a system of mass communication" that offered "entertainment democratized to serve the greatest number, not the favored few." It was only "the fanatic fringe" who criticized this system, Sarnoff asserted. "[T]he vast majority of the people of the nation who form the great radio audience of the United States" were pleased with it, he said, and "support the great industrial structures upon which modern entertainment services are built."[16]

"Mass communication" thus was a term occasioned by the development of radio broadcasting, and that medium provided the original and paradigmatic referent for the new linguistic signifier. Sarnoff was point man in an unorganized terminological vanguard that circulated and defined the term for Americans in the 1920s and '30s. He used it in rhetorical discourses that helped legitimate RCA and NBC as commercial enterprises and which in turn contributed to the formation of a dominant model for what U.S. mass communication through radio would look like—national networks run by centralized private corporations with close ties to the federal government, aiming to turn a profit, while also making some effort to serve the public interest, as defined in noncommercial terms. From the 1920s on, RCA and other American companies and governmental agencies exported the model, as well, to Latin America and elsewhere.[17] In the United States, the broadcasting system set in motion in the late 1920s has both profited its shareholders handsomely and done a great deal to legitimate acquisitiveness, mass consumption, and the cultural stereotypes of the favored groups it has appealed to through its programming over the decades. The public interest component of that system has steadily eroded since the 1980s. To say the least, the broadcasting system could have done the country much better since its formation and early legitimation in the 1920s.[18]

Scholarly Uptakes and Resistances

Beyond advancing the dominant institutional discourse of mass communication, Sarnoff's rhetoric also advanced meanings that came to define scholarly uptake of the new term as well.[19] Radio broadcasting was the technology that occasioned the coinage and initial uptake of "mass communication," and that fact established the parameters for what the new term referred to. Instead of communication from, among, or with the masses, it meant communications broadcast outward, from one centralized point to the masses and great mass audiences. By the mid-1930s, scholars had begun to adopt the term in their publications, initially as a designation for radio and soon as a way to retroactively characterize older communications media as well. Herman Hettinger, an economist who studied radio and had conducted one of the first radio-listener studies in the United States, edited a 1935 volume on radio that observed how the technology had grown from a point-to-point technology to become "the greatest medium of mass communication to be developed since the printing press."[20] Later that year, the sociologist Malcolm Willey, who had written about newspapers, motion pictures, and other means of communication and transport, published perhaps the first significant conceptual piece on mass communication and the "new social environment" it created. In a small overlooked gem, Willey allowed that while "[s]ome degree of mass communication has always existed" (he mentioned physical assembly and the printed page), contemporary mass communication was unique in that "the size of the audience is almost unlimited, and physical assemblage is no longer essential." He called newspapers and periodicals, motion pictures, and radio "the basic three" media of mass communication and then went on to chart social problems and consequences linked to their status as commercial enterprises.[21] Over the next several years, a handful of other scholars picked up the idea of mass communication, which they also used to describe the press, films, and radio—a trio joined by the new technology of television a few years later.[22] All of these media fit easily into what might be called the broadcast paradigm of mass communication—centralized sources distributing identical content to huge, dispersed audiences.

As "mass communication" was emerging as a term to characterize new and older media alike, Princeton University historian Robert Albion made a case for the value of a "not particularly euphonious" label, "the communication revolution," to name and help historians envision "the movement which started with canals and turnpikes and still continues with radio and television." In a lovely and nuanced little 1932 piece in the *American Historical Review*, Albion took the idea of communication and used it for his own retroactive characterization, this one with huge implications for understanding the development of world societies since the early nineteenth century. He conceptualized communication as an emergent social phenomenon, tied to but also distinct from industrial and big business and playing itself out differently in the United States and Europe. Albion didn't refer to mass communication, though he did confess to having "recently 'listened in' and heard the actual words of the Japanese commander broadcasting from Mukden." He did, however, manage to group "canal, turnpike, steamboat, railroad, telegraph, submarine cable, telephone, automobile, wireless telegraph, airplane, and radio" under the umbrella heading of communication, thus keeping a material world of transportation on the conceptual map, even as radio broadcasting etherealized other regions of it.[23] In so doing, he maintained a linguistic usage and scholarly tradition of communications research centered on transport, which economists in the 1930s were still actively cultivating.[24]

That tradition had faded by the 1940s, the decade that saw "mass communication" become a more common scholarly term and a name for an institutionally organizing academic field. One important force behind this development was the Rockefeller Foundation's Communications Group, organized by funding officer John Marshall from 1939 to 1941 and bringing together leading scholars working in the area, including Harold Lasswell, Paul Lazarsfeld, and I. A. Richards. As Marshall told Richards in a letter, "In the last couple of years, it has been increasingly clear that most of my work has been in a field which for a lack of a better name I have come to call mass communications," a field he believed was "hampered for lack of a systematic and disciplined approach."[25] Lasswell, Lazarsfeld, Robert K. Merton, and others would, over the next decade, develop more disciplined and systematic approaches, though it was only after World War II that "mass communication" found real traction as a scholarly term and concept, helping supplant *propaganda* as favored organizing label.[26] Lasswell advanced it through a variety of publications, and Louis Wirth featured it in the title of his presidential address to the American Sociological Society in 1947, the same year that the United Nations Educational, Social, and Cultural Organization (UNESCO) made "the media of mass communication" a central component of its international vision. A year later, Lazarsfeld and Merton weighed in with a brilliant essay on the subject, and the University of Iowa's School of Journalism awarded the first two doctorates in mass communication, a program set in motion during the war by Wilbur Schramm, who in 1949 gave the field its first official collection of readings, *Mass Communications*, published from his new institutional perch atop the University of Illinois's Institute of Communications Research.[27]

Wirth's published Presidential Address gave the clearest and most complete scholarly conceptualization of mass communication to date, articulating a framework both adopted and rebutted in the postwar era. Appropriating rhetorical streams earlier channeled by Sarnoff and Albion, Wirth listed key qualities of the new, generally one-way communication systems and identified their functions in the new mass society that distinguished the modern world from its historical predecessors. "To the traditional ways of communication—rumor, gossip, personal contact, pulpit, school, and forum—we have added in our generation the mass media of communication, consisting of the radio, the motion pictures, and the press."[28] The modernizing world was a more secular one, and one where "the mass" had emerged as a social form that supplanted the small, stable communities of the past marked primarily by face-to-face interaction. Mass societies were characterized by great numbers of atomized, geographically dispersed, heterogeneous aggregates of individuals anonymous to one another, who were lacking common customs, institutions, or defined programs of action. Besides turning the populace into a kind of dispersed crowd, mass societies also favored the creation of organizations "of enormously increased size" across business, labor, government, and religion, including the "giant enterprises" of the new media "dependent upon, and designed to reach, a mass audience" (10). Unlike Sarnoff, Wirth warned of the tendency toward "monopolistic control" of these enterprises, but he agreed that "[i]n mass communication we have unlocked a new social force of as yet incalculable magnitude" (12). This new force could be harnessed for totalitarian ends, as the war had just shown, but it might also be used to bring the "so-called backward peoples . . . within the orbit of a world society resting upon world consensus," and "to supply the means for the furtherance of understanding across the borders of sovereign states" (13). Wirth's characterization provided one baseline understanding for the immediate postwar era.

In the late 1940s and '50s, "mass communication" was disseminated around the world as a term, an institutionalized array of social practices, and an academic field of study, meeting occasional points of resistance along the way. Operating in the Cold War political economy, Wilbur Schramm led other mass communication researchers both to adopt conceptualizations broadly resonant with Wirth's and to direct the new media to the "so-called backward peoples" of the world. Supported by U.S. government agencies and money, Schramm and others took communications research abroad, frequently as part of development or psychological-warfare efforts.[29] UNESCO tried to mobilize the term toward more emancipatory, multilateral ends, and in 1957 it established the field's first important international professional association, the International Association for Mass Communication Research (IAMCR).[30] Translated versions of mass communication named societies and research institutes in Japan, France, and elsewhere. New programs, classes, and textbooks sprung up in the United States, buoyed by a mix of intellectual interest, postwar prosperity, Cold War politics, and social hope. Scholarly accounts of mass communication developed around the globe, in complex interplay with theories of mass society and modernization and guided by critiques of Wirth's picture as well as extensions of it.[31] At the same time, the American sociologist Joseph Ford wondered whether there was such a thing as mass communication (a question he could answer at best with a provisional "yes").[32] Far more consequentially, the British literary critic and historian Raymond Williams forcefully took on the idea in the last chapter of his *Culture and Society* (1958), questioning "whether the idea of 'mass-communication' is a useful formula" for understanding modern media and critiquing it as implicated with the tendency to see audiences as masses to be manipulated.[33]

Led by Williams, cultural studies as it developed in the 1960s and '70s distanced itself from the term, idea, and academic field of mass communication. In Great Britain, American mass communications research came to be viewed as the positivistic, behaviorist, social scientific "other" against which the critical and cultural enterprise took shape.[34] That sentiment found purchase in the United States as well, where James Carey amplified Williams's remark that "the study of communications was deeply and disastrously deformed by being confidently named the study of 'mass-communication,'" and coupled it with comments from Stuart Hall as part of a broader effort to carve out space for a cultural alternative to the dominant social-scientific paradigm of mass communications research.[35] Though a handful of scholars would maintain footing in both, mass communication research and cultural studies operated as distinct sociointellectual formations. Mass communication lay squarely in the domain of the former, while the latter embraced "culture" and "media" as more powerful and less politically encumbered organizing terms and concepts. By the 1990s, mass communication researchers (including Schramm's important student, Steven Chaffee) were themselves beginning to abandon the term on the grounds that it was an obsolete category in an age of new media technologies, niche marketing, narrowcasting, and multichannel households.[36] Mass communication lives on in the names of journals, professional associations, and academic departments, but it lacks the rhetorical and intellectual charge it once had when it captured the energies and political imaginations of some of the great minds of an era.

Activating Repressed Senses

At this perhaps-late date in its social and intellectual history, I would like to take another look at the idea of mass communication and consider some of its meanings and social forms occluded from view by dominant intellectual and institutional forces. Before we toss the term in the rubbish heap or allow it to die on the vine from neglect, let's think about other ways to use it and things it might mean besides the processes tied to the media and mass advertising campaigns of the high years of mass communication from the 1930s through the 1970s. Pivoting back to Sarnoff's invention, we might start by remembering that communications broadcast outward from a centralized source to the masses is only one possible meaning among several. We might also consider crowds, strikes, parades, pilgrimages, and other popular rituals; mass letter-writing; gossip networks; greeting cards; and oratory, among the forms that might be characterized as communication from, among, or with the masses. And if we wanted to get more creative while also returning to the roots of the field, we would also remember that mass transport introduces many more media of mass communication, including subways, railroads, public buses, busy roads, ferries, and, in earlier eras, ships, canal systems, wagon trains, and other means of collective movement. We would also add other traditional entities that roughly fit the broadcast paradigm, but have rarely been considered forms of mass communication—monuments, cathedrals, the empire's flag, and the king's body, for instance. Many of these are social forms with real communicative significance, yet almost all of them have fallen outside the main ken of mass communication study. I'd like to draw creative energies from cultural studies back and mobilize the rhetorical method of definition to draw a different conceptual map, which might, in turn, guide a different kind of field.[37]

Etymology points us toward a more systematic consideration of repressed meanings and referents for a specifically mass communication. According to the *Oxford English Dictionary*, *mass* derives from two distinct genealogical streams, which feed a family of meanings: the Latin *missa* (cult gathering, religious service), and the Greek *maza* (barleycake). Missa, which the Roman Catholic Church decreed the only officially sanctioned cult gathering, entered medieval English as *mæsse* (and Spanish as *misa*, Italian as *messa*, French as *messe*, and Portuguese as *messe*). What we know today as the Catholic Mass is one of the oldest persistent forms of mass communication in the West—and one for which Paul of Tarsus did important conceptual work, as I discuss in the next chapter. On occasion, the Mass grew into great festivals and feast days to which it lent its name: Lammas (the festival of the harvest's first bread), Childermas (the commemoration of the slaughter of Bethlehem's children by order of King Herod of Judea, a ritualized symbol of cultural separation from the Jewish trunk, now known as Holy Innocents Day), and Christmas (the great festival of the Messiah). This linguistic lineage bore the first fruits of compound word combinations, among them mass-bell (the sacred ringing of the bell during Mass), mass-song (the singing or celebration of the Mass), mass-kiss (the kiss of peace among worshippers), and mass-gospeller (a Protestant who hypocritically attends Mass)—all of which await study by some innovative mass communication researcher.

Meanwhile, the second genealogical stream was born from the Greek *maza*, a cognate of *massein*, to knead, the work done to turn flour and liquid into dough that would become the barleycake. The lumplike and unfinished qualities of the dough also characterized potter's clay, called a *massa*, as in the Vulgate translation of Paul's image in Romans: "Has the potter no right over the clay, to make out of the same lump one object for special use and another for ordinary use?" (9:21). Augustine amplified the image to portray *massa damnata* and *massa perditionis*—the condemned, damned, spiritually destroyed mass that made up most of humankind save those chosen few God had destined for salvation.[38] In the sixteenth century, the word took on the additional sense of a large size or quantity, which was extended to describe human beings in the eighteenth and particularly nineteenth centuries—from George Berkeley's "whole mass of mankind" (1713), to Sir Walter's Scott's "close masses of the clans" in *Waverly* (1814), to the American "mass meetings" that found their way into Noah Webster's 1847 dictionary. Beyond totality, the masses also came to reference the unwashed many, a variation on Augustine's damned from the point of view of the elites who gazed upon them—the "masses" as opposed to the "classes," in Gladstone's influential 1886 antithesis. Though generally treated with contempt by elites, the masses found themselves the heroes of Marx's and Engels's revolutionary social theory in the 1840s and Walt Whitman's democratic poetry of the 1850s.[39] It was typically a less heroic view of the masses that made its way into the field known as mass communications research, and by the 1950s it was perhaps not a view of the masses at all.[40]

Taking this opportunity to join these twin inventional streams, I'll identify five senses of *mass*, which map onto five intermingling species of mass communication, the first based on the archaic meaning—*barleycake (maza) communication*, or the communication that occurs around the sharing of bread, whose prior kneading as dough points to symbolic work performed in successful rituals of shared food and table. Maza communication is the communication involved in common consumption of sanctified or secular food. This is the tradition of the banquet, wedding and victory feasts, and Thanksgiving dinners for the poor at churches.[41] It can involve families, friends, and new acquaintances gathered; enemies sharing a meal; or strangers eating in one another's presence. It is a social form that has traditionally carried great moral, spiritual, aesthetic, and political significance whose communicative dimensions are worth greater attention. (Surely it's worth at least informal organizational status in one of the communication associations: The Barley Cake Caucus.) I might call this "mass communication 1," for those scoring at home.

The second sense takes us to *religious or liturgical communication*. Arising from Rome's pagan days, appropriated by the monotheistic state-sponsored church, here is mass communication as Mass communication writ large— communion, liturgy, and similar celebrations of sectarian and civil faiths, with their own gods, cults, and devotional rituals. This species intersects with James Carey's ritual view of communication, which, we can also say, points to an ancient species of mass communication ("mass communication 2").[42]

Third is *large-scale, large-quantity, or abundant communications*. This is the sense that has dominated understanding and research in the twentieth century, but only incompletely. Abundance has been trumped by scale, so that mass communication is primarily that which involves great numbers of people. But even that category-of-the-multitude has been followed through only in part, for we can distinguish among several subclasses based on the relative proximity of the multitudes in space and time. A fourfold table illustrates the possibilities, categorized in terms of the locations of the multitudes involved.[43]

a) Same Time/Same Place
b) Same Time/Different Places
c) Different Times/Same Place
d) Different Times/Different Places

The first combination encompasses large-scale live assembly (crowds). The second represents broadcasting, daily newspapers, and other traditionally recognized species of mass communication. The third includes place-based commemorations or pilgrimages that have occurred over generations. The last combination covers a range of phenomena, from books, motion pictures, and recorded music whose popularity stands over time, to the geographically dispersed rituals of civil and sectarian faiths that persist over generations. To these we might add abundant communications, as in the number of texts, performances, or other discrete communications that go into a broader campaign; the amount of material shipped through a transportation channel; or the copious details that are mobilized to move, inform, or delight an audience in a particular rhetorical appeal—a style famously deployed in Whitman's poetry, as I discuss in Chapter 3 ("mass communication 3, subtypes a–d").

The fourth sense leads us to communication *with, among, from,* or *to the masses,* or *hoi polloi.* Here we adopt the traditional distinction between elite and mass, which is a relative categorization that depends on the particular measure of capital (economic, social, or cultural) deemed relevant for the purposes at hand. *Hoi polloi communication* is that which involves the lower and middle classes, whether they are determined by income, wealth, occupation, social status, or cultural tastes. By definition, *hoi polloi communication* is that in which the majority of a population participates, and which therefore carries a prima facie social and—from democratic and certain religious perspectives—political and moral significance ("mass communication 4").

Finally, there is mass communication that *involves a social totality.* The totality ranges in size, depending on the group or social collective in question. On one end of the spectrum is the universe of all creation through time immemorial, called out in the prayers and rituals of universalistic faiths; on the other end is the totality of introjected personalities that inhabit the psyche of a single human being. "Involving" the social totality can mean addressing them all, representing them all, or giving all of them free play to participate and communicate themselves. Like hoi polloi communication, communication of the totality is a normatively freighted category, and it often functions more as regulative ideal than materialized social fact. Communication involving the social totality is one component of moral universalism, but it is equally at home in schemes of domination and total control as well ("mass communication 5").

Thus we have five species of a rich genus, mass communication, whose social contours and moral significance have been occluded by the rhetorical and institutional processes Sarnoff helped set in motion. These species are not mutually exclusive, and any particular event or process may display qualities of several—for instance, religious gatherings of the many (hoi polloi) that involve vast numbers of people, communicative plenitude, and the sharing of food, a "multiply massed" event like the county fair I describe in this book's Afterword. Like other events and processes that display elements of multiple species, it should be placed high on the ontological ladder of mass communication, as understood through this alternative paradigm generated through genealogy.

Refiguring Mass Communication: A Rhetorical History

Rhetorical definition of genus and species might open imaginative space, but it won't take us far toward considering visions of mass communication different from Sarnoff's. For that project, I propose that we turn to four other individuals and their own figurings about mass communication, now broadly conceived. Sarnoff sets the stage for other stories, having generated a vision of radio broadcasting that served the gods of big business (though he remained personally faithful to the God of his Jewish foreparents). His rhetoric was spoken with an immigrant's accent, though print sanitized its particularistic sounds, while modern public-relations technique insured that it was disseminated widely. His occupational position as vice president of RCA provided the dominant inventional context for his rhetorical vision, and he served as apologist and advocate for the company's corporate mission, organizationally centered in New York City but aspiring to extend itself worldwide.

Paul of Tarsus, Walt Whitman, Charles Cooley, and Robert Merton operated from different places, geographic and cultural, where they struck up different stances toward different forms of mass communication and formulated rhetorical visions thereof. As I have argued elsewhere, individuals like these four serve multiple historiographical roles—as thread ends, agents, representative figures, models, and conversationalists, among others. As thread ends, their lives lead into the fabrics of social practices, cultural understandings, institutional formations, geographic locations, and broader historical events of their eras. As agents, they are seen to have performed actions that were in some sense consequential from the social locations they inhabited. As representative figures, they symbolically stand as condensations of ideas, orientations, activities, institutional formations, and broader identities they participate in. As models, they serve as guides to our own productions of self or action, subjects for what the classical rhetoricians called *imitatio*, or that creative appropriation of past style or substance for present purposes, poorly captured by the English word *imitation*.[44] As conversationalists, they enter contemporary intellectual discussions through texts preserved over time that find their way into our discourse and thought, challenging, extending, or marking off particular positions worth noting and keeping alive across generations.[45]

In the studies that follow, the four featured figures variably play all of these roles. They are thread ends to species of mass communication, agents generating texts, representatives of faiths and ways of being a theorist, models I occasionally channel (consciously or through absorption), and authors I am drawing into the larger conversation about mass communication. They offer alternatives to Sarnoff's faith in capitalism and big business, and they inhabit roles different than corporate apologist. They compose and communicate visions through different rhetorical means than Sarnoff's public-relations driven speeches and press releases and pick out forms of mass communication other than commercial network radio and similar industrially driven institutional processes. The four studies proceed through comparison and accumulation, each one charting inventional contexts that fed particular visions, normative horizons against which they took shape, and species of mass communication conceptualized in the process. I follow in the spirit of C. Wright Mills, who argued that sociological orientations arise in "the interplay of . . . biography and history," extending his insight to orientations toward specific forms of mass communication, as well.[46] I do so both to write a certain kind of intellectual history and to induce some reflexive awareness about our own orientations and conditions of intellectual production as well, impulses that come together in the Afterword on the county fair, intended both to depict an important traditional form of mass communication and to prompt us all to consider our own dwelling places and communicative environments.

One vehicle for accomplishing both historical and theoretical/reflexive ends is a concept that emerged from my research, as I investigated contexts in which ideas were generated and expressed. *Medium of invention* (or *inventional medium*) is a heuristic concept I use to identify enabling contexts and communicative forms through which rhetorical invention occurs. By rhetorical invention (Greek: *heurein*; Latin: *inventio*), I mean the process of (a) finding, creating, or giving discursive figure to (b) topics, ideas, arguments, phrases, and stylistic devices that (c) make their way into a published text or other formal discourse. In the sense that I am using it, invention extends from the earliest stages of coming across topics and ideas, through moving toward composition by engaging in more purposively focused brainstorming, and on to finding particular phrasings during advanced stages of the creative process. I use the word *medium* in three overlapping senses—as communicative mode (for example, speaking, writing, typing), artistic material (as in the medium in which an artist works), and dwelling place (as in the solution in which microorganisms live). Media of invention are the material, social, and cultural places (loci) in and through which subsequently addressed discourse is generated. If part of the aim is to generate alternate visions of mass communication, attending to the process of invention and the settings it occurs is highly relevant.

A full theoretical account of the concept is beyond the scope of this project, but I will suggest that media of invention fall into three broad classes. *Material media* begin with the body, that one persistent medium for all living creatures. They continue out to that inventing body's physical and geographical location, the technologies it makes use of, and the regime of productive labor that frees and constrains its inventive capacities. *Social media* include communicative interactions and relationships with other persons, near or physically distant, real or imagined, that feed the inventive process. They also include the institutional matrices, roles, and structured routines that, like material media, enable and constrain invention. *Cultural media* in turn refer to practices, techniques, symbols, and patterned meanings carried through traditions and emergent cultural formations. These three classes overlap. If we were to consider walking in the woods talking with a valued conversation partner, for instance, as a medium through which ideas are generated, we would need to consider its material components (bodies engaged in movement and speech, preserved forest, leisure), its social components (a particular friendship, interpersonal conversation), and its cultural components (connected to both enacted understandings about conversation in general and the topics under consideration in particular). Traversing political economies of unequally distributed resources and limitations, the three classes broadly mark off the complex totality of the human environment in which rhetorical invention occurs. Any given text is generated through multiple and varied inventional media, which shape both thinking and the physical acts of textual composition. My treatment in these studies is necessarily highly selective, and for each thinker I highlight only a handful of their many media of invention.

While the idea of inventional media points to a complex ecological totality, only through particular cases does it become an illuminating heuristic for bringing out specific contextual components of the inventional process. In each of the following chapters, I highlight the physical places and geographies inhabited by an inventional body, the modes of movement and transportation that help constitute the inventional self, and the compositional technologies it employs. Among the specific media I draw attention to are traveling the open road, walking about town, sitting in an office, lecturing in a smoke-filled room, inhabiting a body drinking single-malt Scotch, conversing with a colleague, taking part in a long friendship, memorizing scripture, composing book reviews for scholarly journals, riding a ferry, preparing for classroom discussion, writing in notebooks, typing letters, observing children at home with a spouse, and attending a county fair. The emplaced body is the context for all human invention, though its corporeal sensations are only sometimes salient in structuring the outcome of any inventional process. Coffee, liquor, a shared meal, the felt stillness of early morning, chronic illness—all can provide psychic structure and sensations that shape the outcome of the inventional process.

Bodies, places, and physical movement (transport) are persistent topics (topoi) I return to in charting these visions of mass communication. By *topoi* (singular *topos*, Latin *loci*) I mean categorical starting points for interpretation and rhetorical invention. Traditionally understood, topoi are conceptual "places" from which to think, organize inquiry, and generate accounts, and they fall into the class of what I'm calling *cultural media of invention*. Richard McKeon expanded their traditional meaning, however, and called topoi "places of things, thoughts, actions, and words," which nicely captures my aspirations for the work done by the inventional media of bodies, geographical places, and transport.[47] Calling attention to them serves both to materialize the rhetorical production of ideas and selves and to draw connections among bodies and their thoughts, actions, and words. Roads, waterways, rails, and airline routes are media through which individual bodies and masses flow, circulating and communicating along the way. They have often served as sites for contemplation and conversation and for means of stretching out social and geographic imaginations. Far-flung mobilities underwrote the visions generated by the figures in my story, adding spatial dimensions to the moral universalisms they articulated. By making them explicit topoi in this book, I also hope to make us more mindful of relationships between communication and transportation and to help ease the latter back into communication and media studies. In the last seventy years, the mass medium of automobiles has done more to rearrange our landscapes than that of television, yet we in communication studies have paid little to no concerted attention.

David Sarnoff's vision of mass communication developed just as the automobile was beginning to rearrange the communicative life of the nation and world. Other visions have emerged from very different cultural, social, and material environments. If we want to understand the genus better, begin to appreciate its variety of forms, and generate different rhetorical accounts of its moral possibilities, we need to look toward other figures and historical moments. Turning back toward ancient roots of the communicative form, we'll move ahead toward alternatives by way of Paul of Tarsus, who bent the universal dreams of the Hebrew forefathers to different purposes than RCA's Sarnoff. Through a letter composed nearly two thousand years ago, Paul envisioned a face-to-face ritual in such a way that it could become the basis for one of the oldest, globally enduring forms of mass communication. To his vision we now turn.

2

Paul's Communicative Figure

> " . . . and greet his mother—a mother to me also. Greet
> Asnyncritus, Phlegon, Hermes, Patrobas, Hermas, and the
> brothers and sisters who are with them. Greet Philologus,
> Julia, Nereus and his sister, and Olympus . . ."
> —Paul, Epistle to the Romans (16:13–15)

Paul of Tarsus was a man of the city who traveled about. Born around the same time as Jesus, Paul was reared in the heterogeneous crossroads city of Tarsus, on the southeast coast of present-day Turkey. Over the course of his lifetime, he traveled thousands of miles across the seas and roads of the region as part of an ancient long-distance transportation system ruled by the force of the Roman Empire. In contrast to the rural Palestinian Jews with whom Jesus grew up, Paul was an urban Cilician. Like other Jews raised in the Mediterranean Diaspora, Paul operated on an everyday basis in Greek, not the Hebrew of his forefathers or the related language of Aramaic spoken in Palestine. He may have known Hebrew scripture directly, but he certainly knew it in its Greek translation, which he cited from memory when making a case to others. He knew Greek ways of thought and translated them into a Jewish cultural idiom. He was separated linguistically and geographically from the main trunk of Judaism, but he also lived distant from the host culture of Tarsus. Among pagans and polytheists, he was a monotheistic Jew. Thus Paul was doubly the outsider.

Though uncontested facts about his life are few and far between, we can say there was a certain mobility to both Paul's character and his body. He grew up privileged enough to be educated, in a family that may have included Roman citizens, a relatively rare legal status for Jews at the time. After joining the Pharisees, a Jewish religious group particularly learned in the law and zealous about keeping it, Paul moved to Palestine. As a Pharisee devoted to orthodoxy and right practice, he chastised those who departed from such and persecuted those who followed the heretical teachings of the charismatic Jesus.

From this position, however, he leaped to the other side, joined the schismatic sect, and took on a life of itinerant physical hardship, low-status subsistence labor, conflict, lashings, and imprisonment. Though he began his life with privilege and centuries later became a central and canonized figure in the Christian tradition, during most of his lifetime Paul was an utterly marginal man outside the confines of a small splinter sect of first-century Judaism.

Paul is thus a fine figure to anchor this unorthodox history, and I will argue that he was one of the world's great theorists and initiators of mass communication. In letters that are the oldest preserved texts of the Christian New Testament, he played the role of theorist in the classic Greek sense of that term, seeing from a distance and offering up interpretations of social practice that helped shape its meaning for participants. Thanks to missionary activity and empire, Paul's letters took on world-historical significance. His theoretical work was interpretive, normative, and rhetorical, generated from the position of an active participant in the Jesus movement of the first century of the Common Era (c.e.). Through discourse addressed to audiences both particular and universal, he offered a vision of customary practice and advocated it as regulative. His letters helped call into social existence one of the oldest and most influential media of mass communication, the Body of Christ. Paul was the ancient world's great medium theorist, and the space- and time-binding Body of Christ was his social object.

I take pains to say that Paul's letters helped call the Body of Christ into *social* existence, by which I mean existence in the practices and shared beliefs of human beings. Christians believe the Body of Christ exists outside human life. Atheists and other outsiders might say it exists *only* in the human realm, and there perhaps as nothing but a fiction, ideological figment, or collective fixation. I bracket this dispute and focus upon what Christians, atheists, and everyone else might together recognize as the sociological and human-communicative elements of the phenomenon.

In this chapter, aided by exquisite scholarship by specialists on Paul, I aim to reread his First Letter to the Corinthians as a classic, originating text in the intellectual and social history of mass communication. Composed by a Jew who understood himself to be working within the Jewish tradition, it came to be one of the canonical texts of a new religion Paul himself had no intention of founding. Generated by a particular enfleshed man, addressed to a particular assembled group, and commenting upon their particular problems, it grew into one of the textual anchors for a global faith, whose images and impulses spilled over to influence innumerable social phenomena in the West and beyond. On the way to sketching his vision of mass communication and aided by experts on the apostle, I reconstruct elements of his communicative world, including selected inventional media and modes of mobility that led into his letter. Outlining the contours of a textually expressed image and the historical bodies behind it, I show how a letter sent to members of Paul's community in Corinth functions as both social description and normative theory, calling its audience to recognize the Body of Christ as a medium for communication among themselves, paradigmatically enacted through eating blessed bread together. Paul's vision was further developed by subsequent generations of believers, who transformed the Body of Christ into a universal, even cosmic medium of mass communication among all the faithful, on earth and in heaven. Officially sanctioned and republished in the Christian New Testament, the Pauline understanding of the Body of Christ became canonical. The form of mass communication he envisioned became a persistent social fact in the world, indexing different moral hopes than do most contemporary mass media.

The Invention of Paul

Though one of the most influential figures in human history, Paul remains something of a mystery. The biographical facts of his life are relatively few. We have seven letters that scholars agree were genuinely his, but they tell us virtually nothing about Paul's upbringing and little about his life. Acts of the Apostles 8–28 gives a fuller picture, but its historical reliability is questionable; its author, traditionally known as Luke, embellished and added elements of good storytelling and mythos to the lives of the figures he chronicled and celebrated. Nonetheless, Paul seems to have grown up in Tarsus, was raised by an observant Jewish family, and acquired a rigorous education in the Septuagint, the Greek translation of the Hebrew scriptures. After becoming a member of the Pharisees, he persecuted or intimidated fellow Jews who had formed a schismatic sect around Jesus of Nazareth, a rural teacher and miracle worker whose life, death, and reported resurrection his followers took as signs that the long-prophesied Jewish Messiah had arrived. Paul subsequently had a life-changing experience that transformed him from persecutor to Christ proclaimer. Much of the rest of his life was spent in announcing the news to all who would listen—the Messiah had come, the rules of everyday living and faith had changed, and the end of the world as it had been was near at hand. He spoke to all comers, but he considered his special mission to be carrying the word to non-Jews or "Gentiles" (*ethnoi* or *hellēnes*), in cities and towns around the Mediterranean. It was in this context of active ethico-religious work that he wrote his letters and, I will be arguing below, conceptualized the Body of Christ as a medium of mass communication that continues to animate and draw together the Christian faithful.

Paul always identified himself as a Jew, a fact often neglected by generations of Christians after him, though recently reemphasized.[1] He never used the word "Christian," which appears just twice in the New Testament and seems to have been forged by Latin-speaking outsiders to the Jesus movement, perhaps as a term of derision, *Christiani*.[2] Rather than seeing himself as helping found a new religion, Paul viewed himself as serving the God of Israel and taking Him to the Gentiles in the final days before the coming of the Lord.[3] To be sure, Paul took Jewish creed and practice in radical directions, but so did others in the first century C.E., when Judaisms were many and the Jesus movement just one among a dozen or so distinct Jewish sects in Palestine and the Mediterranean Diaspora. There was little doubt about his Jewish identity—"circumcised on the eighth day, a member of the people of Israel, of the tribe of Benjamin, a Hebrew born of Hebrews," as he described himself to the Philippians (Phil. 3:5).

According to Acts, Paul hailed from Tarsus, "no mean city," which we can thus think of as among the earliest and presumably most significant of the inventional media that shaped his subsequent intellectual development. A transportation hub, Tarsus sat upon one of the great trade routes of the ancient world, on the edge of the fertile Cilician plain, traversed by a road running east to Syria and north, across the mountains, into central Asia Minor. It lay on the navigable River Cydnus, ten miles inland from the Mediterranean. Thirty miles to the north were the renowned Cilician Gates, a narrow pass through the Tarsus Mountains, which elites had ordered laborers and slaves to widen so as to accommodate greater flows of trade and force. Over four millennia, this strategically situated city had attracted Hittites, Assyrians, Persians, Seleucids, Greeks, Jews, and Romans among many other trading, traveling, and conquering groups. Although Greeks had been in the city since the ninth century B.C.E. (Before the Common Era), their numbers increased in the second century B.C.E., when Tarsus became a Greek city-state (*polis*), and Greek and Jewish colonists were brought in to increase the productivity of the native population (not the last time Jews performed such a function). In 63 B.C.E., Tarsus came under Roman rule, and a decade later it was governed rather indifferently by the subsequently great orator-statesman, Cicero. In Paul's day, the city had perhaps seventy-five thousand inhabitants and, despite two waves of colonization from the West, retained an Eastern feel that reminded one second-century-C.E. Greek observer of the "licentious . . . Phoenicians."[4]

Perhaps Paul's family was among the first generation of Jews transplanted to Tarsus, or maybe they came later, following relatives or acquaintances in a kind of migratory pattern still familiar today. In the first century C.E., there were far more Jews in the Mediterranean Diaspora—perhaps seven million altogether[5]—than there were in Palestine and Judea. Most of them spoke Greek, and their Bible was the Septuagint, to which books had been added since it was translated from the Hebrew Bible in the third century B.C.E., in a rather fluid process of canon formation that came to distinguish the Greek text. (This would serve as the Bible for early Christians before the New Testament emerged in the middle of the second century C.E.) Besides Greek, Diaspora Jews also continued to speak Aramaic or Hebrew as well, which was encouraged in the Torah and functioned to maintain group identity and resist assimilation by host cultures.

Some assimilation was nearly inevitable, though, because anyone who spoke and thought in Greek absorbed some of its concepts and cultural patterns. Interaction with other groups was common. Jews traded and worked with Gentiles, attended the same theater and Games, and sometimes intermarried, all of which also found support in the Septuagint. Monotheistic Jews regularly shared space with pagans and polytheists in the agoras (market places or "town squares") and crowded streets of polyglot Mediterranean cities like Tarsus.[6] At the same time, good Jews worked to maintain a kind of purity—through distinct dietary regimes, celebration of a weekly Sabbath, and circumcision of the penis—that both defined piety and kept the group intact and culturally distinct. It would have been hard to fully avoid all the pagan rituals and deities that dominated the local religious scene, particularly the festivals to the city's patron god, Tarku, with great processions of color, feasting, and drink that surely left impressions on young children from all kinds of the city's families.[7]

While native Cilicians cultivated the crops and raised the animals that prospered on the fertile plain around Tarsus, Jewish immigrants worked among the trades and businesses supported in the city, or as laborers or slaves. In Yuri Slezkine's evocative designation, the Diaspora Jews were the People of Hermes (Mercury), "the god of all those who did not herd animals, till the soil, or live by the sword; the patron of rule breakers, border crossers, and go-betweens; the protector of people who lived by their wit, craft, and art."[8] Paul grew to be such a rule breaker and go-between. Perhaps raised by a tentmaking father who ran a successful workshop that catered to the needs of both Gentiles and Jews, Paul would later work as a *skēnopoios* (Acts 18:3), either a tentmaker or a leather worker. Paul grew up with sufficient privilege to afford the opportunity to pursue a formal education, of which his letters display evidence.

His early education would have focused on learning the Septuagint, through oral and literate learning practices that became cultivated skills Paul would later apply to heterodox ends as well. Jewish learning traditionally began in the home and continued outside it, when, at around age six, a boy "reached the age of training," as Talmudic literature put it. He would be sent to a teacher or house school whose job was to transmit the heritage and initiate young boys into the literacy and learning that marked the people of Israel. Internalization of the word was a primary aim; reading, writing, and recitation all functioned as both memory techniques and independent skills. Reading centered on scrolls drawn from the Septuagint, each carefully copied by a trained scribe whose literacy gave him status in a community that respected the written word. Children learned to treat texts with care and reverence, for reasons of piety and because scrolls were expensive and not easy to procure. There were special scrolls written for young children just learning to read, containing sections drawn from early chapters of Genesis or Leviticus. From the juvenile scroll, they advanced to the Pentateuch (the first five books of the Hebrew Bible—Genesis, Exodus, Leviticus, Numbers, Deuteronomy), the Prophets, and the "Writings." It was customary for synagogues to read completely through the Pentateuch over a period of three to seven years, and schools may have coordinated their reading to follow along. As children learned to read, they also gained competency in writing, using a wax tablet and a stylus or some other technology of the ancient scribal hand.[9]

Memory arts were key in Jewish schools, just as they were in the pagan academies. Quintilian, the Roman rhetor and near-contemporary of Paul, codified the state of the pagan memory arts in his *Institutio Oratoria*. He argued that above all special techniques, "the one supreme method of memory" was "practice and industry" and daily reflection upon it (XI, 2, 40), a component of both pagan and Jewish schooling. While Gentile students in Tarsus memorized passages from Homer, their Jewish counterparts memorized passages from the Pentateuch. Memory was a means of transmitting basic elements of the group's wisdom to boys too young to understand it fully. "One must first learn the text and then enter into the reasoning of it," a fourth-century rabbinic text advised. "One must always go on memorizing—even if he does not understand what he is doing: mistakes will right themselves in good time."[10] In the Jewish schools, practice and industry were joined by oral recitation, chanting, alphabetically based mnemonic devices, and swaying to and fro in rhythm with a verse, techniques of memory still used by orthodox Jews today.[11] Though a People of the Book, the Jews were also a People of the Internalized Word, and Paul benefited from cultivated techniques for inscribing the text upon the souls of the young.

Tarsus was a center of non-Jewish learning in the region, with academies run by Stoics, Cynics, and Sophists. According to Strabo, the city had "all kinds of schools of rhetoric."[12] The Stoic philosopher Athenodorus had grown up nearby and, after serving as Augustus Caesar's tutor in Rome, returned to the city around 15 B.C.E. Apollonious of Tyana, a contemporary of Paul, reportedly went to Tarsus at age fourteen to study with the rhetorician Euthydemus, though appalled by what he saw as the city's hedonistic ways, he left soon after.[13] Some have argued that Paul was trained in one of Tarsus's schools of rhetoric.[14] His letters show that he was familiar with common patterns of rhetorical organization, argumentation, and style. They evince Hellenistic modes of rhetorical comparison, characterization, exemplification, and praise, and are peppered with standard phrases and tropes from pagan rhetoric.[15] He might have learned these by studying with a sophistic teacher of rhetoric and going through the series of pedagogical exercises (*progymnasmata*) that were widely recognized as useful, not just for those who aspired to be elite statesmen or lawyers, but also for those who aimed to become scribes, tax collectors, and bankers, or to pursue other more middling occupations that called for writing and speaking.[16] Beyond a way to educate wise orators, rhetoric was an art of literacy that carried both instrumental value (as a way to secure work) and social status (as a way to distinguish oneself from women, slaves, and the laboring masses).[17] It was also an art defended by the Jewish writer Jesus ben Sirach, in whose treatise (republished and circulated in the Septuagint) Paul would have read, "Do not refrain from speech at an opportune time, and do not hide your wisdom; for wisdom shall be recognized in speech, and instruction by what the tongue utters" (Ecclesiasticus [Sirach] 4:23–24, Jerusalem Bible). Paul may have studied with a teacher of rhetoric, or he could have learned it from one of the many handbooks that circulated in the period, supplemented by watching rhetors perform at festivals or in the town squares of Tarsus. As Dale Martin argues, "it would have been impossible for an urban person of Paul's day to avoid exposure to a great deal of rhetoric."[18]

Paul's relation to rhetoric and the cultivated arts of speech was mixed. Though he never uses the term *rhētorikē* in his letters, he refers to it by other names, distancing himself from it, notably in letters to the Corinthians (1 Cor. 1.17–2.13; 2 Cor. 10:1–11:6). He separates himself from "the debater of this age" (1 Cor. 1:20) and those who speak "in lofty words" (2 Cor. 2:1), issues warnings about those who "by smooth talk and flattery . . . deceive the hearts of the simple-minded" (Rom. 16:18; cf. Thess. 2:3–6), and he presents himself instead as unschooled in speech (*idiōtēs tō logō*) (2 Cor. 11:6), all of which called up contrastive images with sophists, teachers of rhetoric, and those skilled in the arts of persuasive speech.

On the other hand, Paul himself was often eloquent, if not in the preferred style of educated Greek-reading audiences, and, as Johan Vos has brilliantly argued, Paul can be understood as a kind of sophist himself. He makes the weaker argument seem the stronger and uses ambiguity, paradox, false syllogisms, inconsistency, obscurity, strategic deception, and boasting, all of which were techniques associated with sophists since Gorgias and Protagoras. To persuade Jews and Gentiles that an unknown Nazarene was the promised Messiah, a dead body had been brought back to life, the rules of diet and traditional Jewish practice were suspended, and the wisdom of the world had been made foolish and the foolishness wise—these were nothing if not attempts to make the seemingly weaker case stronger, challenging common beliefs of Jewish, Greek, and Roman culture. In practice, Paul was a kind of radical Jewish sophist.[19]

Paul's rhetorical and argumentative capacities to fulfill this role were deepened when as a young man he moved beyond his elementary education and began a more advanced training as a Pharisee. Part religious sect, part social movement, part political interest group, the Pharisees were a Jewish group noted for their rigorous methods of interpretation and argumentation with regard to biblical texts. Although the Pharisees play an important dramatic role in the Christian New Testament as opponents of Jesus and his followers, we have writings of only two people, Josephus and Paul, who called themselves Pharisees—and in Paul's case, this comes only after he has left the group.[20] (Like the sophists, the Pharisees are known mostly through accounts left by critics and competitors.) As a Pharisee, Paul persecuted the followers of Jesus, a fact he referred to frequently in his letters (1 Cor. 15:9; Phil. 3:6; Gal. 1:13; cf. Acts 8:1–3, 9:1–2, 22:4–5, 26:9–11), but also gained the interpretive and argumentative skill that he deployed with great creativity and sophistication. Reading and memorizing scripture, listening and engaging with teachers, arguing with other students, Paul's Pharisaic training stoked his arsenal of invention and helped make him a brilliant and effective rhetor in his adult years.[21]

Our only evidence of Paul's rhetorical abilities, however, comes from after he switched sides in the dispute between the Pharisees, who enforced the law, and the followers of Jesus, who seemed to be subverting it. Acts has the life-changing event taking place as Paul traveled between Jerusalem and Damascus, an overland journey that, like all such travel in the ancient world, was fraught with hardship and possible danger. As Chilton writes, "Journeys produced natural opportunities for vision, bringing the austerity of fasting, night watches, and extremes of temperature to all but the wealthiest pilgrims and travelers."[22] In his mid-to-late twenties, Paul had such a vision, perhaps two years after Jesus was crucified. Although it was a life-altering experience, Paul says relatively little about it in his letters. He reports only having "seen Jesus our Lord" (1 Cor. 9:1) after the crucifixion, though Acts (9:1–22) makes the story vivid with flashes of light, temporary blindness, the voice of God, and Paul receiving the charge to take the word that the long-promised Jewish Messiah had arrived and proclaim it to "the Gentiles and kings and the sons of Israel" (Acts 9:15). Like Hermes, Paul was to be a messenger, not for the Pharisees, but rather for a different Jewish sect, a role that would help set in motion forms of mass communication still coursing about the contemporary world.

Spermologos for Israel's God

Called on the road to Damascus after persecuting Jesus's followers, Paul came to the movement from a distance and spent much of the rest of his life on the road, both physically and communicatively. He understood his mission as proclaiming the truth of the resurrection, which meant that Jesus of Nazareth was indeed the promised Jewish Messiah whose coming indicated the beginning of the world's final days and his imminent return or *parousia* (appearance, presence, or royal visitation), when he would judge mankind and offer salvation for his chosen people. More specifically, Paul interpreted his experience to be a call to preach the news among the pagans. He went to Arabia, returned to Damascus, and then three years later journeyed again to Jerusalem where he visited with Peter and James, Jesus's brother (both of whom surely had their doubts about the motives and character of this former Pharisee persecutor of the sect). He went to Syria and then to his home province, Cilicia, and after fourteen years returned to Jerusalem for a second meeting with the core leaders, where it was agreed that he "should go to the Gentiles and they to the circumcised" (that is, the Jews; Gal. 1:15–2:9). It was in the context of this mission that Paul's letters were composed, and his vision for mass communication manifest.

To carry out the mission, however, Paul had to overcome a core rhetorical obstacle—the question of his status in the movement and his authority to disseminate the word. By the time of Paul's vision some two years after the crucifixion, Jesus's disciple Peter had assumed a leadership position within the sect, assisted by others who had accompanied Jesus during his lifetime. While the disciples could claim a kind of charismatic authority based on having heard Jesus's teachings and bearing witness to his miracles, Paul could not. Unlike the core twelve disciples, Paul never had contact with the fleshly Jesus, the main source of authenticity for those who called themselves apostles. *Apostolos*—literally one who has been sent—is a term that rarely occurs in classical Greek but appears eighty times in some form in the Christian New Testament.[23] It was clearly a social category of significance in the movement. The Gospels of Matthew (10:2–4), Mark (6:29–30), and Luke (6:13, 17:1–5, 22:14) all use the term straightforwardly to refer to the twelve (though Luke 11:49 hints there may be additional apostles in the future). This understanding is also attributed in Acts to Peter, who looks to replace the fallen apostle Judas with one of "the men who have accompanied us during all the time that the Lord Jesus went in and out among us, beginning from the baptism of John until the day when he was taken up from us" (1:21–22). By this criterion, eligibility for apostleship was based on physical and social closeness to Jesus's fleshly body—proximity to charismatic authority, in the Weberian terms. Paul did not meet these criteria and fell outside the social circle of those who did—a point made in characteristically irreverent manner by Slavoj Žižek, who contrasts Paul with Christ's inner circle, whom he imagines "reminiscing during their dinner conversations: 'Do you remember how, at the Last Supper, Jesus asked me to pass the salt?'"[24]

Paul could engage in no such reminiscences. To overcome his marginality in the movement, Paul responded with rhetoric. *Apostolos* appears in five of the seven authentic Pauline epistles,[25] which account for the bulk of New Testament uses of the term. It is absent only in Philippians, an affectionate letter to a group with whom Paul had warm relations, and Philemon, whose primary audience was a core of loyal friends. In the other letters, Paul usually feels compelled to identify himself as an apostle in the opening salutation: "Paul, called by the will of God to be an apostle of Christ Jesus" (1 Cor. 1:1; cf. 2 Cor. 1:1, Rom. 1:1, and Gal. 1:1). Although these were simply reassertions of a status he likely claimed in previous face-to-face conversations with the groups he addressed, they also suggest that his standing was in question.

His correspondence with the Corinthians reveals more general lines of argument upon which Paul drew to establish his apostolic ethos and his corresponding authority to proclaim the truth of the risen Messiah. The central appeal was based on his visionary experience. "Am I not an apostle?" he asked rhetorically. "Have I not seen Jesus our Lord?" (1 Cor. 9:1; see also Gal. 1:15–17). From this perspective, it was not simply proximity to the fleshly Jesus that conferred the relevant status, but also proximity to the risen Christ.[26] The claim remained controversial into at least the third century,[27] which made it necessary to provide additional arguments for support. Paul supplied them, immediately going on to reason from signs of his status and social recognition of it. "Are you not my work in the Lord?" he asked. "If I am not an apostle to others, at least I am to you; for you are the seal of my apostleship in the Lord" (1 Cor. 9:1–2). Here Paul takes the existence of the Christ-proclaiming group in Corinth as a sign of his authenticity, an appeal based on the apparent effect he had had on them and their implicit recognition of it. In a subsequent letter to the same group, he referenced acts he had performed in front of them as further proof. "The signs of the true apostle were performed among you with utmost patience, signs and wonders and mighty works," he wrote (2 Cor. 12:12). Elsewhere, he refers to Andronicus and Junia, who had spent time in prison with Paul and were "prominent among the apostles" (Rom. 16:7), further extending the category so that it might include a woman as well. Taken together, Paul's arguments and subsequent repetition of them broadened the status of *apostolos* beyond the social, geographical, and temporal limits imposed by a definition based on proximity to the human Jesus, which in practice was limited to a few circumcised Jewish males. In Paul's hands, the risen Body of Christ could confer similar status, as could recognition by other believers based on deeds done and relations cultivated. Stated differently, communication with the fleshly Jesus was no longer the singular source of apostolic authenticity. Communication with his postresurrection self or with fellow believers could also bring it about. It was not an uncontroversial move, but it offered Paul and others rhetorical ground upon which to stand in the movement. It was one of several ways that Paul helped the movement break through barriers of space, time, and local networks of communication.

His rhetorical broadening of the category apostolos was of a piece with Paul's more general communicative mission. In Acts, the local Greeks call him a *spermologos* (17:18) and compare him to Hermes (14:12), god of roads, messengers, and rhetorical cunning, among other domains, and, as Slezkine argues, patron for border-crossing groups like the Diaspora Jews.[28] A spermologos was literally one whose speech (logos) was scattered (or perhaps picked up) like seeds (*spermo*, from the root verb *speírein*, to sow). It was the

Greek name for a bird that picked up and scattered seeds, and was a slang term variously applied to gossips, babblers, "word-scats," and "those who loafed about the agora picking up odds and ends."[29] That Paul was a <u>sper-mologos</u> suggests he was a kind of broadcaster—like Jesus whose parable of the sower John Durham Peters has so beautifully read as an image of communication.[30] Paul disseminated his word-seed promiscuously, to all those with ears that might hear it, "to Greeks and to barbarians, both to the wise and to the foolish," to Jews as well as Gentiles, to slaves as well as citizens (Rom. 1:14, 1 Cor. 12:13). A border-crossing, road-traveling, rhetorically able spermologos, Paul was willing to address all, regardless of language, ethnicity, religion, economic class, gender, or social status—the heterogeneous mass of humanity that inhabited cities around the first-century Mediterranean.[31] He had a message to deliver.

In taking the creed to the Gentiles, the Nazarenes (as the followers of Jesus were sometimes called by fellow Jews) were not alone among Jewish sects. The first century C.E. was, as H.J. Schoeps has observed, "the century of Jewish history which fostered universalistic hope without parallel in any century before or since. . . . Whole rabbinic circles were opposed to the particularism of Ezra and insisted that the gates of the law should be opened wide so that the nations of the earth might enter."[32] Paul was one among many first-century Jews to draw upon the broad communicative sentiments of Isaiah and the Psalmists:

> Say among the nations, "The Lord is king!
> The world is firmly established; it shall never be moved.
> He will judge the peoples with equity" (Psalms 96:10;
>   see also Isaiah 2:2–3, 26:2, 56:6–8)

Those, like Paul, who would broadcast the word of Israel's God to all peoples stood in tension with more conservative Jews, who would limit such rhetorical address and group membership to those born into the tribes or brought in through marriage and its transformative rituals. Even within the movement, Paul took up a more radical position, preaching a message of salvation that did not require keeping of the Jewish bodily rituals of meat eating and diet, or the cutting of the male foreskin—customs that represented obstacles to full conversion for some potential audiences.[33] Paul reached out broadly.

He sketches the idealized contours of his communications in one memorable passage in 1 Corinthians, where he reveals what he does to bring the word to various others. "To the Jews I became as a Jew, in order to win Jews," he confesses. "To those outside the law I became as one outside the law . . . so that I might win those outside the law. To the weak I became weak, so that I might win the weak. I have become all things to all people, that I might by all means save some" (1 Cor. 9:20–22). Here the Pauline mission in a nutshell: to be all things and reach all people, for the end is near and time is short.

Paul's Communicative Places

Rhetorical shape-shifter and *spermologos,* Paul the nonparadigmatic *apostolos* disseminated the news of the risen Jewish Messiah with uncommon energy, utilizing a wide range of the available media of his day. Through travel, face-to-face speech, and letters, Paul broadcast the word, and in the process he formulated ideas and phrasings that found their way into his preserved epistles. In the manner of historical sociologists of communication, let's consider some of the media Paul drew upon to communicate, formulate, and refine his rhetorical appeals, to audiences willing and unwilling, in the cities where he traveled and lived.

The first thing to point out is that Paul moved about a great deal. Like other early missionaries in the sect, Paul benefited from relative peace on the roads and seas enforced by Rome throughout much of an empire that ran from Gaul to Judea. Foot was the most common mode of land travel, with distances running some twenty miles per day. Paul traveled frequently by ship as well, braving weather and sea conditions to achieve greater speed. Over the course of his life, he moved through coastal and inland areas of Palestine, Syria, Asia Minor, Greece, Macedonia, and Rome, covering perhaps ten thousand miles. When possible, he and other travelers stayed in private homes instead of the undesirable and sometimes dangerous public houses along the way. Such arrangements established networks of Christ-follower hospitality toward travelers that also facilitated communications in the movement. In the key period of Paul's missionary life, he began or tended congregations of Christ-followers in four Roman provinces (Galatia, Asia, Macedonia, and Achaia), concentrating on the cities in those regions. Greek was still the lingua franca in most of his cities and was spoken by large numbers even in the two, Corinth and Philippi, that had stronger Latin character. Most were commercial cities, and many were transportation hubs, with good-sized Jewish and immigrant populations. Only Philippi was a more agricultural center, and even it included some of Slezkine's People of Hermes, represented in a Latin inscription from the city that was dedicated "to Fortune and the Genius of the Market."[34] Paul and other early Christian missionaries moved about.

Paul practiced a trade that gave him access to travel, semistructured audiences, and social networks. As a tentmaker/leatherworker (Acts 18:3), Paul had means for both sustenance and social mobility. Market stalls, traveling caravans, and great festivals all needed tents. Having the skill to sew tents together, Paul could also mend sails that ripped at sea. Camel caravans took him to inland cities, and ships carried him across the seas. Both served as settings and conduits of communication—media in two senses. These modes of travel took Paul to new cities and returned him to known ones. At the same time, they provided structured opportunities for Paul to speak with fellow travelers—merchants, pilgrims, immigrants, low-level officials, former slaves, camel drivers, soldiers, seamen, pleasure seekers, and, perhaps most receptive of all, fellow prisoners when Paul found himself in jail. Despite relative peace, traveling of all kinds remained dangerous, with thieves on the roads and storms at sea ranking high among the fears.[35] Paul experienced these things first-hand, as he told the Corinthians: "Three times I was shipwrecked; for a night and a day I was adrift at sea; on frequent journeys, in danger from rivers, danger from bandits, . . . danger in the city, danger in the wilderness, danger at sea" (2 Cor. 11:25–27). In the company of captive or semicaptive hearers, away from home and amid fears of the world beyond, Paul had access to potentially fertile ground upon which to make his case about the risen Messiah, the nearing end of time, and salvation in the Lord—becoming all things to all people as opportunities presented themselves.

Beyond according him travel opportunities, tentmaking gave Paul entry into social networks and structured settings of life in the cities. When he arrived in a new place, he could seek out local tentmakers. If they needed help, he gained access to a work scene with its own captive audiences. In comparison with other trades, leather workshops provided relatively quiet settings conducive to talk and gave Paul access to members of the artisanal class and slaves.[36] Corinth had ample numbers of tentmakers, kept in business by the biennial Pan-Hellenic Isthmian Games held nearby. Prisca and Aquila, two early and important members of the movement with Paul, were also said to be tentmakers and to have met Paul this way, inviting him to live in their home, where they could talk together about their mission in the more private contexts of domestic space.[37] Other tentmakers may have served as his host elsewhere.[38] Artisans of one trade sometimes lived in specific neighborhoods, as did immigrants from particular regions. Their trade associations and social clubs provided other settings for talk.[39] Tentmaking thus gave Paul structured spatial and social opportunities to speak with both strangers and acquaintances, and to gain access to social networks. For a man on a mission, who presents himself as forcefully as Paul does in his letters, it's impossible to believe that he didn't try to take advantage of such opportunities.

Communicative access is one thing; communicative success another. There is a big difference between broadcasting a message to all with ears to hear and finding a point of sympathetic reception or moment of audience belief (*pistis*).[40] We need to recall how wild Paul's core message would have sounded to many, if not most, of those who heard him tell it. Pagans would have started the conversation outside the Hebrew culture of prophecies and dubious of the significance of events in faraway Jerusalem. Greeks would have been incredulous of, if not disgusted by, the idea of a dead body in the ground for three days that rose up and walked again. Jews would have been unlikely to believe that an executed but generally unknown radical from Palestine was the promised Messiah. It is little wonder he termed his message "an obstacle (*skandalon*) to Jews and folly (*mōria*) to Gentiles" (1 Cor. 1:23). And given that his letters show that Paul could be difficult, egotistical, and zealous, he probably didn't help his case much with interpersonal charm and conviviality.

If Paul was fighting an uphill battle in the relatively intimate, face-to-face settings afforded a working artisan, his task would have been even more difficult when he spoke in the market places (agoras, which took their name from the verb *ageíren*, to gather together). The classic agora was a site where people congregated to socialize, trade, hear speeches, and attend festivals and public events. They might walk across it on their way to make offerings and worship at one of the several temples around the edge or nearby. The agora was also a place to take in more open air than the cramped housing of closely built towns and cities could afford. Its Latin equivalent, *forum*, signifies "outside" (as in the Spanish *fuera*), and a tower of the winds still stands in the forum in Athens built later by the Romans. Some of the place's characteristic activities are suggested by the more recent verb *agorezein*, meaning roughly "to loaf about,"[41] probably a gendered pastime enjoyed by the men as the women did the marketing, watched the kids, and went home to cook and tend the home. In a literal sense, the agora was a sensational place—one marked by abundant sensations of a sort not experienced in most everyday domestic or work life. Crowds of people standing and milling about; market wares of every sort displayed; colored tents flapping in the Mediterranean breezes above the stalls; temples, shrines, sanctuaries, statues, and sculptures ringing the area, each attracting its own groups of faithful or curious; smells of animals, food, fires, incense, and bodies; the din of voices in conversation, greeting, children playing, selling, speechifying; the best performers—like the teachers of rhetoric who practice their art to attract new students and for fun and honor—attracting a crowd.[42] The agora was a place where members of the heterogeneous masses of ancient cities came together in a spatially structured but also free-moving form.

This is not the kind of setting in which Paul was likely to have prospered, though Acts has him speaking there heroically. In Athens, for instance, Paul was said to have argued "in the agora every day with those who happened to be there," including "some Epicurean and Stoic philosophers [who] debated with him," and was successful enough to have been invited to speak at the Areopagus, the Athenian council that met on the hill of the same name (Acts 17:17–19). Such a description of his activity would have functioned as praise for a Hellenistic audience socialized into the glories of an Athens whose day had by then passed, and we might doubt its authenticity. But there is no reason to doubt that Paul spoke in the agoras of the cities he visited. As a Hellenistic Jew knowledgeable in the rhetorical art, he was socialized to experience some sense of power or opportunity as he took to speech in the public spaces of cities.

That sense may have been regularly accompanied by disappointment, however, for Paul was said not to have been an impressive live orator. Though it could have been merely a rhetorical figure of strategic self-deprecation, Paul described his own appearance to others as unimpressive—"his bodily presence is weak, and his speech contemptible," he reports observers saying (2 Cor. 10:10). In comparison to another itinerant evangelist, Apollos (Acts 18:24–19:7, 1 Cor. 3:4–6), Paul apparently lacked the ability to move others through speech or give spontaneous oratories that some believers took to be a sign of spirit possession and apostleship.[43] Given this general picture—a solid one-two punch of implausible message and perhaps limited oratorical ability in a social setting with plenty of other things for people to attend to—it's not likely that Paul was a stirring rhetorical success in the agoras of the ancient world.

Nonetheless, we might imagine him trying to make his case there, a determined messenger with a cross-cultural education and social experience in a number of cities. Calvin Roetzel, who believes that preaching was Paul's primary apostolic activity and makes a strong case that Paul spoke in agoras, has made a fascinating attempt to reconstruct main themes the apostle might have pursued in his stock public speeches. To reach Gentiles, whom he professed to target in his mission, he needed to draw upon commonplace images and lines of thought with cross-cultural appeal. As a Jew raised in Tarsus, he could have internalized such themes from listening or communicating with the Hellenistic host culture in which he grew up. Roetzel suggests that Paul might have begun his speech with an appeal to "the bondage, helplessness, hopelessness, and despair of his audience" and ended with the promise of salvation and eternal life, themes that might have resonated particularly among those in the more desperate lower strata of ancient cities.[44] With such rhetorical appeals, no doubt invented and refined through repeated attempts, Paul could hope to reach the urban masses in the ancient agora. Of course, the urban masses could also reach back, as they seem to have done on several occasions—as for instance in Thessalonica, where, "with the help of some ruffians in the agora," a mob was formed that "set the city in an uproar" and charged Paul with "turning the world upside down" in his teaching (Acts 17:5–6). And similarly, in Ephesus, where a mob of silversmiths, angered at Paul's condemnation of their trade of forging idols for the cults, dragged his travel companions off to the theater and beat them (Acts 19:23–41).[45]

The agora could be a dangerous place, but so could the synagogues that provided Paul another setting in which to refine and deliver the news that the Messiah had come and the old rules had changed. That danger was painfully obvious on the five occasions when Jewish authorities doled out the traditional "forty lashes minus one" given a heretic (2 Cor. 11:24). Yet despite the inherent dangers, the synagogue (synagōgē)[46] was potentially fertile ground for sowing the apostolic seed. Diaspora synagogues included both Jews and "God-fearers," those fellow-traveling pagan-born followers of the God of Israel who avoided circumcision or dietary regimes, and who offered a particularly promising audience for Paul.[47] In comparison with the public gathered at the agora, the synagogue audience as a whole had the advantage of working from the same grand cultural narrative, defined by the stories and sayings of the Septuagint, which Paul had mastered through argumentative and memory disciplines in his Pharisaic training. As in the agoras, Acts depicts Paul converting synagogue members en masse, another example of the great communicative power the apostle has in Luke's telling.[48] Though one might expect that audiences with an entire synagogue might be hard for a heretic to come by, Paula Fredriksen suggests that traveling evangelists like Paul "found opportunities at the regular Sabbath service to speak, debate, and perhaps demonstrate the authority of their message with charismatic healings and exorcisms."[49] In such a setting, Paul could make close arguments backed by creative interpretation of his storehouse of memorized passages and prophecies from the Septuagint. More than charismatic oratory or charming interpersonal conversation, it was probably such quasi-rabbinical, text-based oral disputation that was Paul's strongest mode of rhetorical address.

Positioned to be the most welcoming of all Paul's audiences were those in the house-based meetings of the Jesus sect, the ekklesiae. In its New Testament usage, ekklesia is usually translated as "church," but this term is misleading insofar as it suggests an institutional or bureaucratic structure or a specially designated building, none of which the Pauline ekklesiae had. "Assembly" is a better translation, for it emphasizes a meeting face-to-face. Ekklesia was a term that classically referred to the political assembly of Greek city-states, and it still may have carried some of that sense when the Nazarenes began adopting it for their own use. Unlike the political ekklesia, which met in public space, the Christ-proclaiming ekklesia congregated in the private household (*oikos*) of one of its members, an assembly situated differently toward the polis.

The ekklesia would assemble regularly in a house large enough to accommodate the numbers of regulars, occasionals, and newcomers who would attend. Established ekklesiae, like the one with whom Paul corresponded in Corinth, might range from thirty to fifty people who came together for a common meal, ritual breaking of the bread, and worship practices that revolved around remembering the risen Christ and anticipating his imminent return. They traversed wealth and social status, and included both Jews and pagans, patterns found in Diaspora synagogues as well. It was part Hellenistic banquet, part charismatic religious event, driven by the Holy Spirit that was made manifest through preaching, prophecy, speaking in tongues, trance, music, and dancing.[50] As a man visited by the risen Christ, Paul had a powerful role to play in testifying to the truth of the resurrection and the coming end of ordinary time. Speaking at the ekklesia afforded Paul the opportunity to address an audience of generally sympathetic listeners—local brothers (*adelphoi*) and saints (*hagioi*), as the faithful called themselves, along with fellow travelers, and curious newcomers in the house that night. Such was the audience for the vision of mass communication Paul presented in a letter.

Figuring the Body of Christ in a Letter: Paul's Vision for Mass Communication

It came to be known as "The First Letter of Paul to the Corinthians," one of the fourteen traditionally attributed to the roving apostle, collected and canonized in the Christian New Testament. At the time of its composition, though, it was simply an occasional communication—from "Paul, called to be an apostolos by the will of God, and our brother Sosthenes, to the ekklesia of God that is in Corinth, to those who are sanctified in Christ Jesus, called to be saints, together with all those who in every place call on the name of our Lord Jesus Christ" (1 Cor. 1:1–2). They addressed the ekklesia from a distance, composing their missive from Ephesus, a port city across the Aegean Sea from Corinth. The Corinthian assembly, which Paul had helped establish a few years earlier, was a diverse and internally divided lot. It included Jews and Gentiles, men and women, laborers, slaves, elites, perhaps some former prostitutes, leaders of the synagogue, and a local government official.[51] Some declared themselves for Christ, while others pledged allegiance to Paul, Peter, or the eloquent Apollos (1 Cor. 1:10–13). Members brought suit against one another in the public courts (1 Cor. 6:1–8). Some engaged in improprieties of sex, diet, bodily adornment, and worship (1 Cor. 5–14). At their regular gatherings, some members of the ekklesia ate and drank hugely, while others went hungry (1 Cor. 11:20–22), perhaps a function of a wealthy host treating his social equals with customary generosity and his inferiors with something less.[52] It was not a good situation.

Paul responded with one of the two key letters of his life, from which anyone who has attended Christian weddings is likely to have heard fragments.[53] Like Romans, his other masterwork, 1 Corinthians includes some of Paul's most beautiful and deeply resonant turns of phrase, including 13:12–13, rendered in its King James English: "For now we see through a glass, darkly; but then face to face"—the deep rhetorical source for a line in Walt Whitman's great poem, "Crossing Brooklyn Ferry," as well as Charles Cooley's idea of "face-to-face communication," invented nearly twenty centuries later. The latter is fitting, since Paul's letter itself was generated through face-to-face communication in Ephesus, a base for apostolic operation well-linked to east and west through land and sea routes.

Though we moderns tend to think of Paul's letters as written texts silently read, in original composition and reception they were deeply oral productions. As was typical in his day, Paul was less a letter writer than a letter dictator, for he used a secretary (*grammateus*) who wrote down what he said out loud.[54] Unlike many readers in classical antiquity, Paul could write and sometimes included in his letters a "greeting with my own hand" (1 Cor. 16:21), but he seems not to have been particularly skillful with script.[55] According to E. Randolph Richards, six of the seven authentic Pauline letters (including 1 Corinthians) utilized a secretary, whom he suggests functioned primarily as a recorder of speech and editor, rather than collaborator.[56] Present during the composition of 1 Corinthians is "our brother Sosthenes," whom Acts (18:17) identifies as a leader of the synagogue in Corinth, as well. Whether Sosthenes or someone else served as grammateus in Ephesus is not clear, but given his status as a Christ-confessing Jew and local leader, it is very likely that he served as something more than simple recorder of Paul's speech. At the very least, Sosthenes would have served as stand-in for the Corinthian assembly, shaping Paul's thinking and speech through social-psychological processes anchored in the two men's physical proximity during the dictation. More likely, the two men talked about the Corinthian situation before the writing commenced and continued their conversation during formal composition. The composition of the letter to Corinth was, in some sense at least, a collaborative affair, built upon intimate, face-to-face speech in Ephesus, sometime in the early part of the sixth decade of the Common Era.

Together, they were guided by the generic forms of both letter-writing and the Hellenistic concord (*homonoia*) speech, the overarching purpose of which was to bring about commonality among discord.[57] Both functioned as cultural media for invention. Letters were becoming a popular new medium among elites and subelites in Hellenistic society.[58] In style, they ranged from the more literary compositions of writers like Cicero to the more utilitarian efforts of officials or private individuals who could arrange to have their missives carried from point to point. Letters often followed customary patterns of organization and appeal taught in schools and in the rhetorical handbooks of the day.[59] With Sosthenes, Paul drew upon these patterns, particularly those of the Hellenistic personal letter, but moved them in distinctive directions, adding an ethos of (contested) apostolic authority and the privileges of instruction that went along with it.

Composed in one city, the written concord speech was transported across the sea to another, likely carried by a trusted and geographically mobile member of the sect who played the role of letter carrier (*grammatophoros*).[60] Corinth was known as the "cross roads of Greece," a place that "receives all cities and sends them off again and is a common refuge for all, like a kind of route or passage for all humanity, no matter where one would travel."[61] It was a multicultural center for trade, travel, and spectacle, a Roman colony since 46 B.C.E., provincial capital, site of the hugely popular Isthmian Games, and the wealthiest and most important city in colonized first-century Greece. It had a sizable Jewish population but was also, from a monotheist's point of view, Sin City. There were pagan cults for Poseidon, Hermes, Zeus, Dionysus, Isis, Serapis, Apollo, and, crowning the city's highest peak, a temple to Aphrodite, patron goddess for one thousand sacred prostitutes, whose presence in Corinth indexed the steady flow of seamen and other travelers through the region.[62] (I like to imagine it as equal parts New York City, Las Vegas, New Orleans, and Tijuana, only smaller and without the cars.)

The letter was carried to Corinth, where it was read aloud at the gathering (ekklesia) that took place in the large home of one of the group's more affluent members.[63] It became a performance that blended reading, oral interpretation, and embodied reception of the word, where it might capture the contingencies of the moment and suggest possibilities not presently realized.[64] "αρακαλω δε υμας αδελφοι δια του ονοματος του κυριου ημων ιησου χριστου ινα το αυτο λεγητε παντες και μη η εν υμιν σχισματα ητε δε κατηρτισμενοι εν τω αυτω νοι και εν τη αυτη γνωμη," the Corinthians heard early in the performance. "And I call upon you, brethren, through the name of our Lord Jesus Christ, that the same thing ye may all say, and there may not be divisions among you, and ye may be perfected in the same mind, and in the same judgment."[65]

Later in the performance, the point was brought home differently, in a manner that I read as the formal literary birth of Christian mass communication. Paul drew attention to the group's shared meal, an event that served as the setting for their reception of his letter. A shared meal carried a sense of commonality among both Jews and Greeks, and the former traditionally began theirs with a blessing of the bread, a practice that schismatic sects like the Nazarenes and Essenes continued in the "messianic banquets" they held in anticipation of the second coming of Christ.[66] The letter called attention to the blessing of the bread and wine, which its hearers had probably just done. "The cup of blessing that we bless, is it not a sharing in the blood of Christ? The bread that we break, is it not a sharing in the Body of Christ? Because there is one bread, we who are many are one body, for we all partake of the one bread" (1 Cor. 10:16–17). It was an image amplified a short while later. "For just as the body is one and has many members, and all the members of the body, though many, are one body, so it is with Christ. For in the one Spirit we were all baptized into one body—Jews or Greeks, slaves or free—and we were all made to drink of one Spirit" (12:12–13). Condensed in this image is the canonical understanding of the Christian Eucharist (later amplified in the Gospels), the core of the dominant theory of the church and Christian society, the seeds of a radical universalism, and the beginnings of what I will call Pauline mass communication. Jew and Greek, slave and free, rich and poor, all were joined together as the singular Body of Christ, both symbolized and enacted through the sharing of blessed bread and cup. "Now you are the Body of Christ and individually members of it" (12:27; cf. Rom. 12:4–8).

So it was in theory, and Paul called for it to be so also in practice, that the Corinthians should come together in concord as the living Body of Christ that they were. He marshaled rhetoric in the service of a kind of immanent critique and normative social theory of the ekklesia and its common meal.

He went further, though, than the mere communitarian reminder that his audience was part of the same corporate body. In a great sophistic reversal that revealed the essence of his social ethics, he elaborated upon the rhetorical image and made a case for the special significance of those who, by the standards of human society, were less honored or even despised. "As it is, there are many members, yet one body," Paul intoned. "The eye cannot say to the hand, 'I have no need of you,' nor again the head to the feet, 'I have no need of you.' On the contrary, the members of the body that seem to be weaker are indispensable, and those members of the body that we think less honorable we clothe with greater honor, and our less respectable members are treated with greater respect; whereas our more respectable members do not need this. But God so arranged the body, giving the greater honor to the inferior member, that there may be no dissension within the body, but the members may have the same care for one another. If one member suffers, all suffer together with it; if one member is honored, all rejoice together with it (12:20–26). Paul's reversal, based on reference to the coverage of genitals by clothing, did not mean that he abandoned all notions of hierarchy within the ekklesia, as he quickly made clear, following up with a sectarian status pyramid in which apostles such as himself sat atop, using the same image of the corporate body to justify patriarchy.[67] There were limits to Paul's egalitarianism.[68]

First Corinthians envisions the Body of Christ as a medium that traverses space and time and binds the faithful together as an intercommunicating community. With Sosthenes, Paul redeployed a common trope and made it the basis for a new collective understanding within the movement. The letter is the oldest preserved document that uses the phrase "Body of Christ," but Paul was drawing upon an orally transmitted cult formula that accompanied the breaking of the bread, which he had learned from Jesus's disciples or others nearer the social core of the sect. He was also drawing upon the image of society as corporate body, a rhetorical commonplace with both Hellenistic and Jewish usage.[69] The genius of the letter lies in the way it links the rhetorical commonplace to the Body of Christ, and the ritually shared bread to the society (ekklesia) of God. The ekklesia was the Body of Christ, a social fact symbolized and enacted through the single loaf ritually consumed. This was the interpretation Paul offered up to the Corinthians, which if they accepted would change their understanding and experience of the ekklesia, its common meal, and their relation to one another and to the risen Messiah.

Through 1 Corinthians, Paul operated as an interpretive communication theorist, weighing in from a distance, and offering the community a new way of understanding and experiencing customary practice. He both identified with the community and stood apart from it, playing out his role as Mercurian apostolos—messenger, organizer, activist—through rhetoric addressed to the ekklesia, which functioned to bring a new social reality into existence. He drew off local understandings, but refigured them so as to lay out a normative vision to guide collective practice.

In the process, Paul conceptualized a very basic, even primitive form of mass communication, which traverses several of the etymologically generated species I laid out in the previous chapter. It was a variation on *maza* (barleycake) communication, centered around its wheaten cousin, the *artos*, but operating from the same deep symbolic structure: eating together the shared loaf, kneaded together from disparate ingredients, and symbolically uniting those who consumed it. As they ate from the loaf, the Corinthians consumed the Body of Christ and drew themselves together as the multi-membered ekklesia of God. This would become the core element of Christian worship, Mass (*missa*) communication, whose human meanings grew out from Paul's letters. It was communication that involved the social totality—the whole of the ekklesia in Corinth, who, despite their (contingent, human) divisions, were in fact members of one body, across lines of difference that included religious origins, cultural orientation, gender, age, and class. And, following Jesus's ministry, Paul's was a vision that made special place for the Corinthian hoi polloi—its laboring classes and slaves, who were full members and even recipients of special consideration in the ekklesia. (Marx would pick up parts of this vision, as would Whitman.) The Body of Christ was the medium of the masses, as much or more than it was the medium of the privileged classes. In Paul's formulation, the Body of Christ was a mass medium in very basic ways—a medium through which the mass of believers were put in communication with one another, across lines, in collective religious affirmation grounded in the sharing of the bread.

If these were its symbolic and social dynamics, we might again remember the experiential contexts that filled out Pauline mass communication in its earliest, Corinthian incarnation, which added elements of a fifth species of the genus, tied to the idea of abundant communications. After the breaking of the bread, the evening moved forward, and Christ's Body emerged in additional sensory ways. Charismatic preaching, speaking in tongues, trances, dancing, chants, incense, prophecy, wine, song—all were media through which the Body of Christ made itself audible, visible, tactile, evident.[70] Paul's letter offered direction and overarching interpretation for a form of mass communication that was anchored in local bodies, whose gestures and vocal sounds were both context and sign for the group's successful communication with more distant realities—the resurrection of Jesus, his nearing return to earth, and the cleansing of the world, all of which were amplified by the sounds and motions of the assembled ekklesia in communication with itself. This is the wild side of what became the Christian tradition and the distant, primal past for the idea of mass communication that emerged in the 1920s. When David Sarnoff hijacked the universal vision of Isaiah to help legitimatize for-profit corporate control of the radio airwaves, he unknowingly tapped into a far different moment: a crazy-eyed evening in Corinth, where Gentiles and Jews ate together, awaited and hoped for the Messiah's return, shouted and professed competing things, were overtaken by the spirit that possessed their bodies, and received a letter from afar that offered them a vision of themselves as the collective Body of Christ, with each individual body counting as much as the others.

Paul's Figure: Reverberations after Corinth

By putting the image of the Body of Christ into writing, Paul and his secretary helped wrest the phrase from its place in the ritual of the shared bread, making it textually available as an inventional resource for subsequent generations of rhetors, theorists, and ordinary believers.[71] Though the apostle devoted much of his adult life to embodied communication in service of the movement, it was through seven preserved letters that he left his mark on history. If he had been simply the virtuoso of the spoken word that his peer Apollos had been, his words would have disappeared, carried on only through testimony and rippling social consequences brought about by those who had heard them—the letter that was the ekklesia itself, as he called the Corinthians on another occasion.[72] As it turned out, owing to historical contingency, divine providence, or some combination thereof, those words persisted. By the time of First Corinthians, Paul had sufficient stature for his letter to be copied and spread through social networks of the ekklesia and its scribes.[73] His letters carried weight and were significant enough to be copied, distributed further, and imitated by others who helped ensure that the Pauline-style pastoral epistle would be one of the distinguishing literary genres of the emerging Christian movement.[74] This is the origin of the so-called "deutero-Pauline corpus," those six letters that most scholars attribute to authors who wrote in the generation after the apostle, but who used his name and style to advance a number of purposes, which ranged from doing honor to a man whose works had influenced them, to clearing up perceived misconceptions about the apostle's position, to mobilizing his ready-at-hand ethos to advance their own particular and sometimes differing agendas.[75] For these writers, Paul's letters served as media of invention.

Some picked up his image of the ekklesia as Body of Christ and broadened the vision for the mass communication it indexed. In the deutero-Pauline Ephesians Christ is "the head over all things for the ekklesia, which is his body, the fullness of him who fills all in all" (Eph. 1:22–23), while in Colossians "He himself is before all things, and in him all things hold together. He is the head of the body, the ekklesia; he is the beginning, the firstborn from the dead, so that he might come to have first place in everything" (Col. 1:17–18). In these redeployments, we arguably see an expanding sect aware of both its grounding in mediated textual authority and its growing geographical range. While Paul tended to use the term *ekklesia* in the sense of a localized assembly, his imitators increasingly used it to reference a far-flung society of the faithful, living and in heaven, both localized and distant. While the Body of Christ in 1 Corinthians had paradigmatically bound together the disparate but assembled believers in Corinth, the Body of Christ in Colossians and Ephesians constituted a dispersed ekklesia and the universe of being that surrounded it. In basic ways, the Body of Christ became a mass medium for a distended society of the faithful, a medium that put them in communication with one another as interrelated members of the same corporate body.[76] Paul and his imitators were some of the original medium theorists of the Western tradition. Like print or television for a much later generation, these early theorists emphasized the transformative power of a new medium, in their case the Body of Christ.

Thanks to appreciative readers and scribes who preserved them, imitators who underwrote their authority by extending them, and church fathers who included them in the New Testament canon, the Pauline letters survived and prospered. In the process, a radical Jewish sophist was transformed into a Christian, and a schismatic sect morphed into its own religion. Early on, the letters were collected and distributed in codex form, the new booklike media technology of papyrus or parchment bound together by leather, favored by the movement, and differentiating it from the Hebrew People of the Scroll. From that status, the letters entered into the new Christian Bible, their authority undergirded by the stylized biography of Paul presented by Luke in Acts of the Apostles, their number standing at an impressive fourteen. As the Roman Catholic Church institutionalized itself over the next millennium, it included the Pauline corpus as part of the regular readings of the Mass, drawing upon Paul's image for its own collective self-understanding and blunting some of the wildness, egalitarianism, and sophistic reversal that had been part of Paul's original vision. In time, the image grew to encompass the kings of Europe, who in medieval social theory displaced Christ as head of the mystical body.[77] Thus deployed, the image served to legitimate and mystify powerful centralizing institutions of church and state, far from the senses it took on in the contexts of the Corinthian ekklesia and its meal.

This is not the end of the story, however, but only one early chapter in it. Thanks to moveable typescript, improvements in print technology, widespread distribution of the word, and expanding popular literacy, Paul's letters entered new cultures, geographies, social networks, and individual imaginations. They became a medium of mass communication in their own right, heard or read by millions, some living, many long departed, some who found them oppressive and others who felt them uplifting. There were orthodox and unorthodox interpretations of them, rhetorical marshalings in new languages and rereadings in old tongues. The Pauline mass communication of the Corinthian assembly had been a semiprivate affair involving a few dozen locals, far different from the great festivals and agoras that represented pagan varieties of the communicative genus. What the new medium lacked in corporeal breadth it more than made up in universalizing normative force, however, for Paul offered a vision in which the socially marginal and downtrodden might be full and complete members of a moral community without geographical, temporal, or social limits. That regulative ideal stands ready at hand for new deployments within the church today—as by those who would argue that homosexuality is precisely one of those human-constructed social categories that Pauline mass communication sought to transcend; and who would urge that Christ-confessing gays and lesbians be granted full acceptance and membership in the church, just as Christ-confessing slaves and Gentiles were granted membership in the earliest days of the movement. And it stands ready, too, for an atheist philosopher like Alain Badiou, who makes Paul into "a new militant figure" and "poet-thinker of the event," who offers the seeds for a universalism that proceeds through human difference.[78] One of the beauties of the rhetorical word is the way that it invites redeployments of many sorts, both within the community of orthodox believers and outside the fold.

Whitman was one member of what he might have called the "audience interminable" for Paul's letters, parts of which he absorbed in the inventional period leading into what he would call his New Bible for American Democracy, *Leaves of Grass*, first published in 1855. Channeling orality, literacy, and rhetorical arts of a different sort, he turned to poetry instead of apostolic epistle as a means of advancing his unorthodox faith, and also expressing himself in the process—not exactly as the "letter of Christ" Paul envisioned in 2 Corinthians, but more as a multitheistic broadcast. Mass communication found place in his religion as well, though of different sorts than Paul's ritual of the bread and Body of Christ. The poet was a different sort of spermologos from the apostle, striking more the classical figure of the loafer in the agora, which Whitman worked out in the walking cities of mid-nineteenth century America and traveling about the country. To his vision we now turn.

3

Whitman's Polytheistic Mass

"Faith is the antiseptic of the soul."
—Walt Whitman, Preface, *Leaves of Grass* (1855)

Walt Whitman moved gladly among people. He walked, ran, and sauntered the streets of Brooklyn as a young boy, and ventured across to Manhattan by ferry when age and inclination allowed. He passed regularly through crowds that captured and enlarged his social imagination. He had feelings for the people he saw, absorbed them into himself, and channeled them back outward in writings later published. He grew up with the laboring classes, with whom he long identified and whom he came to idealize. He was raised in a racially and religiously prejudiced environment but wrote poetry that shed some of those attitudes and depicted a world of acceptance and love (in its many forms) that pushed Pauline moral universalism a step or two further. He entertained dreams of becoming a great orator, a goal he pursued through print-based poetry more than voice and gesture. He took the everyday realities he experienced and imagined something both part of them and better, bound by communicative forms that continue to course through the contemporary world, even if most of us pass through them unawares.

Despite being separated by eighteen hundred years and countless social worlds, Whitman and Paul shared certain things. Both were urban dwellers who got around, although—with a few exceptions—Whitman's movement was more localized and differently driven than the region-spanning apostle's. Paul was a missionary, Whitman a "loafer," but both men articulated universalist creeds and interpreted phenomena we can retroactively see as species of mass communication. Each was a kind of normative sociologist of communication who interpreted common experience and offered visions for what it might be, beyond what it typically was. Each utilized aspects of the spoken word to compose canonical texts that bear the marks of oral address and are arguably powered by it. Each drew upon religious tradition but revised and went beyond it—Paul in the service of the God of Israel, Whitman for a faith in polytheistic democracy.

Whitman's vision unfolds in *Leaves of Grass*, his much-revised master-work, which went through six substantively different editions from 1855 to 1892. I will focus on the early, pre–Civil War *Leaves* (1855, 1856, 1860), when the poet is at his most full-throated democratic self and composes much of his greatest work, and will attend particularly to the first edition. Unlike the elitist European thinkers who gave the masses a particularly bad name over the nineteenth century, Whitman was a man of the people, particularly through the 1850s, and in that period depicts crowds and hoi polloi artfully and sympathetically.[1] Alerting us to some of mass communication's most democratic forms and possibilities, he is both a signal character in its intellectual history and a resonant and inspirational resource for thinking about it today. Through him, poetry takes on some of the functions of social and political theory, just as epistles did through Paul before him—serving as a vehicle for interpretation, representation, reorientation, provocation, practical guidance, and pleasure. His poetry is also part oratorical performance, spiritual hymn, erotic confession, and intimate address, most of which social theory is not (for better or for worse).

In world-historical significance, *Leaves of Grass* is not quite First Corinthi-ans, and Walt Whitman is not quite St. Paul, but both became "cosmopolitan influentials" and are among the great figures in the world's cultural history.[2] Paul had an eighteen-hundred-year jump on Whitman and benefits accorded institutional recognition by the Church, which have allowed him to be more famous and influential on a mass scale, but Whitman has done well himself, attracting readers from around the globe, in numbers that continue to grow. Both men composed texts that have themselves been mass-communicated over time and in the process have attracted thousands of commentaries and criticisms. Though not as abundant as the literature on Paul, scholarship on Whitman is voluminous, and I have drawn gratefully upon it.[3]

My aim in this chapter is threefold. First, I continue my rhetorical-cum-communicative history by sketching select inventional media traversing Whitman's first four decades and contributing to the composition of *Leaves*. Whitman came of age in the era that was retroactively characterized as "the communication revolution"[4] and was one of its many literate participant-observers. He witnessed transformations in the printing and newspaper busi-ness, the development of systems of local and long-distance mass transit, and the invention and popular adoption of new media (including photography and the telegraph), as well as democratic reworkings of older media like preaching, parades, political oratory, and public lectures. Drawing details from Whitman's autobiographical remembrances, newspaper writings, and notebooks from the pre-*Leaves* period, and guided by a number of his biographers, I discuss a small subset of the inventional media he drew upon when he transformed himself, at the age of thirty-six, from a second-rate writer and newspaperman into the author of an edgy and original book of free-verse poetry that "has enthralled readers and influenced almost every major poet of the twentieth century."[5] As with my account of Paul, this story emphasizes literacy and orality, emplacement and movement, modes of transportation and media of symbolic expression. I pay particular attention to Whitman's work as a newspaperman and the walking routines it involved, a long-distance trip he took to New Orleans in 1848, handwritten notebooks, and dreams he entertained of becoming a great orator, all of which contributed to his rhetorical makings.

Next, I move to an interpretation of Whitman's early *Leaves* in terms of the vision of mass communication that I see contained within it. Like Paul's, Whitman's was a vision that took shape against religious horizons, drawing bearings from the Jewish heterodoxy that Paul helped initiate (that is, Christianity), but moving beyond to embrace many gods, all of which might find place within a United States he hoped to chant into being through his rhetorical poetry. This polytheistic ekklesia would be constituted partly through multiple species of mass communication, four of which I go on to parse out and briefly discuss: embodied masses gathered in a crowd, imagined masses inhabiting a geographical place in the future, represented masses depicted through poetry, and introjected masses enfleshed by a polytheistic democratic individual. Whitman advances our story by modeling ways that a poet can be a theorist and by pointing us toward varieties of mass communication less centralized and more democratic than David Sarnoff's broadcasting.

Walt Whitman of Brooklyn: The Making of a Peripatetic Urban Journalist

Walt Whitman grew up oriented toward Brooklyn, Long Island, and Manhattan. He was born in 1819, in a modest two-story home his father had built in rural West Hills, Long Island—"the old native place," the poet would later call it, making a point to return on quasi-religious pilgrimages that put him in a mind toward ancestry.[6] He was the second of eight children born to

Louisa and Walter Whitman, both of whom came from long-settled families, and grew up on small farms in Long Island. Walter the elder was a moody, freethinking Democrat who came from a line of big-bodied alcoholics (he would become one himself), admired Tom Paine, and passed his family's Revolutionary heritage to his children. He was a skilled carpenter who also cut wood and did farm work to support his family. Louisa was six years younger, lively, attractive, and a good storyteller with a gift for theatricality. Walt came to idealize her over time and arguably internalized her feminine and motherly qualities as he developed as a person and poet. Family and nativity would be recurrent themes in his *Leaves*.[7]

The Whitmans moved to Brooklyn when young Walt was four, entering the city amid great fanfare as crowds clogged the roads for a much-anticipated horse race in Jamaica, which was celebrated that night in the streets of town, not far from the family's newly rented house.[8] It was a fitting entry for a future poet of the crowd, taking up residence in what was then a village of about eight thousand. It had "much the appearance of a bustling country town, and partially 'alive,' most of the time, with market and fish wagons, and their proprietors," he wrote in 1861.[9] The Whitmans' first house was on Front Street, "not far from what was then call'd 'the New Ferry,' wending the river . . . to New York City," as the poet later described it. "I was a little child . . . but tramp'd freely about the neighborhood and town, even then; was often on the aforesaid New Ferry; remember how I was petted and deadheaded by the gatekeepers and deckhands (all such fellows are kind to little children,) and remember the horses that seem'd to me so queer as they trudg'd around in the central houses of the boats, making the water power" (before steam-engine ferries, which were soon introduced).[10]

Besides the everyday bustle and crowds of the streets, more occasional gatherings impressed the young boy as well. Revivals, Sunday school processions, and Fourth of July celebrations were all part of his childhood mix. He remembered the great parade for the French hero of the American Revolution, the Marquis de Lafayette, which took place on the Fourth of July, 1825, when the sixty-eight-year-old general came to Brooklyn to lay the cornerstone of a library for apprentices, accompanied by the freethinking feminist Scotswoman, Frances (Fanny) Wright. "The whole village, with all its population, old and young, gentle and simple, turned out en-masse," he wrote.[11] He remembered the town's religious revivals, including one held every night in a nearby church where "a third of the young men in Brooklyn, particularly the mechanics and apprentices, and young women of the same class in life . . . 'experienced religion,'" but where the galleries were also "sprinkled with the mischievous ones who came to ridicule and make sport."[12] Piety mixed with its opposite, as it would in Whitman's poetry.

Indoors and out, he was exposed to oral performances by preachers, singers, politicians, and lecturers. He once said that he was "born, as it were, with propensities from my earliest years, to attend popular American speech-gatherings."[13] He was impressed by the radical Quaker Elias Hicks, whom his parents took him to hear at a Brooklyn Heights ballroom in 1829. Whitman's mother attended a number of churches and exposed her son to what was then one of the most vibrant religious scenes in the Christian world. Revivals swept Brooklyn, home also to some of the leading religious orators of the day, including Henry Ward Beecher, of whom Whitman later published a newspaper sketch. Brooklyn preachers led the way in the development of a more relaxed, anecdotal, humorous, and interactive pulpit eloquence, all of which Whitman admired and took in, among the other speechifying he heard at Fourth of July celebrations and other civic events in his childhood town. Whitman, too, would aspire to be a great orator.[14]

Brooklyn's public spaces were socializing media that helped calibrate an eye that would take crowds and performances as material for art, both journalistic and poetic. He attained requisite literacies through home, schools, work, and library use. His parents read, owned a Bible and a few other books, and subscribed to periodicals. The churches of Brooklyn ran Sunday schools, whose mission included instruction in reading and spelling as well as the Bible. The boy attended the village's only free public school, where the day began with Bible reading, a performance that sometimes gave youthful voice to print versions of Paul's words.[15] Whitman's formal schoolroom education ended when he was 11, and he went to work as an office boy for two attorneys who took interest in their charge. They expanded the boy's literacy by buying him a membership in a Brooklyn circulating library and helping him with his handwriting and composition. Whitman later called the library membership "the signal event of my life up to that time," and he plunged into reading. He took to adventure books and Sir Walter Scott, becoming "a most omnivorous novel reader" and launching an energetic reading career that became increasingly eclectic over the next two decades.[16]

At twelve, Whitman added to his literate self-invention through another social portal when he secured a job as printer's devil at a local newspaper. In that role, as Joseph Rubin writes, Whitman "cleaned the floors, dampened paper, inked type by beating the forms with two ink-soaked sheepskin balls stuffed with wood and fastened to wood handles, and prepared the sheepskins by 'treading out' the malodorous pelts." He sat at the lowest rung of the print-production status chain, far from the creative heights he would eventually inhabit when he became an admired and successful poet. The boy was big for his age, though, taking after his father's people, and had the strength to pull the long handle of the press that created an impression of the typeset. In his assistant's role, he was taught how to sort letters and fonts and eventually worked the typeset composing table himself, which aided his ability to parse and spell (as it would for a young Mark Twain, too). Whitman worked for other Brooklyn printers over the next several years, before he ventured across to Manhattan and became a compositor for one of the Napier steam presses then transforming the printing business.[17]

Besides learning something about grammar, spelling, and the material production of newspapers, Whitman was socialized through his work to a certain way of looking at the typeset published page. He had a deep appreciation for the physical appearance of book leaves and carefully oversaw printing of *Leaves of Grass* through different editions, arrangements, and typesets. As Jerome Loving writes, "as a mature poet, he could never 'finish' a poem without first having it set up in print."[18] Whitman had a craftsman's sense of production, but also developed through the printing trade a reflective understanding of communicative possibilities in book-bound address. "Listener up there! . . . Look in my face while I snuff the idle of evening," he writes in one of many places of direct address in *Leaves*, the voice speaking up to us from the page. "Come closer to me, . . ." it whispers two pages later, "I was chilled with the cold types and cylinder and wet paper between us."[19] Whitman knew those types and cylinders firsthand.

His apprentice work gave Whitman money to ride the ferry across to Manhattan and attend the theater with friends. Both ferry and theater were longstanding joys, and each fed the poetry that emerged from his life. From the time he was a small boy, he traveled the ferries between Brooklyn and New York, the only way across in the era before a bridge linked the two. He often rode with his pilot friends up above, "where I could get a full sweep, absorbing shows, accompaniments, surroundings." He came to call them "living poems" for their "oceanic currents, eddies, underneath—the great tides of humanity also, . . . the river and bay scenery . . . the changing panorama of steamers, all sizes, often a string of big ones outward bound to different ports."[20] The ferry carried him across to performances at Simpson's Park and Hamblin's Bowery, where Whitman would sit with other apprentices on the long wooden benches in the pit. The audience was loud and often unruly, threw food and other projectiles, and generally made its opinion of a performance obvious. He loved that part of the event, almost as much as he loved Shakespeare, minstrel shows, opera, and the other kinds of stage performances of the era. As Ezra Greenspan writes, "Whitman could respond freely to any manner of performance, secular or holy; and in virtually any setting, indoors or out. Theater, opera house, lecture hall, church or synagogue, exhibition hall, parade, Fourth of July gathering—they all charged Whitman with the magnetic force of the performer and the audience."[21]

When the printing business took a downturn in 1836, Whitman moved out to Long Island and took a series of schoolteacher jobs, where he practiced a didactic voice that he refined in later writing. Although school teaching did not particularly agree with the seventeen-year-old, he could still get into New York and attend theater occasionally, thanks in part to the completion of ten miles of the Brooklyn-Jamaica railroad and the stagecoach lines connecting it to points east. He ran a far gentler classroom than the ones he grew up in, refraining from corporal punishment customary in his own schooling. He had philosophical reasons, but he also benefited from being six feet tall and solidly built, which no doubt helped when things got rowdy in the theater pit, too. His physical presence may have played a role in his success as a debater about that time, too. In December of 1837, while teaching school in Long Island, he organized a debating society with ten other young men in Smithtown and served as the group's secretary. According to Rubin, Whitman "kept the minutes for the ten meetings in a script as neat as that of his academy-trained successor, and spoke so forcefully, often against older men who were members of professions, that he won the majority of his debates."[22] Whitman would later write that the poet "is no arguer," but the young man trying to improve himself through the debating society certainly was.

Soon after his short-lived debating society experience, Whitman gave up schoolteaching and returned to the newspaper business, which would be his prime occupation through the 1850s, and the production of the first three editions of Leaves of Grass. He worked occasionally as a printer, but mostly as a writer (for some twenty different papers) and editor, most notably at the New York Aurora (1842) and The Brooklyn Eagle and Kings County Democrat (1846–48). It was a tumultuous time in American journalism, with independent-minded sensationalist penny dailies challenging political party–affiliated newspapers, local news reporting emerging as a practice, and steam-powered presses dramatically increasing production capacity and making mass circulation newly possible.[23] Whitman witnessed and participated in this journalistic culture. As many critics have argued, newspaper work fed Whitman's poetry, influencing its subject matter, form, and style.[24] I want to add here by suggesting that Whitman's newspaper writing also served as an inventional medium for working out ways of representing an urban crowd that directly fed what I will identify as his overarching vision of democratic mass communication.

As I read through Whitman's journalism of the period, two things particularly strike me. One is the range of his subject matter, and the other is the number of stories that mention taking a stroll. His were symbolically expansive and materially peripatetic work routines, which underwrote a rhetorical persona that would address audiences on many subjects and from multiple perspectives. Whitman published on topics that included everything from locusts and boarding houses to public meetings and lectures, the desecration of military graves, Charles Dickens, snoring, theatrical and musical performances, school reform, slavery, abolitionism, the English working classes, festivals, capital punishment, national expansion, literature, religion, elections, party politics, ferries, violent crime, prisons, the Mexican-American War, and strolling. Lots of strolling. The variety of topics stretched his writing self out, making it a kind of symbolic wanderer discoursing on places found along its way.

The symbolic wanderer was underwritten by a corporeal version of the same, represented through the figure of the strolling journalist who made regular appearances in Whitman's stories. Like a number of other writers of the era, Walt Whitman was a sauntering guy.[25] In two months as editor of the *Aurora*, he published some twenty articles that referred to and were built upon walks around the city.[26] He often walked along what he called the "two great channels of communication through the city," Chatham Street and, especially, Broadway.[27] If the term had been coined, he might well have called them channels of mass communication, for they carried that sense for him, and he walked through their crowds as part of his daily routine.[28] He regularly took part in the kind of "promiscuous public sociability" that Mary Ryan describes as part of the "easy, ambulatory space" of antebellum New York, a city still compact enough that one could walk most of it in less than six hours.[29] The journalist made the experience into a subject for his readers and created a kind of poetic sociology of public communication in the process:

> At a little before sunrise, if you are an early riser, you may behold a slight human stream, beginning to set down Broadway. The milkmen's carts, and occasionally a carriage from one of the landings where steamboats arrive early in the morning, dash hastily along the street. The pedestrians are nearly all workmen, going to their daily toil, and most of them carrying little tin kettles containing their dinner; newsmen, also, with bundles of the damp morning

papers strapped to their sides; people now and then, of a more fashionable appearance, who have wisely roused themselves from torpid slumber, and come forth to snuff the morning air. Frequently, too, you may meet a sleepy looking boy, neatly dressed, and swinging a large brass key as he goes along. He is under clerk in some store, and on his way to open the establishment, sweep it out, and if need may be, kindle the fire. Be careful, as you pass, lest you get a sousing from some of those Irish servant women, scrubbing the marble stoops, and dashing pails of water upon the flagging of the side walks.[30]

The description of the street continues through the day, onto the noon hour, mid-afternoon, and sunset, with Whitman depicting the composite mass that populated Broadway as the day progressed. Other walking-about stories depicted a denser-packed "jam" of humanity, which the journalist plunged into with delight. He lit upon and idealized its heterogeneity. "Here are people of all classes and stages and rank—from all countries of the globe—engaged in all the varieties of avocations—of every grade, every hue of ignorance and learning, morality and vice, wealth and want, fashion and coarseness, breeding and brutality, elevation and degradation, impudence and modesty."[31]

He attended to the sounds of the city as well as to its sights and chronicled its other modes of collective movement, too. "The noisiest things which attract attention in that part of Broadway are the omnibusses," he observed of the soundscape from a balcony window of the American Museum. "Rumbling and bouncing along, they come, now and then stopping as some person on the sidewalk holds up his finger—a signal that he wants to take passage. The omnibus drivers are a unique race. Winter and summer, rain or shine, there they are, perched up on the tops of their vehicles, and driving ahead just the same."[32] Whitman would come to befriend the drivers, who invited him to ride up top with them, giving him a high view of the crowds moving about him as they drove down "the whole length of Broadway, listening to some yarn (and the most vivid yarns ever spun, and the rarest mimicry)—or perhaps I declaiming some stormy passage from Julius Caesar or Richard (you could roar as loudly as you chose in that heavy, dense, uninterrupted streetbass)."[33] At its best, movement was a kind of street theater that the roving journalist took in and represented affectionately.

When he assumed editorship of the *Brooklyn Daily Eagle*, Whitman's sauntering about continued and gave him means to survey the world about him, materially and symbolically. With the distinguished journalist-poet William Cullen Bryant, he sometimes "took rambles miles long, till dark, out towards Bedford or Flatbush," with Bryant offering Whitman "clear accounts of scenes in Europe—the cities, looks, architecture, art, especially Italy—where he had travel'd a great deal."[34] Some of Whitman's strolling found outlet in a regular "City Intelligence" column, where he did for Brooklyn's Fulton Street some of what he had done for Broadway at the *Aurora*.[35] Once he described a ferry trip across to Manhattan, where he strolled along South Street and looked out at packet ships from New Orleans and Liverpool.[36] Another time, he reported walking past "several parties of youngsters playing 'base,' a certain game of ball," which prompted a call for more such healthful outdoor pursuits.[37] He regularly ambled down to the Fulton Ferry Salt Baths, a healthful indoor pursuit with perhaps other gratifications for a man among men.[38] He documented Brooklyn's "numerous bands of serenaders who make our thoroughfares 'vocal,' and instrumental too."[39] Strolling for Whitman was both personal predilection and occupational routine.

Two years at the *Eagle* ensconced Whitman as an occupational Mercurian, working between networks of communication distant and local. He monitored and amplified telegraphed news about the war with Mexico along the Rio Grande and described the road between Vera Cruz and Mexico City for his readers in Brooklyn.[40] He read and clipped items from other newspapers and prepared a miscellany of items for the front page. He wrote editorials and other articles on many subjects (politics, education, social reform, and health were all common topics), in what one of his printers described as "a beautiful hand plain as a pikestaff, punctuating it all the way through," and afterward carefully checked over his compositors' work.[41] He read, reviewed, and recommended a great array of books.[42] He wrote about performances, including the Oratorio of St. Paul, performed by the New York Tabernacle, which he listened to with eyes closed to go "with Saul on his wicked journey" till "the still soft voice of God spoke by the way side, and a bright light shone around."[43] He wrote about the city on the Fourth of July, with its different lights, having witnessed it from the streets, taking in the sites and sounds and urban crowds.[44]

Whitman's urban strolling might remind one of the *flâneur*, that ambling French idler of the same era who walked about Paris and took in its sights, made famous by Charles Baudelaire (1821–67) and amplified in Walter Benjamin's brilliant essay, "On Some Motifs in Baudelaire." With feints toward Hegel, Engels, and especially Edgar Allen Poe, Benjamin meditated on the urban masses of the nineteenth century and the figure of Baudelaire's *flâneur*, noting, "Fear, revulsion, and horror were the emotions which the big-city crowd aroused in those who first observed it"—a statement made with Whitman nowhere in view.[45] The attitude was represented in one way in Poe's "Man of the Crowd" (1840), which Baudelaire translated. Poe's short story has some catalog-type similarities with Whitman's writings, but its gothic portrayal of a man behind glass peering out into the crowd before being drawn into it has none of the joy (if all of the rambling) of Whitman's city strolls. One critic calls it a "tale of incommunication, and existential loneliness," which no one could say of Whitman's urban journalism, or most of his crowd poetry that followed it.[46]

As Benjamin notes, the *flâneur* was no man of the crowd, even if Baudelaire saw fit to equate the two. In Poe's character, "composure has given way to manic behavior," while the *flâneur* is a strolling man of leisure who takes in the scene, but does not fully give himself up to it.[47] Baudelaire himself wrote of the "singular intoxication" and "ineffable orgy" that came from walking among the multitudes, though he allowed that it "is not given to everybody to bathe in the man-ocean."[48] His stories more often depict a narrator who stands as a lone figure distant from the ills of modern life, apart and alienated from the crowd.[49] As Benjamin wrote, the *flâneur* becomes the crowds' "accomplice even as he dissociates himself from them. He becomes deeply involved with them, only to relegate them to oblivion with a single glance of contempt."[50] Though it made its appearances, the glance of contempt was not central to Whitman's repertoire, nor was estrangement from the urban scenes around him, or hesitance to embrace its masses. Bathing in the man-oceans was closer to the mark. In this regard, Whitman's crowded streets differed from those represented by Baudelaire, Poe, and subsequent major writers on crowds. Unlike those alienated, appalled, or otherwise distanced from the crowd, Whitman embraced it.

Whitman's sensibility was arguably a reflection on his class position, politics, pattern of personal mood, and physical size. Unlike most of the literati and intellectuals who wrote on the crowd, Whitman grew up in a producer-class household with democratic sympathies, which he further cultivated in adulthood. He was a member of hoi polloi who grew up in Brooklyn crowds and seems to have been drawn to them from an early age. To be sure, New York had violent crowds, and Whitman witnessed and wrote about these as well,[51] but he seems not to have been haunted by their specter. Dispositionally, he knew oceanic, world-embracing moods, and civil crowds could bring this out in him. He was also a healthy, white, native-born man, six feet tall, and weighing between 180 and 200 pounds—quite large for his day. This meant that Whitman could move comfortably through street jostling with a sense of riding upon a human sea, a feeling indexed to bodies tall enough to rise above it, strong enough to feel safe, and not marked as culturally different so as to stand out as objects of ridicule, prejudice, or violence. Consequently, the crowd experience could be different for him than it was for members of those groups not favored in the same ways—blacks and ethnic minorities, women, the smaller-bodied and infirm, all of whom were comparatively disadvantaged. Whitman could move with maximal freedom through the streets, making them a more fertile inventional space for crowd-embracing sentiment and writing built upon it.

Embrace of the crowd sometimes extended to embrace of a reading public beyond it. This was particularly true when Whitman became editor of the *Brooklyn Daily Eagle*, the Democratic party paper in his home city.[52] "There is a curious kind of sympathy (haven't you ever thought of it before?) that arises in the mind of a newspaper conductor with the public he serves," Whitman wrote (using a name for his job that nicely blurred the boundaries between communication and transport). "He gets to *love* them. Daily communion creates a sort of brotherhood and sisterhood between the two parties."[53] To be sure, Whitman struck relations to his public rather different from partaker in daily communion (a bragging self-promotional stance among the more notable),[54] but he was probably expressing a genuinely felt mood, which in turn pointed to an evolving social psychology of public address that newspaper work allowed him to develop. Early as editor of the *Aurora*, he had observed to his readers, "The consciousness that several thousand people will look for their *Aurora* as regularly as for their breakfasts . . . implies no small responsibility upon a man. Yet it is delightful."[55] He discharged his delightful responsibility in many ways, one of which was occasionally to address a reader directly, almost like a friend: "Well (are you interested, dear reader?)"; "Reader, was you ever so unfortunate as to be locked out, and put up at some lodging house where, much to your dismay, you are packed in a room containing some five or six single beds?"[56] Newspaper writing had Whitman taking up multiple communicative positions toward both the assembled crowds he wrote about and the dispersed audiences he addressed.

Travel, Notebooks, Oratory

Whitman's personal dispersal received a boost in February of 1848, when he and his brother Jeff set off for New Orleans, where Walt had been offered a job working on a newspaper. He had been fired from the *Eagle* in December, after he had endorsed Congressman David Wilmot's proposal that "neither slavery nor involuntary servitude" should ever exist in territories acquired from Mexico, whom the United States was at war with and had invaded.[57]

Whitman energetically supported expansion and seizing territory from Mexico, but opposed the westward extension of slavery, and he pushed the cause in a number of editorials that upset more conservative members of the local party, who in turn pressured for his firing. (Whitman may also have kicked a prominent local Democratic politician down a flight of stairs.) He seized the chance to work for the *New Orleans Daily Crescent*, a paper about to begin publishing and in need of experienced newsmen.[58] Although he had roamed Manhattan, Brooklyn, and a good deal of Long Island, he had never been further from home than Montauk Point. He was about to start off on a journey he would count as "crucial to his development as a poet."[59]

The trip to and from New Orleans and the time Whitman spent there provided inventional media for filling in and expanding his geographical, social, and moral imaginations alike. He recorded and made sense of his experiences through writing and notebooks, staples for working journalists and aspiring literary figures like the twenty-eight-year-old Whitman. It turned out to be a liminal journey, which brought him face-to-face with slavery as an institution and human beings who were slaves.[60] Before going to New Orleans, Whitman opposed the institution and the slave trade on the grounds that it was immoral and lowered the dignity of labor (of white working men), but he did not support the abolitionist movement, and, like the vast majority of whites in his era, he harbored racial prejudices against blacks. According to Loving, though, Whitman's position on slavery had begun to shift in his last weeks at the *Eagle*, prompted by attending his first abolitionist lecture, "The Worth of Liberty," delivered by the Irish-born Unitarian minister, Henry Giles. In a review for the *Eagle*, Whitman called it "one of the most powerfully written and warmly delivered speeches we have ever heard. Rarely have the divine proportions of liberty been praised by more eloquent lips: rarely, if ever, has the accursed nature of tyranny and slavery, in all their influences and results, been pourtrayed [*sic*] in words more effective and clear, or in a manner more enthusiastic! The lecturer's picture of a slave, the thing without the feelings of a man—not a husband, not a parent, not a wife, not a patriot—and impossible to be either, in its proper sense—was burningly fearful and true. It will long live upon our memory, and we doubt not, in the memories of many a man and woman who heard it," he wrote.[61] Giles's eloquence seems to have seared into Whitman's awareness a picture of the dehumanization wrought by slavery—"not a husband, not a parent, not a wife, not a patriot," the slave was treated as nothing more than "the thing without the feelings of a man." As Loving interprets the episode, the journalist seems to have "suddenly broken away from the nineteenth-century stereotypes about the slave as less than human to see blacks in the context of citizenry and social roles he had championed for whites in his editorials throughout the 1840s."[62] Such was at least the germ of an attitude as the brothers set off for New Orleans.

Walt would keep a journal of the trip, which he would convert into a three-part narrative of technologically enhanced sauntering, published by his new paper as "Excerpts from a Traveller's Note Book." From New York, the brothers traveled five hours by train to Philadelphia, and from there to Baltimore, where they spent the night. At seven the next morning, a Saturday, they boarded another train that took them west to Hagerstown, where it then hugged the Potomac as it climbed into the first great mountains they had ever seen. They stopped and ate dinner in the spectacular setting of Harpers Ferry, where the houses seemed built one atop another, and then pushed on to Cumberland, western terminus of the railroad, "the great rendezvous and landing place of the immense Pennsylvania wagons, and the drovers from hundreds of miles west." The wagons put Whitman in the mind of caravans crossing the Steppes. "Hundreds and hundreds of these enormous vehicles, with their arched roofs of white canvas, wend their way into Cumberland from all quarters, during a busy season, with goods to send on eastward, and to take goods brought by the railroad."[63] With night falling around them, the Whitmans got into a four-horse stagecoach with seven other people and climbed into the mountains ("these mighty warts on the great breast of nature"), stopping to change horses every ten miles. They stepped out into the cold February night and into long, one-story public houses, sometimes coming upon "ten or twelve great strapping drovers, reclining about the room on benches, and as many more, before the huge fire." Bidding adieu to the strapping drovers, they pressed on through the night into Uniontown, Pennsylvania, at daybreak Sunday, and then slowly from there to Wheeling, Virginia, on the banks of the Ohio River, which they reached at ten that night.[64]

At the river they found the freight-and-packet boat *St. Cloud*, down from Pittsburgh, steamed up and bound ultimately for New Orleans. They awoke the next morning to the sound of the ship's breakfast bell and took in their first daylight view of the Ohio. "There is no romance in a mass of yellowish brown liquid," Whitman wrote, reacting to the gap between image and reality of the great western river.[65] He marveled, though, at the abundance gathered and transported on the packet: "barrels of salt pork, flour, and lard, bags of coffee, rolls of leather, groceries, dry goods, hardware, all sorts of agricultural products, innumerable coops filled with live geese, turkeys, and fowls . . . divers [*sic*] living hogs, to say nothing of a horse, and a resident dog."[66] The packet hugged the Kentucky border, and Whitman spent hours listening to slave workers talk as they 'wooded up' the boat, stripped to the waist, shoulders padded with empty salt sacks, carrying cords of wood across a plank laid between ship and shore, stacking it on deck or near the furnaces.[67] Since pulling out of Wheeling, the *St. Cloud* had been steaming down a river whose left shore held slaves, but whose right shore did not. When they hit Cairo, Illinois, and turned south on the Mississippi, the unslaved side vanished, and they plunged deeper into the region, past Memphis and Mobile, sighting grand plantation houses and squalid slaves' cabins. On Friday afternoon, the dome of New Orleans's St. Charles Hotel came into view, and after several more hours of picking its way through the assemblage of ships and flatboats clogging the river, the *St. Cloud* pulled into port. On a rainy night in February, the boat disgorged itself upon docks filled with slaves carrying freight, mules pulling carts, and two brothers trying to find their way among them to a boarding house in a crowded and unfamiliar city of 125,000.[68]

New Orleans was a remarkable place in the late winter and early spring of 1848. Thousands of soldiers from the Mexican campaign, wounded or healthy, were housed there or passing through. The Lenten season was upon the city, punctuated at one end by the carnivalesque Shrove Tuesday celebrations and at the other by the great Cathedral Masses of Passion Week. Walt and his brother wandered the city, passing through Lafayette Square and the French Market, along Canal Street and the levee. Whitman's walking now took him through crowds of a different sort, made up of blacks, mulattoes, octoroons, Indians, Creoles, and whites of various ethnic backgrounds. At indoor performances and in the streets, he heard the city's musical rhythms, accents, and languages. In late March, news of revolution in France came telegraphed through the newly finished line from Mobile. Incoming ships brought follow-up reports and kept the city "in a perfect ferment," with nightly gatherings in Jackson Square and banquets of celebration that Europe's autocratic rulers and kings appeared to be falling. "The whole civilized world is in commotion," Whitman wrote. "Everywhere the people have risen against the tyrannies which oppress them."[69]

Not quite everywhere. Organized white violence and its threat had been largely successful in keeping American slaves from rising up en masse against the tyrants. Although slavery was not a subject Whitman could address in the pages of the *Crescent*, it was an inescapable part of daily life. The paper ran announcements of upcoming slave auctions—"Sarah Ann, 17 years, house girl, and her infant girl, fully guaranteed"—and woodcut images of runaway slaves with offers of rewards for their capture. Each night at eight he heard the toll of the Market House bell that warned slaves to leave the streets—an ominous form of sonic mass communication backed by state-sanctioned violence of a particularly cruel sort. At Banks's Arcade, which served as a newsgathering center, Whitman would likely have witnessed a scene of human beings auctioned and sold as wealthy planters lounged at a bar on the side. When a northern visitor came to New Orleans the next year, "a tour of the Arcade shocked her into declaring that no orator could indict the institution of slavery with the power of an hour spent at this auction."[70] Walt's brother Jeff was appalled by the spectacle of Mass in the city. "Everyone would go up and dip their fingers in the holy water and then go home and *whip* their *slaves*," he wrote to his family.[71] Seven years later, Whitman would deploy the image of a slave at auction in the most morally searing poem of the first edition of *Leaves of Grass*, which I return to below.

In late May, the brothers were steaming back north, driven by a combination of events that included Jeff's homesickness and dysentery, and perhaps Walt's firing. Owing to the recent completion of the Illinois and Michigan Canal (the last major canal project of its sort in the United States), they could head home by a different route and be among the first travelers to do so. They passed through St. Louis and switched there from the *Pride of the West* to the *Prairie Bird*, which took them up the Mississippi to the Illinois River at Alton, and then on to the new canal that joined it and carried them one hundred miles east to Chicago. The Whitmans tramped about the fast-growing city, then nearing thirty thousand inhabitants, and boarded a steamer to take them across Lakes Michigan, Huron, and Erie, passing through Mackinac Island, Detroit, Windsor (Ontario), Cleveland, and, by coach, Niagara Falls, before riding the railroad to Albany. They caught a boat down the Hudson to New York, where they pulled into the docks on June 15, three weeks after setting off from New Orleans.[72]

The trip furnished the writer a storehouse of images, in addition to a corporeal sense of the geographic expansiveness of the country. He channeled some of this material into the programmatic prose Preface to the first edition of *Leaves of Grass*. The poet's "spirit responds to his country's spirit. . . . he incarnates its geography and natural life and rivers and lakes. Mississippi with annual freshets and changing chutes, Missouri and Columbia and Ohio and Saint Lawrence with the falls and beautiful masculine Hudson, do not embouchure where they spend themselves more than they embouchure into him . . . He spans between them also from east to west and reflects what is between them . . . the New-York firemen and the target excursion—the southern plantation life—the character of the northeast and of the northwest and southwest—slavery and the tremulous spreading of hands to protect it, and the stern opposition to it which shall never cease till it ceases or the speaking of tongues and the moving of lips cease" (7–8).

While Whitman could have composed these lines without ever passing through the places he mentions, the fact is he did pass through a number of them and wrote as an eyewitness. He had seen seventeen of the nation's thirty states, set foot in Canada, lived at the gateway point to Mexico, and been brought face-to-face with both slavery and the stern opposition to it. The ambling journalist had stretched himself out along the country's expanding transportation system and crossed over the sectional divide that threatened union of both party and nation. Gregory Clark has argued that travel can function as "a fundamentally rhetorical experience that prompts individuals to make themselves over in the image of a collective identity that they find symbolized in their national landscape."[73] Such seems to have been the case with Whitman's ramble to New Orleans. His picture of the nation was sensorially enriched by the journey, and he came to draw upon pieces of it in the poetic identification with the nation that he forged in *Leaves of Grass*.

Notebooks played an important role and allowed Whitman a place to work out his thoughts and phrasings. It's not clear when he began keeping the notebooks (the earliest surviving one dates perhaps to 1847), but they served a number of functions, from personal and journalistic *aide de memoire* to medium of literary invention—material form for figuring *logoi* through pencil or pen on paper, hand moving across the page and leaving traces of an embodied mind.[74] Although some notebooks focused topically on particular subjects, most were more miscellaneous collections of notes on everything from money he owed people, to short observations on subjects, lists of men briefly identified by appearance or occupation, dicta to himself, and beginnings for stories and poems. He sometimes kept very small notebooks, which could easily fit in his pocket, but also worked with loose paper more haphazardly collected over the course of time—lined white paper, leftover pink and green wrapper stock from the first edition of *Leaves*, blue tax blanks perhaps provided by a printer friend, letterhead from government offices. His writing changed as he aged, from the small neat hand of a younger man to a looser and more flowing script as he aged. He often wrote haphazardly on a page and crossed out very often. When using the notebooks to compose poems that would find their way into *Leaves of Grass*—"Song of Myself," for instance—he painstakingly wrote and rewrote. "He could hardly write five words without crossing out three," Edward Grier observes.[75] While Paul of Tarsus talked his vision out to his secretary, Whitman of Brooklyn wrote his out longhand on leaves of notebook paper.

Notebooks provided a medium through which Whitman worked out a desire to become a great orator, another inventional stream feeding composition of *Leaves of Grass*. One critic calls the book "a shrewd blend of platform speaking and journalistic prose" bound together by "new use of old rhetorical rules."[76] Whitman learned and reworked the rules through a version of the traditional rhetorical commonplace book, collections of quotations organized by topic headings that furnished material for subsequent rhetorical production. Whitman had a sheath of papers he labeled "Oratory," which consisted of notes copied or paraphrased from other sources, along with his own thoughts on the subject.[77] He copied a passage from Thomas Sheridan's *Lectures on Reading* (1775), for instance, which offered a picture of speaker and audience that updated and electrified the Pauline trope of the common body: "The organs of the body attuned to the exertions of the mind, through the kindred organs of the hearers, instantaneously, and as it were, with an electrical spirit, vibrate those energies from soul to soul. Notwithstanding the diversity of minds in such a multitude, by the lightning of eloquence, they are melted into one mass . . . and have but one voice," Whitman penned.[78] He would go on to "sing the body electric" in his *Leaves of Grass*, and through multiple means give poetic voice to the multitude.

The expansive first-person narrator of that book would encompass a democratic multitude by making them part of his extended self—a kind of crowd within that was evoked in another passage that Whitman paraphrased for his "Oratory" sheath: "The greatest orator, actor is he who contains always a crowded and critical audience in himself, and plays, speaks to that invisible house more than to any other, with unflagging vitality and determination in every assertion, flight, suggestion, hazarding, withdrawing, inquiring, rebuking moroseness, poetic &c of an oration, as shown and ejected in the vocalism of every word expressing those parts—that is what makes the main of a great speaker."[79] Whitman's journalism carried intimations of a developing social psychology of the crowded audience within. His urban and long-distance rambling, meanwhile, furnished him characters and social types that filled out the "invisible house" he might play to when he broke out in oratory.

Whitman seems to have undertaken rhetorical study with the hopes of being an orator himself. According to his brother George, while Walt was living at home in the 1850s, he "had an idea he could lecture . . . [and] wrote what Mother called 'barrels' of lectures."[80] He drew up plans for a lecture tour, "North and South, East and West—at Washington,—at the different State Capitols . . . promulging [*sic*] the grand ideas of American ensemble liberty, concentrativeness, individuality, spirituality &c &c."[81] He had ideas about how to carry it off. "Talk directly to the hearer or hearers: *You so and so* . . . From the opening of the Oration & on through, the great thing is to be inspired as one divinely possessed, blind to all subordinate affairs and given up entirely to the surgings and utterances of the mighty tempestuous demon."[82] He imagined "founding a *new school* of Declamation Composition far more direct, close, animated and fuller of live tissue and muscle than any hitherto—entirely different (of course) from the old style."[83] Animated, muscular, direct, and promulgating the ideas of ensemble liberty et al., Whitman's imagined oratory resembled the poetry that came from him.

Whitman did not become a great orator, but from "imagining himself in that role," C. Carroll Hollis has argued, he "created the persona that dominates the first three editions" of *Leaves of Grass*. "Oratory was the dream, and writing and printing were the actual production."[84] Emerson had proclaimed that the orator must be "to a certain extent, a poet," and teach his audience "to see . . . thing[s] with his eyes."[85] Whitman reversed the equation, becoming a poet who was to a certain extent an orator, but still offering us ways to see. As Hollis demonstrates, *Leaves of Grass*, particularly the edgy first edition, is marked by oral syntactical patterns and styles. Ellipses run throughout the book, taking the place of written punctuation, and arguably serving as reading marks to pace spoken delivery. Like Paul's letter to Corinth, Whitman's *Leaves* was a kind of oratory by other means, designed to communicate with a diverse audience held more-or-less in mind.

Chanting Polytheistic Democracy

Whitman channeled his oratorical dreams into *Leaves of Grass*, where he offered what we can retroactively characterize as both a vision for mass communication and an example of it. The first edition was published in early July of 1855, after Whitman had walked his manuscript down to the Rome brothers' print shop on Fulton Street and helped them set it in type during free moments between their commercial jobs. The title called up Isaiah 40:6 ("All flesh is grass, and all the goodliness thereof is as the flower of the field"), as well as printers' slang for compositions of questionable value that they wrote up and set in type during idle moments.[86] The slender volume ran ninety-five pages and consisted of twelve unrhymed and untitled poems preceded by a rambling prose preface that announced a vision of America, the poet, and the divinities of people. The volume grew exponentially, and poems gained titles and were arranged into clusters over the next five years. The second edition came out in 1856, expanded to thirty-two poems spread over 340 pages, and the third in 1860, with a whopping 178 poems over 456 pages. The poet would later say that "the religious purpose" underlay all others in the composition of these early editions, something particularly true of the third edition, which Whitman considered, at least for a time, as "*The Great Construction of the New Bible* . . . the principal object—the main life work."[87] Focusing especially on material composed for the first edition (supplemented with passages from 1856 and 1860), I want to characterize the religion of Whitman's early *Leaves* as a heterodox (or post-) Christianity I'll call *democratic polytheism*, anchored in an idealized America and marked by a kind of sophistic embrace of contradiction. In this section, I will sketch the contours of that faith and unpack media of mass communication that might constitute it.

The religious Whitman isn't as familiar to us today as the gay Whitman, the erotic Whitman, the political Whitman, and of course the poetic-literary Whitman, but this hasn't always been so. The *Christian Spiritualist*, for instance, called the book's first edition "a prophecy and promise of much that awaits all who are entering with us into the opening doors of a new era" (while also allowing that it "abounds in passages that cannot be quoted in drawing-rooms").[88] "The whole body of these Poems—spiritually considered—is alive with power," a reviewer of the 1860 edition wrote.[89] Although more conservative Christians were less effusive (one called the book "impious and obscene"), a friend of the poet would call Whitman's religious sentiment his "leading characteristic."[90] "I too, following many, and followed by many, inaugurate a Religion," the opening poem for the New Bible of 1860 declares. "I see the following poems are indeed to drop in the earth the germs of a greater Religion," a claim that a small group of his disciples would take very seriously.[91] Looking back late in life, the poet said, "I claim everything for religion: after the claims of my religion are satisfied nothing is left for anything else: yet I have been called irreligious—an infidel (God help me!): as if I could have written a word of the Leaves without its religious root-ground. I am not traditionally religious—I know it: but even traditionally I am not anti: I take all the old forms and faiths and remake them in conformity with the modern spirit, not rejecting a single item of the earlier programs."[92]

We might characterize *Leaves of Grass* as one of a number of U.S.-hatched heterodoxies of the era, perched midway between Joseph Smith's *Book of Mormon* (1830) and Mary Baker Eddy's *Science and Health* (1875), and like them mobilizing the printed word to formulate and disseminate a new kind of faith. Whitman's was a variation on second-generation Transcendentalism, refracted through a working-class sensibility and embracing the city and democratic masses that another second-generation figure, Henry David Thoreau, distanced himself from in his literary experiment at Walden Pond (1854). As Michael Robertson writes, "Emerson promoted an individualistic spirituality that, to many people later in the century, seemed to find its highest expression in *Leaves of Grass*."[93] Whitman did his compositional work as Karl Marx was busy in Europe working out his own heterodox faith in the masses, figured through dialectical philosophy and economic materialism instead of a free-verse oratorical poetics fed by broad cultural absorption.[94]

Unlike more orthodox Christians and Jews, Whitman pledged singular allegiance to no one God. In comparison to Paul, the vigilant monotheist, Whitman was a loose-limbed polytheist open to heterogeneity in all realms of life, or what Phillip Rieff once called "the polytheism of experience."[95] Leading into the first edition, he wrote in his notebooks: "How full of Gods is the world—There are none greater than these present ones—Why has it been taught that there is only one Supreme?—I say there are and must be myriads of Supremes. I say that is blasphemous petty and infidel which denies any immortal soul to be eligible to advance onward to be as supreme as any—I say that all goes on to be eligible to become one of the Supremes."[96] When an edited version of the passage found its way into a kind of thesis poem of 1856, Whitman added a descriptor of the multiple Supremes: "One does not countervail another, any more than one eye-sight countervails another, or one life countervails another."[97] He had been reading about the history of the world's gods; "supposed to be about one thousand religions," he wrote in a pocket-sized notebook, "Phtah Isis Osiris . . . Jehovah Adonai Christ Brahm Bhudda, Ormuzd god of light Ahrimanes god of darkness . . ."[98] A list of world gods made it into the first poem of *Leaves*, where the great poetic "I" takes them "all for what they are worth." The poet goes on: "My faith is the greatest of faiths and the least of faiths,/ Enclosing all worship ancient and modern, and all between ancient and modern," and following with a list of worship practices from across world religions, from tribal practices through the great monotheistic faiths, to atheism."[99]

The polytheism played itself out in a heterogeneity of embraced ideals, social entities, and animating myths, well-evidenced in the closing poem of the 1855 edition, which opens: "Great are the myths. . . . I too delight in them,/ Great are Adam and Eve . . . I too look back and accept them." He would praise "risen and fallen nations, and their poets, women, sages, inventors, rulers, warriors and priests" and a dizzying array of other entities: liberty, equality, the current age, democracy, reformers, sailors, "yourself and myself," youth, old age, day, night, wealth, poverty, expression of speech, silence, "the greatest nation" (presumably America), the earth, "the quality of truth in man," language, the law, "marriage, commerce, newspapers, books, freetrade, railroads, steamers, international mails and telegraphs and exchanges," justice, goodness, wickedness, the eternal equilibrium of things, the eternal overthrow of things, life, and death (156–60). Attending to the polarities of some of the things he was praising, the poet asks and answers himself: "Do you call that a paradox? It certainly is a paradox" (159). Earlier, near the conclusion of the book's opening poem, he had cheerfully admitted, "Very well then. . . . I contradict myself;/ I am large. . . . I contain multitudes" (95). Poet of body and soul, man and woman, young and old, wise and foolish, "[o]f every hue and trade and rank, of every caste and religion" (46)—he is the poet who contains multitudes, including some who seem contrary to one another.

There is a kind of sophistic embrace of contradictions in this stance, one that plays upon Protagoras's idea of *dissoi logoi*—whose narrow translation is "countervailing arguments," but which can be taken more generally as competing or seemingly contradictory accounts or perspectives. Protagoras suggested that *dissoi logoi* were an inescapable part of the human epistemological condition, which his students might sort through and argue about with regard to a particular issue.[100] Whitman is pushing the idea into realms of social and individual being, as well as ethical and spiritual life. In Whitman's world, contradiction is something to be embraced and lived with, drawn into a larger composite identity that might find room for all.

In creating what he later called "the thread-voice, more or less audible, of an aggregated, inseparable, unprecedented, vast, composite, electric democratic nationality,"[101] Whitman used a decidedly heterodox version of the Pauline image of the universal Body of Christ, sensualized and identified with the body of the orating poet. This is clearest in "Poem of Many in One," the 1856 thesis poem made from the 1855 Preface. The poet, making room for near and far, spans the nation from east to west, touching all in between, incarnating the land, "Plunging his semitic muscle into its merits and demerits,/ Making its geography, cities, beginnings, events, glories, defections, diversities, vocal in him."[102] With help from his semitic muscle the poet would give voice to the nation's diversities. "By great bards only can series of peoples and States be fused into the compact organism of one nation," he announced, substituting the body of the poet for the Body of Christ as that which binds together the far-flung ekklesia.[103]

While the erotic and polytheistic elements of Whitman's faith clearly distinguished him from Paul, he nevertheless maintained elements of continuity with the Christian tradition. The universalism of Whitman's poetic project, his effort to "reject none, accept all," resonated, for instance, with Paul's evangelism, while his special concern for the meek and shunned found precedent in the ministry of Jesus. "I am for sinners and the unlearned," Whitman wrote in his notebooks.[104] "Through me many long dumb voices," he promised in the poem that became "Song of Myself," voices of prostitutes, the deformed, diseased, despairing, dwarves, and thieves (54). Champion of the vulnerable, needy, different, and despised, Whitman also followed Jesus and Paul—and the sophists before them—by upsetting traditional categories of sacred and profane. He would channel culturally forbidden voices, of sex and lust, flesh and appetite, and thus push beyond where Paul was willing to go, setting a symbolic table more radically inclusive than his predecessor's could be. "This is the meal pleasantly set. . . . / for the wicked just the same as the righteous," he wrote. "I will not have a single person slighted or left away"—kept woman, sponger, thief, slave, venerealee, "There shall be no difference between them and the rest" (47–48). At the social level, polytheism played itself out as a radically egalitarian pluralism, symbolized by the table pleasantly set for all, with special places reserved for the socially despised and degraded. It was a social and symbolic order that embraced contraries, with the longer-term hope of creating something greater than had been known before.

That greater moral order extended to slaves, a point forcefully made in the fifth poem of the 1855 edition, titled "Poem of the Body" a year later. Opening with an eroticized version of the poet's universal body ("The bodies of men and women engirth me/and I engirth them") it proceeds through a catalog of people, female and male, immigrant and slave. "Each belongs here or anywhere just as much as the welloff. . . . just as much as you,/ Each has his or her place in the procession" (134) From the inclusive procession, the poem turns back to the particular—a slave at auction, a man, his body, his fatherhood; and then a woman at auction, her body, her motherhood. With complex and searing detail to which I cannot begin to do to justice here, the poem takes the reader through a moral argument, from particularity and the body to universal identification. A woman's body at auction, a mother— and then he asks us directly, "Your mother . . . is she living? . . . /Do you not see that these are exactly the same to all in all nations and times all over the earth?" (135–36). Like *Leaves of Grass* as a whole, "Poem of the Body" laid out a normative vision that exceeded social reality, serving at once as critique and moral ideal.

Whitman held hopes that the United States might someday house the greater ethico-spiritual order his *Leaves* envisioned, even as he was acutely aware of the crisis and moral disorder that would eventually bring civil war. More than its concrete political realities, it was the nation's promise, common people, and ultimate principles that animated his hope. "As he sees the farthest he has the most faith," he wrote of the poet, and of himself as well (9). He held high the Declaration of Independence, the Constitution, and the nation's unofficial motto, *e pluribus unum*, even as he was recoiling from the party system in which he had long participated. Like others in the 1850s, he grew cynical about politics as usual, a point made abundantly clear in a scathing unpublished treatise he wrote in the summer of 1856, which characterizes the parties and nominating conventions as run by "robbers, pimps, . . . malignants, conspirators, . . . slave-catchers, pushers of slavery, . . . gaudy outside with gold chains made from the people's money and the harlot's money twisted together," among other human sorts.[105] It was not politicians who would redeem the nation, but poetry and the people. "[T]he great mass of mechanics, farmers, men following the water, and all laboring persons . . . are in fact, and to all intents and purposes, the American nation, the people," he wrote.[106] "Washington made free the body of America," he penciled to himself. "Now comes one who will make free the American soul."[107]

For Whitman, America and democracy were deeply interwoven and together anchored his freer-floating polytheism in particular (if idealized) places and forms of life. "America does not repel the past or what it has produced under its forms or amid other politics or the idea of castes or the old religions," the 1855 Preface begins. Rather, it had absorbed and actualized inherited currents of humanity. "Here is not merely a nation but a teeming nation of nations," he wrote (5). Its genius lay not "in its executives or legislatures, nor in its ambassadors or colleges or churches or parlors, nor even in its newspapers or inventors . . . but always most in the common people." They and their ways were "unrhymed poetry," waiting for a commensurate bard who might "give them reception for their sake and his own sake" (6). *Leaves of Grass*, as Betsy Erkkila argues, would be politics by other means.[108] Whitman would set out to represent the whole of the nation, its people and places, things public and private, each finding room in an oratorical poetry that might stitch together the many as a pluralistic one and point it toward a better version of itself. As he would later write, "the fruition of democracy . . . resides altogether in the future," and the same was true of the American nation where it took root.[109]

In the 1850s, Whitman's hopes for a better America ultimately rested in a kind of spiritualized democracy materialized through poetry and the people, hoi polloi, the demos. After the outsetting bard had returned from New Orleans, Loving notes, "the democracy he had so studiously attended to during his *Eagle* days began to take on aspects of divinity."[110] The masses became almost holy in his poetry. Working, procreating, sauntering, odorous, sensual, embodied, a collective made through individualities, they were an object of democratic faith: "Endless unfolding of words of the ages!/ And mine a word of the modern . . . a word en masse/ A word of the faith that never balks" (53). In his new polytheistic order, they would make up the "the gangs of kosmos and prophets en masse" who would take the traditional place of the priests. "Through the divinity of themselves," they would be "interpreters of men and women and of all events and things" (25).

And Whitman would be the interpreter of them. "I am the bard of Democracy," he wrote, "I alone advance among the people en-masse, coarse and strong . . . solitary chanting the true America, . . . suffused as with the common people. I alone receive them with a perfect reception and love—and they shall receive me."[111] It was a statement of hope—hope that his poetry would be absorbed by the common people just as he had absorbed them, a communion of poet and audience that would both symbolize and bring about the sort of polytheistic democratic America he envisioned.

A shameless self-promoter since his early days as a newspaperman and writer, Whitman wasn't going to leave the dream of popular reception to chance. In the months in 1855 after 795 copies of the book were printed (and precious few sold), Whitman penned three anonymous reviews of the volume, using a variety of techniques to drum up interest. He lauded its originality ("Nature may have given the hint to the author of the *Leaves of Grass*, but there exists no book or fragment of a book, which can have given the hint to them"). He praised the author's brawniness ("No sniveler, or tea-drinking poet, no puny clawback or prude, is Walt Whitman"). He praised the author's soul ("He is the true spiritualist . . . [and] the largest lover and sympathizer that has appeared in literature"). He even praised the author's stoic, hands-off attitude toward the success of his book ("Walt Whitman, the begetter of a new offspring out of literature, taking with easy nonchalance the chances of its present reception").[112] When he received a note of congratulations on the volume from Emerson, who did not know its author, Whitman passed it on to be printed by the *New York Tribune*, without bothering to ask permission from the Concord sage. He would go on to print a short excerpt of the letter—again without permission—in gold letters embossed on the spine of the 1856 edition: "I Greet You at the / Beginning of A / Great Career / R W Emerson." The Emerson letter itself appeared at the back of the volume, followed by Whitman's own twelve-page "Letter to Ralph Waldo Emerson." It gave a sense of personal correspondence, but was no such thing (Whitman still had not sent Emerson a personal reply to the original letter). "HERE are thirty-two Poems, which I send you, dear Friend and Master," it opened. The two men had met once.[113]

There was something fitting about Whitman's New American Bible being enmeshed in a culture of do-it-yourself public relations. Whitman himself had observed that the American union was "swarming with blatherers," and at times he was one of them, deriving his impulses as much from the Penny Press and P.T. Barnum (whom Whitman had once interviewed) as from the great prophets of history.[114] Publicity and self-promotion too would be central elements of the great religion of American democracy, from Whitman's time through our own.

Varieties of Mass Communication in Whitman's *Leaves*

The polytheistic democratic ekklesia that Whitman hoped might find place in the United States would express itself through multiple media of mass communication. Four seem to me of particular significance. Each can be described in terms of the crowds through which he loved to move. One is the materially assembled crowd, bodies brought together in spatial and temporal proximity. The second is that aggregated crowd that assembles in one place over time—past, present, and future. The third is that mass of humanity represented through art—poetry and journalism being the two media at which Whitman himself was particularly adept. And the fourth medium of mass communication, also indicated in *Leaves of Grass*, is the individual human person, channeling the voices of the world. "Whitman comes to us—perhaps not a discoverer, but certainly a grand interpreter," one of his early readers observed, and such is the case with regard to these four media.[115] He neither discovered nor invented them, but he did interpret them grandly, and in so doing brought them to light in a new and compelling way.

Like Pauline mass communication, each of Whitman's four types is marked by a kind of love. Not surprisingly, Whitman's love differs from Paul's. It might be described as a blend of eros, care, and complacency (*complacentia*), all of which course through his representations of the crowd and, arguably, the feelings that fueled it. Eros, in both its sexualized and sublimated versions, is the love of desire that powered both particular attractions and a kind of primitive, orgiastic "we-feeling" that sometimes attached itself to sociality en masse. Care is the love of friendship and responsibility, directed especially toward individuals nearby and known but extending also to the distant and unknown. It is the love of *ethos* and ethical action, anchored like *eros* in the bodies of humans, but extending also to their souls and marked as much by willful restraint as onward urge. The third, *complacentia*, is the least familiar of the three, defined by the Thomist philosopher Frederick Crowe as the "faculty of affective consent, of acceptance of what is good, of concord with . . . [or] natural gratitude for the universe of being."[116] Free from the striving and willfulness found in the other two kinds of love, complacency in this sense is a variation on what William James called "the feeling of sufficiency of the present moment," which he associated with Whitman loafing on the grass on a summer morning, overcome with "the peace and knowledge that pass all the argument of the earth."[117] We can find elements of all three kinds of love in Whitman's accounts of the crowd—which James believed the poet "felt . . . as rapturously as Wordsworth felt the mountains, felt it as an overpoweringly significant presence."[118]

"Here is what moves in magnificent masses, carelessly faithful of particulars," Whitman wrote, describing both the strolling antebellum crowd and the nation he idealized. "Here the flowing trains—here the crowds, equality, diversity, the Soul loves."[119] The diversity and rough spatial equality of the antebellum streets, as experienced by a big-bodied man who moved comfortably about them, served as both experiential rootground and synecdoche for the democratic ekklesia Whitman sensed possible. Moving among masses, *carelessly* faithful of particulars—here the moment of democratic *complacentia*, when the jam of the streets is sufficient unto itself for the sauntering democrat. In these moods, he finds evidence of divinity in the people he passes: "These faces bear testimony slumbering or awake,/ They show their descent from the Master himself" (140).[120] At other times, the poet carves a space of particularizing care out from the crowd: "All day I have walked the city and talked with my friends, and thought of prudence,/ Of time, space, reality—of such as these, and abreast with them, prudence."[121] Here is the man of the city, strolling with friends, attending to prudence—the careful, judicious, and provident. But this moment, too, passes, and gives way to another, when longing and desire make themselves felt in the streets: "Among the men and women, the multitude, I perceive one picking me out by secret and divine signs. . . . / I meant that you should discover me so, by my faint indirections."[122] Here the glistening eyes of another, the well-muscled limb, the delicate step, the unexpected sight that captures and captivates. All of these things and more were possible in the crowd, that great form of bodily mass communication actualized through urban arteries and other common spaces and customs well alive in Whitman's time, and even more in his poetry.

Beyond assembled crowds, one can also find in *Leaves* crowds dissembled over time, passing along through a particular place. There was some hint of this in a journalistic series Whitman published in 1849, when he sat at the Croton Reservoir on Long Island and thought forward one hundred years hence, considering the others who would look upon the same scene he was surveying.[123] It came into further focus in a trio of 1856 compositions. A magazine essay, "Broadway, the Magnificent!," takes the reader from the present-day street "ebbing and flowing with American men, women, and with strangers," to a past not obvious to those strolling today—to the days of the Dutch administrations and De Heere Straat, with whipping post, pillory, stocks, and a market that auctioned Indian and African slaves.[124] The historic account calls one to the possibility of dwelling with the dead who had peopled the place earlier. He made the point more explicitly in "Poem of the Road" (1856): doors, steps, arches, gray-stoned pavement, "From all that has been near you I believe you have imparted to yourselves, and now would impart the same secretly to me,/ From the living and the dead you have peopled your impassive surfaces, and the spirits thereof would be evident and amicable with me."[125] The material elements of the space he inhabits cue the strolling poet to those souls, dead and still living, which have passed by them before.

In "Sun-Down Poem" (1856), later re-titled "Crossing Brooklyn Ferry," he adds those who will come after him. Standing atop the ferry as the sun nears the horizon, he sees the crowds on deck below and thinks ahead: "you that shall cross from shore to shore years hence, are more to me, and more in my meditations, than you might suppose." He continues on, dwelling upon the swift-moving current past dawn, the ferries, the transport ships, the islands in the distance, the ties he feels between himself and future generations: "Fifty years hence others will see them as they cross, the sun half an hour high,/A hundred years hence, or ever so many hundred years hence, others will see them."[126] As it has turned out, with car-filled bridges and subway trains having replaced the ferries that Whitman rode, and Manhattan shipping largely a thing of the past, few in recent decades have had the chance to ride the flood tide running off the shore of Brooklyn, the sun half an hour risen. Predicting the future is generally less reliable than excavating the past.

The point is less about accuracy, though, and more about moral and spiritual communion. In these poetic and journalistic moments, Whitman is pointing to a kind of place-based mass communion with those past and those yet to come. It shares certain similarities with Pauline communion, which also connects the individual to a temporally dispersed collectivity, but Whitman's is geographically localized and carried out through individual rumination instead of communal ritual. That said, Whitman's rumination lends itself to ritual form, be it the regular practice of an individual or the formal enactment of a group. He is, I think, drawing our attention to the fact that places construct their own ekklesiae, to which the faithful are called to tend. There can be rituals of remembrance for the scenes that marked those places in the past, and for the people who inhabited them. And there can be rituals of mindfulness for those people who will pass through or dwell there in the future, and for preservation or building that might serve them well. ("You are more to me than you might suppose.") Such place-based mass communion is part of all those faiths with holy sites visited by the devout, but it seems to me that there is a proto-environmental consciousness implicit in Whitman's, which moves toward making all places potentially holy and worthy of care.

If fleshly crowds and proto-environmental place-based communion were two media of mass communication suggested by Whitman's *Leaves*, the most notable is the poetry itself, mediated through the orator-poet. In Whitman's hands, print-based, free-verse literate art becomes a medium through which the masses are lovingly represented and communicated to readers. The *Christian Spiritualist* had something like this in mind when it called Whitman's song "highly mediatorial." There were different sorts of media, the journal observed, the greatest of which would materialize in some rapturous future and allow the love and wisdom of heaven to flow by "divine influx" into humans on earth. In the meantime, "many varieties of Mediumship must be expected," it wrote, and Whitman's was one. "He accepts man as he is as to his whole nature, and all men as his own brothers," it went on. "The lambent flame of his genius encircles the world—nor does he clearly discern between that which is to be preserved, and that which is but as fuel for the purification of the ore from its dross." To the *Spiritualist*, this lack of discernment was a shortcoming, which put Whitman on a lower plane than Emerson, who mediated only "the upper mind-sphere of the age."[127] In contrast, Whitman mediated the whole shebang.

Whitman mediates and poetically represents the multiplicity of things that find place in a polytheistic democratic ekklesia. Things animal, vegetable, and mineral, contemporary and historical, material and spiritual, profane and sacred—and, particularly, things human—the low, the high, and everything in between. Perhaps the most notable means for such mass representation are his catalogs, long lists carelessly faithful to particulars, mobilized as magnificent masses that, like the human crowds they mimic, carry a sense of both collectivity and assembled individuality. Scores of catalogs are scattered throughout Whitman's *Leaves*, giving voice to the array of things that find moral place in his idealized ekklesia: contralto, carpenter, married and unmarried children, pilot, mate, duck-shooter, deacon, spinning-girl, farmer, lunatic, printer, anatomist, quadroon, machinist, driver, half-breed, marksman, immigrants, woollypates, dancers, youth in a bed, reformer on a platform, squaw, connoisseur, steamboat deckhands, young and older sister, one-year wife, Yankee mill girl, dying woman, pavingman, canal-boy, conductor, child being baptized, drover, peddler, daguerreotypist, opium eater, prostitute, the President, five friendly matrons, fishing crew, Missourian, fare-collector, floormen, pikefisher, squatter, flatboatmen, coonhunters, patriarchs and great grandsons, husband and wife—to condense one catalog from the poem that became "Song of Myself" (41–45). Drawing from both experience and imagination, Whitman gives us a long series of human figures, scattered about the country, engaged in wildly diverse activities.

Here is mass communication as communication of the masses—a representation of the democratic many, artfully rendered, and informed by ideals of egalitarianism and inclusivity. Catalogs are one way this is accomplished, based upon the rhetorical technique of copiousness that Thomas Sloane has equated with "stoking the mind with variety."[128] Stephen Hartnett calls them "a utopian form of synecdoche, [where] Whitman promises to reveal the brilliant master plan that unites all individuals (parts) in a kind and generous nation (whole)."[129] The catalogs haven't appealed to all of Whitman's readers (Emerson compared them to warehouse inventories), but they can serve to stretch out the social imagination and draw attention to both particularity and collective heterogeneity through adding example upon example. In addition, by grouping together accepted and rejected, high status and despised, the cataloged *copia* have the effect of communicating symbolic equality, so they carry a certain democratic über-message. This representative mass communication, in turn, is built upon an understanding of the poet as a mass medium of sorts—"the channel of thoughts and things without increase or diminution, and . . . the free channel of himself," who does his work by "flood[ing] himself with the immediate age" and addressing his readers with the hope that "his country absorbs him as affectionately as he has absorbed it" (14, 24, 27).

Finally, *Leaves of Grass* points to the individual person as a medium of mass communication, each of us enfleshing an introjected ensemble of voices, images, signs, experiences, sensations, and personalities. Many a catalog each of us carries, below the surface and sometimes consciously. Whitman once called his book "the song of a great composite democratic individual, male or female," which is a figure stunningly portrayed through "Song of Myself."[130] This is the kind of individual the book aims to cultivate, something we readers must do, each in our own way. Every individual is a medium, composite made, embodying countless catalogs, and it is up to each of us to determine how we deal with that fact. "Every existence has its idiom . . . every thing has an idiom and tongue," Whitman tells us (143). The poet absorbs and responds to the idioms of existence, and in the art that is living, we all might do the same: "He resolves all tongues into his own, and bestows it upon men. . and any man translates. . and any man translates himself also:/ One part does not counteract another part. . . .He is the joiner . . . he sees how they join" (144). Man or woman, this is the condition of the composite democratic individual, translator and joiner, the singular channel that speaks many voices. "They shall arise in the States, mediums shall," the poet prophesies. "They shall train themselves to go in public to become oratists (orators and oratresses,)/ Strong and sweet shall their tongues be—poems and materials of poems shall come from their lives—they shall be makers and finders."[131] Makers and finders, orators and oratresses, channels of communication through which an ensemble of idioms might speak—this is the task that *Leaves of Grass* sets before us.

"I enforce you to give play to yourself," we are told near the end of the 1860 edition, the poet giving musical form to the mission for the composite individuals who would populate Whitman's polytheistic ekklesia. What this might look like is left open for future generations to determine for themselves, through the songs they sing and the idioms they channel. It is a vision that places the burden of democracy upon embodied individuals and the *ethē* that rhetorically shape them. To be sure, institutions would be part of the process, but it was the individuals who guided them in whom Whitman placed his hopes. They would be the ones to make up the crowds and appreciate their polymorphous beauty through all types of love humans properly feel. They would be the ones who cared for particular places and dwelled on their pasts and futures. And they would be the ones who created the art and lived the lives that mediated the variety of human and nonhuman things that would find place in the world Whitman hoped to chant into existence.

Winding Down, Wending On (Absorbing Whitman)

In the years following the release of the 1860 edition of *Leaves of Grass*, Walt Whitman of Brooklyn became Whitman of Washington, D.C., and then Camden, New Jersey. The poet went to the capital in late 1862, looking for his brother George, whom *The New York Herald* listed as wounded in the Battle of Fredericksburg. Walt decided to stay in the Washington area, volunteering in the Civil War hospitals, where he wrote letters for and read to the wounded and dying and supported himself as a part-time government clerk. He captured aspects of the war and his shifting moods about it in poems collected as *Drum Taps* (1865), called by one critic "the finest war poetry written by an American." There, through poems "more concerned with history than the self, more aware of the precariousness of America's present and future than of its expansive promise . . . Whitman projects himself as a mature poet, directly touched by human suffering, in clear distinction to the ecstatic, naive, electric voice which marked the original edition of *Leaves of Grass*."[132] He would revise and reorder *Leaves of Grass* for a far less ebullient fourth edition (1867) and three more that followed (1871–72, 1881–82, and 1891–92), but by 1865, most of his greatest work was done.

Whitman stayed in Washington until 1873, when he suffered a stroke and moved in with his brother and sister-in-law in Camden. He would partially recover, but suffer several more strokes over the next twelve years, which limited his sauntering and darkened his mood for extended periods of time. Although his vigor diminished, his reputation grew, and his poems were translated into French, German, Danish, Russian, and Spanish. In spite of his weakened state, he wrote regularly to support himself, maintained an active correspondence, and rode the ferry for pleasure between Camden and Philadelphia. He managed two more long-distance trips in 1879 and 1880, one to Ontario and the other west to Missouri, Kansas, and Colorado, which gave him his first look at the Great Plains and Rocky Mountains.[133] In these later years, he gathered around himself a circle of male friends who served as defenders and disciples and fought off critics who continued to find fault with Whitman's poetry, on both moral and artistic grounds. A cult of sorts grew up around the poet, spearheaded by Richard Maurice Bucke, a Canadian physician and student of the mind who had discovered *Leaves of Grass* in 1867 and who in 1872 had a mystical experience, complete with light and inner fire, after an evening of reading Whitman—spiritually confirmed when he met the poet in person and was put in a state of "mental exaltation" that lasted six weeks. Bucke would later compare Whitman to Jesus and the Buddha.[134] William James wrote about the cult of Whitman in *Varieties of Religious Experience*, where he portrayed the poet as an exemplary figure in "the religion of healthy-mindedness" and saw in him "the undifferentiated germ of all the higher faiths." Elsewhere he called Whitman "a contemporary prophet," an opinion shared by the sociologist E. A. Ross, who wrote about the same time, "The soul of religion lives on in the teachings of Jesus, the theology of Paul, and . . . the poetry of Walt Whitman."[135]

Others found a less spiritual core to Whitman's poetry. In 1882, the district attorney of Boston called *Leaves of Grass* "obscene literature" and the state attorney general (supported by noted vice-crusader Anthony Comstock) banned sale of the book in the state; Wanamaker's, Philadelphia's most famous department store (and future employer of David Sarnoff), followed suit. Public controversy ensued, pressed by critics and defenders in the newspapers. Sales of the book skyrocketed, fueled by the free publicity.[136] In Ann Arbor, Michigan, Charles Cooley acquired a copy of the 1884 edition (published by Philadelphia's David McKay), perhaps aware of the controversy it had stirred. Cooley was twenty when that edition came out, and he would use Whitman periodically to illustrate the views of self, democracy, and communication he would work out as a sociologist two decades later. Cooley did not count Whitman among his most beloved authors, identifying more with the "aloof and fastidious" Henry David Thoreau, but he took as the literary representative of democracy "Whitman, who had joy in the press of cities, and whose passion was to 'utter the word Democratic, the word En Masse.' His chants express a great gusto in common life."[137] Later in his life, Cooley called *Leaves of Grass* "good democratic art," but noted that "there is nothing especially democratic about the crudity that impairs it."[138] A younger version of Cooley's readerly self might have been less put off. He had once placed Whitman among those authors whose "'I' is interesting and agreeable," so that "we adopt it for the time being and make it our own. Then, being on the inside as it were, it is our own self that is so expansive and happy. We adopt Montaigne, or Lamb, or Thackeray, or Stevenson, or Whitman, or Thoreau, and think of their words as our words."[139]

Death came to Whitman in Camden in late March of 1892, the same year Cooley would begin work on a doctoral thesis that would feed into the first major social theory of "communication" (so named) in the United States. The Good Gray Poet played no major role, but Cooley's occasional adoption of Whitman's agreeable "I" provided fodder for developing an account of what he called "the communicative life."[140] We might ask ourselves, as amateur or professional theorists, what reading Whitman and adopting his "I" might do for our own understandings and accounts of communication. This question in turn raises the issue of poetry as a kind of theory, and the poet as theorist— one who offers up a vision and perspective, artfully rendered, which casts phenomena like crowds, places, and mobile individuals all in distinctive light and helps us to interpret, experience, and perhaps act in fresh ways. I note that the condensed language of poetry can serve as a human creation that reveals things not fully sensed by the poet him- or herself, not to mention being good to read and think with. "My voice goes after what my eyes cannot reach," Whitman tells us (57).[141]

Whitman's was perhaps the first great positive democratic vision of crowds and masses, entities not much celebrated in social thought since then. As worked out in the early editions of *Leaves of Grass*, it is a vision that is at once radically inclusive and egalitarian, open to finding symbolic place for all the people, activities, and things that exist in the nation, and the kosmos writ large. At the same time, it puts extra normative shine on the common people—craftsmen, laborers, farmers, ordinary mothers and fathers—whom it counts as the moral and political soul of the country and the world. The peaceable, heterogeneous, perambulatory crowd is the figure through which Whitman's vision is refracted and expressed. The sauntering urban journalist grew into the sauntering poet, big-bodied and expansive when he hit the right mood, making crowds emblematic and constitutive of the pluralistic many-in-one that the American ekklesia is supposed to be. He saw darkness and evil, and drew that, too, into his poetic catalogs, just as he made room for competing ideals and cultural currents in what I have called his sophistic embrace of contraries. Social theorists after him would attend disproportionately to the dark side of crowds and the uncultivated or disorganized side of the masses. Raymond Williams, another working-class–raised theorist, would eloquently rebut those tendencies when he wrote that there were no such things as masses, only ways of seeing people as masses, thus drawing attention to the elitism and condescension of 1950s mass society theory.[142] If we were to adopt the perspective of the early Whitman's "I," however, we might say that seeing people as masses is not so bad after all.

In comparison with Pauline mass communication, the sorts suggested in Whitman's writings are both more and less expansive. Normatively speaking, Paul remained a vigilant monotheist, while Whitman was open to multiple gods and moral supremes. The Pauline Body of Christ is open to all Christ-confessing believers and thus pushes toward a universalism that transcends human difference. Whitman's poetry and crowds, however, push even further, rejecting none, embracing all, and generally making space in the grand procession. As enacted through the breaking of the bread, Pauline mass communication is tied to a localized, communitarian ritual, but reaches out toward God's creation writ large. Whitman's crowds and composite individuals are in comparison more mobile, but they lack the transcendental dimension Paul provides. Whitman's place-based communion, meanwhile, is anchored to particular geographies, while its Pauline counterpart can take place wherever the faithful might assemble.

As a way of seeing, communicated in a manner whose aesthetic appeal increases the likelihood of its rhetorical uptake, Whitman's poetry offers us a normative ideal to draw upon in evaluating and guiding communication in our own day. *Leaves* provides a model for inclusive, egalitarian representation of the diverse array of particulars found in any given society, group, institution, or geographical place. "For these and the like, their own voices! For these, space ahead!" This remains a powerful democratic ideal, recognized but inadequately realized in print, broadcast, and electronic media today, not to mention the communicative practices of governments and organizations at all levels of society. Whitman provides us a vision with which to evaluate newspapers, radio and television systems, legislatures, boards of directors, public spaces, live assemblies, and the moral imaginations and communicative patterns of individuals and collectives alike. His is not the only ideal we should use to evaluate those practices ("There can be any number of supremes"), but it remains a powerful one, particularly for social entities professing to abide by democratic principles.

Though he brought the ideal to bear on the United States, Whitman provides guidance for polytheistic democracy wherever it might bloom, and for the individuals who embrace and populate it. He calls those individuals to lovingly enflesh a kind of mass communication with the diversities of the world—making room for near and far, high and low, female and male, gay and straight, souls and bodies, spirits and things, and people of every ethnicity, occupation, religion, and political orientation to be found. To anchor their polytheism of experience, he advises such selves: "Keep your places, objects than which none else is more lasting."[143] Geographical places matter, as do the bodies that move through and care for them. Self-fashioning citizen-poets we might all be, lovers of earth and sun and animals, defenders of the poor and weak, companions of "powerful uneducated persons and . . . the young and . . . the mothers of families," open-air readers of his *Leaves:* then, he tells us, "your very flesh shall be a great poem and have the richest fluency not only in its words but in the silent lines of its lips and face and between the lashes of your eyes and in every motion and joint of your body" (12).

4

Cooley's Transcendentalist Quest

"Nothing keeps one young like hope."
—Charles Horton Cooley in his journal, April 13, 1914

Charles Cooley was a constipated child. Or so goes a story put into print by a former student in 1942. Actually, he wrote that his teacher had suffered "obstetative elimination" as a child, which is apparently the indirect bowel phraseology of a more restrained era. From the age of eight or ten until he apparently cured himself walking in the Tyrolean Alps at nineteen, Cooley is said to have suffered. "It seems a long time indeed, from early childhood to post-adolescence, for an extremely sluggish system to become normally active," the former student observed, venturing into still-new Freudian territories. The condition was likely "psychogenic," and it "accented tendencies he had already early manifested and probably left additional scars on his personality in the form of intermittent irritability, obstinacy, and a high sensitiveness to encroachment on his domain of thought and power," traits that "manifested themselves again and again throughout his life."[1] While Whitman's and Paul's followers made out the poet and apostle to be venerated spiritual figures, Cooley's student worked different rhetorical territory.

Cooley did not influence the development of a great religion like Paul or write one of the masterworks of world literature like Whitman. He was not important in the same way they were, but was instead a character about whom one might remark that he was a constipated child, in the contexts of considering his contributions to sociology and related academic fields like political economy, social psychology, and communication. Over the course of a four-decade scholarly career, Cooley (1864–1929) published work in those fields, some of which proved germinal, but within far more localized spheres of influence than Paul's and Whitman's. He is remembered today as one of the founding fathers of American sociology, a classic figure in symbolic interaction and reference-group theory, and the creator of two concepts that made their way into the broader social-scientific lexicon—"the looking-glass self" and the "primary group."[2] Obviously, these fall into a different league from Paul's and Whitman's contributions.

Yet Cooley belongs in this book, too, not as the cultural equal of his two predecessors here, but as another figure on the grander historical stage who plays a role and that advances the story. The man from Ann Arbor—the Michigan college town where he was born and lived—was among the first people in the English-speaking world to develop an extended theory of something explicitly called "communication," from a position of employment in a modern university. Indeed, though John Dewey and George Herbert Mead have generally accumulated the credit, Cooley was the one who led the way in the academic study of communication so named, during its earliest phase in North America, from the 1890s through the 1910s. Cooley's was the first significant social theory of communication in the United States, developed through articles and a trio of books that charted the ways in which selves, small groups, and society writ large were constituted through "communication," an idea and rhetorical god term that also gathered Cooley's moral and spiritual hopes and served as an engine for his faith. He worked out a vision that has not been adequately recognized by scholars, within the contexts of a life whose contours furnished inventional media that, like his predecessors', spanned places and mobility, speech and writing, interpersonal relationships and embodied solitary reflection.

Within the field of communication, the constipated Cooley has taken his place alongside other less-than-favorable images to create a composite portrait that doesn't exactly serve as a rousing call to read the man's work. Daniel Czitrom gives Cooley credit for being one of "a trio of American thinkers [who] began the first comprehensive reckoning with modern communication in toto as a force in the social process," but Czitrom also presents him as a tongue-tied dreamer, philosophical idealist, and borderline solipsist who got the idea of communication from his teacher, John Dewey—a picture of influence Dorothy Ross amplified nine years later, writing that "virtually all the distinctive lines of analysis in Cooley's sociology were articulated first, albeit briefly, in Dewey's lectures."[3] (Ouch.) Dewey is the hero of Czitrom's history, as he was in James Carey's celebrated essay, "A Cultural Approach to Communication," which opens with a line that blends a storyteller's eloquence and an ethos of wisdom that has stuck in many a readerly craw: "When I decided some years ago to read seriously the literature of communications, a wise man suggested I begin with John Dewey."[4] Cooley receives just three passing references in Carey's *Communication as Culture* (once as Dewey's student, once as his descendant, and once as his scribe), which is one more passing reference than he earns in Dan Schiller's *Theorizing Communication: A History*, where we learn that Cooley believed "Teutonic village communities . . . had furnished America with its institutional and racial inheritance."[5] John Durham Peters's more nuanced and extended read of Cooley in *Speaking Into the Air* doesn't exactly make us rush to the library to read, either. Instead it deepens the picture Czitrom had established of Cooley as a "clear idealist" and "high point of theoretical disembodiment," who "makes communication indistinguishable from a solipsistic pas de deux," and whose "great failing is his Victorian insistence that embodiment does not matter."[6]

Cooley's work is not without problems, I'll readily admit. He can seem like a dilettante and is often maddeningly vague. Though he wrote well (much better than Dewey), his occasional tone of seemingly ungrounded knowing can irritate. His works are peppered with weird, vaguely sexual Victorian phrases like "ejaculatory biography" and "fluid impulses propagated by simple contact."[7] Although he had important insights into what he called "the communicative life," his preference for armchair sociology and his relatively sheltered adult life afforded him neither formal nor quotidian methods to make contact with social realities beyond his immediate, quiet and relatively sheltered experience. As a result, he could make claims that were at best projections from his own social position and at worst dead wrong. Though liberal by the standards of his era, his attitudes about race, culture, and ethnicity sound conservative today. He had faith in social progress, and he believed that communication technologies were among its most powerful engines, sentiments not widespread now among contemporary intellectuals and students of media. He had a bourgeois moral sensibility that idealized the nuclear family and a late Victorian bias toward "civilization," which privileged literate North Atlantic societies over against so-called "primitive" oral cultures. He can seem like a square, whose works call to mind what Theodor Adorno sardonically called "the social-democratic ideal of the personality expounded by heavily-bearded Naturalists of the 'nineties, who were out to have a good time."[8]

But as Cooley himself said, in an early meditation on Emerson, "It is the affirmative, not the negative, that is in the end important," and in reading we should estimate an author "by what he is rather than by what he is not."[9] It seems fair to apply Cooley's dictum to his own writings, and a good means of clearing the decks and setting the record straight about his contributions. Instead of a constipated, Teutonic-loving, body-denying Victorian idealist, I'd suggest that Cooley was the last of the nineteenth-century Emersonians, working in Ann Arbor, instead of Boston, Concord, or Brooklyn, and operating in the academic fields of political economy and sociology instead of the more public arenas of lectures, essays, and poetry.[10] Instead of the derivative follower of John Dewey, I'd like to show that Cooley actually led the way in developing the idea of communication, central in the sociological trilogy of *Human Nature and the Social Order* (1902), *Social Organization* (1909), and *Social Process* (1918). Dewey discussed communication only in passing before 1916, and, while he was the more astute philosopher of communication, · he never wrote about the subject with the sociological and cultural range of Cooley.[11] Cooley would write about communication in face-to-face settings, history, primary groups, institutions, literature, cultures, social classes, public opinion formation, and fame—in addition to charting what he called the "material communication" involved in transportation and storage. Out of reading and thinking, he covered a lot of important ground and gave the fullest Progressive Era account of communication. He was the first American to chart ways that "communication" created selves, social institutions, communities, and culture—a marriage of Emersonian expressivism, sociology, and political economy in his figuring of it. He is also one of the central figures of his era, and thus helps fill out the larger story. Both his insights and blind spots are productive to think with.

What I'll read as his vision of mass communication—a term he does not use—develops as an offshoot of his vision of communication more generally, and I trace the latter to get at the former. Jean Quandt wrote what remains the best intellectual history of Cooley's sociology of communication, which I reference and supplement by throwing his work into different historical and philosophical relief, at once more expansive and more particularizing than her excellent but standard history of ideas.[12] On the one hand, I put him in play with Whitman and Paul, as part of a longer-standing lineage of thinking about mass communication, its media, and the faiths they might serve. Raised in a Protestant culture, Cooley channeled Pauline images of "face-to-face" and universal community in the direction of communication itself, whose developing media he thought enlarged the world, both socially and morally. Brought into a literate culture, he read Whitman's poetry, but distanced himself from its promiscuous, polytheistic embrace of social and experiential heterogeneity. Cooley would study communicative dimensions of the composite self Whitman poetized (and William James psychologized), but in more staid, disciplined, and domesticated form than we saw from the Brooklyn poet. Communication was for him at once social concept, mode of personal therapy, and repository of spiritual hopes. While Paul had faith in the God of Israel and the Risen Messiah, and Whitman had faith in poetry and the masses, Cooley put his faith in communication itself and drew out ways that it might actualize a kind of mystical "Great Life" of social communion over generations, people, and places. Instead of an apostle composing letters or a poet penning poetry, Cooley was an interpretive sociologist writing humanistic prose, communicating a late Transcendentalist vision mostly composed in a college town in the provinces. In contrast to Paul's apostolic activism and Whitman's efforts at mass public address, Cooley played out the theorist's role in a more contemplative manner, writing for an educated reading public with college-based audiences at its core.

As I did with Paul and Whitman, I consider how Cooley's vision materialized rhetorically by attending to a few of the inventional media through which it came into being. The story runs through his home in Ann Arbor, and his father, Judge Thomas MacIntyre Cooley, a prominent and in some ways towering figure whose letters, presence, and material success all contributed to the son's discovery of communication, and invention of himself. As a boy, maps and trains expanded Cooley's sense of distance and place. As an adult, Cooley's wife and children were key social media, creating a domestic space of conversation, observation, and production that was Cooley's base of inventional operation. He was a man of neither cities nor streets and was neither absorber nor activist. His eklessiae were the classes he lectured in and the Great Life he felt himself part of. Like Whitman, though, he dreamed he might be a great orator and wrote regularly in notebooks, both of which moved him toward finding and figuring the idea of communication. Political economy was another key inventional route—government and academic research about transportation and railroads, which led him to Albert Schäffle and the image of society as a corporate body bound together by communication.

The Early Making of Charles Horton Cooley

Charles Cooley had a successful father, whose shadow cast further than the house that they shared in Ann Arbor. The judge would prove instrumental to his son's development as a theorist of communication, an occupation that was both an outgrowth of his father's life and a reaction against it. Thomas McIntyre Cooley was an upstate contemporary of the downstate Whitman, born on a farm near Attica, New York, five years after the Long Island–born poet (1824) and dying six years after him (1898). Both came from longtime Yankee clans, had fathers active in Democratic party politics, worked for a time as newspapermen, and praised poetry that in the words of Thomas Cooley "made the world feel that all honest occupations are equally honorable."[13] Whitman composed languishing lines such as "I loaf, and invite my soul," but while the elder Cooley dabbled in poetry, he loafed not, living instead by Thomas Carlyle's dictum that "in Idleness alone is there perpetual despair." From the farm he moved to Palmyra, New York, an Erie Canal town where he worked as a clerk in a law office. From there in 1843 he joined the human stream that passed by daily and rode by barge and then steamer across Lake Erie to Adrian, Michigan. There, he read for and passed the Michigan bar; practiced law; married a sixteen-year-old local girl, Mary Horton; fathered two sons; used his limited disposable income to accumulate books; and by the early 1850s had became one of the town's leading citizens. He was assigned by the state legislature to compile Michigan's laws in 1857, became court reporter for the newly established state Supreme Court in 1858, was hired as one of three professors to teach in the University of Michigan's new Law Department in 1859, attended Abraham Lincoln's presidential inaugural in 1860, and was elected justice to the state Supreme Court in 1864. That same year his fourth child was born, Charles Horton. Four years later he published *A Treatise on the Constitutional Limitations Which Rest upon the Legislative Power of the States of the American Union*, a legal text with as great a national circulation as any between 1850 and 1900. It became the canonical source for understanding procedural interpretations of due process of law and was widely used by legislators drafting state constitutions, country lawyers, law students, and judges from the local level to the U.S. Supreme Court, where Judge Cooley had aspirations of one day serving. Cooley's father was famous.[14]

Judge Cooley traveled frequently when Charlie was a boy, off to Lansing for Supreme Court duties or elsewhere around the country, to give speeches or attend meetings, often in his capacity as an emerging expert on the regulation of railroads. When away from home, the father sent the son letters, which served as portals into places distant from Ann Arbor. "We are full of business here," the judge wrote from the bench in Lansing, in a clean hand addressed to seven-year-old Charlie. "A lawyer is talking to us now, but I have no difficulty in hearing him and writing this."[15] (It was an early lesson in high-level multitasking the boy never quite grew into.) A year later, he wrote from Philadelphia in the middle of February and instructed his son directly: "I should like to have you find on the map the road I took to get here. I will name the places I passed through:

Wayne, changed cars.
Monroe, stayed over night.
Toledo, passed a day.

Monroeville, changed cars and stayed a night.
Shelby, changed cars.
Delaware, changed cars.
Columbus, passed a night and day.
Newark
Pittsburg, changed cars.
Altoona, near the summit of the Alleganies.
Harrisburg
Lancaster
Philadelphia.

Vividly, sometimes poetically, the father described his travels. "We came into Pittsburg [as it was then spelled] in the night, but the iron furnaces are kept at work the whole 24 hours, and at night the fire blazes out of the chimneys, and in some places you can see streams of melted iron being run into great moulds, and glowing so bright as to dazzle the eyes."[16] Written in cursive script, which the boy could not yet read, the letter was meant, like Paul's, to be read out loud, while Charlie pored over a map in the family's home—an activity that would grow into a personal ritual that was among his favorite childhood pastimes.

Charlie had an active imaginative and literary life, but trouble with speech. The family read novels together aloud, and the children took advantage of their father's growing library. Charles Dickens was one of the judge's favorites, and he passed his appreciation on to his son. ("Dickens always makes me weep," Charles would write.) When he was just six, his father allowed him to spend an entire day alone fishing in a boat in the middle of a lake and to travel by himself across the state by train.[17] He often sat alone. "A great part of my mental life was spent in imagining situations where I was the glorious hero," he later wrote. "I confronted lions escaped from their cages, while the terrified crowd wondered, or I dauntlessly entered burning buildings or jumped into the river and saved the drowning." He was "remarkably deficient in command of language" and could compose sentences (and move his bowels) "only with great effort." Still, he maintained ambitions and found himself "passionately eager for applause." He dreamed of greatness in singing, but he "had not voice enough for continuing conversation and no ear for music." He recalibrated his sights and set them on becoming "a great orator," a dream that he "for many years cherished fervently."[18]

In January of 1882, as a seventeen-year-old student at the University of Michigan, Cooley began keeping a notebook in which, like Whitman three decades earlier, he recorded his thoughts and efforts at learning the rhetorical art. "When men are thoroughly earnest they instinctively trust to experience," he proclaimed, in an Emersonian mood. "Success is not attained by following a theory, but the theory is rather drawn from the observation of success."[19] For a model of success, Cooley turned to Demosthenes' "On the Crown," which he translated from the Greek and committed to memory, as he had read that the great English orator William Pitt had done. He translated sections of Cicero's *De Oratore*, spelled out his own system for readying oneself for a public discussion, gave speeches on current topics before local audiences, and critiqued his efforts afterward.[20] As winter dragged on, though, he began to doubt himself: "I am too cold to be an orator. I lack enthusiasm, vehemence and imagination, the *adorem quenquami amoris* of Crassus."[21]

His body was not cooperating. Charles had his father's delicate frame, but not the old man's energy and hard-driving disposition, and had contracted malaria the previous year, probably on one of the nearby waters he liked to boat. As he was trying to internalize principles and models of oratorical greatness, he was forced for the first of several times to drop his classes and seek health through higher altitude and vigorous exercise. Financed by his father, he turned to travel and stretched himself out geographically along the way. By train he ventured to St. Louis, Kansas City, and Denver, staying in railroad hotels along the way, taking in the great bridge across the Mississippi and thirty-six hours of the Great Plains across Kansas and Eastern Colorado. He worked with a survey crew outside Leadville, the 10,000–foot mining town, and nearly died in a hotel fire, where it was reported by newspapers that Judge Cooley's son had escaped peril. "I find my name a password to the affections of half the lawyers in the West," he wrote his mother. Two months later, he confided, "I should like as an experiment to get off somewhere where Father was never heard of and see whether anybody would care about me for my own sake."[22] The following summer he did more of the same in the Appalachians, "running into his father's reputation," as Vernon Dibble puts it, as he sought respite in the mountains of Tennessee and North Carolina. Europe proved curative in 1884, giving Cooley a chance to steam across the Atlantic, pay homage to the statue of William Pitt at Westminster Abbey, take courses at Ludwig-Maxmillian University, and find relief in the Alps from his sundry bodily ailments.[23]

Cooley returned to the University of Michigan in the fall of 1885, the well-traveled twenty-one-year-old son of the judge. He spent time that year with a group called the Samovar Club, named after the large pot in which they brewed hot chocolate to drink as they read and discussed works by the Russian authors Turgenev and Tolstoy. Also in the club were Elsie Jones, daughter of the dean of the Medical College, her friend Alice Chipman, and a twenty-six-year-old instructor in philosophy, John Dewey.[24] Cooley would marry Jones, Dewey would marry Chipman, and the four would know each other as peers on the scene in Ann Arbor. Cooley continued his well-rounded undergraduate work, which had him studying languages (Greek, Latin, French, and German) and history, before taking a degree in mechanical engineering in 1887, the same year he published a short piece in the student newspaper on Emerson, whom he admired. "To think is to stand alone, and nature plainly intends for the most part men should move as a mass," he wrote. "The man who can stand upright in this surging mass grows like a seed that has got itself planted and becomes of more import than a million of the germs that once seemed like him."[25] Though he hoped to grow like a seed, when Cooley graduated he took a job as a draftsman in Bay City, where he read Herbert Spencer and worked out his attraction to both science and poetry. "The man of science discovers the law," he wrote in his journal. "The poet reveals its full meaning. The two work from the same instinct but the energy of the former is so absorbed in the labor of discovery that he cannot communicate, indeed does not know, the real significance of what he has done."[26] Cooley held out hope that he could communicate and reveal meaning. He quit his job and returned to the familiar student's life in Ann Arbor.

Judge Cooley was not pleased. Appointed first chairman of the Interstate Commerce Commission (ICC) in 1887, the self-made man was now living in Washington, D.C., and growing impatient with his third son's retiring and bookish ways. In March of 1889, he mailed a letter:

> Dear Charley,
> My opinion is very clear and decided, that for your own good you had better come on here *at once*, and stay for 6 or 12 months. You will learn more here that will be valuable to you as a teacher *five times over* than you will in Ann Arbor. If you think otherwise after you get here, you can leave any day. You will make a great mistake if you do not come.
> Yours ever,
> T. M. Cooley.[27]

The judge had been charged with bringing regulatory order to the American railroad system, which had grown from a scattered array of 9,000 miles of track when he was practicing law in Adrian in 1850 to an interconnected network of nearly 160,000 miles when he joined the ICC. Like President Cleveland, who appointed him, Judge Cooley was a reform-minded Mugwump intent on serving the public interest against threats posed by commercial monopoly and unregulated railways.[28] Safety was one of several of the ICC's concerns, and as a trained engineer with knowledge of statistics, Charles could conduct research for the Commission's reports. He heeded his father's call, moved to Washington, and spent two years collecting data and preparing reports on railroads for the ICC and Census Bureau. This was the beginning of his formal communication research.

Cooley compiled statistics on the nation's street railways and authored a report about safety regulation for the railroads, in addition to writing a paper to deliver at the 1890 meetings of the American Economics Association, held locally in Washington. The association gave him a small public gathering (ekklesia) of a professional sort in which to read his paper, "The Social Significance of Street Railways." It set statistical data about speed, ridership cost, and the influence of city rents on urban transport within a broader organic-functionalist picture of society borrowed from Herbert Spencer. Cooley called "the system of urban transportation a definite social organ, having for its function the distribution of population about industrial centers," and urged municipalities to take into account not just the revenue generated but also the public service provided by their transit systems.[29] Lester Ward, the sociologist-geologist-paleontologist whose *Dynamic Sociology* (which Cooley did not yet know) had briefly addressed the idea of communication, heard the paper delivered and complimented the young man, while Columbia's Franklin Giddings offered what Cooley called "kindly encouragement to my sociological aspirations."[30]

He remained torn between competing ideals and pursuits. "I am over sensitive to the contagion of the world," he wrote in his journal in 1890. "My 'active life,' that is my life among men, will surely absorb all my energy unless I show remarkable self control. It looks as if I would have to withdraw from active life, for a time at least. 'But you would be unhappy; you are made for such a life.' I am made for other things also." The objecting voice was his father's, whose embodied version was deteriorating through a series of strokes that would send the formerly robust judge into retirement a year later. Charles tried to straddle ideals as he planned his writing. "Work ahead, finishing up studies in rapid transit and writing a monograph on the question," he wrote to himself. "Meanwhile, I shall probably make use in some form of the material I have collected in my journals."[31] The journals had evolved from the rhetorical commonplace books they began as in 1882, aiding the aspiring orator in his training, and were now guided more fully by the example of Emerson, who, Cooley wrote, "practiced and taught this habit that many look upon as unsocial and self-conceited. 'Pay so much honor' he says 'to the visits of truth to your mind as to record them.' Holding that 'He who writes for him-self writes for an eternal public' he wrote down day by day the thoughts he needed for his own use and afterward arranged them into essays as best he might. He gives his own experience as a student and practitioner of life and pretends to do no more."[32] Cooley would marry this expressivist writing to the sociological project, guided by ideals of scientific investigation inspired by Darwin and his dicta of "copious collecting, accurate recording, and much thinking."[33] Along the way, as Glenn Jacobs has argued, Cooley would shift his writerly identity from oratorical to literary.[34] Beyond wedding expressiv-ism to sociology, Cooley would also marry former Samovar Clubber Elsie Jones, in whom he found his single most important conversational partner and an inventional collaborator for the remainder of his life. A sensitive and indefatigable reader with a love for languages, Jones taught high school after graduation and took part in an active epistolary relationship with Charles when they were apart. She helped him gather transportation data in the sum-mer of 1890, and from then on was "of great service as a sympathetic critic of his writings" and "of the utmost importance to his development," in the words of their nephew.[35] Though a student reported that Cooley gave his wife "generous credit" for her contributions to his work,[36] formal acknowledgment is pretty well absent from the published record of thinking that he has gotten credit for, and that she made possible (not unlike Paul's secretaries, in this regard). Unlike her husband, she was outgoing and energetic, but Elsie Jones Cooley gave up her career and, in the words of her nephew, "so ordered her life as to free him from worry . . . and kept others from encroaching on his quiet mode of living."[37]

"My First Real Conquest"

The Cooleys returned to Michigan in 1892, after leaving Washington and taking a six-month trip to Europe, and Charles was admitted to the doctoral program in political economy and appointed half-time instructor. He pur-sued minors in statistics and sociology and started work on a thesis over the Christmas break that year, drawing on his "educative experience" in Wash-ington for a project that became *The Theory of Transportation*. In 1893, he undertook "an arduous perusal of the first volume of [Albert] Schäffle's *Bau und Leben des socialen Körpers* [*Structure and Life of the Social Body*]," which would be a crucial moment in the development of his early communication theory.[38] Now all but forgotten, Schäffle (1831–1903) was a former journalist and publicist whose book was "known by name to everybody in this country who has pretended to study sociology," as Albion Small wrote of it in 1896, and was considered "one of the epoch-making treatises in sociology" as late as 1938.[39] Schäffle's role in the development of thinking about communication in the United States has been as undervalued as John Dewey's has been overestimated.[40] As the title of his book indicates, Schäffle was in the long line of thinkers, from the Stoics and Paul of Tarsus on, who conceived of society as a collective body, and in fact he opened *Bau und Leben* with an epigraph of Paul's own image of such (1 Cor. 12:12). Against Herbert Spencer, who argued that the collective body had no unifying consciousness (a theoretical point that helped support his laissez-faire individualist politics as well), Schäffle argued that the social body was bound together by its lines of communication, which functioned as a collective nervous system. As Cooley wrote in his reading notes, Schäffle's insight made society "a true body or aggregate as such," connected not so much physically as psychically. "It works by means of ideas, and these are communicated by symbols and by technic or arts. Language, speech, gesture, writing, means of communication and transportation, the arts; these are the vehicles of the ideas that connect the parts of society."[41] Unified by such a communicative nervous system, the collective social body was as real as any other, and more than the sum of its individual parts. Schäffle provided what Cooley called "a basis upon which to work out my plan" and "write a theory of transportation from a sociological standpoint."[42] Reading the German's book was a key inventional medium for development of Cooley's subsequent theory.

As he was studying Schäffle and working up his thesis, Cooley sat in on lectures in political philosophy given by his old friend, John Dewey, in the fall of 1893. He took careful notes, preserved among his papers, which form the evidentiary base for the claim that Dewey led Cooley to the idea of communication. Like Schäffle, Dewey rejected Spencer's idea that there existed no mechanism for collective consciousness within a society, arguing, "Language does for the social organism what the nervous system does for the physical. It is a means of communication back and forth from the individual to the whole, and an organ of registration. Functionally speaking, language *is* the nervous system of society—the sensorium."[43] About the critique of Spencer, Cooley later remarked, "I had already arrived at a somewhat similar view," and suggested more generally that Dewey influenced him more "by his personality . . . than by his lectures."[44]

Indeed, in the fall of 1893, Cooley was further along than Dewey in the study of communication, owing to his railway work, and his careful study of Schäffle, whose extended treatment of communication offered far more in the way of conceptual help than did Dewey's brief mention in a lecture, and which Cooley seems to have encountered before he heard that classroom performance. Also, Cooley would almost certainly have run across the section on communication in Ward's *Dynamic Sociology*, as he belatedly familiarized himself with the work of the man who had encouraged him at the American Economics Association meeting.[45] Indeed, it is as likely that Dewey was brought to the idea of communication from his younger Samovar Club friend as it is that Cooley came to the idea through Dewey. For three years, Cooley had been enmeshed in it, through his studies of the railways.[46]

Regardless of who found the theoretically inflected idea of communication first (my bet is that Cooley did, or that they came to it about the same time on independent tracks), Cooley was the one who began to hammer out a social theory of it, two decades before Dewey's first significant writing on the concept. Thinking gathered in 1893 and bore public fruit in 1894. Cooley's thesis, *The Theory of Transportation*, is the key work and one of the founding texts in the academic study of communication. He followed it with lectures in a course he developed and gave in the fall of 1894, Principles of Sociology, the first of its kind at Michigan, and an article he coauthored with his father. Cooley's account of the course gives retrospective sense to the inventional process as it unfolded that year:

> Probably the most distinctive part of this offering was that dealing with transportation and communication. It is my observation that anything like an original view always comes gradually and as a result of working through some sort of experience, rather than by the mere pondering of second-hand ideas. I had just had an educative experience of this sort in regard to transportation, with which I had for two years been concerned at Washington. My Doctor's thesis, on the Theory of Transportation, had been an attempt to interpret this function in terms of an organic social whole. But while working in this region, I could not fail to reflect also on the psychic mechanism, embracing all sorts of language and the means of its transmission and record, whose function was analogous to that of transportation and even more intimately concerned with the social process. So I pursued these two mechanisms through history and contemporary life until I could see them and their social implications in something of the vividness and detail of actuality, acquiring thus a base from which I could develop my exploration of the social organism in any direction I wished. Communication was thus my first real conquest, and the thesis a forecast of the organic view of society I have been working out ever since.[47]

Building upon his railway investigations, supplemented by Schäffle and other relevant writers, Cooley wrote a thesis that appeared as *Publications of the*

American Economic Association, IX, No. 3 (May, 1894). He received the first printed copy September 1, as he was preparing to teach Principles of Sociology and lecture about communication and transportation to a mix of undergraduate and graduate students.[48] We can do worse than calling 1894 the birth year of the field of communication in the United States.

I cannot do justice to *The Theory of Transportation* in brief discussion. It is an overlooked gem in the intellectual history of communication, which also gives lie to some of the inherited images of Cooley as communication theorist. The idealist Cooley is well known. *The Theory of Transportation* is the materialist Cooley, operating from the grid of political economy, trying "to write a theory of transportation from a sociological standpoint" (17). It contains some remarkable insights (along with errors, objectionable statements, and other chaff among the digestible wheat) and lays down grander theoretical riffs of a musical score that the political economist Harold Innis would play with greater brilliance and acclaim half a century later. It's a significant work not adequately read today and a starting point for Cooley's broader theory of communication.

In it, Cooley considers transportation from multiple perspectives. He attends to the physical dimensions ("movement of things—masses of any sort" over physical terrain), but is particularly interested in what he calls "the social relations of transportation," including the functions it serves and the institutions it evolves with, which he divides into four classes—military, political, economic, and "ideal," the last of which encompasses what we would call culture (religion, science, literature, art, thought; 39–42). In the process, he makes a large and important claim: The mechanism through which society organizes itself and extends its relations "is Communication in the widest sense of that word; communication of ideas and physical commodities, between one time and another and one place and another" (40). The claim births a heuristic scheme of analysis:

> The mechanism of material communication:
>> Place communication—transportation.
>> Time communication—storage and the like.
> The mechanism of psychical communication:
>> Place communication—gesture, speech, writing, printing, telegraphs, mails, etc.
>> Time communication—writing and printing regarded as means for recording and preserving thought for considerable periods of time; custom, imitation and heredity as conservative agents. (40–41)

He doesn't systematically follow out his scheme, but instead considers relationships between communication (material and psychical) and the development of military, political, economic, and cultural institutions over long historical time. In brief, he considers everything from military roads and signaling to ceremonies of the political state, "the medium of fairs and religious meetings," markets, cathedral squares, pilgrimages, books, ecclesiastical documents, traveling clergymen, special messengers, postal systems, universities, learned societies, the coercive state, formal organizations, periodicals, bibliographies, wagon services, newspapers, letters, railways, canals, telegraphs, and telephones (42–62). Reading through it today, we can hear anticipations of Innis, Foucault, and Carey.[49]

Cooley offers what is perhaps the earliest explicit vision for the study of communication as a distinct field. He classes it as a branch of social psychology, a "field of inquiry which embraces language as an instrument of social organization and all the material agencies that language employs" (61). Though Peters has characterized Cooley as an unrepentant idealist who ceded body, place, and materiality as fundamental components of communication, *The Theory of Transportation* puts forward a different picture. It operates within the frameworks of political economy, recognizes both material and "psychical" communication, and embeds the latter in the material agencies of language—media, bodies, events, and institutions.[50]

Cooley closes the thesis with a thoughtful consideration of markets, private organizations, and government regulation of transportation. He makes a case that transportation is different than other industries because it "is one of several fundamental social processes" (104), which means that it is subject to "the aims and methods of public control" (112), including government regulation in the name of the public good (103, 109, 114) and "publicity" ("collecting, arranging, analyzing and communicating all those facts which throw light upon any matter with respect to which a question of control arises" [113]). Though cautious about making political recommendations within the thesis (62), he depicts a transportation and communication system regulated through a blend of private initiative, the market, publicized statistics and other factual findings, and government action in the name of the public good. Unfortunately, the first two have come mostly to control the U.S. media system.

The thesis and Principles of Sociology course fed a third 1894 attempt to work out the idea of communication, directly connected to his father. The judge had been asked to write an entry on transportation for a massive three-volume government compendium of knowledge about the nation. An expert now himself, the son joined the project, which was published as Cooley and Cooley. Beyond surveying the state of transportation in the United States, the article extends some of the grand theoretic impulse of Charles's thesis, sharpens his dialectic of transportation and social change, and haltingly pushes the communication idea forward. "The thought of our time, whether taking the form of literature, science, the fine arts, or political discussion, is evidently molded in great measure by the spectacle of the industrial revolution and of the phenomena induced by it," the article proclaims. "None of these changes are more characteristic . . . than those in the methods of moving men and things from one place to another, and of communication between men in places distant from one another."[51] Charles amplified his own travel experiences, social hopes, and growing sense of the changes wrought by mobility, making a case about communication and the industrial revolution similar to the one Robert Albion would offer in the 1930s (see Chapter 1): "The development of great inland cities like Denver and Kansas City, the opening up to profitable culture of vast areas of land inaccessible to water, the enormous augmentation in the movement of persons from place to place, the quick interchange of thought throughout the world, causing a more vital self-consciousness in nations and facilitating the unity of great political aggregates like the United States, these are only a few of the more obvious of those features of the life of to-day that did not originally belong to the industrial revolution, but were added to it as secondary and unforeseen results of changes in transportation" (69). Drawing from the image of the collective social body and its communicative nervous system, the article suggested that "thought-transportation" through newspapers, cheap mails, telegraph, and telephone "tend to produce something like unity and self-consciousness in industrial society," which in turn could provide the basis for reform (132).[52] Charles had once attached a hope like this to oratory. From now on he would tie it to the agencies of communication writ large.

A plaintive footnote ends the article: "Owing to the illness of Judge Cooley, . . . he was unable to take an active part in the preparation of the preceding paper. It has, however, been read and criticized by him, and some expressions altered to meet his view. As here presented it has his full approval" (133). One can only guess what the episode meant to the son, for he destroyed his journals from this period.[53] When the judge died four years later, after nearly a decade of illness, Charles barely noted the event in his journal, but his father remained a presence for him. "I hope to do better than my father in having clearer and higher aims of *art*," the son wrote as he was working on his first book. "He fixed his mind too much on a success too dependent on people and so not restful."[54] Cooley believed his father worked himself to death, and he vowed to live a quieter life, for which the son was well disposed. But he also built upon his father's projects. His idea of "communication" arose from this matrix—marked by filial ambivalence, moral hope, and theories of material and symbolic transportation in society.

An Unfolding Vision: Communication and "The Great Life"

In the hands of its leading first-generation American theorist, communication grew out of political economy and statistics, the railroad business and government regulation, investigating social problems and trying to develop more general theories, writing research reports and journal entries, family connections and fatherly pressures, personal ambition and contemplative retreat. After 1894, Cooley developed a theory that emphasized what he called the "ideal" side of communication more than the material. He moved further from Washington and railway research and settled into a domestic existence with Elsie and their children in Ann Arbor. He assumed the role of college professor and settled into a kind of late Transcendentalist intellectual life within the emerging research university and professional systems. In that context, he developed a kind of secular faith in communication as an idea and social process, which he was working out through his writings.

In an important article and his trilogy of books, between 1897 and 1918, Cooley turns from transportation to what he once called "psychical communication," and lays down bases for a full field of communication study, from interpersonal and small group through organizational and public communication, media studies, and the history of communication. Sketching how "the communicative life"[55] constitutes selves, societies, and social institutions, the theory blends Emersonian expressivism with interpretive social science, refracted through an unorthodox religious sensibility that came to identify with a semimystical "Great Life" of communicative humanity. It was a descendant of Pauline universalism, house-based in its own way, which saw particular communications as part of a grander transhistorical interconnectivity and onward march, a kind of overarching universalist Mass experienced through moments of reflective awareness by observers like Cooley. Communication and the Great Life were elements of Cooley's secular faith, marked by their own kinds of quasi-religious participation and spiritual hope. In the context of this book, I want to lay out the contours of Cooley's theory, presenting a synoptic picture across those two decades of writing that led into a kind of vision of mass communication.

Cooley's theory was indexed to his personal life in its composition and style. "My thinking and writing, are well knit together and grow naturally out of my life," he observed in the spring of 1897. "My journals are but the fuller and more definite continuation of meditations begun in early childhood, and my social studies accomplished and projected, are the continuation, enlargement and verifications of my journals."[56] The self-conception aligned with observers' comments on Cooley's style, which George Herbert Mead called "Emersonian" for the way it reflected the author's structure of thought more than "any closely knit concatenation of elements which analysis presented."[57] Cooley envisioned his sociological writing as an outgrowth of his personal writings, which gave them a certain first-person quality, even when the "I" was formally muted. This tied into his understanding of sociology as a discipline and his method of pursuing it. "[T]he sciences that deal with social life are unique in that we who study them are a conscious part of the process," he wrote—articulating an essentially interpretive or hermeneutic view of the human sciences, as Schubert has observed, and extending the first-person-inflected essay tradition of Montaigne and Emerson, as Jacobs has detailed.[58] That view helped justify a method he called "sympathetic introspection," whereby a researcher puts "himself into intimate contact with various sorts of persons and allow[s] them to awake in himself a life similar to their own, which he afterwards, to the best of his ability recalls and describes," a method he believed gave access to the thought worlds of "children, idiots, criminals, rich and poor, conservative and radical—any phase of human nature not wholly alien to [the researcher's] own."[59] It's easy to see the epistemological shortcomings and naïveté of the method, but it did provide a means for him to call out and describe his own (socially generated) images of others' worlds, which means his applications of it can be read as accounts of his internalized ideals, fantasies, and ideological distortions. The method meant that his writings serve as entry points toward the contexts of his life in Ann Arbor.

Cooley's books and papers were produced in a home created by his wife, Elsie, who fed Charles's opportunity to write, read, and reflect. With Elsie as confidante, intellectual conversationalist, and editor—in addition to wife, mother, and household manager—Charles led a rich scholarly life. Almost every morning of his adult life, often as early as four o'clock, "he retired to his study to put down fresh thoughts on small slips of paper," as his nephew remembered.[60] His book-making rough work included piecing together fragments of journal entries and "bibliography cards," each with a brief thought penned on it, in a compositional process he divided into nine sequential steps.[61] Cooley's books show signs of this process, with chapters divided into shorter clusters topically related to one another, but often standing, too, as more or less self-contained thoughts.

He likened composition to the carpentry he practiced with great care and skill. He had talents for what he called "hand work" and as a boy had built small boats and other wooden products, taking sensuous pleasure in the process. As an adult, he delighted in watching his Ann Arbor home being constructed and did some of the carpentry himself. He later built the family a vacation cabin, on Crystal Lake, a distant quotation of Thoreau's Walden, manifest through the emergent culture of bourgeois vacation properties. "It is joyous work," Cooley wrote one summer while building a porch for the cabin, "the sensuous delight of touch, sight and smell in wood, tools, paint etc. . . . I love to handle my saws, planes, chisels and hammer, to see the wood take shape, to spread on the paint . . . [with] consciousness that I am creating something of use for those I care for."[62]

The craft of woodworking informed Cooley's understanding of the compositional process and served as a sort of medium of invention for him. "Making an essay, or a book, is very much like the job of carpentry, such as making the book-shelves that stand in our hall," he observed. "One must do much rough sawing and planing and sandpapering, and, especially, keep a clear plan before them. The rough work is not unpleasant, if done in the right mood and if one knows that it all counts toward the whole." As it had been for Emerson, mood was key for Cooley: "It is delightful to think if one's experience suggests and the mood inclines; but hateful to force a systematic essay from an unwilling brain."[63] (To which I say, "Amen.") Consistent with the craft ideal, he considered his sociological writings as "a peculiar kind of art, seeking a peculiar kind of beauty, not one of the popularly recognized branches" as he described the best of them in 1898, under the spell of Goethe's idea of the artist.[64] As an aid to its composition, he imagined as an audience "a conclave of the great and wise spirits of the past. They will take plenty of time; they will not overlook any merit; they will see thro' everything, and consider the man behind it. They will not expect omniscience, will not reprove enthusiasm, will value hope."[65]

Cooley was flush with hope, but aspects of his day job as a professor crimped his Emersonian style. Dispositionally, he was a mildly narcissistic, easily upset, controversy-averse, administratively incompetent man working in a professionalizing discipline, and his performance there was mixed. He taught the introductory lecture course on sociology, whose enrollments numbered in the hundreds, where he spoke nervously with what a former student described as a "thin, somewhat weak, slightly feminine" voice, and with mannerisms that "an unsympathetic undergraduate might find irksome."[66] He was not particularly effective at training his graduate students to do research, and he never expended the energy to create a sociology program at Michigan in the way others did at Columbia and Chicago. He took no interest in faculty meetings or matters of university policy, leaving his colleagues to do the tasks he avoided. He disliked attending professional meetings of the American Sociological Society (ASS), which he ambivalently helped form in 1905. "After a day or two I hate it desperately," he wrote of attending them. "I think I should not come if I did not partly forget how painful it is."[67] His intellect suffered as much as his psyche. "I am very commonplace after my convention. Emerson, whom I have just taken up, seems far over my head. This talk, talk, is only drifting. Thought is extremely dilute and *das gemeine* [the commonplace] eats up more and more of us."[68]

From his domestic and professorial perches, Cooley envisioned *communication* as a kind of sociological god term that animated human life and its development. "Society is a matter of the incidence of men upon one another, and since this incidence is a matter of communication, the history of the latter is the foundation of all history," he wrote, in one kind of expansive mood that grew from the impulses of *The Theory of Transportation*. As communicative environments changed, so too did human existence, an argument he deployed against laissez-faire versions of social Darwinism in his day.[69] The insight opened up space for considering the development of communications media over time, which in Cooley's progressive teleology made for a story of human advance from speech and gesture to printing and newer media.[70] Communication held a central place in history because it was the medium through which minds developed and manifest themselves publicly. He called communication "the mechanism through which human relations exist and develop—all the symbols of the mind, together with the means of conveying them through space and preserving them in time."[71] It was the creator of all thought. "[T]he mind lives in perpetual conversation. . . . The impulse to communicate is not so much a result of thought, as it is an inseparable part of it."[72] Individual characters, social groups, institutions, and traditions represented communication that had organized itself. In his view, a communicative environment was "a progressive invention, whose improvements react upon mankind and alter the life of every individual and institution."[73] Communication, in other words, was a process that helped constitute the social life of which it was part.

Cooley explored different aspects of "the communicative life," from personal thought to large-scale media. In *Human Nature and the Social Order* (HNSO, 1902), the emphasis falls on the individual and intimate, face-to-face interactions. Important sections of the book are built upon observations that Charles and Elsie made of their children, whom Cooley wrote of affectionately in his journals. As Jandy writes, their house became "a domestic laboratory for the observation and study of the genesis and development of personality," with the parents watching and taking extensive notes, which they also made available to other researchers.[74] The experience provided a social medium for invention of Cooley's theory of the communicative self, growing through interactions with real and imagined others. "The creation of imaginary companion seems to arise from the need of communication," he wrote in his journals about his son. "He talks constantly to other people when with them and keeps it up when they are gone. In both cases his talk is simply thinking aloud and does not presuppose any definite qualities in the interlocutor."[75] In his first book, Cooley lays out a developmental account of the communicative self, peppered with short transcriptions of notes about his children. "It is by intercourse with others that we expand our inner experience," he observes, going on to introduce his idea of "the looking-glass self," created through "the imaginations of our appearance to the other person; the imagination of his judgment of that appearance; and some sort of self-feeling, such as pride or mortification" (HNSO, 69, 152). Such selves also identify themselves with groups and construct honeycombed social identities in the process. "A man may be regarded as the point of intersection of an indefinite number of circles representing social groups, having as many arcs passing through him as there are groups," he suggests (114), a condition he later captured with the idea of the "nucleated" individual.[76] Moreover, "there is no separation between real and imaginary persons" (60), he writes, mutely testifying to his own childhood dreaming; "the dead, characters of fiction or the drama, [and] ideas of the gods" all are real members of society insofar as they are imagined (88). The book offers the starting point for a dramatistic theory of social interaction, which Cooley would develop further in subsequent writings. "Every social situation is of the same general nature . . . [and] must be understood, if at all, as a dramatic whole—as you would understand, say, 'Macbeth,'" he observed in his journal.[77]

In *Social Organization* (SO, 1909) and *Social Process* (SP, 1918), Cooley builds upon notions of the communicative self and moves outward, toward small groups, institutions, public opinion, and other social entities and processes. The building begins with "the primary group," defined as "those characterized by intimate face-to-face association and cooperation"—family, play group, and "neighborhood or community group of elders" being core examples (SO, 23–24). These intimate, spatially circumscribed groups are sites through which individuals interact in face-to-face conversation and develop a "we-feeling" that incubates moral ideals like solidarity, justice, freedom, autonomy, and service (ibid., 26–50). As Schubert puts it, "In primary groups individuals gain social competencies and experience normative ideals that are a prerequisite for social democratization."[78] In Cooley's telling, the groups were seedbeds of democratic moral life. He believed that developments in communication technology made it possible to extend those ideals to encompass ever larger populations, across lines of social difference, thus bringing distant others into one's circle of imagination and care and laying the groundwork for a new moral and political commonwealth. As Helen MacGill Hughes would observe, Cooley had faith in "a 'trend toward humanism'—meaning an extension of the sentiments developed in intimacy to include wider spheres."[79]

Public opinion would play a part in that development, and Cooley offered a communicative theory of it as well. His treatment is nuanced, and in certain regards it is superior to the more famous accounts by Gabriel Tarde, Walter Lippmann, and John Dewey.[80] For Cooley, public opinion is neither aggregated individual opinions nor broad agreement. As a "product of communication and reciprocal influence," public opinion is a process, "as different from the sum of what the individuals could have thought out in separation as a ship built by a hundred men is from a hundred boats each built by one man" (SO, 121). It takes many forms, and he distinguishes general public opinion from the public opinions of particular groups—"of the family, the club, the school-room, the party, the union, and so on" (126). Public opinion arises through a blend of elite and specialist discourse on the one hand, and the more diffuse "sentiment" and "judgment of persons" contributed by the group Cooley variously called "the masses," "the handworking people," and "the humbler classes" on the other (135, 139, 140, 142). "The thought of the undistinguished many is . . . not less important, not necessarily less original, than that of the conspicuous few," he writes (135). Cooley was no Whitmanesque popular democrat, but he gave the masses a positive role in the public-opinion process and cashed out ways that newspaper publicity of institutional transgression generated variable public sentiment and organized social action (132–33). Though Cooley often stressed the ideal of moral unity, there is also a significant pluralism in his social theory, manifest, among other places, in his account of public opinion.

Like other cultural processes, public opinion "is of the nature of a drama, many characters taking part in a variegated unity of action," Cooley writes (SP, 378). Public opinion is not about agreement, he insisted, but rather "divergent and often conflicting [characters], interact[ing] upon one another," and creating a scene the audience fills in (378). Though he emphasizes them far less, disagreement and difference are as fundamental to the process as cooperation and consensus. "Communicated differences are the life of opinion, as cross-breeding is of natural stock," he goes on (379). He was particularly interested in nonconformists and minority positions as basic elements in the process. "The choice of to-day is important; but the inchoate conditions which are breeding the choices to come are at least equally so. We shall be interested to find whether Democrats or Republicans win the next election; but how much more interesting it would be to know what obscure group of non-conformers is cherishing the idea that will prevail twenty years from now" (380; on nonconformity, see also see HNSO, 267–74).

Hero worship and fame also play parts in the communicative life, providing ways that ordinary people participate in the broader cultural order. "We feed our characters, while they are forming, upon the vision of admired models," Cooley writes, laying down a position that sat somewhere between the traditional rhetorical concept of imitation and the sociological idea of role models. He calls the character-forming process "hero-worship," and suggests that "it merges insensibly into that devotion to ideal persons that is called religious" (HNSO 280). The line between secular and sacred is blurry, just like that between real and literary characters. Hero-worship is related to fame, a communicative status Cooley links to the symbolic needs of the present. ("It is, then, present function, not past, which is the cause of fame" [SP, 115–16]). Fame operates as a means "for impressing certain ideas and sentiments and arousing emulation," he writes, also noting that it is caused as much "by publicity, by dramatic accessories, and by . . . luck" as it is by just desserts (SP, 122). Through fame and "hero worship," distant individuals enter the collective life of a community.

Language for Cooley was a multiply communicative medium that fed his social mysticism and sense of connectedness across time. "A word is a vehicle," he writes at his poetic best, "a boat floating down from the past, laden with the thought of men we never saw; and in coming to understand it we enter not only into the minds of our contemporaries, but into the general mind of humanity continuous through time" (SO, 69). "Thought . . . is communicated by words, and these are freighted with the net result of centuries of intercourse," he says elsewhere (HNSO, 105). The view at times spills over into a kind of spiritually infused, post-humanist account of language: "When

I speak, or even when I think, language lives in me, and the part that lives in me is acting upon other parts living in other persons, influencing the life of the whole of which I am unconscious" (SP, 6).

On occasion, Cooley writes in a more critical voice about communication, and points to its role in serving power, maintaining the status quo, and promoting less than ideal forms of social solidarity. "Dominated by the habits which it has generated, we all of us, even the agitators, uphold the existing order without knowing it," he observes (SO, 276). "Newspapers are generally owned by men of wealth, which has no doubt an important influence upon the sentiments expressed in them; but a weightier consideration is the fact that they depend for a profit chiefly upon advertisements," he observes elsewhere (270). These qualities go toward creating a communicative "upper-class atmosphere" that "[m]ost of us exist in," which makes it difficult "to understand or fairly judge the sentiment of the hand-working classes" (272).

The political economist in Cooley never wholly disappeared and got occasional space in articles and in sections of his last, and least read, book, *Social Process*. In a discussion that one could use to peel back some of the more upbeat moral idealism of his early communication theory, for instance, Cooley unpacks what he calls "valuation as a social process." He attends especially to economic values, but he also weighs in on valuing more generally, addressing a subject central to pragmatist thought.[81] Calling them "a system of practical ideas or motives for behavior" (SP, 283), he argues that "[a]ll human values are more or less mediated by special social conditions" (287). He breaks down the process of valuation in terms of organisms, persons, groups, institutions, situations, and objects. Value is generated with regard to particular objects (stocks, books, doctrines, people) in the contexts of situations "in view of which the organism integrates the various values working within it" (284). He goes on to show how valuation occurs consciously and unconsciously, both by the technical classes with special knowledge and institutional access (334–35), and by the wealthy and powerful upper classes, who exercise "a dominating and somewhat monopolistic influence over values," particularly those connected to the market (308). "Power is concentrated about the functions of the dominant institutions, and the powerful class use it consciously or otherwise, for their individual class advantage," Cooley warns (308). About the business system in particular, he notes that "the class in power, in spite of constant changes in its membership, is for many purposes a real historical organism acting collectively for its own aggrandizement," a process that is "for the most part unconscious" (305–306). Here is the basis for an account of how the values of a particular segment of a social organism come to dominate the whole. Unfortunately, Cooley didn't follow through with it. He paid insufficient attention to ways that injustice and domination were communicatively constituted as well and limited the kinds of ethico-political progress he saw as communication's rightful ends.

Cooley instead envisioned mostly the positive moral possibilities of communication, cultivating a kind of secular faith that merged into the semi-mystical social totality he called "The Great Life." His faith courses across his writings but was particularly pronounced from *Social Organization* on to the last chapters of *Social Process*, where it helps provide the crescendo for the final volume of his trilogy. I might call the faith a late-Transcendentalist, freethinking Protestant universalism, which served as a substitute for what he saw as the faltering religions of the world. "The existing creeds, formulated in a previous state of thought, have lost that relative truth they once had and are now, for most of us, not creeds at all, since they are incredible," he writes. In this context, formulating new creeds was "as natural and useful as any other kind of invention," the task of "competent men" who would devise ways of thinking about "the larger life and our relation to it" (SO, 375–76). I would suggest that Cooley's sociology was precisely such an invention for seeing larger wholes, and the relations of individuals to them. As he wrote in his journal in 1913, "It is the religious bearing of my work that arouses me. It helps me to see life as an onward, growing, unpreaching whole. I might call my book God in Human Life. To understand and expound the social manifestation of God is my religious function."[82]

The Great Life gathered a family of terms, ideas, and social processes into an object of faith in Cooley's secular religion of communication. In journals and published writings, he refers to "the great life," "larger life," "greater Life," and similar terms, all of which capture some of his sense of being part of a grander flow of social, moral, and spiritual life brought about through communication. It is closely tied to his belief in progress, whose reality he believed was itself "a matter of faith, not of demonstration" (SP, 408). Progress means "growth, renewal, onwardness, [and] hope" for Cooley, all ethical categories cashed out through the expansion of social identifications, moral concern, and democracy as a way of life. Far from determined and linear, progress is "essentially tentative, . . . we work it out as we go along." It is "a process rather than an attainment, . . . an upward struggle toward a good which we can never secure, but of which we have glimpses in a hundred forms of love and joy" (SP, 408). The idea of the Great Life is part of Cooley's this-worldly theism, which transferred hopes for a future life onto the unfolding collectively fashioned ethical life of humankind. "Of a further individual consciousness after death

I have no expectation. Yet I feel that life, *our* life, the Great Life, is somehow good beyond our dreams. Great things are doing and we help them on."[83]

Like everything else for Cooley, the Great Life expressed itself communicatively, and he experienced it in a variety of ways. "In childhood, music, poetry, in transient hours of vision, we know a fuller, richer life of which we are part," he writes. "It seems to me that back of all this must be a greater Life, high and glorious beyond my imagination, which is trying to work itself out through us" (SP 408). Reading gave him access and made him a participant in the process. "The best way to feel the great life is through the fellowship of those who have lived in and for it; thus faith can become a tradition, a social atmosphere. Who can think on Dante and not believe in God?" he wrote in his journals.[84] He found glimpses of it, too, observing "the stream of young men and women that flows through my classes—from three to four hundred a year—[and] is a part of the current of the life of God . . . I float on it as much as guide it."[85] He found it, too, in sociology, which he conceived as a kind of "religion" that offered "a way of seeing life as an onward whole, as the manifestation of God."[86] In a more general phase, the Great Life worked itself out through progressively enlarged social identifications. "[T]he community, the nation, the Commonwealth of Man, merge indistinguishably into the conception of a greater life" (420). He believed that "it is only a continuation of this enlarging membership and service to go on, by the aid of symbols and worship," from more specific social identifications "to the Great Life in which our life is merged" (421).

The Great Life can be read as a kind of mass communication writ large, a communicative totality of cultural and moral striving that encompassed and was born through the individual and collective efforts of humanity past, present, and future. Cooley experienced it as real, but participating in it required the right sensibility. It served as an object for spiritual contemplation, grounded by faith in the possibilities of communication. Society is "a complex of forms or processes each of which is living and growing by interaction with the others, the whole being so unified that what takes place in one part affects all the rest," he wrote (SP, 28). The Great Life captured this interrelatedness and inflected it with ethical, cultural, and aesthetic energies. Art contributed to it, including craft production, the art of democratic living, and any work suited to a person and performed in a manner that "takes delight in the whole to which it contributes" (416). Though merging into mysticism, Cooley's was a humanist ideal tied to the hope that individuals might find meaningful place in larger communities and see themselves part of a greater, better, unfolding social reality. It was a dream that resonated with Paul's and Whitman's, and, like theirs, called up images of the common body. Its moral core consisted in a "sense of community, or of sharing in a common social or spiritual whole, membership in which gives to all a kind of inner equality, no matter what their special parts may be" (SO, 180). Mass communication as represented by the Great Life was both all-encompassing and internally pluralistic: "Let there be 'diversities of gifts but the same spirit'" (242). Cooley's own gifts were writing and reflection, but he also contributed to the Great Life through marriage, parenting, teaching, woodworking, and countless quotidian communicative productions that did their small parts to constitute a greater communal whole.

At the same time, Cooley clearly wanted to keep material distance from certain characters and groups, even if they found some remote space in his mystical totality. Though "the masses" played an important role in his broader theory of democratic communication, he was no fan of crowds, nor did he seem to have moved gladly among them. He isolated them in his mind, symbolically and geographically, and struck up distance. "We find the mob and the mob-like religious revivals in the back counties rather than among the cheerful and animated people that throng the open places of New York or Chicago," he claimed (SO, 153). And while he took a relatively liberal position on race and understood it to be partly constructed through attitudes and "the total situation" of a social environment, in addition to biology (SP, 276), he advocated separation of black and white, and his writings show little evidence of making "sympathetic contact" with the African-Americans being lynched in the South. Addressing "Oriental immigration" specifically, he confidently wrote that there are "excellent grounds of national policy for preventing [the races from] mingling in large numbers in the same state" (SP, 280). Cooley had his limits and, unlike Whitman, envisioned the mass of humanity from afar.

In comparison with the sorts of mass communication we find in Paul and Whitman, Cooley's Great Life is, like its author, pale and slender. Paul rhetorically conceptualized a communicative form materially embedded in ritual and communal religion, while Whitman's were made manifest through print-based poetry, assembled crowds, geographical places, and mobile bodies. In contrast, the Great Life, though ubiquitous in some ways, is fleeting and evanescent, sensed by individuals in some moments, but disappearing in others. He ties it to a faith in moral progress that is similarly less institutionally anchored than faith in God or democracy. As with his predecessors' versions, there is universalism in the semimystical mass communion represented in the Great Life, but it doesn't favor the masses or energetically embrace the shunned and socially despised in the same way Paul's and Whitman's do. Perhaps fitting a far less illustrious figure, Cooley's vision of mass communication doesn't stack up to the others'. His significance, however, lies elsewhere—in crafting a theory of communication as such.

Staying Put and Moving On: Parting Thoughts on Cooley

In December of 1910, at the ASS meetings in St. Louis, Charles Cooley was offered a job at Columbia by Franklin Giddings, Chair of the Department of Political Economy. Cooley was a year removed from publication of *Social Organization*, which sold more than a thousand copies its first year out. After the University of Chicago, Columbia was the second major center for the study of sociology in the United States. Among its faculty members was Alvan A. Tenney, a young assistant professor, who at the time was teaching his students to conduct basic content analyses of newspapers.[87] Joseph Pulitzer had agreed to fund a new School of Journalism at Columbia, which would open in 1912. Though Chicago with Robert Park is far better remembered, Columbia was, through the 1920s, an important location for the sociological study of newspapers.[88] Giddings had told Cooley that he had some 160 graduate students working with him, and he needed assistance in teaching them, but he wanted Cooley to do his "own sort" of work.[89] From our vantage point today we can see that hiring Cooley would have brought the leading American theorist of communication to a department establishing new methods for its empirical study.

Cooley considered the offer, but the thought of moving overwhelmed him. He was neither Whitman from Brooklyn nor Paul from Tarsus, but Cooley from Ann Arbor. "There is an idea abroad that it is a good thing for a man to change his habitat," he wrote in his journal. "If he aims to be a complete man of the time and of the world, perhaps it is; but for depth, significance, flavor, he would better root himself somewhere and grow with the neighborhood," he continued. "I can be a distincter man here than transplanted: I see myself clothed in a tradition, a reputation, in local associations that I could not carry away with me. I should half die in moving. Here I have incarnated myself."[90] Cooley was more emplaced than mobile, as a theorist and as a man. Instead of moving to New York, he would continue plunging what Whitman called his semitic muscle, late-Victorian style, into his incarnated places in Michigan.

World War I broke out in 1914, setting in motion a series of events that would change the way people understood communication and practiced its techniques. Cooley wrote in his journals that he had "little enthusiasm" for the war and continued to hope for a "sense of solidarity" among nations, but he was not among those like John Dewey who weighed in publicly with their views.[91] Instead he moved forward writing *Social Process*—revising it at Crystal Lake in the summer of 1917 by reading it out loud to Elsie—a book that would advance his faith in progress, renewal, onwardness, and hope. Meanwhile, a generation of men was being wiped out by machine guns and mustard gas in Europe, in a war popularly legitimated and stoked by the organized propaganda of the warring states. Cooley's vision was more than a little out of step with the moment.

When *Social Process* came out in 1918, younger men who would shape thinking and policy about communication in the next decade were doing very different kinds of work than Cooley. Walter Lippmann, who grew up on New York's Upper East Side and was part of Harvard's famous class of 1910, was recruited to help start a propaganda bureau in the Army's Military Intelligence Branch, and he would become one of the country's leading journalists and syndicated columnists after the war. One of his classmates, the radical journalist John Reed, had moved on from championing the cause of the Mexican revolutionary Pancho Villa to working in Moscow for the Bureau of International Revolutionary Propaganda. Reed died in Russia in 1920; Lippmann wrote the most important American work on media in the 1920s, *Public Opinion*. Together they signaled the coming of organized propagandas that swept across the world over the next three decades.[92]

The leading scholar of those propagandas, Harold Lasswell, was entering the University of Chicago in 1918, a brilliant sixteen-year-old undergraduate who became probably the single most influential thinker in the nascent fields of propaganda and communications research in the 1930s and early 1940s. Described by one of his closest colleagues as "a kind of Leonardo da Vinci of the behavioral sciences," Lasswell was a lot of things Cooley was not: a towering and energetic intellectual polymath, methodologist, "tireless quantifier, early interpreter of Freud, and lively bon vivant."[93] Lasswell studied with the political scientist Charles Merriam, whose published 1919 empirical study of war propaganda was perhaps the first of its kind. Lasswell took propaganda analysis to new levels of empirical and methodological sophistication and scholarly self-consciousness over the next two decades, from his published dissertation, *Propaganda Technique in the World War* (1927), to subsequent studies of revolutionary and other political propaganda and two mammoth annotated bibliographies of writings in the field.[94] He wrote at a furious pace, in ways few of his peers could fully understand or build off, and with a rigor of the sort Cooley had little talent for.

Meanwhile, in 1918, David Sarnoff was working for the American Marconi Wireless Telegraph Company, which operated a technology that handsomely benefited from a world at war. Wireless was used to communicate with off-shore ships, coordinate attacks, and transmit reports from Europe that helped create what Lippmann would call the pictures in the heads of publics around the world.[95] In 1917, the U.S. Navy installed the most powerful transmitter to that point built, strong enough to carry a human voice across the ocean—which it did for President Wilson's Fourteen Points speech, articulating a vision for peace after the war. After the armistice, and with support from the U.S. government, General Electric bought out American Marconi and formed a new subsidiary, the Radio Corporation of America. Sarnoff rose quickly in the company, and, as I sketched in Chapter 1, played an important rhetorical role in legitimating the for-profit broadcast network RCA was establishing. He took Cooley's god term, *communication*, with its emerging moral energies, and yoked it to *mass*, which could suggest a great service for the people. In the process he helped justify an institutional apparatus that only occasionally served the moral and democratic ends Cooley hoped for.

While Lippmann, Lasswell, and Sarnoff were busy making their professional lives in the 1920s, Cooley was winding his down. Glad to be free of the self-imposed pressure to complete his three books, he entered what he called the happiest years of his life. He bought his first automobile, a Studebaker, and in September of 1923 drove it through regions his father had passed through by train, and Walt Whitman by stagecoach—Pittsburgh and Uniontown, on the way south to the Blue Ridge Mountains.[96] Motoring was still an adventure, with bad roads, frequent collisions, and high fellowship among drivers on the open roads. Cooley wrote about the automobile in his final book, *Life and the Student*, his most personal effort and the one closest to his journals in form and subject matter.[97] His optimism about new technologies of communication persists there, and he proclaims the "wonder of spontaneous adaptation [that] is a town full of automobiles." Like "all of our modern means of communication," he predicts, the automobile will "facilitate democracy by multiplying contacts," in this case "by causing all classes actually to rub against one another, as it were, on the open road" and becoming "a flying shuttle that weaves the strands of our life into a broad and flexible fabric."[98] Automobiles have surely multiplied social contacts of some sorts, but Cooley was—as usual—blind to or mute about the other side of the technology: its propensity to isolate travelers in cocoons of mobile domesticity and tear them out from the social fabric in and around their homes.

Cooley was diagnosed with cancer soon after *Life and the Student* was published, at a time when he himself was turning attention to the question of methodologies in social research.[99] His sociology trilogy had sold more than

33,000 copies, and he was considered by his fellow American sociologists as perhaps the most influential author in the field.[100] Diagnosed in March, Cooley was dead by early May, 1928. He went out with his literary boots on:

> I look from my window out into the lovely April landscape, the busy men at work on the new building, the flood-roots in the garden below and think: This is our world, the world of the social heritage and the cumulative achievements of men, of great traditions, of history, literature and arts, of great men, great hopes and great endeavors; the world which has been growing from immemorial time, and will continue to grow for unmeasured time to come.
>
> I think also: This is my world, the world in which from earliest childhood I have rejoiced to live and strive and have a part. Where I have learned and experimented and aspired, begotten children, formed and executed projects, failed and succeeded, made on the whole a helpful and honorable incarnation of myself. In this world I shall go on living, for the immediate future in my known works, and in the memories of men, for all time as an influence absorbed into the whole.
>
> The change which is about to take place is this: that my organism, and my consciousness which is a part of it, will dissolve, leaving that separate and precarious height of being attained and exhausted during the years of my life, "immerging again into that holy silence and eternity out of which, as a man, I arose." This is a notable change, but in so far as I have lived and do live as a man, in our world, in the great world, by no means a calamitous one; for what I care most about shall not die but live hopefully on.[101]

Fittingly, the Emersonian sociologist paraphrased Emerson ("The Method of Nature") in his final journal entry.

Though he is rarely recognized as such, Cooley was probably the most influential of the pre-1920 communication theorists for the generation that established U.S. mass communications research in the 1940s and '50s. He established terms, concepts, and baseline understandings that became "an influence absorbed into the whole" as advanced by Edward Shils, Helen McGill Hughes, Robert K. Merton, Paul Lazarsfeld, David Riesman, Donald Horton, Elihu Katz, Kurt and Gladys Lang, and dozens of others. The idea of the primary group was particularly influential in mid-century research, and served as a seedbed for understanding flows of media influence and the broader shape of mass society.[102] At Columbia, students were exposed to it in Merton's lectures, where he offered his take on a figure he had first read during an undergraduate education that began in the fall of 1928, five months after Cooley died. Together with his colleague Lazarsfeld, Merton would address the idea of "mass communication" so named, borrowing occasionally from Cooley, but operating out of very different intellectual and geographical places.

Though he had his limits, Cooley figured important insights into "the communicative life," and deserves credit for doing so. He viewed his written publications as art and was guided in their composition by a craft ideal and essayistic style that represent a model of academic production not dominant today. He moved slowly and took care with his work, publishing four books and twenty-odd articles over nearly four decades of scholarly publishing. I admit to feeling some nostalgia for these ideals, as I feel nostalgia for an era of transportation before automobiles, anchored in foot, horse, and railway, and materializing communicative worlds less dispersed and frenetic than our own. Cooley's writings offer thread ends into different ways of social being, while also giving pleasure through their readability and frequent artfulness (in contrast to those published by the *spermologos* Dewey, who consistently turned out work that would have benefited from editing and revision). Those writings also serve as substantive starting points for conversations that can be cashed out in a number of different conceptual currencies. Try substituting words like *culture*, *ideology*, or *collective representations* when he says "larger mind," and Cooley's ideas will seem less distant.

Cooley's achievement lay in his ability to draw upon the found materials of his inventional environments to figure the idea of "communication" as a major concept with which to interpret, analyze, and normatively guide the human makings of the world. His hopes for communication can seem blind and woefully out of touch with domination and darkness wrought, but this makes him a good starting point in the longer conversation we are part of, which has challenged and refined his descriptive and normative claims. What I've identified as his vision of mass communication, tied to the Great Life, is less significant than the fact that he played an important role in making communication a topic of scholarly consideration and considered it in a re-markable array of forms—from transportation to interpersonal, small group, and public communication, and across media ranging from speech to print, telegraphy, art, and automobiles. Cooley's vision is embedded within an over-arching faith that channels Pauline universalism and Emersonian expressivity into humanistic prose of a sociological sort. In this blending, he stands as a theoretical hinge figure, drawing the inherited biblical, Enlightenment, and Romantic traditions into a university-based scholarly matrix that gathered and grew in the twentieth century. He is historically significant, and he is still good to think against. For those interested in the idea of communication, one can do worse than start with Cooley's work, even if it wasn't a wise man who suggested it to you.

5

Merton's Skeptical Faith

"Faith in the continued disclosing of truth through directed
human cooperative endeavor is more religious in quality
than is any faith in a completed revelation."

—John Dewey, *A Common Faith* (26)

Robert K. Merton was a reader, born to freethinking Russian Jews, in a country and time with more personal freedom than most. He grew up Meyer Schkolnick, and though as an aspiring magician he shed his birth name, it indexed his destiny. *Schkolnick* means "schoolboy" in Russian, and for everything else he became, the schkolnik in him never vanished. He would become one of the most important sociologists of the twentieth century and a key, if ambivalent, figure in the development of research into "mass communications" so named. He seized openings in his cultural moment to craft a hugely successful professional career, blending himself into a multicultural milieu that included Gentiles and Jews, white people and black, women and men. Born on the Fourth of July to working-class immigrants, he became an American success and carved out his place in an intellectual ensemble that included Talcott Parsons, Paul Lazarsfeld, Harold Lasswell, Herta Herzog, Max Horkheimer, Theodor Adorno, Leo Lowenthal, David Riesman, Edward Shils, C. Wright Mills, and Marshall McLuhan—Jewish- and Protestant-born, two Catholic converts, elites and working-class kids, Americans (Northeast, Midwest, West), Austrians, Germans, a Canadian, and an honorary Englishman. Together they helped jump-start the organized academic study of "mass communication."

Collectively, these and other scholars brought dialectical scrutiny to an idea and social practice that had been granted rhetorical and institutional flight by David Sarnoff and other forces in the late 1920s—mass communication, classically understood as social processes instantiated through radio broadcasting, motion pictures, and broad-circulation print. The scrutiny had begun by the 1930s, and a decade later an institutionalized field was settling into place, scattered across research institutes and universities in New York, Chicago, New Haven, Washington, D.C., and state colleges of the Upper Midwest (especially Iowa, Minnesota, Illinois, and Wisconsin). The rise of this dispersed institutional nexus is a tale involving funded intellectual work, government, war, politics, competing philosophical frameworks and methodologies, and some larger-than-life personalities. I tell one small part of that larger tale through the figure of Merton, best remembered as a leading architect of structural-functionalist sociology, "middle-range theory," and as an author of classic works in science studies, social deviance, and medical education. As I show in this chapter, he also did important work in the sociology of mass communications and sat near the institutional birthplace for some of the most important and lasting research on the subject from the pivotal decade of the 1940s.

Merton (1910–2003) was a complex figure: a social scientist with an ample humanist side, a modernist who sometimes anchored himself in history, an architect of objectivist sociology whose communications research had critical dimensions, and an outsider who became the consummate professional insider from his position at Columbia University. He was an eloquent speaker good on the mechanical typewriter, a fast driver and suburban commuter who did the bulk of his longer-distance traveling by book. He directed the vast majority of his writing toward academic audiences, through journal articles and book chapters, and through his book-length collections of them.[1] Yet he invented or helped invent concepts that became phrases now common to everyday parlance—*self-fulfilling prophecy, dysfunctions, focus group, public image*, and *role model* among them.

By the time Merton came to start writing about mass communication in the 1940s, he was three decades into a nearly ninety-three-year life marked by direct experience with a huge array of media. He knew the urban motion-picture house in the era before "talkies," sold daily newspapers on the street as a young boy, benefited from the free public library funded through the capitalist-derived beneficence of Andrew Carnegie, built and used a series of amateur radio sets, used manual and then electric typewriters with dexterity and speed, conducted empirical research on the Philadelphia press while an undergraduate in college, listened in with the great radio audiences for Franklin Roosevelt and the World Series, tuned in to shortwave radio broadcasts from Europe during World War II, conducted propaganda research for the government and marketing research for businesses in the 1940s, negotiated automobile traffic on a regular basis, examined patterns of interpersonal communication in public housing projects, looked at mass letter-writing directed to heroes and political leaders, addressed parts of the nation on NBC radio's University of Chicago–sponsored *Round Table of the Air*, delved into educational television for a time as moderator on WNDT–New York's *Court of Reason*, debated Marshall McLuhan in more than one setting, oversaw the continued development and specialization of scholarly journals, traveled by air as planes supplanted railroads and ships, and experienced the beginning of the digital age through electronic word-processing, email, and the internet. Some were significant to the development of his thinking, others peripheral. Collectively, these communicative forms and many others entered the warp and weave of his life and the public texts that arose from it.

This chapter continues my story about the development of visions of mass communication, the faiths and rhetorics that animated them, and the social forms they index. After two unorthodox Christians in the previous two chapters, Meyer Schkolnick of Philadelphia returns us to Paul of Tarsus and unorthodox turns in the Jewish Diaspora. Merton and Paul were both city kids who moved among cultures, knew multiple languages, and grew to embrace universalisms different from those of their Hebraic forefathers. Whereas Paul continued to serve the God of Israel, Merton put his faith in science and secular learning instead. Paul's epistolary vision of mass communication was orally delivered and argumentatively based upon memorization of the sacred texts of Israel. Although the spoken word still had a place among Merton's media of invention, he brings us into an era of advanced professionalized literacy shaped in the contexts of the modern research university, Version 2.0, a generation and a half past Cooley's. Merton kept abundant typewritten notes of his thoughts and reading, which he stored in notebooks in his office. Whitman had his reporter's notebooks and sheaths of paper, and Cooley his journal, both written by hand; neither approached in sheer quantity the output of typewritten reading notes, research memos, letters, and manuscripts that Merton produced over his lifetime.[2] Merton was also master of a form Cooley dabbled with and Whitman and Paul didn't know—the footnote. Merton's are a thing of beauty (at least for footnote geeks such as myself) and remind me of a kind of Talmudic disputation carried on beneath the main text and running parallel to it. Whitman and Cooley had both aspired to be great orators, but Merton developed his public persona through youthful ambition in a different performing art, magic, which he practiced occasionally in adulthood as well. He composed most of his work in a home office in the suburbs, commuting to Columbia by car down the parkway from Hastings-on-Hudson. Without overstating the case, one might say that there was a homology of sorts in the spatial distance that ran between Merton's suburban home and the city (*polis*) on the one hand, and the symbolic distance that ran between Merton's mature sociology and the exigencies of contemporary political life on the other.

That distance opened markedly after the 1940s, the main decade for his communications research, which I unpack by way of some of the inventional media Merton drew upon in creating the rhetorical self and vision he manifests in that corpus. I focus on the young Robert Merton (and the Meyer Schkolnick who preceded him), sketching a route from Philadelphia to Harvard, New Orleans, Columbia, and suburban Hastings and outlining the skeptical faith that he came to embrace in the 1930s and '40s. His was one of the "common faiths" that John Dewey hoped would inhabit the modern world, supplanting inherited theological orientations with secularized evolutionary outgrowths.[3] In contrast to Cooley's tender-minded humanistic faith in communication, Merton's was a tough-minded scientific alternative, guided through his thirties by left-liberal and social democratic sympathies, but intent on cutting through platitudes and analyzing the social world in its pluralistic complexity. We might call young Merton's a skeptical left-leaning faith in science and disciplined sociological inquiry.

During the 1940s, Merton brought this sensibility to bear in sorting through and conceptualizing a number of species of mass communication, paradigmatic and nonparadigmatic. Many were in some form dominant or ideologically dominating—government-sponsored wartime propaganda, commercially sponsored radio networks, daily newspapers, public opinion polls, celebrity entertainers, and popular heroes. Others were grassroots alternatives like letters to leaders written by large numbers of ordinary citizens and, I will suggest, quotidian spaces inhabited by residents of an interracial housing project in Pittsburgh. His vision differed from that of his predecessors, and he took up a different stance toward being a theorist. While Paul, Whitman, and Cooley all largely identified with the forms of mass communication they theorized, Merton inhabits a position of greater symbolic distance, playing the role of a kind of modernist, social scientific Socrates, dialectically scrutinizing the popular art of rhetoric in Plato's *Gorgias* and *Phaedrus*. While his predecessors all found moral dwelling places in the species of mass communication they depicted, Merton's home lay elsewhere—in the wandering logoi of skeptical inquiry and the collective project of a professionally identified sociological science.

I call Merton's a multifocal vision of mass communication, attuned as it was to actors differently situated in the social structure and managing as it sometimes did to remain faithful to the creed of objectivist social science while also casting critical attention upon the moral and political deformities of the processes he studied. As Johnny Cash might've said, Merton walked the line, keeping both eyes open, addressing different audiences around him, and finding ways to describe the newer mass media with some of the nuance and complexity they deserved. Given a personal trajectory that took him from working-class-Jewish origins to a central position among the mostly Protestant-born Ivy League elite, Merton came by his multifocality honestly.

I sketch portions of the inventional route Merton followed in developing his vision and bringing it to bear on mass communication in the 1940s. In doing so, I draw from published and unpublished writings and piece together parts of a life that as yet has no biographer. I also draw selectively from a literature on Merton that lies volumetrically between those on Paul and Whitman on the abundant side, and Cooley on the sparer. Though a great deal of ink has been spilled on Merton's ideas, he has attracted little attention from historians outside the ranks of sociology, and only slightly more from historians within.[4] My understanding of Merton has been guided in key places by the intellectual historian David Hollinger's superb analyses of modernism, universalism, and Jewish-American history,[5] and it also builds off several essays I have published on Merton's communications research, the writing of which served as serialized inventional media for this chapter.[6]

Meyer Schkolnick of Philadelphia

Meyer Schkolnick came into this world by way of a Yiddish-speaking Russian mother, the former Ida Rasovskaya, who received important early assistance from her husband, Aaron Schkolnickoff. The couple's first child, Emma (named for her mother's anarchist heroine, Emma Goldman),[7] had been born eleven years before in Russia, perhaps in the Ukrainian city of Lviv. The young family traveled to the United States by way of Southampton, England, and arrived on June 11, 1904. At the port of entry to the United States, the father was officially identified as Harrie Skolnik, a tailor from Russia and a Hebrew.[8] They were three of the nearly 1.3 million Jews who left the Russian Empire between 1897 and 1915, more than a million of whom came to the United States. (Between 1881 and 1924, more than 2.5 million emigrated to the United States, giving it the largest Jewish population in the world.) Like the vast majority of Russian Jews, the Schkolnickoffs had lived in the "Pale of Settlement," an area consisting of twenty-five provinces in Poland, Lithuania, and other western regions of the Russian Empire where Jews were allowed to settle, under one of thousands of discriminatory laws that made the phrase "excepting the Jews" a legal commonplace. With the ascension of Czar Alexander III in 1881 (which took place at the time Cooley was dreaming of becoming a great orator in Ann Arbor), a bad situation worsened, and Jews became the targets of organized massacres known as pogroms, a word that means "devastations" in Russian. Jews emigrated in large numbers, a movement that accelerated during a series of deadly pogroms between 1903 and 1906. There were at least forty pogroms in 1904, the year the Schkolnikoffs migrated to Philadelphia. The Ukraine was particularly hard-hit.[9]

Turn-of-the-century Russian Judaism was a complex and vibrant affair. Traditionalisms blended with currents of the Jewish Enlightenment (*Haskalah*). Enlightenment Jews (*maskilim*) held out ideals of secular learning, encouraged the study of science and foreign languages, and developed what David Biale calls a "culture of self-criticism" that infected revolutionary political and scientific movements alike.[10] Zionists looked toward the Holy Lands, late Romantics toward the Yiddish-speaking shtetl, and cosmopolitans toward the universal horizons of science, socialism, or secular philosophy. Among many others, the culture bore the literary greats Tolstoy and Dostoyevsky, the composer Tchaikovsky, and the chemist Mendeleyev.[11]

Merton's family emerged from this cultural mix and participated in its great transplantation to America. If Lviv was in fact their home—the handwriting on the immigration documents is hard to read—then they were coming from what one scholar calls "a precursor model of the modern multicultural city."[12] It was a center for Jewish printing, education, culture, and enlightenment, and a point of connection between Poland and Germany to the west and Russia to the east.[13] Merton's family was not religiously pious. His mother "attended night school far more religiously than the synagogue," her son later wrote, and young Meyer never had a bar mitzvah. This was not unusual among East European immigrants, "a disproportionate number" of whom "had abandoned their faith years earlier," as Jonathan Sarna puts it. With Emma Goldman as her heroine, Ida Schkolnick had freethinking radical sympathies, though she may have tried to maintain the traditional dietary regime, like other "unsynagogued" socialists among the immigrants.[14] The 1910 census reports that Merton's mother and father were both literate and could speak enough English to communicate with the census taker.[15] The parents spoke Yiddish with each other and "English of a sort" with their son. Ida also read Russian.[16] The family provided cultural-border-crossing momentum to the son.

Merton's childhood provided a number of important media for subsequent self- and rhetorical invention. At home, he was the adored boy of a loving mother, a father he described as "remote," and a sister eleven years older. His mother was a reader and socialized her son into "the glories of the book."[17] She played a central role in developing her son's self-confidence, work ethic, and love for learning, all of which he would draw upon throughout his adult life. Their inexpensive row house on Wilder Street included "an occasionally used parlor and a diversely used dining room," where the boy engaged an interest in technology and built a series of radio sets that he listened to as a young "radio ham."[18] A coal-burning stove in the kitchen provided heat for a house illuminated by gas lights, which sat a few paces away from a backyard privy.[19]

A series of institutions stood within walking distance of the house, including the Young Men's Hebrew Association, which Meyer did not frequent; a settlement house, where he sometimes took classes; the John Hay Grammar School, which he attended from 1916 to 1923; and a free public library, which was perhaps the key place for him outside home and school. The library, funded by the Irish-born, Pittsburgh-based industrialist Andrew Carnegie, boasted multiple attractions for young Meyer, who was allowed to walk there alone by the time he was six. One was, of course, the hundreds of books free to be borrowed and read by blossoming bibliophiles like himself. A second was the building's electric lights, both brighter and more novel than the dim gaslights the family had at home. And the third emerged from "the tender facilitating attentions" of the attentive and dedicated women librarians who took an interest in the precocious young reader. They helped him cultivate tastes for biography, history, and literature, all lifelong favorites that made their ways into the research and sociological writings he would eventually produce. It was through this local branch of the Carnegie Library that he developed an interest in French modernism and first read Laurence Sterne's *Tristam Shandy*, a book that he periodically reread and which inspired his minor classic, *On the Shoulders of Giants* (1964).[20]

As it had in different ways for Paul and Whitman, the city provided Merton's overarching developmental medium as a child. He had enough freedom to ignore family wishes and hustle newspapers on the streets near City Hall when he was seven or eight, paying cash up front and hoping to sell enough papers to get his money back and turn a small profit (an early firsthand experience with the media business as it penetrated down to the street level).[21] He bought cheap seats with his friends to attend Philadelphia's Academy of Music, where he remembered "the charismatic Leopold Stokowski . . . scolding the Philistine audience for noisily objecting to the new complex music of a Schoenberg, Varèse, or Alban Berg." He heard orchestra players talk baseball afterward at "the lavish Horn and Hardart Automat" and cultivated a love for the game himself.[22] He played Tipcat in the streets[23] and ran with groups of boys in a neighborhood that included Irish, Italians, and Russians. "Our membership wasn't ethnically restricted," Paul Lazarsfeld remembered him saying.[24] Based in a multilingual immigrants' home in South Philadelphia in the 1910s and '20s, Merton traversed cultural worlds of literature, modernist art, people of different backgrounds, and baseball, all of which he embraced longer term.

Domestic location and Sister Emma brought Meyer his first key male role model, Charles Hopkins, or "Hop," a neighbor whose family's house shared a wall with the Schkolnicks'. The families were said to have met when Hop's white mice ran through the Schkolnicks' dwelling. The mice turned out to be part of Hop's magic act, and their escape was the auspicious start of two relationships—one between Hop and Emma, which led eventually to marriage, and the other between Hop and Meyer, a friendship that soon helped the boy become Robert K. "Bob" Merton, performer of enchanting mysteries and typographic man.[25] Ten years older than Meyer, Hop was something of a big brother and a male guide "far more important than my father," Merton later wrote, and "everything my Americanizing self could admire."[26] A successful magician respected enough to be profiled by a Philadelphia newspaper, Hop was a self-taught polymath whose family had emigrated from Russia a few years before the Schkolnicks. Hop brought Meyer into the disciplined art of prestidigitation. "To become even a routine amateur took countless hours, almost like becoming a pianist or violinist," Merton said. "Hop gave me a sense of discipline of what's needed." Meyer became good enough to perform at birthday parties and bar mitzvahs, help support himself in college, and become a member of the Society of American Magicians, a craft guild that required a potential member to perform a new trick or sleight of hand. He aspired to greater success as a magician, but began to think otherwise after performing one summer with a traveling carnival. "I was good at close-up magic, but with bigger audiences, it was different. I was a big failure," he later remembered.[27] Appealing to large public audiences was never Merton's forte.

Under Hop's influence, Meyer adopted a stage name, Robert K. Merton, which reportedly came to him after a brief stop at "Robert Merlin," quickly declared too hackneyed. The precedent of a famous figure played some role, too, when Merton did a school report on Harry Houdini, born "Eric Weiss, son of eminent talmudist" (as he recorded on a typed note card still preserved among his papers), which apparently served as confirmation to a young man who typed his name, "R.K. Merton, 12-B," on the research cards.[28] If a rabbi's son could reinvent himself as Harry Houdini from the all-American-sounding town of Appleton, Wisconsin, then surely Meyer Schkolnick could become Robert K. Merton, man of the world.

Beyond initiating him into magic, performance, and renaming, Hop also mediated Merton's way toward skepticism, typewriting, speed, and travel, all of which fed lifelong inventional streams. Like other magicians of the era, including Houdini and Charles Fulton Ousler, Hop was a man skilled in the arts of illusion who lent his talents to those bent on unmasking claims made about supernatural phenomena.[29] Ousler worked with Houdini to expose fake mediums and organized a committee that offered ten thousand dollars to anyone who could demonstrate a supernatural phenomenon.[30] Hop operated in lower-profile circles, but he too mastered both skepticism and the production of artifice, each of which would mark Mertonian sociology. That sociology was composed through typewriting, an art Hop passed on to his younger charge and which Merton did with great precision as an adult. Hop also gave Meyer rides on a motorcycle that introduced him to speed (Merton was always a fast driver) and offered him early experience being on the road (the two of them went to Massachusetts one summer to sell a new kind of telephone directory Hop had invented). Hop probably also offered encouragement for the hitchhiking trip west that Merton took when he was 14, staying overnight for free in jails or with accommodating strangers and encountering a farmer's daughter named Nebraska along the way.[31] He didn't have access to a deep-pocketed father like a young Charles Cooley did, but Merton managed to get around, and apparently had a good time doing it. He was even on the highways during the same years that Cooley was motoring about. (I wonder if Cooley picked up hitchhikers and saw them as roadside manifestations of the Great Life. I wonder who had more fun on the road. I wonder what happened to Nebraska.)

R. K. Merton was listed as "Myer R. Schkolnick" in the Philadelphia newspaper that identified him as valedictorian of the Southern High School class that graduated in December of 1927. The public high school provided Merton four years of Latin, two of French, and a solid scientific curriculum of chemistry, physics, and math. He was one of twenty boys to graduate in three and a half years, and his record was strong enough to win him a scholarship to attend Philadelphia's Temple College, established for the city's poor and laboring classes by the Baptist minister and orator Russell Conwell. Merton delivered the valedictory address, "Appreciation of School Endeavor."[32]

At Temple, Merton would develop the next in a series of significant inventional relationships with slightly older men, this one drawing him into what became his lifelong field of study, sociology. The man was George Eaton

Simpson, an Iowa boy who had gone from Coe College and the University of Missouri to the University of Pennsylvania, where he was still working toward his doctorate while serving as an instructor at Temple. Simpson became Merton's teacher, mentor, friend, and "principal drinking and talking companion,"[33] and he set his charge on a sociological path. In Merton's meticulously typed class notes for Simpson's introductory course, he noted that sociology deals with "[o]rigin, development, structure and functioning of social groups," and that science was "accurate, tested and systematized knowledge . . . [whose] purpose is to scrutinize alleged facts to discover whether or not they are facts."[34] Origins were not a Mertonian priority (he largely left his own behind), but structures and functions were, and he would go on to develop the most influential conceptual framework for analyzing them sociologically by taking the scrutinizing impulses of science as his guide. He found sociology both interesting and enlightening, and later remarked on "the joy of discovering it was possible to examine human behavior objectively and without using loaded moral preconceptions."[35] In other classes he learned that crime was a category defined simply by the conventions and "prevailing ethical standard" of a society, vice an "action injurious to [an] actor and offset by no social gain," and that "[s]in is a religious concept and not a sociological one."[36] Merton was swimming in waters beyond the bounds of Cooley's moralized and expressive link to the culture at large.

Simpson enlisted Merton to serve as research assistant for his dissertation, a study of depictions of African-Americans in the white Philadelphia newspapers. It would eventually be published as *The Negro in the Philadelphia Press* (1936), where Simpson argued that "[t]he use of the newspaper, the radio, and the movie in modern propaganda and modern education make it appropriate for social scientists to undertake studies of the roles which these agencies play in the formation of public opinion."[37] He drew upon research methodologies developed at Columbia in the 1910s and '20s, designed to analyze newspaper content in a systematic way.[38] Merton was set to work "classifying, counting, measuring, and statistically summarizing all references to Negroes over a span of decades in Philadelphia newspapers," as he later described his job.[39] But Simpson's research assistant (like Paul's secretary, perhaps) did more than record the facts or mediated logoi, and Simpson thanked him for having "contributed a number of important suggestions during the course of the study." The research tested the perception "that the Negro is generally ignored in the large metropolitan newspapers, but that when any attention is given him it is usually of an unfavorable nature," and through interviews with reader-experts, sought to determine how such coverage affects racial attitudes.[40] The book is among the earliest systematic studies of portrayals of minorities in mass media. In participating in it, Merton unknowingly began his career in communications research.

Merton succeeded at Temple, driven in part by an internalized standard of excellence that would press upon him for the duration. A short poem he wrote in a notebook gave some indication:

MEDIOCRITY

Ah words, you scorn my pleading search,
You resist and bid me silent be,
My hopes must hide themselves
In sad nonentity ~ ~
So much to tell, yet cannot say,
Words, Words, Words. ~ ~ ~

As an adult, he would name the internalized voice that insisted upon excellence "The Examiner." It could be relentless in its judgments and helped create a perfectionist self that Merton's students sometimes found debilitating. It drove him to become a master of words, among other destinations.

More nurturing than this inner voice was the relationship he cultivated at Temple with Suzanne Mae Carhart, like Merton a working-class–raised high school valedictorian, but otherwise coming from a far different cultural milieu. An only child, Carhart grew up in Tuckerton, a small fishing community of perhaps thirteen hundred on the southern coast of New Jersey, which in the 1920s boasted a huge radio tower that could send shortwave transmissions to Europe. While Merton's family had arrived from Russia just two decades earlier, Carhart's family were English Methodists who had lived on the Jersey coast since the seventeenth century. Although her mother was agnostic, the larger clan was intensely religious and filled with missionaries. "I was an uncommon specimen when Sue first brought me there," Merton said of being brought home to meet the family in Tuckerton. "What brought us together was the Bible. When they discovered I read the Bible, not religiously, we could argue and debate and so on."[41]

Sue Carhart graduated from Temple with Distinction in English, serving as treasurer of the College Women's Club and vice president of Phi Delta, writing for the student newspaper, and participating in Le Cercle Français and the Writers Guild.[42] She and Bob would marry in 1934, becoming one small data point within a still-rare social phenomenon Merton would later study—intermarriage.[43] She was a social worker in the 1930s, but from the 1940s on, Sue Merton made it her business to raise three children and maintain the family's household, with help from her mother, who lived with the family. Like Elsie Cooley, Sue Merton supplied the domestic labor that freed her professor husband to go about his intellectual labors undisturbed.

If Sue Carhart from Tuckerton stretched Merton out culturally in one way at Temple, George Simpson did it in others. Race was Simpson's main area of study, and he drew Merton into "new social and cognitive networks," with both African-Americans and professional sociologists. Through Simpson, Merton came to know Ralph Bunche, E. Franklin Frazier, and members of "the reclusive Negro Philadelphia élite of physicians, lawyers, writers, artists and musicians."[44] He also came to know Alain Locke, the great Harvard trained African-American philosopher, aesthetician, and race-theorist, most widely known for editing *The New Negro* (1925), the compilation of writings that named and gave shape to the Harlem Renaissance. With encouragement from Simpson, young Robert Merton invited Locke up from Washington to speak to the undergraduate sociology club. The Philadelphia-born Locke had gone from a local college to Harvard, taken his doctorate in philosophy after a Rhodes Scholarship and more study in Europe, and then converted to the Baha'i religion, which emphasized the unity of humanity, met in interracial groups, and promoted race tolerance. He and Merton struck up an epistolary and occasional face-to-face friendship following. First-rate thinker and cosmopolitan, Locke encouraged Merton and gave him confidence when the undergraduate decided to go to graduate school.[45] Merton, too, set sights on jumping from an unaccredited Philadelphia college to Harvard. He had been taken by the "dramaturgic and dramatic self" and "inadvertently recruiting sociological voice" of its Russian émigré sociologist, Pitirim Alexandrovich Sorokin, whom Merton heard when Simpson took him to the 1929 meetings of the ASS.[46]

Skeptical Left-Democratic Faith: Invention in Cambridge and New Orleans

Robert K. Merton enrolled at Harvard in the fall of 1931. With his mother's blessings, he had legally changed his name at Temple. Genteel Harvard was worlds away from South Philadelphia. It was still governed by a quota system, instituted in 1922, limiting the number of Jews it would admit, and administered through an application form that included questions concerning religious preference, mother's maiden name, birthplace of father, and "change, if any, [that] has been made since your birth in your own name or that of your father? (explain fully)."[47] Jewish graduate students had more leeway, particularly in the new science of sociology, and "Robert Merton" was a good assimilating name. Except when hailed as such by his professor Carle Zimmerman or the anti-Semitic secretary of the department, "I wasn't experiencing myself as Jewish," Merton told me.[48] At the same time, he was living out one way of being Jewish in America in the 1930s—"[s]huffling cards of identity, switching and disguising names as declarations of independence in a society that might reward nobodies, putting on masks amid the fluidities of class and status," and generally taking advantage of a moment "where any barrier dividing them from their neighbors became so easy to surmount that it was sometimes difficult to notice," as Stephen Whitfield has described it.[49] Like Paul and, to a lesser extent, Whitman, Merton was a border-crosser—in his case one of a class of Jewish-born, Enlightenment-inspired, cosmopolitan freethinkers, with little interest in Judaism, who brought what David Hollinger has called "a skeptical disposition into the American discussions of national and world issues that had been the all but exclusive domain of Protestants and ex-Protestants."[50] In the 1930s and '40s, Merton brought this disposition to bear on discussions of, among other topics, science, propaganda, and mass communication.

At Harvard, Merton would come to solidify a skeptical faith in rational inquiry and science. It was a recognizable outpost of the Jewish Enlightenment, pushed to its secular limits, and inflected with modernist sensibilities. Science provided at once epistemological orientation, quasi-religious moral source, and object study for Merton's sociology. Reflexivity was built in, though rarely trumpeted. Merton was aware of its artifice—scientific concepts that give facts shape, research that is guided by human purpose. He was aware of its nonlinearity, concealed by the neatness of scientific publications that present a different image. The dream of a science of society was a long one. Merton would channel it to a high-modernist sociology with epistemological debts to pragmatism and a clean analytic structure far more economical than the positivist and encyclopedic variations of the nineteenth and early twentieth centuries. It was a hopeful but not triumphal faith, aware of contingency, irony, and unanticipated consequences. In the 1930s and '40s, it was informed by socialist and left-liberal politics (which in the 1950s eased into the liberal-establishment center).

I can't begin to tease out the intricacies of Merton's epistemological and ethico-political orientation, but I'd like to sketch its contours with reference to a few inventional media that contributed to building it. One revolved around the ambivalent interpersonal relationship he cultivated with his advisor, Pitirim Sorokin, the writing-and-performing sociological voice that drew

Merton to Harvard. Sorokin was a Russian émigré whose *Leaves from a Russian Diary* (1924) grippingly portrayed the Revolution from the perspective of an anti-Czarist, anti-Bolshevik, romantic nationalist and member of the Orthodox Church, jailed by both sides in the conflict.[51] At Temple, Merton had read at least the bulk of the corpus of American sociology, but Sorokin drew him toward Continental thinking, which the student took to. Merton enrolled in Sorokin's seminars and served as his teaching and research assistant. He was exposed to the long and wide view of sociological thinking "from Confucius, Plato, Aristotle, Ibn-Khaldun and Vico to Comte, Spencer, Tarde, Marx, Durkheim, and Pareto," among others.[52] A review Sorokin had agreed to do, but sloughed off on his student, brought Merton up to speed with recent French sociology and drew him into Durkheimian waters he would swim in much further.[53] Through Sorokin, Merton was hearing that "[a]ll socio-cultural phenomena, even the criteria of truth and of science . . . are directly—and often mainly—conditioned by social reality or the social milieu."[54] Developing that idea, Sorokin enlisted Merton to research social rates of scientific discovery, technological invention, and fluctuation in adherence to scientific theories over time.[55] By January of 1933, Merton was telling Sorokin that his "primary interest is a study of *The Sociology of Invention*."[56]

Merton's own intellectual self-invention developed ambivalently through Sorokin. The professor's old-school European expectation that students would "become his disciples, echoing his words and thoughts almost as though they were their own" sat uneasily at Harvard. Instead of becoming disciples, Merton and others like him internalized "the same critical stance toward aspects of Sorokin's work as he, in the capacity of role-model, was taking toward the work of others, both contemporary and bygone."[57] Merton did not adopt Sorokin's cyclical model of sociocultural systems and scientific change, and he would go on to reject grand theories like Sorokin's, in favor of his famous "middle-range" variety.[58] Feelings of ambivalence were mutual and captured in an inscription to a book Sorokin sent Merton some twenty years later: "To my darned enemy and dearest friend Robert—from Pitirim."[59]

Another key interpersonal relationship for Merton's intellectual self-invention occurred with George Sarton, the great historian of science whom, like Sorokin, Merton would both draw on and depart from. On the one hand, Sarton brought the young sociology student "across academic boundaries into the then hardly institutionalized discipline of the history of science," mentoring him "as student and apprentice, then as journeyman and junior colleague." He offered Merton a desk in his large workshop-office in Widener, the centralized spatial medium in which Sarton and his research associates did their own work and published *Isis*, the journal he had founded in 1912. Merton "was allowed to move freely through the fabulous bibliographic files, asked to serve as a referee for the few manuscripts with a sociological tinge, and enabled to read selectively in the galleys of the forthcoming contents." Even more enduringly, Sarton provided Merton a model of scholarly care and steady, high-level productivity while also bestowing what Merton called other "threshold gifts" that made a material difference to Merton's career and development. On the other hand, what Merton termed Sarton's "Edwardian" thought style manifested itself in a late Comtean positivism "temperamentally averse to the explicit use of analytical paradigms," as well as a long-held desire to write "an encylopaedic history of science" that would encompass European, Islamic, and Asian civilizations. "This attitude of mind was far removed from the sort of sociological framework adopted in my dissertation," Merton wrote, and "even further removed from my later efforts to develop what I described as 'paradigms,' as in the 1945 'paradigm for the sociology of knowledge.'"[60] Merton's was not the Edwardian positivist's faith that knowledge could be built from the ground up, but rather a modernist variation, aware of its own artifice. As he put it in a revealing but little-read 1941 paper, "an explicit conceptual outfit, a part of theory, is necessary even for fruitful discoveries of fact."[61] Since becoming a magician and adopting a stage name, Merton was well aware of the powers of artifice in perceiving the world.

Merton departed from Sarton's thought style, but he took full advantage of other inventional resources the historian of science provided him. These revolved around Sarton's two-room Widener Library office suite, which provided Merton direct and easy access to an amazing collection of books and journals bought or received by *Isis* and Sarton, not to mention the stunning library stacks in Widener. It was a reader's delight. Sarton made Merton an associate editor of the journal, which in turn got him reviewing books, something he did with great frequency in what Merton called "the half dozen or so years of my novitiate" with Sarton.[62] Reviewing books was a high-level literate practice that gave Merton the chance to engage with and discourse upon the published text. Notes and book reviews gave Merton a structured context for reading and focused his mind toward summary, evaluation, and communication for an exquisitely knowledgeable international audience of scholars. He learned to do it very well. (Florian Znaniecki called a review Merton wrote of his book "one of the best pieces of interpretive and constructive scientific criticism I have ever read."[63]) One review allowed him to display his talents for New Testament exegesis.[64] Later in his life, New Testament discourse played a central role in Mertonian theory, in the form of "the Matthew Effect."[65]

The book reviews allowed him to begin mastering an interpretive practice that John Murray Cuddihy would describe as "Merton's Talmudic *explication de texte*."[66] This was another high literate art, fed by long-cultivated practices of reading and worked out both in print and orally, for his students. Cuddihy was one of scores of Columbia graduate students enraptured by Merton's lectures on sociological theory. Merton began developing his lecturing skills to undergraduates at Harvard, where he performed thinking and gained practice with an oral form that would lead him to reflect on the way speaking "can provide for the discovery of thoughts barely conceptualized before they were put into so many words before an evocative group."[67] The lecturer announced to one class in 1937 that a "piece of research does not progress in the way it is 'written up' for publication," giving voice to a phenomenon he published on decades later.[68] In another class, he spoke on the social figure of the Jew, his "readiness of eliminating visibility," willingness "to discard many of the loyalties obscuring his intellectual perspective," and being possessed with a creative insight "not unrelated to his geographic and social mobility, to the fact that he is a peripheral man, and thus obtains relativistic perspectives which enables him to see old problems in a new light."[69] These were ideals Merton himself held, as he developed an ethos that downplayed his visibility as Jew, discarded inherited loyalties in the pursuit of social scientific truth, and developed creative analytic schemes for understanding old problems in new sociological ways, typically with multifocal awareness of different positions in the social structure.[70]

Teaching in the provinces in State College, Pennsylvania, in the summer of 1938, Merton reported a different, but no less revealing, sort of classroom performance to his friend Read Bain:

> [E]ach day I conscientiously spend some ten minutes in preparation for lectures, but the unmitigated stupidity of my summer session clientele responds only to ad libing. I have a large class, as summer classes go,—40—and as I tear their ethnocentric illusions into unrecognizable shreds, they sigh, weep and shudder, only to cheer me on as they take hold of the new faith of nominal objectivity. Willy-nilly, I am their very own prophet and theirs is the joy of the convert. Now they too sit high above the social universe, surveying all, judging none. A passionate neutrality is their sole guide, and they will probably become very unhappy neurotics.

Through irony and wit, Merton offered an exaggerated portrait of critical objectivity and personal mission, alluded to elsewhere in the letter in a huzzah to his friend: "May the red-radical flag of sociological operationalism wave over the length and breadth of this unfortunate land."[71] Wit distanced, but Merton also broadly subscribed to the ideals of science and socialism, which he tempered with skepticism

Science in fact made skepticism a virtue, as Merton had made clear in a paper he delivered six months earlier, in the aftermath of a trip to Austria and Germany. Among other points he made, he critiqued the idea that the social effects of science must be good in the long run, calling it "an article of faith [that] performs the function of providing a rationale for scientific research . . . [and] manifestly not a statement of fact." The proper scientific attitude was more iconoclastic and involved "latent questioning of certain bases of established routine, authority, vested procedures and the realm of the 'sacred' generally." Every institution, Merton said, involved "a 'sacred area,' which is resistant to 'profane' examination," and science itself had such an area. But scientific investigation was also different: "whether it be the sacred sphere of political convictions or religious faith or economic rights, the scientific investigator does not conduct himself in the prescribed uncritical and ritualistic fashion. He does not preserve the cleavage between the sacred and the profane, between that which requires uncritical respect and that which can be objectively analyzed."[72] His words were as much exhortation as description, delivered within a dialectical-analysis-cum-praise of science as institution, orientation, and method of inquiry.

In the spring of 1939, Merton accepted a job at Tulane University in New Orleans, joining a two-man department alongside Harlan Gilmore, whom he described to a friend as "a forty-two-year-old nonentity, with special interest in population."[73] In early October, Merton filled out the Faculty and Staff Biographical Record for the Tulane University News Bureau. He identified himself as a Quaker, whose hobbies were carpentry and tennis.[74] A twenty-eight-year-old rising star sufficiently youthful to be mistaken for an undergraduate, Merton enjoyed New Orleans with Sue, took in the local cultures, and pushed ahead as a sociologist. He was appalled by popular politics ("The electioneering here defies any and all descriptions—apes, prisoners, and bloody shirts are all used as electioneering symbols"[75]) and ambivalent about rituals of social decorum at the university. But as he did in State College, he found ways to address his students in the classroom and "tear their ethnocentric illusions into unrecognizable shreds." On his first day teaching at the all-female Sophie Newcomb College, for instance, Merton responded to a roomful of white Southern women (half of them knitting) by launching a discussion of "Negro-White intermarriage," a subject he was conducting research on, which was illegal in thirty states and taboo in all forty-eight—

Louisiana most certainly among them. The knitting needles stopped.[76] One might say he was practicing a kind of piecemeal quotidian left politics, seizing an opening provided by the classroom.

About that time, Merton was identified by his friend Granville Hicks as "a sociologist, a man who has been considered, whether or not he considers himself, a Marxist."[77] Hicks, the critic and literary editor of the Communist Party's *New Masses*, had sent out a mimeographed letter in early 1940, after the American Left had been thrown into disarray by the Nazi-Soviet nonaggression pact in the fall of 1939. He sent it out to friends, asking them "what they thought ought to be done to unify and advance the radical movement in the present moment of disorganization."[78] Merton was among the fifty or so who received Hicks's letter, which was followed by five more, sent to a growing number of people, and including letters and excerpts sent in from Hicks's correspondents. Merton typed and mailed his thoughts, which Hicks identified as taking "a point of view somewhat farther to the right, I think, than any that has yet appeared in these bulletins."[79]

Merton's statement, a portion of which Hicks reproduced, began,

> I *know* that I am dissatisfied with many features of our social life. I don't like to see families attempting to subsist on $500 a year and I don't like the conspicuous waste of our Bourbons at Miami Beach; I don't like to see the collapse of morale on the part of men who have no employment; I detest war and exploitation of racial and economic groups.

Everyone shared these sentiments, he said, but there were differences when it came to what should be done about the situation. Some were true believers in grand solutions. Merton was not. There are people "who are convinced that we KNOW just how these problems can be solved," he wrote, and who variously advocate "a 'classless society'; socialization of property through expropriation of private owners; liquidation of those who are too stupid or too vicious to see the necessity of these changes; a vigorous, united organization in which the party line is strictly defined for all members (differences of opinion breed weakness); clearcut definition of the conflicting interests and the basic cleavages in society." These were the dogmas of socialists, communists, fascists, eugenicists, and objective political analysis. "As any faith, they minimize anxieties, and as any faith, they produce, in some measure, 'results.' But those of us who have not been converted—and I use that term in its strict sense—to this faith, are still beset by doubts." Merton was skeptical: skeptical that "large-scale changes can be for the first time deliberately and consciously guided"; skeptical of the "all encompassing aspirations of the C.P.

or, for that matter, the Socialist Party"; skeptical of their attempts to reshape values wholesale. "Call it education or, if you prefer, propaganda; both are equally ineffective if they do not draw upon the immediate experiences and sentiments of their audience."[80]

Merton had personal talent in appealing to audiences, but his faith lay not in rhetoric but in skeptical inquiry, which he attached to the projects of science and nondoctrinaire socialism alike. He was no populist, but he paid attention to "the symbols and values of the great bulk of our population" as a structure that could not be predictably reengineered.[81] He found evidence for his views on a research trip/driving adventure to Mexico in the summer of 1940.[82] Propaganda drew his attention. He followed the shortwave radio broadcasts from war-torn Europe, at once satisfying the radio ham, citizen, and social scientist in him. He wrote George Simpson that the broadcasts offered him "valuable propaganda material," and said that he was "gradually becoming convinced that the field of propaganda, with all its implications, is practically the field of social psychology."[83] He pursued the proposition in a course he co-taught in the spring of 1941, Social Psychology, which had propaganda as a major topic. Exercising his multifocal analytic vision, Merton considered unanticipated consequences he called "boomerang propaganda," "latent and manifest functions," and the idea of "ambivalence"—oral publications of concepts that would become staples of Mertonian sociology.[84] In late April of that year, he was offered a job by the Department of Political Economy at Columbia, which had been looking for an assistant professor to teach urban sociology. Unlike Cooley, Merton jumped at the chance of moving to New York.[85]

Figuring Mass Communication from the Suburbs

Actually, the Mertons moved to the New York suburbs—Hastings-on-Hudson, seventeen miles north of Columbia by car on Sawmill River Road and the Hudson River Parkway. Bob would be teaching urban sociology and living a suburban life, offering "Growth of the City" his first semester while experiencing some of his subject matter firsthand via his thirty-four-mile roundtrip commute. For a kid who had grown up in a row house with an outdoor privy in Philadelphia, though, he had hit the suburban jackpot: six rooms, twelve trees, thirty kinds of birds, six squirrels, a four-minute walk to the woods, and views of the Hudson River. "I relish too the opportunities for hand-work," the proud new resident reported, "the cutting of boughs, destruction of monstrous weeds, building of book-cases, invention of shelves, the simple joys of homo faber."[86] As *homo faber*, Merton was no Charles Cooley, nor was he able, as his predecessor was, to walk to his job. Talcott Parsons observed to his friend, "You seem to choose the pattern of commuting."[87]

A "pattern of commuting" underwrote Merton's work as a theorist of mass communication in the 1940s, when he brought his disciplined mind to bear on the study of microprocesses and larger patterns of radio, motion pictures, and print media. At Columbia, he fell into an opportunity structure organized around Paul Lazarsfeld, Herta Herzog, and their Office of Radio Research (ORR), a research institute affiliated with the university but dependent on outside sources for its funding. Its primary benefactor had been the Rockefeller Foundation and its grants officer, John Marshall, who organized an important Communications Seminar in 1939–40, aimed at supporting the ORR's radio research and remedying the fact that "there is no general body of theory about mass communications in American culture."[88] Besides Lazarsfeld, formally hired into the Department of Political Economy the same spring as Merton, the seminar also included the Columbia sociologist Robert S. Lynd and adult educator Lyman Bryson from its Teachers' College, among other notables, such as I. A. Richards and Harold Lasswell.[89] The Seminar represented by far the most significant focused scholarly attention yet on "mass communication" so named. Over the next decade, the bulk of the most important work on the subject was done through institutions and interpersonal networks connected in some way to Lazarsfeld, the high-powered intellect and institutional operator who beat the streets to keep his research institutes funded.[90] Merton grew to be a major, if sometimes ambivalent, intellectual player in this matrix.

He fell into it serendipitously. In early November of his first semester at Columbia, Merton worked himself into exhaustion severe enough that he was granted a leave of absence from teaching for the rest of the semester. Two weeks later, he and Sue were invited to dinner at the apartment of his new colleague, Lazarsfeld, and his wife, Herta Herzog. Likely with at least some feeling of unease at having to take a leave from his new, high-powered job, Merton drove into Manhattan with Sue, parked, walked up to the apartment building at 252 W. 85th, and headed up to 8B. Lazarsfeld met his new colleague at the door, explained that he had been called to a test of a war-related "morale program" down at the CBS radio studios and asked whether Merton would like to join him. The two men left their wives and caught a cab down to Midtown.[91]

Lazarsfeld worked closely with CBS and its research director, Frank Stanton. Together they had created the Program Analyzer, a test device to gauge audience reactions to radio appeals that resembled a primitive polygraph device with response buttons and fountain pens. It was the first time in a radio studio for Merton, the former radio ham who earlier that year had taught a course examining propaganda. Fifty years later, he still remembered the scene: twenty men and women, instructed to push a green button if they heard something they liked and a red button for something they disliked, an assistant following up with questions about what it was they specifically responded to, Merton finding fault with the questioning, Lazarsfeld offering him a try in the seat. Afterward, the two men went out to the Russian Bear to drink champagne and eat caviar. The latest in a string of slightly older men with whom Merton developed an important friendship, the interpersonally co-optive Lazarsfeld seized the opportunity to recruit Merton to work with him at the ORR. Merton called it the beginning of a "rather ambivalent collaboration."[92]

Two weekends later, the United States was at war. On a Saturday afternoon, Granville and Dorothy Hicks had driven down to Hastings from their farm outside Troy, New York, worried about Merton's health. They spent the night with the Mertons, catching up with old friends while their two daughters (both named Stephanie) played together. On Sunday afternoon they all tuned in to hear Benny Goodman on the radio and learned that Pearl Harbor had been bombed. Granville Hicks's face turned green. "Bob and I took a walk, to try to come to terms with the news, and then we all listened to radio broadcasts, which became more and more repetitive and less and less coherent as the evening passed, until we all had a laughing jag," Hicks remembered.[93] Merton had favored U.S. entry into the war for more than a year and blamed American individualism, blindness, and lethargy for conspiring "to destroy the last safeguards of moderate decency in the Old World."[94]

Pearl Harbor mobilized the nation and launched Merton's career as a theorist of mass communication. By February, he had recovered from his exhaustion and was reintegrating into the department, though the civilian rubber shortage was threatening to deflate his commuting routine. ("The tire situation grows formidable and we might have to move into the city, but we're reluctant to confess it."[95]) Lazarsfeld had ensnared him in "program analysis work" for the ORR and requested that Merton conduct four tests, develop categories for analysis, and prepare a paper that might "induce the government to allow us to go on with another four tests."[96] Merton's inventional contexts at the time are well-indicated in an excerpt from a letter he wrote Hicks:

> I have not yet learned how to say "NO." As a result, I am working night and day—for three weeks, I haven't gotten to bed before two—on a detailed analysis of the "effectiveness" of the new government all-network radio program,

"This Is War." It's an interesting problem, especially if I can bring some of the radio-research boys at NBC and CBS to the point of seeing that sociological theory-in-practice can supply them with significant questions and help formulate some useful answers. They're somewhat limited in their perspectives—they come from an advertising background—and fail to see much that is patently involved. Then again, there are the purely "artistic" criteria of Corvin, Maxwell Anderson, etc. who are writing the scripts, and these don't always coincide with the propaganda-effectiveness criteria. . . . Simultaneously, I have been roped in on an as yet utopian attempt to get at the effects of Axis occupation upon the social structure of occupied countries, in terms which may be of use to the COI. However this grandiose project actually turns out, it calls for more of my virtually non-existent time and energy. And of course, there's still this damned "prediction" study for the Social Science Research Council. All this, and a half-dozen theses to be looked after. What dubious fun to have one's every hour taken with "busy work" with seldom a glance to inquire into its further purpose.[97]

I have quoted at length because the letter reveals a good deal about Merton's personal trajectory into propaganda and mass communication research, and his multifocal perspective on the subject. Over six sentences, Merton shows himself ensconced with government agencies, radio networks, advertising, script writers, social scientists, and audiences, and gives evidence of considering radio propaganda from the perspectives of all of them—whether he really wanted to or not. When I read his account, I am filled with something like the opposite of the nostalgia I get when I think back to Cooley's leisurely pace of intellectual production. I feel dread and exhaustion. Merton drove himself hard, with an internalized work ethic and standard of judgment additionally fed by talent and institutional demands, and domestically enabled by a wife and live-in mother-in-law who raised the kids and ran the household.

Though science and assimilation suggested a certain universalist path, Merton's was always a pluralistic sociological vision, attuned to different points of view and perspectives, operating within distinct institutions, and serving more than one cultural logic. In his mass communications research of the 1940s, he was able both to work for "The Man" and to voice doubts about him; to do his patriotic duty while maintaining cosmopolitan identifications; to unleash his skepticism without sacrificing epistemological and political hope; to attend to the perspectives of insiders and outsiders, locals and cosmopolitans, agents engaged in purposive social action and bystanders narcotized by the greater mass communication system; and to craft a theoretical orientation that drew eclectically from both European and American traditions. It was also a vision with its blind spots, incomplete in the ways it conceived mass communication, and benefited in multiple ways from work done by largely unacknowledged women.

Over the next several years, Merton cast attention on several species of mass communication, from the dominant ones of his day to other, more vernacular and nonparadigmatic sorts we can retroactively find in his writings. His investigations grew from the matrix of classic Lazarsfeldian "administrative research"—empirical work done "in the service of some kind of administrative agency of public or private character" that funds and has a stake in it, aiming to learn how better to use media as a tool for their preestablished purposes.[98] Conducting administrative research, particularly for the government during the war, led Merton into more general considerations of mass communication in society, and to his first book, a case study of mass persuasion through radio broadcasting and celebrity.

In 1942, Merton had allowed himself to become enmeshed in war-related work for the government. He conducted a series of audience tests for "This Is War," the radio program being produced by the Office of Facts and Figures, predecessor of the Office of War Information (OWI). He considered an offer to head up the research sections of the OWI in Washington, but was sufficiently horrified by the "chaos and inefficiency of the organization" that even though he was "primed to accept" the offer, he turned it down, as the émigré Frankfurt School scholar Franz Neumann had also done, for similar reasons.[99] That summer, Merton traveled to army bases testing the effectiveness of propaganda films shown to incoming soldiers that explained why the nation was at war and also informally analyzed a Communist Party appeal made at his front door[100] (a door that led into a new suburban paradise the Mertons inhabited in Hastings, "replete with barbecue-pit, minute fish-pool, . . . and innumerable bathrooms").[101] In the fall, he worked for a time at "the wholly fantastic Pentagon Building," having temporarily accepted a position in the Psychology Division of the Office of Strategic Services (OSS), before returning to New York in early November and directing a number of radio studies for the War Department. In the midst of it, he cultivated backstage cynicism, writing Granville Hicks that sixteen-hour days spent analyzing fifteen hundred hours of radio program materials, overseas propaganda, and rumor-combating techniques "will result in a mess-age [sic] for the government files. Some of it may escape immediate burial and result in minor changes of policy, but for the most part, the lot of government researchers is activity capped by frustration. I suspect that if the truth were told, much the same would be said of Goebbel's outfit."[102] Needless to say, working in these contexts gave Merton a very different observational position upon mass communication than Paul's, Whitman's, or Cooley's.

By the spring of 1943, Merton was angling to pull back from OWI research, as he expected to be drafted in August or soon after and wanted to leave his work in order. He was overseeing a study of magazine readership and social influence in Dover, New Jersey, sponsored by *Time* magazine, and was also winding down an attempt to "codify some of our experience" in ORR research for a formal publication of the sort Lazarsfeld had in mind when he originally enlisted Merton, regarding a method they were calling "the focussed group interview."[103] The ORR had been profiled in *Life* magazine.[104] In June a film Merton had worked on, Frank Capra's *Battle of Britain*, was due out in theaters, the fourth in the government's "Why We Fight" series. He had recently met the radio correspondent Edward R. Murrow, who was just back from London and left Merton with a gloomy picture of the war and nation. "Full-page advertisements remind us that it is Chrysler and Ford and GM who are 'really' winning the war, despite interference from Washington," Merton wrote in June to his friend Richard Deninger. "Not a single newspaper carries the story of the actual issues in the coal controversy; organized business systematically builds up distrust of labor, particularly of organized labor."[105] Several years later, he would make a related point, expressed in the form of a critically tinged scholarly observation: "Since the mass media are supported by great business concerns geared into the current social and economic system, the media contribute to the maintenance of that system. . . . To the extent that the media of mass communication have been an influence upon their audience, it has stemmed not only from what is said, but more significantly from what is not said."[106]

Such observations were still incubating in the fall of 1943, though, when Merton delivered a paper to the Anthropology Section of the New York Academy of Sciences, published shortly thereafter under the authorship "Lazarsfeld and Merton" (though there are indications that Merton was the lead composer). Previously delivered to the Writers Congress in Los Angeles, the paper was addressed both to writers of propaganda who wanted to do their job better and to social scientific researchers who wanted to determine "the ascertainable effects of particular propaganda documents."[107] It laid out a novel methodology that combined "content-analysis" (the term was Harold Lasswell's) and "response-analysis" (audience interviews), as a way to determine "whether propagandists have achieved their aims." While allowing that their systematic approach could not "recapture the deft rhetoric and impressive rhythms which enter into dramatic effectiveness" or teach writers their craft, they argue that "propagandists often cannot gauge the psychological effects of their products without using techniques such as we have described." To gauge those effects, they identify six sorts of content-analysis of scripts and films, to be followed up with what they called "interviews of a special type, . . . the 'focused interview.'"[108] Thus went one of the rhetorical birth moments for what later became known as the focus group.[109]

Lazarsfeld, Merton, and, by unacknowledged proxy, Herta Herzog—whose longer-standing role in developing the focused interview was not acknowledged by coauthorship—were essentially channeling a dream, influentially articulated in Plato's *Phaedrus*, whereby rhetoric might be built upon the solid foundations of knowledge and truth. This dream is amplified in the final pages of their paper, which call for "propaganda of facts" as an alternative to that which "obviously seeks to 'sway' or 'stir' people by general appeals to sentiment." A propaganda of facts "does not seek so much to tell people where to go" as "show them the path they should choose to get there," and thus "preserves the individual's sense of autonomy," free from "the hammerlike blows of frenzied oratory."[110] Merton and Lazarsfeld held out hope that propaganda could proceed ethically and that science could contribute to the effort.

At the same time, Merton and Lazarsfeld recognized limits in both propaganda of the facts and systematic social-scientific testing of persuasive appeals. Fully a quarter of the paper is devoted to "boomerangs," an unanticipated consequence whereby the actual audience response is opposite that intended by the propagandist. "Material which is effective for one segment of the audience may produce opposite effects among another segment which is socially and psychologically different," it observes, amplifying their pluralistic view of audiences. The impact of those boomerangs is magnified by the fact that they typically "diffuse far beyond the person who experiences them initially," through subsequent conversation and interpersonal contact. Although systematic pretesting could go some distance in controlling the frequency and social amplitude of boomerangs, it could not eliminate them. Moreover, no amount of pretesting could make propaganda all-powerful. Merton and Lazarsfeld close the paper by warning their audience "not [to] exaggerate the role of propaganda," which is "no substitute for social policy and social action" and cannot "prevail if it runs counter to events and forces underlying these events as the fascists have begun to discover."[111]

In brief form, Merton and Lazarsfeld had conceptualized one subspecies of mass communication, the discrete and purposive persuasion campaign. In later years, the kernel of what they said here would be expanded into what became known as "the limited effects paradigm" of mass media, which

portrayed media influence as refracted through people and discussion—
the "two-step flow of communication"—that in turn suggested localized
safeguards against propagandistic domination from afar.[112] Whereas there
was some positive spin on the idea in 1943 (the fascist propagandists' day of
reckoning would come), there was a certain pathos, as well, especially when
we remember that the ORR consulted for public campaigns against prejudice and discrimination, where they found boomerangs and limited positive
results as well. The 1943 picture of the two-step flow, not yet named, is less
cheery than the one that would emerge in the mid-1950s. In 1943, Merton
was attuned to the fact that boomerang responses can diffuse through a kind
of interpersonal contagion. Face-to-face discussion might only amplify the
unintended racist response to a campaign promoting tolerance and understanding. Two-step flows might simply make things worse. Operating as a
mass communication theorist in the administrative role, the former magician kept a number of balls in the air—social scientific findings, practical
and bureaucratic demands, ethical principles, and the need to communicate
with multiple audiences and organizations.

Even as Merton was offering his services and insight to those producing the
ideologically charged propaganda that underwrote the American war effort,
he also continued to reflect upon the broader cultural order in which it all
took place. In a rather remarkable 1943 document that formed the basis for a
class lecture, "Institutional Ideologies and Propaganda," he distilled his thinking in a theoretical mash of Durkheim, Marx, and Kenneth Burke. Working
at his typewriter, he readied to tell his class how ideologies included "a creed:
articles of faith [and] a symbol-structure in which the emotive overtones are
far more significant than its strict denotation." Ideologies and their creeds
are not fixed, unchallenged, or homogeneously shared by all members of a
society, he observed, but they play important functions in shaping perceived
reality and asserting its legitimacy. Institutional ideologies "at once 'explain'
the social structure and 'reaffirm' its validity by doing so," he typed. They
"structure our evaluations by supplying us with a ready-made vocabulary of
encomium and opprobrium" that nominally describes, but actually evalu-
ates, situations, events, persons, and behavior; and they include rhetorically
loaded epithets—which in the U.S. context included "un-American, radical,
red, nigger, [and] agitator." Dominant creeds could be challenged, but as with
propaganda more specifically, there were limits to symbolic action. "What
is decisive for the failure of . . . ideologies and counter-ideologies," he wrote,
"is the underlying conditions of power and organization."[113]

The lecture points to a Merton relatively little known today—attending critically to the larger cultural realm, freely using the word "ideology," and generally letting his Marxissant hair down a bit. This voice would mostly be muted by the 1950s, but we can hear it occasionally in his early cultural sociology (for example, "Social Structure and Anomie" [1938]) and in places in his mass communication research. I think it's a great version of Merton, which reaches its peak in the mid-1940s, and more specifically between the 1943 ideology lecture and the 1948 publication of "Mass Communication, Popular Taste, and Organized Social Action," his classic piece coauthored with Lazarsfeld.

Fed by a memo Merton typed in 1946, which set the agenda for a field that never quite materialized,[114] the 1948 essay is the best example of what Gabriel Weimann and I have called "critical research at Columbia." I won't repeat our argument in detail, but we show how that essay gives lie to received wisdom about Columbia mass communication research as characterized by "the search for specific, measurable, short-term, individual, attitudinal, and behavioral 'effects' of media content, and the conclusion that media are not very important in the formation of public opinion."[115] Led by Merton, "Mass Communication, Popular Taste, and Organized Social Action" discusses, among other themes, the commercial ownership of American media and its role in what today we would call capitalist hegemony and the structured silencing of system-challenging critique.[116] As Lazarsfeld and Merton concluded their frequently reprinted piece, "the very conditions which make for the maximum effectiveness of the mass media of communication operate toward the maintenance of the going social cultural structure rather than toward its change."[117]

In addition to everything else it is, "Mass Communication, Popular Taste, and Organized Social Action" provides the best example of Mertonian middle-range theory as applied to mass communication. This falls in a four-page section of the paper which was Merton's alone, "Some Social Functions of Mass Media." Here Merton introduces three general functions of mass media, which operate across any particular social context: the enforcement of social norms, the status conferral function, and the narcotizing dysfunction. Each echoes an unnamed theorist—Cooley, Weber, and Marx, respectively— whom Merton deftly extends. The enforcement of social norms refers to the way that journalistically publicized wrongdoing has the effect of reinforcing the norm violated, a refinement of Cooley's functional account of newspapers as "organized gossip."[118] Status conferral names the way that appearing in the mass media gives individuals, ideas, institutions, and groups a prima facie significance or social standing, which extends Weber's account of status and the ways it is generated. And, most intriguing of all is the narcotizing dysfunction, a variation on Marx's idea of religion as opiate of the masses, which calls attention to the way that mass media do not promote action and engagement, but instead lull their audiences into passivity and, through a wealth of news, promote quiet resignation. The narcotizing dysfunction complemented earlier observations in the paper—that those "who would control the opinions and beliefs of our society resort less to physical force and more to mass persuasion," and "media have taken on the job of rendering mass publics conformative to the social and economic *status quo*."[119] This was a sentence underlined by the original owner of the 1948 volume in which the paper was originally published (Priscilla A. Marsden, Baltic, Conn.). She appreciated this Mertonian voice, here at its critical democratic, social scientific best, forging concepts for a theory of mass communication and ideological hegemony.

That Mertonian voice makes intermittent appearances in the crowning jewel of his mass communication research, *Mass Persuasion* (1946), his book-length study of the popular celebrity Kate Smith's live, eighteen-hour radio war bond drive. It was Merton's first published book,[120] but very much a product of the Office of Radio Research, which changed its name to the Bureau of Applied Social Research during the three-year period between start and publication of a research project whose working title was "Swayed by Smith." That project began as an opportunistic study funded by CBS's Frank Stanton, whom Lazarsfeld approached. Merton led the eight-woman, one-man research team who conducted lengthy focused interviews with bond-purchasers in the New York area, categorized the topical content of Smith's eighteen hours of scripted appeals, and conducted a survey. They put out their research report for CBS, "The Effectiveness of the Kate Smith Bond Drives," which analyzed resistance to purchasing bonds and made concrete suggestions for rhetorical appeals that might overcome that resistance in future drives.[121]

The research also included symbolic analysis of Smith's appeals and "public image" (a term whose first extended published use perhaps comes in this book), which Merton did through the kind of Marxissant-Durkheimian-Burkean lens he displayed in the "Institutional Ideologies and Propaganda" lecture (1943). Conversation with local Frankfurt émigré Leo Lowenthal also aided the inventional process.[122] The book was unique in the ways it brought together team-generated empirical research with critical cultural analysis and middle-range theoretical concepts (including the brilliant "pseudo-Gemeinschaft"),[123] and it was trailblazing in its analysis of celebrity, popular culture, and the images real-life audiences have of people they know through mass media.[124]

"Swayed by Smith" was a title that revealed Merton's unease with the event. For him, to be "swayed" was not to be led syllogistically by a propaganda of facts, and Kate Smith, a popular lower-brow entertainer, was not the sort of figure he admired. To be sure, Merton the baseball fan and son of the working class was not allergic to popular culture in the same way that other intellectuals of the era were, but he was no admirer of Smith's art or persona.[125] He saw her as a manifestation of some of the ideological contradictions and social tensions inherent in American life. Smith's fans were disproportionately from the working classes, and Merton explored the way she served as "compensation" for their poverty, an "Ideological Balm for the Underprivileged," as he put it in the draft title of one important chapter. Her apparent embodiment of "the homespun virtues of charity, generosity, sympathy for the underdog, disinterest in sex, love of God, the American home and the Stars and Stripes," Merton argued, compensated those shut out from material success with an alternative scale of valuation and self-assessment. At the same time, she was a figure who consistently affirmed that despite challenges and changes in America, "*our basic institutions remain sacred and stable,*" and her ongoing messages as a radio personality reinforced the "great social institutions. . . . of business, private property and free enterprise," as Merton wrote in the draft (emphasis in original).[126] Just like commercial mass media, Smith functioned to maintain the status quo.

Merton aspired to reach a larger public with "Swayed by Smith" and so sought a slightly different style and voice than he did for more straightforwardly academic writing. To achieve that goal, he enlisted the aid of his friend Granville Hicks—writer, critic, journalist, editor, and teacher of literature. Merton mailed Hicks drafts, and Hicks marked them up "more or less as I would go through a college student's themes." Besides helping with sentence structure and tone, Hicks made an observation that would rankle. He accused his friend of "labor[ing] points that the layman would take for granted. . . . [A] journalist would drop in a depreciatory phrase or two to make it clear that he knows he isn't telling the reader anything new, but you hit the reader over the head. You don't have to omit your arguments and proofs, but perhaps you do have to adopt a less solemn tone towards them."[127] Three nights later at 2 A.M., Merton typed back a reply, both agreeing with his friend and insisting that the points he was trying to make were "neither obvious nor unimportant. The persistence-of-tension theory, for example, is one of the most significant findings in gestalt psychology in the past couple of decades, and it took a hell of a lot of experimental work to confirm this theory. . . . I suppose my discussion sounds pompous, strenuous and pedantic to the layman, that's because I was talking at that point to the professional."[128]

If there was tension in anything, it was a project that aimed at once to address researchers and practitioners of organized persuasion ("the professional"), and general readers as well. After several months of struggle, Hicks asked his friend, "Do you really want to reach a wider public?"[129] Merton seems to have had doubts he could pull it off.[130] In May of 1945, he dropped the manuscript at Columbia University Press, which in early June agreed to publish it, though owing to the war-induced paper shortage, they wouldn't be able to do so until the following year.

Edited, severely in places, the manuscript once known as "Swayed by Smith" was published a year later, retitled *Mass Persuasion*, and put out not by Columbia but rather in a series edited by Lazarsfeld at Harper and Brothers, "Publications of the Bureau of Applied Social Research." Between the time he dropped it off at Columbia and the book's publication the next year, Merton had tried to exercise his public self in a different way, by writing Harold Laski in England to ask for a job "studying the 'effectiveness' of the Labor Party program of education and propaganda." Observing that it was "a sad commentary on 'social science' that its skills have been put in the service of testing the effectiveness of advertisements, but not of progressive political and economic propaganda," Merton pursued an opportunity that didn't materialize.[131] Meanwhile, through either self-censorship or pressure from Lazarsfeld or Harper and Brothers, many of the edgiest, Fellow-Traveler–sounding passages of "Swayed by Smith" were dropped from the manuscript, and the figure of Kate Smith pushed from the center of the book. "Although her name inevitably recurs time and again throughout the book, this is *not* a study of Kate Smith," *Mass Persuasion* tells us. Nor for that matter was it a study of "Kate Smith as a Symbol in American Culture" or "Ideological Balm for the Underprivileged," as Chapters 5 and 6 of "Swayed by Smith" had been titled. Their more Marxian passages deleted, the two chapters were merged into one, and given the neutral-sounding title "The Social and Cultural Context."[132] Something had happened.

I don't have hard evidence, but my theory is Lazarsfeld exerted his sometimes coercive interpersonal influence in the process of publishing the book with his series. Though a former Socialist in Europe, Lazarsfeld rigorously separated objectivist research and critical observation, and he didn't engage in much of the latter when he emigrated to the United States. Though he had a position at Columbia, he was a socially marginal man—an immigrant, obviously Jewish in a time of significant discrimination, self-conscious of his status.[133] The Bureau was a financially precarious organization, and after the war it was again dependent on private and commercial contracts to keep it afloat. Lazarsfeld might have been nervous about a BASR book that seemed too radical, or even implicitly called into question the legitimacy of the commercial or national creeds. Talk of "ideological balms" smacked too much of the Reds. The Cold War hadn't been declared yet, but Lazarsfeld was sensitive about offending his funders. Critical research at Columbia was never given free rein.

In the longer history I am tracing, *Mass Persuasion* stands out as a kind of vision of a feminized common body, enacted through the figure of Kate Smith and actualized through the medium of a live network radio broadcast. Though it lost some contact with the body when it transformed itself from "Swayed by Smith," the book was a multiply feminized study that gave voice to women's experience and collectivity, even as it repressed those same elements. Smith was a female icon, the most popular entertainer on radio, and a special favorite of middle- and working-class women, who tuned in religiously to her midday talk and advice show. They listened to her bond drive and called in their pledges. Female interviewers from the ORR went out to talk with these women—eighty-eight percent of the focused interviews were conducted with women listeners, a fact mentioned only in the book's appendix—and record their affections for the folksy entertainer one called "plain, fat Kate Smith" (147). The listeners "stayed by her side" through Smith's eighteen-hour ordeal on the air, hearing the feeling in her voice and wondering if she could hold up till the end. "Listeners clearly felt that they were witnessing or even participating in a special event," (24) a live ritual of sorts, dispersed around the country, and dramatically organized around the voice and (dis)embodied performance of Kate Smith, who testified and exhorted in the name of the symbolically sacred boys overseas. Smith's broadcast voice dispersed her body to the nation and served as locus for a kind of mass communication in which women participated disproportionately and created their own understandings.[134]

For *Mass Persuasion*, those understandings were worked out in important ways through the face-to-face conversations that took place between the women who interviewed for the ORR and the women who were listeners and fans of Kate Smith. "For the exceptionally difficult interviewing we are indebted to Lillian Mintz, Joan Doris, Jeanette Green, Helen Kaufman, Carol Coan, Patricia Salter and Alfred Etcheverry," Merton typed, giving only the barest hint of the human interactions that gave the book its social base. (Etcheverry, the only man in the group, would die in the war, and the book about war bonds was dedicated to his memory.) Snippets quoted from focused interviews that could last several hours give a sense of the feeling that the women had for Kate Smith. They also give a sense of the rapport cultivated by talented young women like Joan Doris (Goldhamer) from Brooklyn, one of several Jewish-born college-educated New Yorkers who went out in the boroughs to interview the largely working-class Catholics and Protestants who had phoned in their pledges. To his credit, Merton would take a stab at analyzing the symbolic gender dynamics enacted through Smith (see esp. 146–51), but he couldn't do justice to the richness of social experience uncovered and created through the interviews (including one three-person conversation between the interviewer, a dime-museum freak, Reptilina, and her personal attendant [!]).[135] Like Paul's secretary and Cooley's wife, Elsie, the women interviewers of the ORR were bodies whose communicative labor made possible the published work others received credit for.

Though constructed from female labor, the gendered components of *Mass Persuasion* were, like Merton's Jewishness, removed backstage, driven there by a blend of universalist aspiration and patriarchal privilege. Amplification and repression of gender was a component of Bureau research writ large and played central parts in other key publications.[136] The book was part of its cultural moment, prejudices and possibilities alike. In execution and writing, the study displays Merton's composite intellectual style. It brings social theory (Marx, Durkheim, Dewey) and disciplined empirical methodologies (focused interviews, survey data, and content analysis) together with rhetorical sensibilities (symbolic analyses of Smith's appeals, references to classical rhetorical texts, clear and sometimes elegant writing), administrative support (CBS), bureaucratic structure (ORR/BASR), critical-left sensibilities (toned down along the way), gendered labor (at home and work), and personal ambivalence (about even doing the project). It channels these currents into a multiperspective account of one engineered episode in mass persuasion, which concludes with an appeal to professional persuaders ("technicians in sentiment") and the researchers who study them (especially the positivists), warning against the idea of "value-free" social science and the potentially long-term harms caused by morally reproachable advertising and persuasive technique.[137] The book would provide a model for David Riesman, who looked to its interviews and theoretically informed empirical work as models for *The Lonely Crowd* (1950), his best-selling study of American social character.[138] *Mass Persuasion* is an elegant little study and a unique vision of broadcast mass communication.

Beyond his multifocal analysis of dominant species of mass communication, Merton conducted research into what we can call nonparadigmatic species as well. I'll mention two studies, both unpublished, but multiply noteworthy. One was *Mass Pressure: The 1948 Presidential Draft of Eisenhower*, a book-length study of thousands of letters written to General Dwight Eisenhower, urging him to run for president in 1948. This was a variant of mass communication as communication *emanating from* the masses, made material through handwritten and typed notes mailed to the general. Letters were an ancient art, and in the nineteenth and twentieth centuries, they became a mass medium as well, sent by the thousands to politicians, movie stars, sports figures, and other celebrities. Mail studies were an ORR/BASR staple, conducted almost exclusively by women researchers before Merton got involved, prompted by one of the Kate Smith interviewers, Joan Doris Goldhamer, who drew his attention to then-President of Columbia Eisenhower's cache.[139] Merton saw the letters as an alternative to public opinion polls in gauging public sentiment, images, and rationality-in-process. "If 'Society exists in and through communication,'" as Merton quoted John Dewey saying, "then content analysis of any and every type of communication is an important technique for converting the 'stuff' of social life into the 'data' of social science."[140] Written spontaneously or in response to a campaign by radio commentator Walter Winchell, the mail was a form of more-or-less bottom-up mass communication, sociologically rich and politically significant. Leila Sussmann, who took part in the Eisenhower study, would write a dissertation and book on such mass communication, which was an important effort to understand a truly significant species of the genus.[141]

The other nonparadigmatic species I want to draw from Merton's corpus occurred in a laundry room of an interracial public housing project in Pittsburgh, Addison Terrace, circa 1948. The Columbia research team called it "Hilltown." It was one of three planned housing communities they were studying, along with a workers' community in New Jersey (Winfield Park, or "Craftown") and another interracial project in New York City (Manhattanville, or "Rivertown"). With Marie Jahoda and Patricia Salter West, Merton authored, but did not publish, a fourteen-chapter manuscript, *Patterns of Social Life: Explorations in the Sociology of Housing*.[142] Part applied urban research, part Middletown-style community study, and part intervention into the politics of race in the 1940s, the housing study was rich, multipurposed administrative research conducted with a grant from the Lavanburg Foundation, and the centerpiece of the urban sociology Merton was originally hired to teach.[143] As with his propaganda research, he would investigate the phenomena with one eye toward social science, the other toward politics broadly conceived—public administration and housing reform. He supported racial integration and maintained a cautious hope that social research could aid "continued mutual accommodation between the races now in process."[144]

The architectural structuring of community interested the researchers. "We shape our buildings and afterwards our buildings shape us," Merton wrote, quoting Winston Churchill.[145] This drew them to Addison's laundry facilities, situated in the basement of every eighth building, where black and white women socialized with one another as they waited for machines or folded clothes. The researchers found that these were the sites where the tenants came to know one another, more than through the organized activities held at Addison's community center. They were places where the women of the community, some trailing small children, negotiated the use of a scarce resource (laundry machines) and found quotidian openings to speak with one another. It could be a starting point for friendships, or slowly confirm new social images of difference, making the public housing community a space for what the researchers called "that kind of sustained interracial contact which displaces racial stereotypes."[146] Involving the working classes ("masses"), the laundry rooms were spatially structured media of communication, operating in the contexts of a mid-century public housing project.

As seen up close and from afar by the Columbia research team, the interracial planned community was no utopian form of mass communication—no Body of Christ, democratic free verse, or contemplative Transcendentalist faith. But they held out moderate hopes for it and its designed spaces, where bodies from different races might interact face-to-face, instead of merely from a distance, through mass media and social stereotypes, which were a particular obstacle for white people, since most black people had no choice but to interact with whites. As Merton understood better than most, racial prejudice was a problem emanating from the cultural worlds of majority groups, not from the society's various out-groups. The face-to-face was a place, maybe, to break through stereotypes, over time and with effort. Planning, design, and creative social research could all help the process. The residents of Addison Terrace would bring it to life.

Concluding Merton

After 1949, Merton had little to do with mass communications research.[147] He had moved his family to a grand Tudor home in Hastings, which symbolized his remove from the cultural world of mass communication and popular

sentiment and his strengthening identifications with science and the professions. He worked at home, in an office that was a window-ringed back room
of the second-floor master suite he and Sue shared, his day typically beginning at 4:30 A.M. The office afforded a splendid view of the Hudson River
beyond. Surrounded by bookshelves and filing cabinets, a large wooden desk
sat near the center, within arm's reach of the Oxford English Dictionary and
dozens of other reference books. He kept a bottle of single-malt Scotch in a
drawer and sometimes sipped from it as he composed. Sue Merton and her
mother raised the kids and took care of the house, freeing Bob to work long
hours, unimpeded by extensive domestic responsibilities. The upstairs office
remained Bob's chief seat of intellectual production and spatial medium of
invention from the summer of 1950 until he left his wife and moved out of
the house in the spring of 1968.

His suburban neighborhood did afford him occasional political opportunities, however. The Mertons had been able to buy the grand house for a
good price, because the previous owner had been set into a panic when he
saw African-Americans moving into the neighborhood. Real estate agents
in the area tried to "bust" the neighborhood, contacting white homeowners
and trying to frighten them into selling by saying that property values were
dropping. Convinced this was true, the previous owner became a fleeing
white man who accepted a low price, thinking it inevitable—a classic example
of a Mertonian "self-fulfilling prophecy."[148] Four months later, an African-
American psychology professor whom Merton knew moved his young family
into a house across the street, encouraged by his new neighbor. On Christmas
Eve, Merton showed up at their door leading a caroling session to welcome
Kenneth and Mamie Clark and their children to the neighborhood.[149] The
Mertons would go on to convene a homeowners meeting at their house, to
address the attempt to bust the neighborhood. Merton and Kenneth Clark
went door-to-door persuading people not to sell. A crisis was averted, and
the neighborhood remained one of the most integrated in Hastings.[150] One
Sunday some time later, Clark brought a manuscript over to Merton's house.
The two men sat in the English garden, drinking coffee and talking out the
draft. Its working title was "Social Science Statement Concerning the Effects of Racial Segregation," a subject Merton knew something about from
his housing research. He was also a famously good editor of other people's
work. Revised, the draft became the Social Science Brief for *Brown v. Board
of Education* and helped alter the face of American society.[151]

Working from the Tudor home, Merton turned his attention from the
sociology of mass communications, public housing, and race to the soci-

ology of medical education, the professions, and, most belovedly, science, while also continuing to build middle-range sociological theory of concepts like role sets and status sets. His career continued to take off. He served as president of the soon-to-be American Sociological Association, moved among ultra-elites in the social and natural sciences, and solidified a status far removed from his South Philadelphia roots. Insofar as he was interested in communication, language, or rhetoric it was generally the sorts practiced by elites, not the popular masses.[152] His politics eased from left-democratic to centrist liberal, perhaps hastened in 1952 when he was publicly chastised for trumped-up versions of youthful dalliances with radicals. Coincidentally or not, he removed some of the indexed references to "ideology" for the second volume of Social Theory and Social Structure (1957).[153]

A few graduate students he taught in the 1940s and '50s went on to make contributions to mass communication research—Warren Breed, Rolf Meyersohn, Thelma McCormack, Leila Sussmann, Charles Wright, and, especially, Elihu Katz—but Merton's mind was elsewhere. When he and Robert Nisbet put together a popular textbook, Contemporary Social Problems (1961), they didn't bother to include mass media, perhaps not recognizing that, like transportation, drug addiction, and the family (three topics featured in the book), the media created social problems, too. That same year, Newton Minow—as FCC Chairman no less—was declaring television a "vast wasteland." The Merton of "the narcotizing dysfunction" was long gone. A textbook that helped socialize a generation of students into thinking about society's problems missed the opportunity to put the problems of media on the agenda.[154]

Though Merton was not discussing the problems of mass media in his scholarship or teaching, he did do his small part to address them through television. From September 1962 until the following April, he was moderator for Court of Reason, a production of WNDT ("New Directions in Television"), the independent "educational" channel in New York. The show probed controversial questions with a small group of expert discussants. As moderator, Merton set the tone and regulated the discussion. "We should remember that this is a Court of Reason, not a Court of Rhetoric," he wrote in notes used for the opening of the show. "We look for sound arguments, not merely noisy ones. It is our assignment to raise questions that will search out weaknesses in each case and to search out strengths. We take no sides in order that we can probe each side."[155] It was the perfect role for the late-Enlightenment liberal. He moderated discussions of Red China, censorship, the military industrial complex, Webster's Third Dictionary ("Is English Changing or Being Corrupted?"), birth control, the death penalty, automation, social revolution abroad ("Should U.S. Foreign Policy Encourage It?"), educational testing, integration, religion—and mass media, among other topics. Guests included Dwight MacDonald, Daniel Bell, Malcolm X, Gore Vidal, William Rusher, and Ernst Nagel. The show ran weekly, on Wednesday nights from 8:30 to 9:30, opposite *Dobie Gillis* and *The Beverly Hillbillies* on Channel 2. The week that *Court of Reason* talked about whether the United States should encourage social revolution abroad, Channel 2 had faux-beatnik Maynard G. Krebs drinking a potion that turned him into an intellectual.[156]

Highbrows generally liked *Court of Reason* and wrote reviews and letters of appreciation. The liberal *New Republic* appreciated its discussion of censorship and pornography and compared WNDT favorably to the work done by British historian Richard Hoggart in writing the "Pilkington Report" about British television.[157] One viewer called the episode on mass media and mass culture, with Daniel Bell and Dwight MacDonald, "one of the best programs I've ever heard in my life; maybe the best."[158] Robert Lynd praised "the fine clarity" of Merton's thinking, which he thought could "make an important contribution to the public's efforts to understand."[159] David Boroff, writing for the socialist *New Leader*, was less convinced. He found *Court of Reason* "tiresome" and "in a sense, too reasonable." "TV is all wrong as an intellectual forum," he wrote; "the middlebrows and hucksters have a more realistic appreciation of its possibilities."[160]

Commercial television broadcasters started to get nervous, however, about the new competition they faced from "educational television." NBC chairman Robert Sarnoff, inheritor of his father, David's, throne, made a $100,000 contribution to WNDT president Samuel B. Gould, thanking Gould for his plan to focus "the bulk of its service" on programs with "a specific teaching function"—by which he meant the dull classroom lectures long a staple of educational TV. Richard Heffner, the WNDT station manager, had different ideas and wanted to enliven and enlarge the programming, with *Court of Reason* one step in that direction. Heffner objected strenuously to Gould's announced policy decision, leveraged by Sarnoff's payment to the station, and Heffner was fired by the station's board of directors. Merton resigned in protest over Heffner's dismissal, and his television experiment came to an end.[161]

If he couldn't improve mass media by hosting his own television show, Merton might at least try to pin down the chattering guru on the subject, Marshall McLuhan. When WNDT invited him to take part in a ninety-minute televised symposium in 1966, "McLuhan on McLuhanism," Merton accepted. The two had sparred when the University of Toronto English professor had given a paper at Columbia in 1955, when McLuhan was just beginning his explorations of media and had not yet become a celebrity.[162] Merton prepared for the television appearance by reading McLuhan's *Understanding Media* (1964) and typing up notes. "MM busily engaged in writing exotic, or, in this electric age, shd we say, way-out aphorisms pour épater le bourgeois, or as we should say in mcluhanese, 'to electrify the squares.'" He allowed that McLuhan had taken hold of "sound and penetrating ideas" developed by Harold Innis and Lewis Mumford, but that he transformed "some old-fashioned, carefully crafted truths into new-fashioned, grotesquely exaggerated half-truths."[163]

The show opened with a half-hour introductory lecture by McLuhan, "a la the format followed in The Annenberg School of Communication recent 'From Gutenberg to Batman' confab, tricked up this time with various slides (a copyright symbol, a pair of pliers, a 'talking tooth,' punctuation marks, fingerprints, etc.)," which McLuhan called his "probe-provokers," according to a Philadelphia television critic who watched the WNDT debate.[164] *Court of Reason* style, Merton then entered into cross-examination, which a sociology professor admired from California, as he described to Merton in a letter:

> What has exasperated me about him [McLuhan] is not so much the bland way in which he confidently mixes his insights with misleadingly half true or totally false generalizations, but even more, the insultingly blithe way I have seen him evade his critics with "witty remarks" in situations much like the one in which you appeared with him. I think you caught him; his attempt to evade in his usual style seemed stale and pallid; and his teetering on the edge of real anger indicated that you had got through to his soft underbelly, and that he and everyone else knew it. I have admired your keenness before, but I don't ever remember *identifying* with you before. But as you got to him, I kept saying silently: Go, Merton, Go.[165]

Merton's performance generated identifications in a few, as Kate Smith's had done for a larger and different group before. For those with a taste for analytical precision, dialectical scrutiny, and scientifically cultivated epistemological cautiousness, Merton was their man, a figure to root on against the talking tooth and evasive wit of the probe-provoking McLuhan. Merton played Socrates to McLuhan's Gorgias, and the fans of dialectic loved it. Afterward, Merton returned to his life as a professionally identified sociologist. McLuhan was interviewed by *Playboy*.

Twenty years earlier, Merton had worked out a very different account of mass media, operating in a far different style from McLuhan's. As I have tried to show in this chapter, in the 1940s, his was a vision informed by a faith that made skepticism a virtue, but tempered it with (cautious) hopes for a better social-democratic future. He was not a preacher or a poet or a mystico-contemplative humanist. He was a mid–twentieth century social scientist committed to mapping the communicative phenomena he studied with a blend of empirical rigor, advanced methodologies, and multidisciplinary social theory. He moved in his mass communications research from particularity to generality—from questioning an assembled test audience of 20 listening to a single radio program in the CBS studios, to overseeing a research team investigating the Kate Smith radio event, to making observations about the ways a commercial mass media system reinforces the ideological status quo. In producing his cumulative theoretical vision, he moved between roles as teacher, colleague, administrative researcher, middle-to-more-general-range theorist, and, once in a while, citizen-critic. The accounts he gave were nuanced, and suitable for a pluralistic society marked by complex social processes.

In contrast to Paul, Whitman, and to a certain extent Cooley, Merton's theoretical vision of mass communication was more descriptive than normative, seeking to explain the way the phenomena do work, not hold out a picture for how they should. At the same time, middle-range concepts like the narcotizing dysfunction and pseudo-Gemeinschaft carried with them elements of critical judgment and value, which revealed that his mass communication theory had its normative elements, too, supplied by something more than the norms of objectivist science that he famously spelled out. Still, in comparison with his three predecessors in this book, Merton struck a greater symbolic distance from the forms of mass communication he conceptualized, while the other three came to identify with theirs morally and spiritually. His was a different kind of theoretical figure.

At the same time, I am struck by ways that Merton, too, was an Emersonian inventor of self, like Whitman, Cooley, and, in his own way, Paul, that name-changing cosmopolitan from Tarsus. Robert King Merton, aspiring magician, transferred his self-creating talents to the performative arts of sociology instead. While not expressive in the more direct ways of Cooley's prose, Whitman's poetry, and Paul's letters, Merton's sociological writings were put together with exquisite craft, and they gave typographic voice to an unfolding logos. He was known to go through ten or more drafts of his papers and compose footnotes that are models of scholarly elegance, displaying a craftsmanship Cooley would surely have admired. Though the first-person "I" was generally forbidden in the genres Merton wrote in, his work was as much a product of a particular self as those of his predecessors. The professional organization and pace of his life separates it from the others' (and invites the mood of exhaustion and dread I mentioned earlier), but those too were expressions of a cultivated self. In his case, it developed from the particular stock of Jewish Russian immigrants, grafted onto cultures of assimilation, knowledge, and professional success in pre–World War II America. His friend Read Bain, who had a bit of Emerson in himself as well, recognized Merton's self-creating talents in 1938, and offered a prediction in a letter:

"You will play your concerto of the cortex according to the basic Mertonic scale; you will never long remain a devotee of Pete, or Talcott, or Larry, or Sarton,—or Bain, to drop to the ridiculous—but will always return to yourself—you, as the lens thru which all these wandering rays, these partial gleams, will be focused to produce your own bright burning point of intellectual energy. You will learn a lot from many sources, but at long last, you will be your own Master."[166]

There are worse things to be.

Assembling through a Fair

"It's because we ourselves are so divided by so many
contradictory attachments that we have to assemble."
—Bruno Latour[1]

The vision I would figure started off with a sound. It came wafting through the window one night in late August of 1996. Amplified music drifted in from a distance as I lay in bed in a new place, in a house with my family. We had moved in a month earlier, and my wife and I were still in a state of mild shock from transplantation to Meadville, an economically depressed town of fifteen thousand in the rambling foothills of northwest Pennsylvania. I was about to start my first job out of graduate school, at a small liberal arts college. We bought a house on the outskirts of town, set on a two-lane state highway, near the crest of a steep hill where cars and pickups accelerated hard on their way to rural areas east. It was a modest place with a big back yard and a second garage out back, where the guy before us had fixed up cars, and where I set up an office. Our boys were 2½ and 20 months old, and sleeplessness was a fact of life. The small master bedroom sat at the front of the house, and road noise came in when the windows were open. We regularly heard the sounds of traffic. That night we heard music instead. The fair was in session.

I would come to recognize those amplified sounds as a symbolic bellwether calling the local ekklesia to gather, though from where I lay that first night they were more like a slightly distorted soundtrack for a geographical-and-existential transition still very much in process. The composer and sound theorist F. Murray Schafer talks of "sacred noise": loud sounds—often the loudest in an area's "soundscape"—that are immune to cultural censure. Historically, he suggests that the loudest sounds regularly heard in traditional societies were made by festivals and other religious events; in medieval Christendom, by the church bell outdoors and by its organ and singing voices indoors; in the industrial revolution, by factories in towns and cities and the railroad in rural areas; and in the last fifty years by the collective sound of traffic.[2] On an everyday basis, the local soundscape made sacred the gods of traffic and indoor media (radio, music, and television). During the fair, a different order reigned, though supported by the ordinary one, in the form of traffic to and from the event.

The fair made the sacred noise for the county, and I came to see it as a paradigm for an important species of democratic mass communication, characterized by pluralistically structured, large-scale ritual assembly of a representative cross section of a local population. To close this book, I want to lay out a modest vision of this communicative event and species, rounding off my history of four envisioning figures by performing the role myself and offering a sometimes-stylized account of the fair. I believe the fair is an important manifestation of what Cooley called "the communicative life," and want to give it its due. I'd also like to cue you to your places and the forms of mass communication you find there, so that this Afterword might play a maieutic role, midwife to insights on your side of the text.[3] As a figure in this longer tale, I identify most with two minor characters in the Merton chapter—Harlan Gilmore, the colleague at Tulane Merton described as a "42–year-old nonentity, with special interest in population"; and Maynard G. Krebs, after he drank the potion and temporarily became an intellectual. I count myself a Latter Day Gilmore, who occasionally lets his hair down as Maynard G. Krebs.

This Afterword brings me into new inventional space. Instead of published and unpublished writings, archives, oral history interviews, and biographies, I draw here upon a participant observation that informally began that first night from my bedroom. The participant observation grew more formal over the next three years, peaking in 1999, and continuing steadily, though less intensely, since. Before 1999, I had volunteered at a fair booth as a board member for the local Big Brothers agency and attended with my family. I took interest in fairgoing as a public and sensory experience and began observing in earnest, taking field notes and keeping an ethnographic journal. I was reading Whitman at the time, learning about ritual and thinking about crowds and mass communication. Teaching helped focus my thoughts, and good students served as sounding boards and conversation partners. Crowds intrigued and sometimes captivated me, in part a reflection on the fact that they were relatively rare in the small-town life of the area. Whitman was a key inventional medium, refracted through longer-standing populist sensibilities, and sympathies toward what William James called the varieties of religious experience. I gave a couple of conference presentations on the study and one public lecture, which was taped by the underfunded and limited local cable-access channel and seemingly replayed on a continuous loop. We moved away from town before fair time in 2000, taking up residence down the hill from the old Addison Terrace housing project in Pittsburgh, but we bought a small run-down cabin twenty miles outside Meadville, which kept me connected to the region and provided a launching pad for fairgoing. A few years later, we moved to Colorado, attending the fair got harder, and I reflected on it from greater distance. The heart of my account was invented in a position of proximity, but it accumulated additional interpretive layers since then, less emotionally invested, and distilled through the media of very different social and geographical places.

This Afterword focuses on the fair, which I argue represents a form of mass communication significant in its own right and suggestive in more general ways, too. I read the fair as a ritual for the ekklesia of a local democratic public, which by gathering bodies together does communicative work not easily accomplished by other media. In a very literal way, events like the fair are assemblies of an area's res publica—its public things, in this case the living bodies of that ethico-political entity we call "the public." Drawing a broad-based cross section of the local population, the fair corporeally indexes a more general public, while also serving as gathering place for people to do various kinds of public work, ranging from displaying and beholding products of agricultural and domestic skill to conducting the work of commerce, consumption, entertainment, education, political campaigning, evangelism, health care, nonprofit outreach, family and friendship networks, and institutional image management, among other activities. In reading the fair as a popular ekklesia of sorts, I offer a sketch of its ritual structure, the various cultural gods it serves, and the people it attracts and moves through its midst. I amplify both material realities and moral possibilities grounded in this nonparadigmatic form of mass communication, intending some of my observations to apply to similar popular rituals elsewhere—for instance, urban street fairs and festivals, where a cross section of a local public assembles, shares space, and finds opportunities to pursue a range of projects. I then close by drawing together the preceding chapters of the book, reflecting on the figures and communicative forms discussed in them, and wrapping up this unorthodox history.

A Ritual of Democratic Mass Communication

The county fair provides a paradigm for one important type of democratic mass communication, the embodied ritual gathering of a broad local public.

As a ritual, it falls into a class of events the anthropologist Roy Rappaport considers *the* basic social act, "the foundry within which the Word is forged." Ritual—"the performance of more or less invariant sequences of formal acts and utterances not entirely encoded by the performers"—"is a special medium," Rappaport explains, "peculiarly, perhaps uniquely, suited to the transmission of certain messages and certain sorts of information." Rituals enact public liturgies, *leitourgiai*, from the Greek *laos* (people), and *ergon* (work, function). A liturgy is the work of a people, a product and deed that needs to be performed to be made real (*res*), evident, publicly obvious.[4] As media, rituals communicate through words, gestures, objects, and places that are often distinct from the everyday. Rituals like the fair are time-out-from-time events, which call attention to themselves in multiple and redundant ways. As a result, they become nearly unavoidable communicatively.

The county agricultural fair hosts liturgies of multiple sorts. Agriculture, domestic production, commerce, and entertainment all have their spaces. Politics and sectarian religion find spots as well. Competition cuts across many spheres, balanced by the peacefulness and respect of the civil crowd that assembles to witness it. Though U.S. farm life is not what it once was, county fairs continue to celebrate and support agriculture. Farm families spend the week at the fair, camping in trailers near the animal barns and relishing "the real fair" that happens only after the gates have closed and the fairgoers have cleared out. They bring cattle, pigs, horses, mules, goats, sheep, chickens, and rabbits. White-shirted, black-trousered boys and girls eight or nine years of age tug and cajole calves as judges call out their names over a loud but grainy public-address system, while a recent agricultural science grad from the state university appraises their animals and showmanship. Outside a cow pisses (what a river it sounds to ears not accustomed). Large and small animals, fruits and vegetables, maple syrup, outdoor agriculture bleeding with fruits of indoor labors—baked, canned, and sewn goods, photography and crafts. 4–H and the Grange sponsor contests, like the "Nearing Y2K" theme of 1999, with children-made bulletin boards and organized displays of Y2K necessities and advice (including, "Pray for God's wisdom and direction"). In a culture of consumption and corporate conglomeration, the fair stands as testament to the small production and craft talents of individuals and families, organized by local voluntary associations working the civic grassroots.

Leslie Prosterman beautifully details the production and judging in *Ordinary Life, Festival Days*, her fine ethnography of Midwestern agricultural fairs. She sees exhibition and judging as "the heart of the fair," which she calls "a festive commemoration of the raising of food and the activities connected with it, loosely interpreted." Her fieldwork reveals the intricate webs of local knowledge, care, and social interaction that produce the agricultural and domestic displays. Through face-to-face rituals of reciprocity and sociability, fair participants—those who enter the exhibitions and displays identified in a fair's "premium book"—build the bonds of local community and reinforce categories of value and judgment that lie at the core of key agricultural and domestic practices. For Prosterman, the animals, vegetables, flower arrangements, and other things displayed at the fair are vernacular forms of art, beautiful in their own right and anchored in the aesthetic judgments of a knowing local community. The fair is a celebration of the raising of food, she tells us, and when in good order, it plays an important role in the life of rural communities.[5]

But small-scale production is not the end of the story, for the county fair celebrates consumption, spectacle, commerce, and, to lesser extents, political and religious life as well. Lurking high in the center of the fair are the rides of the Midway, where the pastoral and the domestic give way to the carnivalesque, the sexualized, and the seedy. The wholesome image of four-year-olds playing near their farm families in bulb-lit cow barns is supplanted by baggy-jeaned tattoo boys and tube-top girls in tight pants, traveling carnies (only some of whom look like they might be on speed), and the insulting clown at the dunking booth. "Hey Chubby, you need a training bra!" "You going to try again, Ugly?" (Ugly nails target. I join crowd in cheering.) The Midway with its mechanical rides and rumored-to-be-rigged games of chance has long stood as the symbolic Other to the agricultural exhibits at the American fair, but as nearly everyone realizes, the two feed off each other and allow the fair to channel both Apollonian and Dionysian impulses. At the edge of the Midway sit the grandstand and track, where national music acts play, the Miss Crawford County Scholarship Pageant occurs (won here in the late 1970s by future Hollywood star Sharon Stone), the souped-up tractors and trucks deafen those near, and the demolition derby and fireworks bring the week to a splendid popular conclusion.

Under the grandstand is the main civic area of the fair. Democrats and Republicans are stationed at opposite ends. During election years, they are brimming with stickers and literature, and candidates who periodically appear. Other civic and nonprofit groups have their tables as well: a labor union, an agency for seniors, a branch campus in the state university system, a Christian school. Commercial booths sit cheek-by-jowl in this variegated space. A guy selling "indoor environment cleansers" and recruiting new distributors tells me that a baby crawling across a dirty carpet is the equivalent of that baby smoking four cigarettes. I like to talk with everybody, but the political booths are especially fun. It's a strong Republican region, working-class white, though the Democrats have a presence, too, and good potential in bad years for Republicans. They act as small, vernacular public spheres of the sort Jerry Hauser has championed.[6]

I always try to talk with the Republicans, usually with my boys in tow. I like to think of it as dialogue and debate, all in good fun, but also making a point. "You basically have one idea that you repeat over and over again," my nine-year-old tells me one year. My eleven-year-old eggs me on, though, so (yet again) we stop by the Republican booth. I exchange greetings with my interlocutor, a white man who looks to be in his late sixties, and I ask as nicely as possible, "So, are you still supporting the president on the war in Iraq?" It is August 2005, the U.S. death toll is inching toward two thousand, and Cindy Sheehan has captured national attention by bringing her antiwar vigil to President Bush's ranch in Crawford, Texas.

"Yes," he answers, promptly and strongly.

"Why?" I ask.

"Because he's my president," he says.

"Did you support everything Bill Clinton did when he was your president?" I come back. (I feel very clever.)

"Not quite as much," he says, grinning.

A red-headed high school boy working the booth then kicks in, as do two middle-aged women a little older than me. We go at it, civilly but with feeling, for ten or fifteen minutes (my boys later say we were there longer than we were at the Midway's Ride-a-Rama), then we wind it down and shake hands. I'm about to leave when somehow we get back into it, and I bring up the point that this president avoided military service himself but is now sending American men and women to die. One of the women says to me that Bush didn't avoid service, but her heart's not in it, and her facial expression lets on that she knows I'm right. "He has no honor," I intone. "Shame on him." She doesn't say anything back, and immediately I feel like I've pushed it too far, the moralistic college professor going after someone who is volunteering her time. Shame on me.

I try to keep myself in check, but talking at the booths can be too engaging to resist, at least for curious fairgoers like me. I ask the guy in charge at the cable-television provider's table if they could start opening up their cable-access show more, and funding it better, and one year get the idea that it would be great to have a media-reform table there as well. Politics at the social-movement level is mostly absent at the fair, except through the various Christian organizations that have tables or their own buildings. An Our Lady of Fatima Catholic lay representative is there every year, with scores of brochures and pamphlets representing an array of Catholic teachings and devotions, including some on abortion and sexuality. One year, early in my study of Paul and the Body of Christ, I picked up his brochures on the Eucharist. The representative tells me the bread is the real Flesh of Christ and goes on to describe the bedroom of an ill girl in Connecticut, where a poster of Christ is dripping a liquid substance, and where four miracles have thus far occurred.

The Protestants have their own buildings, one an old wood-framed Full Gospel building from the late 1940s, which offers free cold water and a handful of chairs for tired fairgoers to sit in. Lying near one of the fair's busiest intersections, the building has an old-timey feel and hosts traditional gospel singing by small performing groups who stand just outside it. Members of the Christian Laymen's Gospel League, a prison ministry in the area, also give their testimony and leave brochures. The tradition of Paul lives here, in this newer-style agora of a sort the Apostle would surely have sought out, were he ministering today. It's a place of the testifying spirit and of reaching out to all souls, whether they seek salvation or simply solace. The politics of the day is not the focus here.

The Word comes out differently a hundred yards further, in the newer Citizens for Life building, whose most obvious outdoor identifying sign reads "Free Face Painting." I wander in, where ten kids wait in line for the bright-colored treatment, standing beneath a row of "Choose Life" posters. Across the room is a series of low tables with small, realistic, life-sized models of the human fetus as it develops from the embryonic stage. "Please Hold," a sign reads. I pick one up, and it fits easily into the palm of my hands. I wander over to two people standing behind a table of literature, a man of about my age and a woman slightly older. I have recently been talking about abortion with a friend, an African-born Roman Catholic priest, who has told me the Biblical evidence for the antiabortion position is very thin, so I ask the volunteers about it. They paraphrase Jeremiah 1:5 ("Before I formed you in the womb I knew you, and before you were born I consecrated you."). I shift ground a bit and tell them I think there's a difference between stem-cell research and abortion. They tell me there isn't. We'll go nowhere, it seems. I thank them for being volunteers out there talking to us, shake the guy's hand, and move on down the line.

This fair I am participating in is a distant genealogical relative of the pagan festivals and markets for which Paul made tents. In one form or another, fairs and agricultural festivals have been part of world civilization for thousands of years (one sign it's a good and resilient ritual form). In the Roman world, *feriae* signified "feasts," which indexed the fact that the earliest fairs were held during the festivals of the warm season or at the beginning of harvest. The Catholic Church suppressed some of the pagan origins; when fairs took place in Germany, they were called "Messen" (as in the liturgical Mass).[7] As they developed in Europe, fairs were periodical gatherings of buyers and sellers in a place identified by decree or custom, often involving pleasure as well as commerce, and linked to holidays, festivals, and frequently carnivals as well. They were popular events, attended by a cross section of the local population, and especially hoi polloi.

Nineteenth-century Americans bent the traditional form to their own purposes and set off a domestic process of evolution that led to the fair as I witnessed it. American agricultural fairs date back to the 1810s, organized initially by agricultural groups like Elkanah Watson's Berkshire Agricultural Society, which in 1811 organized a livestock judging competition in southwestern Massachusetts. Drawing on the example of English agricultural fairs of the eighteenth century, American societies sponsored fairs aimed to improve local agriculture through education and contest. While English agricultural societies were filled with gentlemen landowners and often functioned as debating societies, their American counterparts were composed of working farmers and informed by Jeffersonian ideals. Practical education, wholesome pride, and Protestant restraint characterized the early fairs, though spectacle and popular pleasure played parts as well, with parades and, more controversially, horse racing. Fairs spread across Upstate New York and western Pennsylvania, and one was organized in Crawford County in the 1850s, as Walt Whitman was composing his *Leaves* four hundred miles east in Brooklyn, and Thomas MacIntyre Cooley was practicing law some three hundred miles northwest in Michigan. By the early twentieth century, carnivals, mechanical amusements, and electric lights had made nighttimes at the fair alluring, while political speeches were sandwiched among horse races, high-wire walkers, baseball games, and, increasingly, automobile exhibitions. By then, the Grange, the Farmers Union, and the agriculture departments of land grant colleges had joined the fair's associational mix.[8]

When a teenage Merton the Magician was trying his hand at fairs and carnivals one summer in the 1920s, 4–H Clubs ("Heart, Head, Hands, Health") had sprung up around the country and organized youth competitions at county fairs. The clubs were a Progressive Era attempt to tie together agriculture, public education, and moral uplift, and they had the additional aim of promoting new agricultural methods to young people as a modernizing end-run around the more recalcitrant adult population. (Nebraska, the farmer's daughter Merton met, might have been a card-carrying member of the 4–H.) The Future Farmers of America began in 1928 and established an organization for rural boys and their agricultural education that was active in Crawford County in 1946, when the County Park and Fair Association (CPFA) bought sixty-seven acres of land on the plateau northeast of Meadville and began a new county fair. While Merton was writing about newer media like radio and motion pictures from his house in Hastings and investigating an interracial public-housing project ninety miles south in Pittsburgh, the CPFA was laying the foundation to revive an old medium of mass communication here. The new iteration of the fair maintained a decidedly traditional moral code: no gambling, no alcohol, and no immoral exhibitions. It still maintains the same basic rules.[9]

Though the form has evolved over time and will continue to do so, it has evolved a characteristic and recognizable series of elements and sequence of events. Mornings are devoted to judging events, which occur throughout the day and into the evening. Evenings are dominated by the Midway, food stands, and grandstand entertainment. Participants and fairgoers mark their weeks differently, but each has an established temporal pattern. In Crawford County, that pattern extends over eight days, from Saturday through Saturday. Baked goods, floral arrangements, and other home-economics judging occurs on the first day, when items are fresh. Sunday traditionally includes an interdenominational church service in the morning, which marks the official opening, and religious music is performed that night in the grandstand. Monday night is the scholarship pageant. Tuesday through Friday alternate national music acts (country or pop) with motorized sporting events (hot-rod truck and tractor pulls). The fair ends Saturday night with a local demolition derby and fireworks display.

Like other good mass rituals, the fair is, practically speaking, communicatively unavoidable for the ekklesia it calls out. To be universally known is a rarity in the segmented media cultures of today, but the fair pulls it off. Six months or more beforehand, the newspaper announces the celebrity performers who will descend upon the event, attract widespread attention, generate excitement, and spur fans to buy advance tickets when they go on sale in April, prompted by free publicity in the newspapers and radio stations. Hard-core fans and devoted fairgoers line up hours and sometimes days ahead of time.[10] For the devoted, obvious and redundant signals of the fair's imminent arrival are communicated around the area, beginning in early August. Posters appear in store windows around the county and into the neighboring ones. Restaurants use paper placemats that print the fair's schedule and include advertisements from some of the exhibitors. The fair becomes a topic of everyday conversation, particularly for the nontrivial number who will take their vacations during fair week. The local newspaper begins running stories about preparation of the fairgrounds, painting and sprucing up. The radio stations announce that, as usual, they will be broadcasting live from the fair. Directional signs go up on all the main routes into town. Nearer the fairgrounds, traffic patterns change, and anyone driving past can see the campers arriving on Wednesday and Thursday. On Friday, the day before opening, the grounds are abuzz as vendors set up their stalls, carnies assemble the rides, and the products of domestic economy come in for judgment. The newspaper publishes a special pullout section with details of all the week's activities. Opening day arrives, and for the next eight days the fair is the front-page story in the newspaper. People ask their doctors for sick notes so they can skip work to attend. In public places around town, the fair joins the weather and sports as topics of conversation among strangers. Business signs around town read, "See You at the Fair." All week, sounds cascade outward from the plateau at night, reminding a considerable area within earshot of the gathering then occurring. Traffic thickens along all the arteries into town and toward the event. The fair has become the heart of one geographical area's collective social body.

Though agricultural fairs like this one officially honor rural and domestic production, they are also grand celebrations of mass consumption of a relatively affordable and largely vernacular sort. Consumption and commerce are of course longstanding elements of fairs, which developed historically as places to conduct trade and sell food. Commercial entertainment in some form has also long been part of the fair and festival mix, with rhapsodes, musicians, orators, poets, prostitutes, and actors collecting money for services rendered near or on the fairgrounds. This fair extends those traditions (minus, so far as I know, the poets and prostitutes), with a range of consumptive activities that both index and add to the event's collective significance and festivity.

Celebration of the fair involves eating publicly with others. Consumption of food is widespread and popular and a frequent topic of conversations around the county—sausages, barbecue, chicken dinners, corndogs, pizza, fresh-baked pies, and a cascade of deep-fried foods (onions, potatoes, vegetables, funnel cakes, Oreos, Twinkies . . .), all of which are relished with joy or guilty pleasure in a time-out-of-time from regimes of health, diet, or routine. The scents of cooking meats and frying oils perfume the air, like some kind of incense calling a congregation of meat-fat-and-sugar-eaters into the night. Ribs on a grill, chickens on rotisseries, sausages on steam tables, carmelizing kettle corn, sizzling ostrich burgers, fried sweet dough, fresh ice cream, sit-down spots and walking food, an eight-foot-high painted wooden chicken, the Methodist ladies and their amazing pies (blackberry, gooseberry, rhubarb, cherry, lemon meringue, coconut cream, raisin, burnt sugar, apple . . .). Out-of-town commercial vendor trailers compete with wooden buildings run by locals and their voluntary associations. You can eat well for relatively little here—6 bucks for a plate with five baby back ribs and two side orders from a guy with a smoker; $8.50 for a half chicken and three sides at the Chicken Shack; $1.60 for a two-fried-egg sandwich at Art's Place. That still puts full dinners out of easy reach for some families in this hardscrabble area, but they can eat their dessert here. Eating is a huge part of the event, done among intimates and strangers, tastes and smells adding considerably to the multisensorial ritual experience.

Consumption at the fair also takes the form of the buying of nonedible objects and services. Scattered across the grounds, one can find opportunities to buy everything from Tupperware to tractors. Water softeners, wood stoves, Amish-made outdoor furniture, airbrushed T-shirts, Mary Kay Cosmetics, NASCAR paraphernalia, POW/MIA gear, flags (American or Confederate, some with a ten-point buck deer imaged against them), hats, jewelry, retirement home plans, chiropractor visits, investment advice, cell phones, satellite dishes, hearing aids, aluminum siding, modular homes, and gazebos. Like the food, the commercial vendors are a mixed band of locals and out-of-towners.

The Midway, of course, represents its own brand of consumption, well-known in the American collective psyche through tradition, media representations, and firsthand experience. Depending on the time of day, the Midway is populated mostly by young adults, teenagers, or families with young kids (though I once saw a fifty-something-year-old guy going through them alone, looking grimly determined to achieve something). Carnies do their bit to lure the locals to drop some cash on games of chance, while across the way the Yo Yo, Zipper, Tilt-a-Whirl, and Ring of Fire call those looking for thrills of embodied, mechanically induced speed and dizzying rotation. The neon-lit carnival on a late summer evening in the Great Lakes region is impressive indeed. It is also a good place to drop money fast. The rides are run on a ticket system, which keeps the carnies from pocketing money and also masks the cost of each ride. Tickets are sold from booths and cost 75 cents a pop (a hard number to multiply) if you buy $20 worth. Rides require four or five tickets, which means that every time I put my two kids on a good one, I'm spending $7.50 for about five minutes. In-the-know locals on a budget get around the ripoff by bringing their kids to one of the three afternoon Ride-a-Ramas, where, between one and five, $8 buys unlimited rides. One year I can't make the afternoon session and burn through more than 20 bucks in fifteen minutes. Next thing, I'm dragging the boys off to argue with the Republicans.

The biggest, most expensive and concentrated mass consumption of enter-tainment occurs at the grandstand events, where tickets to the country music shows can run up to $50, cheap by national standards, but no trivial amount in this county. The money indexes both a market and the cultural significance of the out-of-town celebrities, whose performances, like the truck and trac-tor pulls, are given the privilege of breaking local sound ordinances. For the fans who gather, both concerts and loud engine sports invite remarkable and thrilling sensations, experienced as a crowd, en masse. People come locally and from some distance to be among the three thousand or so who gather to witness national acts like George Jones, Toby Keith, the Beach Boys, and other country or pop acts that will attract fairgoers. One year, at the George Jones concert, I see a woman on a portable hospital bed on the track in front of the stage, lying there as if to be healed. Another year I watch a dozen middle-aged women approach the stage one at a time to make offerings to their beloved Vince Gill (wrapped gifts, plates of cookies, a framed photo-graph of his children) and hear him say, "Thank you, Darlin'" to each. Waves of music crash against the aluminum grandstand and the bodies seated in it. We are set to vibrating at the same sonic frequency, a collective sensation that mystics might groove on.[11]

After out-of-town music performers and professional hot-rod trucks have set the grandstands vibrating Tuesday through Friday nights, the fair returns to its vernacular roots for its culminating event, the Saturday night demolition derby. Demolition derbies are spectacles of automotive reversal—strip the shiny parts off, disguise the old beater with a racy new paint job, and slam it freely into other cars around you. Together we bear witness to a stylized form of conspicuous waste, gendered and embraced by gearheads and the working classes. Participants often labor for months. They find a good car (big American ride on the far side of useful) and then pull out all the glass and get it rumble-ready, often with buddies or family members. They find sponsors, whose names are painted on the car ("SIGNS BY RENEE"), along with shout-outs to family and friends ("THANKS HUEY") and a number (every year lots of "69s"). Some paint other messages as well: "DRIVE IT LIKE IT'S STOLEN," "MIA/POW YOUR [*sic*] NOT FORGOTTEN" "LET'S ROLL," and—on a car by one of the few women drivers in the evening session—"KISS THIS." Owing to its popularity, there is also a Saturday afternoon demolition derby, which includes an all-women's heat. ("Eight bad ladiezzzz," the announcer growls.)

It's 6 bucks to get in, and the night starts with the national anthem. The event is sponsored by a county Ford dealership, which the announcer reminds us of frequently: " . . . a HUUGE collection of used cars at Lake View Ford . . . Who's got a FOOORRRDD!!?!!" (Loud boos from Chevy, Dodge, and GMC owners.) It's me and the boys, as the wife has decided the derby isn't her thing. The announcer asks, "Who wants to drive a demolition derby car?" About twenty people in the stands respond, including a solidly built crew-cut guy in front of me, who whoops loudly. He and his heavy-set wife hold young kids on their laps (only two tickets to buy that way) and she talks cars all night. "I wonder if they pulled the 410 out of that. . . . They CAN'T disqualify you if your wheels are still spinning." Four heats, twelve cars each, the last three standing in each round moving on to the finals, called the Feature Event. The volunteer fire department stands ready, in case a car catches fire, which happens twice tonight. There is a lot of banging. Occasionally a car is knocked onto two wheels. The crowd tightens and releases with the most spectacular collisions, letting out great yells as cars settle. Between heats, survivors pry back bent metal and replace blown-out tires. Twelve twisted winners from previous heats reappear, missing a trunk or other part, but ready to roll. Winning is a blend of car, driver, and good fortune. Spectators pick their favorites and predict the winner. After ten or fifteen minutes, only one car is left moving, the official waves his checkered flags, a driver climbs out through his car window, cheers go up, a trophy is awarded, and fireworks begin. They last a good long time, light up the night sky, and sonically mark the ritual's public culmination. The fireworks illuminate a crowd walking out to their cars, or standing a while longer on the grounds of the fair.

Materializing the Local Public

Over the course of the week, the fair's greatest spectacle is the crowd itself. According to a marketing survey, the single most popular aspect of the fair is "the people."[12] Looking at faces, clothes, and bodies is a significant part of the collective social experience. Within the bounds of the demographic attributes present in this rural community, one sees a great deal of variety among the people present. Bodies are overwhelmingly white, but one sees scattered faces, too, of African-Americans, South and East Asians, Native

Americans, Hispanics, and apparently mixed-race people. By the standards of multiethnic cities and regions, the population here is quite homogeneous, but on the local scene, this is the place for gathering the greatest heterogeneity. Stylistically, the crowd tilts working-to-middle class, though one sees a few upper-middle professional types, too, along with sometimes striking—especially to outsiders—rural poor in from the outlying area. All ages are represented, with roughly even mixes of men and women, some elderly and disabled people moving in wheelchairs. These are the people of the county. Durkheim believed that the very act of congregating was itself "an exceptionally powerful stimulant."[13] The Crawford County Apollonians don't get very Dionysian at their late-summer harvest festival, but sensing public bodies adds energy to the event. It is supplemented by the attendance figures that appear daily in the newspaper, running up to 175,000 (in a county of 90,000) over the eight-day event and, as McLuhan would say, extending the crowd's tactile sense of itself by means of number.[14]

There is a human plenitude here that Whitman would have loved, like the glorious jams on Broadway he sauntered through with relish. I see a teenage girl in gold lamé, a grandmother in tie-dye, others in blue jeans, short shorts, sweatsuits, well-paunched stretch pants, dangling golf shorts, pressed khaki Dockers, cargo shorts, hoodies, Hawaiian shirts, Izods, scoop-necked tees, bustiers, sundresses, shoulder purses, bead belts, fanny packs, work boots, cowboy boots, high heels, tennis shoes, sandals, red-flashing sneakers, hats of many varieties. I see bodies moving pigeon-toed, knock-kneed, palsied, striding, sashaying, meandering, purposeful, pushing strollers, riding electric scooters, young, old, infirm, free-breathing, or hooked up to oxygen. I see evidence of muscles taut from physical labor, strengthened through weights, shrunken from apparent anorexia, hidden beneath layers of fat in bodies far beyond obese, drawn and sinewy in the skinny bodies of women smokers. I see the barrel-chested, sunken-chested, flat-chested, and seemingly implant-chested; grandmothers' bosoms, grandfathers' laps, fathers' shoulders, mothers' arms; kids cautious and curious; bodies on the far side of birthing babies without time or inclination or money for health clubs or exercise; fertile bodies moving through the Midway; working farm bodies in the barns; bodies bent over picnic tables, kicked back in lawn chairs, entering and exiting the outhouses, standing in line for ice cream. A woman with one crutch, a man with two; a sleeveless full-zip, neck-plunging leather shirt on a lady in her sixties; pink golf shorts on a guy in his forties. Streaked hair, rinsed hair, receding hair, no hair, long hair, ponytails, buzz cuts, flat tops, Afros, and mullets. All find place in this great mass, where particularity communicates up close and vividly, and the collective local body bears witness to itself.

When I hit the moment right, Whitman's aesthetic hits Cooley's social mysticism, and I can pretty well feel the democratic ekklesia I'm now describing at my keyboard. As Emerson realized, there's a "power of moods, each setting at nought all but its own tissue of facts and beliefs."[15] When I'm in a mood of the yea-saying, street-strolling Whitman, the crowd gets bathed in a sea of fondness, its composite humanity is made moving and beautiful, its pulse electrifying, its fluidity alluring. I can sense it with a kind of Jack Kerouac beatitude. The crowd becomes a palpable manifestation of Cooley's Great Life, each individual a sociospiritual thread end to places beyond, but all connected through this space. In these moments, I can see the signs of familial love and civic friendship through the strolling fairgoers and the volunteers all around them. I can appreciate from a distance its pockets of sexualized adolescent energy, fitfully working its way out through a new generation. There seems something holy in the moment, not all good but all human, and the fact of sharing democratically structured civic space with strangers and friends seems a wonderful collective accomplishment to be part of.

But it's easy to find other moods as well, which plunge the fair into well-different tissues of Emersonian fact and belief. My wife hits the less-than-yea-saying moods faster and more regularly than I do, which explains why she doesn't attend it as religiously. "America didn't look so good last night," she tells me the morning after her last demolition derby. She is a physician, and the obesity stands out to her. It stands out to me, too, when we move away to Pittsburgh, and even more after I've been visually socialized into the conspicuous fitness of Boulder, Colorado. One can follow this darker mood to a reading of the fair as an orgy of high-fat consumption that literally feeds the collective obesity of America, through fried food, high-fructose corn syrup, and pieces of the highly processed corpses of industrially produced animals—tokens of a regime of food production that has driven small farmers like those celebrated here out of business and into commuting many miles to low-paying jobs with no health care or benefits. These, too, are truths of the fair, as is the fact of its gendered symbolics and divisions of labor, which both index and uphold a social order that favors men as a whole. Though the fair places value on women's work and performances, men command most of the higher-status positions, while women take up roles as elected queens and princesses put on public display, or pass as adolescent fairgoers through its sexualized pockets, touching a culture that may well make them physical victims, if it hasn't done so already. Meanwhile, the few black people in town either stay home or brace themselves for a plunge into a white sea they know has an ample number of racists swimming in its midst, some of whom identify with the Confederate deer-hunting flags sold by a vendor. Or so goes the start of a different vision of the mass communication occurring here, born out of moments of passing through it, too.

Somewhere between aesthetico-mystical yea-saying and harder-edged critical analysis, I say that the crowd gathered at the fair serves as a material index of the local public. As Walter Lippmann long ago realized, the public is a largely imagined entity known mostly through representation and abstraction. At events like the fair, which attract a broad cross section of a local population, the public assembles and is made flesh. The public is given a face—many faces, connected to many different bodies. It is made real, *res*. A public is materialized, yielding a kind of literal res publica, a public thing made from local bodies now inhabiting common and more-or-less equal ground (no cheap and expensive seats, no economically based spatial segregation). The mass assembly that occurs here creates the most detailed available fleshly representation and index of the local population, which in turn makes up its democratic public. This crowd shows what that public looks like, and assembles its members together in a complex enactment of collective communication.

Rhetorically speaking, the public gathered here as a crowd communicates with vividness (what the Romans called *evidentia*) and copiousness that reside in the gestures and gaits of particular bodies, fluidly arranged in this ritual setting of time-out-from-routine-time. Individuals stand in composite testimony to the lives of particular others in the area. As a result, the fair provides very literal grounds upon which to enlarge and populate one's social imagination. Here I am thinking of Hannah Arendt's idea of an "enlargement of the mind" that consists of taking into account the thoughts of others by imagining their judgments of particular things. "To think with an enlarged mentality," Arendt wrote, "means that one trains one's imagination to go visiting."[16] Live mass assemblies like the fair provide corporeal cues for an enlarged mentality tied to a particular place. They provide materials for adjusting one's social picture and correcting the inevitable demographic biases it contains, based on one's routine and interactional circles. Copious particular others "stoke the mind with variety," just as rhetorical *copia* like Whitman's catalogs do something of the same.[17] This process is considerably deepened through conversation and interactions afforded by the fair's pluralistic structure, which offers space for those willing to talk with people oriented differently and formally representing a range of *logoi*. That most fairgoers don't take advantage of these opportunities is, from my perspective, a loss, but it does not refute the possibilities structured here, awaiting moods and dispositions that might follow them out.

Less subjunctively, we can say that the public gathered at the fair is sign and incubator of the "social capital" of the area. Robert Putnam defines this somewhat protean concept in terms of "the collective value of all 'social networks' (who people know) and the inclinations that arise from these networks to do things for each other ('norms of reciprocity')."[18] As Prosterman shows in her study, and as I found in mine, county fairs are built upon the labor and care of exhibitors and volunteers who work with one of the many organizations that create the fair each year—from the fair's board of directors who oversee operations to the agriculture clubs, fraternal organizations, churches, and volunteer fire departments that bring it off annually. Fair volunteers are enmeshed in social networks whose ties are strengthened and extended through their participation. They organize and take part in cooperative activities that contribute to shared public goods. Fairgoers too are drawn into these socially capitalizing processes. The social ecology of rural fairs like this one is such that locals almost inevitably run into friends and acquaintances walking by. Brief, unplanned conversations move information and reconfirm social ties, both of which are important elements of civil society. When they walk past the exhibits of agricultural and religious organizations, political parties, social service agencies, unions, and hunting and conservation groups, they learn or are reminded of voluntary associations in the area. When they buy pies, chicken, or french fries from a fraternal or religious organization's stand, they come face-to-face with a local volunteer, and, not infrequently, someone they know.

If the fair is a site for enlarged imagination and social capital now, in the future it could also be a place for what Bruno Latour has called *Dingpolitik*, a politics of things. Responding to a widely felt sense that politics as usual (*Realpolitik*) is inadequate to the pressing needs of the present, Latour has sketched an alternative, based on the idea of *Ding*, a German word that refers to both a kind of archaic assembly and an object or thing. *Dingpolitik* will be a politics of assembly and gatherings and will attend to things— polluted rivers, beheadings in the Middle East, the Islamic veil in France. It will require "a *new eloquence*" to go with it and new or retrofitted forms of assembly as well. He identifies scientific laboratories, technical institutions, marketplaces, churches and temples, financial trading rooms, and Internet discussion sites as "some of the forums and agoras" in which *Dingpolitik* might occur. In Latour's vision, *Dingpolitik* would be driven not by a sense of human knowledge, power, or sovereignty, but instead by awareness of our disabilities and handicaps. Our condition calls for gatherings of many sorts. "If we are all handicapped, or rather politically-challenged, we need many different prostheses."[19]

The American county fair has the potential to be one of these political prostheses, new agoras that could play one role in the multimodal communicative process. Though politics and deliberation are currently only trace elements in the celebration of the fair, they could grow to be more. Political candidates have long worked fairs, but there is grassroots space as well, which the antiabortion group uses in Crawford County. Conservation and hunting groups also make their cases heard, as do businesses like the cable television provider who uses the fair to legitimate its view of media. What is currently lacking, in this and no doubt other county fairs around the country, is a progressive grassroots voice that might reach out to ordinary people (hoi polloi) in a region. Conservative fair boards and gatekeepers of display space may well be skeptical and hesitant, but all that means is that progressive groups face the rhetorical challenge of showing how giving space to their cause contributes to the mission of the fair and the common good of citizens in the county.

Media education and reform would, it seems to me, be a perfect cause to take to fairs. There is a great deal of popular criticism about "the media," anger about cable television and internet service–provider rates, preference for locally owned and operated media, and concern about the quality of news and other programming. So far, the media reform movement has been very good at building a base and appealing to progressives. The next step is to reach out more to moderates and cultural conservatives, as fellow citizens sharing common concerns and speaking language that ordinary people can understand. Education is one important route—disseminating facts about things like media conglomeration, federal policy (for example, the Fairness Doctrine, obscenity standards, cross-ownership), media practice (for example, with regard to public service and news programming), and citizen action (for example, names and contact information for all sorts of media-related citizens groups, progressive and conservative alike) and inviting conversation with members of the public. Such education would be a new version of Merton's propaganda of the facts. It would also represent a start for a new eloquence of the kind Latour calls for, one concerned with *things* (our communications media) and worked out in *gatherings* (a county fair, with its popular cross section of a local public), where at least brief dialogue is possible.

With media reform and a few more social-movement and civic-affairs booths added to the mix, the county fair has the potential to grow into a new agora that allows citizens even greater opportunities to engage and build their communities. One of the beauties of this agora would be the way it mixed so many realms—agricultural and domestic production, commerce, religion, politics, consumption, education, competitive contest, and much entertainment. It would build on its tradition of being a place of strolling and loafing about (*agorezein*) and offering a diverse but (mostly) wholesome array of ideas and activities that appeal across age groups and interests. Like other agoras, it would be a place for both doing public work and taking time off from it, here in a ritual context enacted one week a year. The fair is already festive, which makes it a social magnet that attracts crowds who venture there to take in its offerings and also to behold themselves. I don't want to make too much of its possibilities (or maybe I do) but offer only a sketch for what it might be.

In the alternative paradigm I've been filling out in this book, the fair represents mass communication of several varieties. It is a ritual of civic communion for the local body public, where strangers and social intimates eat outdoors together. It is a communicatively abundant event, marked by sensory and symbolic plenitude, far greater than that available through most media channels. It draws a generally representative cross section of the social totality in the area, tilted toward the working and middling classes (hoi polloi). For minds readied for the occasion, it also provides grounds for cultivating an enlarged mentality of moral inclusivity from the material particulars of the event—the bodies that enflesh the souls who assemble here together, offering human points of departure for analogically working out toward otherness beyond this place, lived variety in all its varieties, horizons of experience we can never reach, but that we can try to make room for. Those, I would suggest, are some of the less-obvious features of gatherings like the fair.

Past and Prologue: Final Reflections on These Figures

The fair brings this book to a close, but it also launched the broader project of considering nontraditional species and theorists of mass communication, and was thus among the study's key inventional media. I spent time there as I began my first serious reading of Whitman, and the two experiences cross-pollinated one another. The twin efforts to consider social forms and thinkers emerged from that point, holding together across two moves and time zones in a region-skipping motion of professional mobility that carried away from the immediacy and public feelings of the fair as a local presence. With distance gained from those moves, I'd like now to conclude by speaking across the six essays of this book, drawing together threads and key ideas, and reflecting on what I see as the significance of the reclamation project I've tried to conduct.

I began by revisiting the rhetorical origins of the term "mass communication" in the 1920s and '30s, primarily through the person of David Sarnoff but also through some of the scholars who began organizing a field around it. That historical moment gave rise to what I called the "broadcast paradigm of mass communication," defined from radio broadcasting outward to analogous enterprises that produced and distributed identical content for huge, spatially dispersed audiences. Tapping into "communication," an idea with growing cultural cache, the new compound term helped legitimate the for-profit industries of RCA, NBC, and American commercial media more generally, presenting a favorable alternative to circulating alternatives like "toll broadcasting," "chain broadcasting," or "a monopoly of the air." Expanded to include motion pictures, newspapers, magazines, and television, mass communication grew into a topic of public and scholarly discourse, and by the late 1940s was coming to name an institutionalizing academic field, aimed at studying, guiding, and occasionally criticizing the processes and institutions that fit the broadcast paradigm. Mass communication research originated in the United States but expanded quickly overseas in postwar contexts that ranged from reconstruction, occupation, development, and knowledge exchange to cold war propaganda and psychological warfare. By the 1970s and '80s, a rhetorical backlash had developed against mass communication, which came to serve as a symbolic boundary object that separated cultural studies from social scientific mass communication research, both intellectually and politically. In the same era, "the media" emerged as a term of public discourse that encompassed a part of what mass communication had covered in its heyday; while cable television, satellites, VCRs, niche marketing, and the internet ushered in a new, seemingly post-mass era. In this context, I have set out to reinvest in mass communication, refigure its meanings, and add to our knowledge of its history and social forms.

One might ask, though, at the end of the day, why bother with such a rehabilitation project? What does it get us? How does it contribute to understandings or practices? I would answer that, at its most modest, the book has been simply an effort at enriching conversations about communication and its media—adding historical characters, texts, and a few new ideas into the mix, as a way of contributing variety of perspective while others move forward with critical, cultural, and social scientific projects more at the center of current work in the field. At the very least, I would say, we can benefit from outlying perspectives on the subject, just like city dwellers can benefit from a visit to the country, or country dwellers to the city—as a way temporarily to inhabit different space and recalibrate the senses before returning to more familiar environs. Or, to shift the analogy, perhaps the book enriches ongoing conversations like an inflatable radish does when passed from deep in the bleachers during a baseball game, adding color to the spectacle as it lands gently on the playing field, before being carted away by a dutiful member of the stadium grounds crew.[20]

I would argue that refiguring mass communication is more than an inflatable radish at a ballgame and point out that this book has contributed to a number of projects. They include sketching new methodological directions for communication history; adding to our substantive knowledge of the intellectual, rhetorical, and social history of mass communication; preserving and conceptually refurbishing a historically significant term of art and theory; reweaving webs of connection among communication, transportation, and religion; expanding the categories of communication theorist and communication theory; inviting reflexive awareness in amateur and professional participant-observers, critics, and theorists of communication; and calling attention to overlooked communicative forms that carry ethical, spiritual, political, aesthetic, and environmental significance—and which are therefore worthy of further attention by citizens, seekers, scholars, and, perhaps, slackers and cynics alike.

As it has played out, the book has revolved primarily around portraits of four individuals who came variously to theorize mass communication. In a pragmatist leveling move, I have broadened the idea of theory to include all manners of reflective interpretation-cum-representation of communicative phenomena. In a rhetorical definitional move, I have broadened the idea of mass communication by attending to repressed meanings of the term *mass*, which, I argue, index important species of the genus. These dual broadenings gained structure through the four portraits, designed both to illuminate historically specific contours of the rhetorical production of ideas and to cast a series of exemplars in comparative intellectual and sociological relief. To further cinch the potentially unlimited expansion opened by the dual broadenings, the portraits have attended analytically to four topics (*topoi*) that have cut across the studies and also point to questions that we theorists might ask ourselves with regard to our interpretive productions: (1) In what role(s) do we perform our theoretical activity? (2) What inventional media guide the development of our visions? (3) What kinds of communication do we attend to? (4) What moral orientations or normative horizons—secular or sacred faiths, or functionally defined gods—inform and are served by our accounts? I'll review some of the answers to these questions as they played out through Paul, Whitman, Cooley, Merton, and the fair.

Each of the figures I've sketched took up a particular ideal-typical stance toward mass communication in one or more of its varieties. Paul was the apostolic activist, devoting his adult life to pursuing his convictions and doing work that contributed to a greater movement with which he strongly identified. He offered a critique of practices of public communication in the ekklesia in Corinth and laid out a vision for just and normatively sound action and social identifications. Whitman was the journalist-poet, who forged an art that at once represented, idealized, and critiqued the communicative practices of his day. His was an aestheticized vision intended to constitute a new, polytheistic democracy. Cooley was the sociologically minded humanist, an Emersonian social philosopher who contemplated ideas, imaginations, and experiences from his personal spaces in Ann Arbor, and who managed to express himself in the process. Merton was the social scientist, who skeptically probed social realities and beliefs through disciplined methods and middle-range sociological theory that served scholars, practitioners, and administrative funding agencies alike. The role carried him out of his customary personal spaces to investigate mass communication as experienced by actual people in the world and then took him back to his office to figure out an account that would withstand critical scrutiny and epistemological challenge. The analytical distance he took with regard to the communication he interpreted suited him for observation, critique, and the accumulation of knowledge. If I were more of a media-reform activist and carried through with my idea of pitching the cause at the fair, I would have taken up aspects of all four roles in my own envisioning. As it stands, this Afterword has blended elements of humanistic reflection and qualitative fieldwork with aesthetically tinged rhetorical depiction of a partly idealized social reality. As theorists, any of us might blend impulses of the activist, artist, philosopher, and social scientist, along with other impulses, reflective and spontaneous.

Proclaimers and observers, skeptics and believers—the four main figures were mobile men who participated in the transportation systems of their days. Paul walked the roads and sailed the seas of the Mediterranean, along the way experiencing their dangers, people, and visions. Whitman ambled about the sidewalks and countryside of Manhattan and Long Island, rode high upon their ferries and coaches, and witnessed the development of the railroad. Through railway, stagecoach, and riverboat, he stretched himself out through a long-distance transportation system that brought Europeans deeper into the continent's heartland and drove the people of the first nations toward destruction and death. Cooley grew up in a world increasingly networked through railroads, with street railways in cities and towns, and long-distance routes spanning the country. He observed the coming of the automobile and watched it become a national commonplace that moved through an expanding system of roadways. A teenage Meyer Schkolnick took advantage of that system by hitchhiking a route then known as the Lincoln Highway, which passed through his Philadelphia and took him out among the Gentiles of the American Midwest. Streetcars and trains were still favored modes of urban and longer-distance transport, but Merton himself rode the wave of the future by embracing the ways of the car-driving commuter. He came of age at a time when ships linked the globe's continents, but he advanced his career in the era of commercial airline travel. A world of automobiles and jets is one that many of us living now have always known, having come on the scene after most of the urban streetcars of the nation were scrapped in favor of the buses that carried those who resisted, out of choice or necessity, the regime of automobility. That regime regularly provides the loudest aggregated noise heard on an ongoing basis in most of the populated soundscapes the world now inhabits, while jets command the sonic heavens and index a different branch of today's transportation system.

Methodologically, sketching these stories has involved me in a distinct kind of rhetorically informed communication history, told through the lives of individuals and calling attention to the places and contexts from which their ideas emerged. I have suggested that individuals serve as thread ends into the communicative fabrics of their eras, which means that they provide entry points into rhetorical, intellectual, social, cultural, technological, and institutional history. I have tried to make some of those connections in the condensed rhetorical biographies I have written, guided in part by a concept that emerged in the course of researching the book, *media of invention*, or the structured contexts for generating addressed discourse. I will develop the concept further in future work, but here it has served as a heuristic device for organizing and reflecting upon the material, social, and cultural places through which communicated visions of mass communication have arisen. Those media have included bodies, workplaces, oral performances, modes of physical movement, reading, conversational relationships, and technologies of literacy, among other enabling-and-constricting media. The concept is not intended to reduce rhetorical discourse to its productive contexts, but rather to aid comparative, analytical, and reflexive thinking, as well as purposive rhetorical action. As it has played across these studies, the *topos* of inventional media has led through embodied performative arts that shaped the characters (*ethē*) of the four figures I've followed, from Paul's internalization of the Septuagint and dictation of letters to a secretary, through Whitman's perambulatory journalistic absorption of Broadway and longhand composition of print shop-destined poetry, Cooley's home-based journal writing and conversational observation of his children with his wife, and Merton's early magic and later classroom lecturing and typewritten analysis, among other activities and places. I have also sketched ways that their inventing bodies moved over distance, expanding themselves spatially, rhetorically, and sometimes spiritually in the process.

Their visions, I have suggested, can be retroactively understood as attending to, interpreting, and representing multiple species of the genus *mass communication*. These species traverse the five senses of *mass* that I parsed out in Chapter 1—those involving barleycakes and banquets, liturgies and religious rituals, large scales and abundance, hoi polloi and ordinary people, and the totality of some social collective (creatively identified as "mass communication 1–5"). Paul's Body of Christ partakes of all five, so serves in its own way as multiply paradigmatic: grounded in bread and banquets, grown into a widespread liturgical enactment, encompassing millions upon millions of people scattered widely in time and space, normatively favoring the poor and humble, and in principle open to anyone who proclaims Jesus the Messiah—the totality of the Christian ekklesia. Whitman's poetry, meanwhile, moves in the direction of representing the totality of America and the cosmos beyond, through the depiction of copious particulars normatively weighted toward the democratic masses. It hints at how crowds, place-based contemplation, and compositely formed democratic individuals can all be media of mass communication. Cooley then advanced the story by theorizing "communication" itself and showing it to be so ubiquitous and socially interconnected that we can view all symbolic interaction as part of one interconnected totality, a universal mass communion he sometimes called the Great Life. Operating in the era of mass communication so named, Merton saw how radio and celebrity could advance the dueling faiths of American nationalism and capitalistically driven consumerism, but also turned his attention to more vernacular forms, including mass letter writing and interracial public housing communities. A contemporary manifestation of the traditional agricultural fair then rounded out the mass communication forms whose histories I have sketched, one that features food, ritual assembly, communicative abundance, and ordinary people, and that provides material foundation for building social imaginations that open out toward the totality of a local population and points beyond.

Across these studies—and again veering toward questions we might ask ourselves, too—I have characterized what I have called the faiths that informed the visions of mass communication for each figure. This *topos* has allowed for its own threads of comparison and accumulation. Heterodoxies cut across the book, from the heterodox Judaisms of Paul and Merton to the heterodox Christianities of Whitman, Cooley, and perhaps my depiction of the fair. Beyond his own more orthodox Judaism, David Sarnoff had faith in capitalism, while Paul had faith in the God of Israel as manifest through His recently Earth-sent Messiah, Whitman had faith in poetry and polytheistic democracy, Cooley in "communication," and Merton in skeptical science and disciplined critical inquiry. All harbored moral universalisms of a sort, manifest through chosen varieties of mass communication. In his role at RCA, Sarnoff channeled his universalism in commercial directions, imagining a company with global dimensions, controlling radio and television networks that delivered giant audiences to sponsoring advertisers. The other four figures point us in different directions, mobilizing their faiths to represent forms of mass communication whose inclusivity serves other purposes and gods. While not absent their own structuring exclusions in conceptualization and practice, their nonparadigmatic forms were marked by impulses to make room for the many at the communicative table, both symbolically and materially. This is true of the Pauline Body of Christ (open to Jews and Greeks, slaves and free, women and men, the privileged and the socially shunned), Whitman's democratic free verse (rejects none, accepts all), Cooley's Great Life (a cultural procession of humankind, past, present, and future), Merton's Addison Terrace housing complex (inclusive of black and white during a segregated era), and a thriving popular fair (attended by a broad cross section of the local population and making representative space for many cultural activities). We need to keep these and other forms alive and do what we can to bring out their full normative potentialities.

Though mass communication in the broadcast paradigm has typically burst the boundaries of locale to reach a geographically scattered audience, a refigured mass communication partly reverses that tendency, reminding us of morally significant forms organized around particular places and the assembly of bodies therein. From the house-based ekklesia in Corinth to the county fair in Meadville, from Whitman's New York streets through the laundry rooms of Addison Terrace, we've seen that place-based mass com-

munication can be a medium for working out politics, community, spirituality, and the aesthetic dimensions of human life together. When places are
taken as sites extending backward and forward in time, new dimensions of
mass communion emerge, as we saw suggested in some of Whitman's writings. Imagining past and future, we can invent solitary and collective rituals
of remembrance for peoples and place-scapes that preceded us and of moral
consideration for the generations that will follow. Religious pilgrims can
feel some of this cross-generational communion when they visit their holy
sites, but place-based mass communication can also contribute to a kind of
environmental piety as well. Prepared minds in particular locales can use it
to help invent rhetorical means to communicate care for our places.[21]

As the environmental movement has put us in position to see, the earth itself
is the ultimate medium of mass communication, binding the world together
in a single interconnected system of climate, air, water, and soil. Managing
that mass medium requires concerted action at the highest institutional levels
of government and business, but it also requires mindfulness and ongoing,
quotidian action on the part of ordinary people scattered everywhere. Caring
for the universal place of the globe is partly a matter of caring for an infinite
number of small places around it, each of a size that can be tended by local
governments, citizens groups, families, and individuals. Mass communication in the service of the environmental health of the planet requires many
hands and talents—activists and citizens with Paul's conviction, artists with
Whitman's imagination, scientists with Merton's critical intelligence, and a
legion of ordinary people with some of Cooley's moral hope.

That said, it's time now to shut me up and return to your own figures
and places.

Notes

Introduction

1. Wirth, "Consensus and Mass Communication," 10.

2. Simonson, "Writing Figures into the Field," drawing upon Abbott's superb "Historicality of Individuals" and influenced by Marvin, "Literacy's Corporeal Constant."

3. Nerone, "Future of Communication History."

4. Taylor, *Sources of the Self*, 3–52.

5. Dewey, *A Common Faith*, 28.

6. Whitman, in Stovall, ed., *Prose Works 1892* (PW 1982) II, 725.

7. Mailloux, *Reception Histories*, ix; see also Leff, "Hermeneutical Rhetoric"; Eberly, *Citizen Critics*; and Mailloux, "Re-Marking Slave Bodies."

8. Rorty, "Inquiry as Recontextualization."

9. See, for instance, Emerson, "Eloquence"; Burke, *Attitudes Toward History*; Carey, *Communication as Culture*; West, *American Evasion of Philosophy*; and Peters, *Speaking Into the Air*, and *Courting the Abyss*.

10. There are signs of contemporary resurgence, however; see, e.g., Hoover, *Religion in the Media Age*; Morgan, ed., *Keywords in Religion, Media, and Culture*; Horsfield, Herr, and Medrano, eds., *Belief in Media*; and Clark, *From Angels to Aliens*.

11. James, "The Social Value of the College Bred," in *Writings 1902–1910*, 1245.

12. Sloterdijk, *Critique of Cynical Reason*, 22.

13. Cooley, "Some Teachings of Emerson," in *On Self and Social Organization*, 35. Cf. Sue Curry Jansen's "hermeneutic golden rule" in Park and Pooley, eds., *History of Media*, esp. 97–100.

14. On communication and transportation, see Mattelart, *Invention of Communication*; Packer and Robertson, eds., *Thinking with James Carey*. On rhetoric and place,

see McKeon, "Creativity and the Commonplace," in *Rhetoric*, 25–36; Clark, *Rhetorical Landscapes*; and Blair, Dickinson, and Ott, eds., *Places of Public Memory*.

Chapter 1. The Rhetorical Invention of "Mass Communication"

1. Sarnoff, "Radio Progress Passes in Review," *New York Times*, September 18, 1927: R10, R19; "New Milestone of Radio Progress in 1927," press release, Radio Corporation of America; David Sarnoff Publicity (DSP), Box 4, Folder 15, David Sarnoff Library (hereafter, DSL), Princeton, N.J.

2. Douglas, *Listening In*, 55–82; McChesney, *Telecommunications, Mass Media, and Democracy*, 12–29; Hilmes, *Radio Voices*, 34–74; Barnouw, *A Tower in Babel*, 105–88.

3. A tale compellingly told in Slezkine, *The Jewish Century*.

4. Lyons, *David Sarnoff*, 5–6, 26–34; Lewis, *Empire of the Air*, 89–95; see also the excellent Web site of the DSL (http://www.davidsarnoff.org/). For corporate public relations in the era, see Marchand, *Creating the Corporate Soul*.

5. Sarnoff was actively addressing strategic and general publics through speeches and articles by 1922. Thirty-three of his early speeches (1922–33) were collected by the RCA publicity department and bound as Addresses by David Sarnoff (ADS) I, DSL.

6. Sarnoff, as told to Mary Margaret McBride, "Radio," *The Saturday Evening Post*, August 7, 1926, 141–42; rpt. in part in Sarnoff, *Looking Ahead*, 22–23.

7. Lewis, *Empire of the Air*, 106–7; Alexander B. Magoun, Director, DSL, personal communication, July 8, 2004.

8. Barnouw, *Tower in Babel*, 105–7, 186.

9. Sarnoff, "The Progress and Direction of Radio Development," address delivered December 17, 1925 to the Boston Chamber of Commerce," DSL, ADS, I; "The Development of the Radio Art and Radio Industry Since 1920," address delivered to the Harvard Business School, Cambridge, Mass., April 16, 1928. DSL, ADS I.

10. Sarnoff, "Relationship of Radio to the Problem of National Defense," address delivered January 31, 1927, to the Army War College, Washington, D.C., DSL, ADS I. Part of this schema morphed into "The Voice of America" radio system that played an active role in American Cold War politics and that Sarnoff reportedly envisioned and named; see Sarnoff, *Voice of America*.

11. Sarnoff, "How Radio Developments May Affect the Auxiliary Language Movement," address delivered to the International Federation of University Women, London, July 31, 1926, DSL, DSP, Box 3, Folder 26. Esperanto was concocted in Bialystok, Russia, by Ludwig Zamenhof, a Jewish student (Slezkine, *Jewish Century*, 64, 98–99).

12. Sarnoff, address to Atlantic City Chamber of Commerce, January 26, 1923, DSL, Source Book for Early Reports II.

13. "Sarnoff Takes Issue with H.G. Wells on Value of Radio Broadcasting," RCA press release, November 28, 1927, DSL, DSP, Box 4, File 8. Sarnoff's speech generated

letters of support, including one from an Esperanto member, who asked that Sarnoff "use the Esperantists throughout the country for broadcasting speeches, recitals, songs and music so that our neighboring countries may understand us"—one of several universalist dreams attached to broadcasting (Ruth Davis Fillisti to Sarnoff, April 30, 1927, ibid.).

14. Sarnoff, "Radio and Our Daily Life," *New York Evening World*, September 15, 1928 (DSL, DSP, Box 4, File 31). Susan Douglas argues that as late as 1930, there was "still not one 'mass' audience" but instead "many listening publics with ongoing, warring ideas about how to listen and what to listen to" (*Listening In*, 79).

15. McChesney, *Telecommunications, Mass Media, and Democracy*, 27–28.

16. Sarnoff, "In Television Sarnoff Sees a New Culture," *New York Times*, July 13, 1930, 115.

17. For the formative years of this story, see Schwock, *American Radio and Latin American Activities*.

18. See McChesney, *Rich Media, Poor Democracy*.

19. Some of the most important books of the era did not use the term *mass communication*, including Lippmann, *Public Opinion* (1925); Dewey, *Public and Its Problems* (1927); Lasswell, *Propaganda Technique in the World War* (1927); Cooley, Angell, and Carr, *Introductory Sociology* (1933); Willey and Rice, *Communication Agencies and Social Life* (1933); Lasswell, Casey, and Smith, *Propaganda and Promotional Activities* (1935); and Cantril and Allport, *Psychology of Radio* (1935).

20. Hettinger, "Forward," *Annals of the American Academy of Political and Social Science [Annals]* 177 (1935): ix; see also his article for that volume, "Broadcasting in the United States." Hettinger (1902–72) conducted a radio listener study in Philadelphia in 1928, took his doctorate in economics from the University of Pennsylvania (1933), served as the first research director of the National Association of Broadcasters (1934–35), and remained active in listener research until 1938. He went on to serve as economic consultant for CBS, NBC, and the Newspaper-Radio Committee, and also served as a special consultant to the Federal Communications Commission in 1936–37.

21. Willey, "Communication Agencies," 194.

22. See e.g., Riegel, "Nationalism in Press, Radio and Cinema"; Rice, "Quantitative Methods in Politics." For the introduction of television into the narrative, see Sarnoff, "Possible Social Effects of Television" (1941).

23. Albion, "The 'Communication Revolution.'" Of the revolution's social consequences, he observed: "It has widened the horizons of every community, partly through the rapid dissemination of news and partly through the breaking down of provincialism with new facilities for travel. It has been of vital importance in opening up the wilderness and in linking together the far-flung possessions of the world empires. It has made possible far greater centralization in commerce and in government and it has also had important consequences in the art of warfare" (718–19).

24. As revealed by a JSTOR search of "communications" in the economics journals

of the era. This is the tradition that Harold Innis came into, as did Charles Cooley (see Ch. 4). Some sociologists in the 1930s also continued this older usage, centered on material transportation; see, e.g., Willey and Rice, *Communication Agencies and Social Life* (1933).

25. John Marshall to Ivor A. Richards, August 16, 1939, folder 2672, box 223, RF 1.1, Rockefeller Foundation Archives, Rockefeller Archive Center, Sleepy Hollow, N.Y. For Marshall and Rockefeller's role in the development of mass communications research, see Gary, *Nervous Liberals*, 85–129; and Buxton, "From Radio Research to Communications Intelligence."

26. On propaganda research giving way to the study of "communication," see Sproule, *Propaganda and Democracy*, esp. 217–23; and Cmiel, "Cynicism, Evil, and the Discovery of Communication." Sproule reports 1948–49 as "the pivotal point at which the aggregate number of citations in *Psychological Abstracts* to 'persuasion,' 'communication,' and 'information' regularly exceeded those relating to 'propaganda'" (217).

27. Lasswell, Casey, and Smith, *Propaganda, Communication, and Public Opinion* (1946); Wirth, "Consensus and Mass Communication" (1948); Huxley, *UNESCO*; Lazarsfeld and Merton, "Mass Communication, Popular Taste, and Organized Social Action" (1948); and Schramm, ed., *Mass Communications* (1949). For Schramm's role in establishing the Iowa doctoral program, see Rogers, *History of Communication Study*, 3–29. For mass communication more generally in the period, see Peters and Simonson, eds., *Mass Communication and American Social Thought*.

28. Wirth, "Consensus and Mass Communication," 10 (subsequent page references in text). For a fine commentary on Wirth's lecture, see Rothenbuhler, "Community and Pluralism."

29. Simpson, *Science of Coercion*.

30. Nordenstreng, "Institutional Networking."

31. The most important internal critique from within American sociology was Katz and Lazarsfeld, *Personal Influence* (1955), on which see Simonson, ed., *Politics, Social Networks*. The international history of the field has yet to be pieced together; for a start see the entries on "Communication as an Academic Field" in Donsbach, ed., *International Encyclopedia of Communication*, II, 591–645, 675–88, 757–71.

32. Ford, "Is There Mass Communication?" (1953).

33. Williams, *Culture and Society*, 301.

34. Recently, Paddy Scannell confessed, "I had avoided reading American mass communication sociology for at least 30 years because I thought it was boring uncritical 'mindless' empiricism. That was the received wisdom in Britain when I first began teaching 'media studies' in the mid-1970s" (*Media and Communication*, 71).

35. Carey, "Mass Communication and Cultural Studies" (1977), in *Communication as Culture*, 40.

36. Chaffee and Metzger, "The End of Mass Communication?" (2001).

37. On definition as a means of rhetorical invention (one of "the 'places' of argu-

ment"), see Quintilian, *Institutio Oratoria*, V.x.20, 54–64, which lays out two of the definitional methods I draw upon in the next several pages—etymology and genus/species. See also Perelman and Olbrechts-Tyteca, *New Rhetoric*, 210–14.

38. John Carey, *Intellectuals and the Masses*, 217.

39. For Marx and Engels's take on scattered and assembled masses, see "Manifesto of the Communist Party," 480–84. Note also claims about developments in communication, e.g., "the improved means of communication that are created by modern industry and that place the workers of different localities in contact with one another" (481; see also 475–477).

40. Scannell, *"Personal Influence and the End of the Masses."*

41. "[W]hen you give a banquet, invite the poor, the crippled, the lame, and the blind," Jesus proclaims in the Gospel of Luke (14:13), as part of a broader teaching and parable of the banquet (14:1–24).

42. Carey, "A Cultural Approach to Communication," in *Communication as Culture*, 13–34.

43. Cf. Peters's typology in "Witnessing," 721.

44. On imitation, see Leff, "Hermeneutical Rhetoric," 199–204.

45. Simonson, "Writing Figures into the Field."

46. Mills, *Sociological Imagination*, 4.

47. McKeon, "Creativity and the Commonplace," in *Rhetoric*, 33. For good introductions with bibliographies to the concept of *topoi*, see Jasinski, *Sourcebook on Rhetoric*, 578–82; and Bloomer, "Topics"; see also Eberly's extension in *Citizen Critics*, 3–6.

Chapter 2. Paul's Communicative Figure

1. Boyarin, *Radical Jew*.

2. Chilton, *Rabbi Paul*, 104; Freed, "Christian."

3. For a good brief summary of Paul's beliefs about the impending coming of the Lord, see Sanders, *Paul*, 32–40.

4. Gasque, "Tarsus"; Roetzel, *Paul*, 12–14; Murphy-O'Connor, *Paul*, 32–46; Chilton, *Rabbi Paul*, 3–8. The "licentious Phoenicians" quote comes from a second-century-c.e. text by Dio Chrysostom and is quoted in Murphy-O'Connor, *Paul*, 33–34.

5. Chilton, *Rabbi Paul*, 28.

6. Roetzel, *Paul*, 17; Meeks, *First Urban Christians*, 9–50; Wallace and Williams, *Three Worlds of Paul*, 95–116.

7. On Tarku and other pagan aspects of Tarsus, see Chilton, *Rabbi Paul*, 9–12.

8. Slezkine, *Jewish Century*, 7–8.

9. Morris, *Jewish School*, 42–63, 71–74, 80–83. The Talmudic "age of training" saying is quoted on 59.

10. Quoted in Morris, *Jewish School*, 125, 129. For complementary discussions, see Yates, *Art of Memory*; and Ong, *Orality and Literacy*, esp. 33–36, 58–68, 141–47.

11. Morris, *Jewish School*, 131–45.

12. *Geography* 14.5.13, quoted in Chilton, *Rabbi Paul*, 24. The discussion of Athenodorus of Tarsus occurs in ibid., 22–24.

13. An account found in Philostratus's *Life of Apollonius of Tyana* and recounted in Gasque, "Tarsus," 334.

14. See, e.g., Hock, "Paul and Greco-Roman Education"; and Murphy-O'Connor, *Paul*, 49–51.

15. For good entries into discussions of rhetorical technique in Paul's letters, see two recent collections: Sampley, ed., *Paul in the Greco-Roman World*, esp. Chs. 4, 5, 7, 8, 10, and 15; and Eriksson, Olbricht, and Übelacker, eds., *Rhetorical Argumentation in Biblical Texts*, Chs. 13–21. Other studies I have benefited from include Ramsaran, *Liberating Words*; Martin, *Corinthian Body*, 55–68; Hughes, *Early Christian Rhetoric*; Fiorenza, "Rhetorical Situation and Historical Reconstruction"; Kennedy, *New Testament Interpretation*; and Judge, "Paul's Boasting."

16. Morgan, *Literate Education*, 196–97. Drawing upon evidence from papyri, Morgan nicely describes the *progymnasmata* on 198–225.

17. "[W]idely (though not universally) regarded as the culmination of *enkyklios paideia*"—the Greco-Roman "rounded education"—rhetoric was promoted by its many admirers as that art that separates those who know it from those who do not, the latter groups "identified variously as barbarians, peasants, slaves, illiterates, children and women" (Morgan, *Literate Education*, 190, 235). On the social status of rhetoric and rhetorical education, see also Martin, *Corinthian Body*, 47–52.

18. Martin, *Corinthian Body*, 49.

19. Vos, "'Weaker Argument'"; see also Given, *Paul's True Rhetoric*; for Paul's reversals of wisdom and foolishness, see 1 Cor. 1:18–2.14, 3.19, 4.10.

20. Anthony J. Saldarini, "Pharisees," *Anchor Bible Dictionary*, Vol. 5, "Pharisees," 294, 300–303. According to Josephus, the Pharisees were a group "priding itself on its adherence to ancestral custom and claiming to observe the laws of which the Deity approves" (*Jewish Antiquities* 17 §41, quoted in Saldarini, "Pharisees," 293).

21. For a discussion of Paul's interpretation and use of Hebrew Scripture, see Hays, *Echoes of Scripture*; for a rhetorical take on Paul's use of quotations, see Stanley, *Arguing With Scripture*.

22. Chilton, *Rabbi Paul*, 48.

23. Betz, "Apostle"; and Roetzel, *Paul*, 46.

24. Žižek, *Puppet and Dwarf*, 10. Žižek sees Paul's outsider status as a fundamental condition for Paul's particular formulation of the faith. The classic discussion of charismatic authority is Weber, *Economy and Society*, 212–51, 952–55, 1111–56.

25. Of the fourteen letters declared authentic near the end of the fourth century and included in the Western biblical canon, the seven generally agreed to be authentic today are Romans, 1 and 2 Corinthians, Galatians, 1 Thessalonians, Philippians, and Philemon. For a discussion of the other seven, see Collins, *Letters That Paul Did Not Write*.

26. Cf. Orr and Walther, *First Corinthians*, 101, which argues that Paul made a case

for his apostleship based on God revealing his son "in" Paul, not "to" him, based on their reading of the Greek preposition *en*.

27. According to Roetzel, third-century Pseudo-Clementine Homilies "reveal an earlier tradition profoundly critical of the claim by Paul to be called by revelation of Christ to be an apostle" (*Paul*, 50).

28. Slezkine, *Jewish Century*, 4–39.

29. Chilton, *Rabbi Paul*, 87, 277 fn. 6; and Meinardus, *St. Paul in Greece*, 49. The image of agora loafer sits uneasily with the picture of a hard-working, embattled apostle that emerges from Paul's letters—and applies far better to Walt Whitman, as I discuss in the next chapter.

30. Peters, *Speaking into the Air*, 51–62. The parable is found in Matthew 13:4–23, Mark 4:1–20, and Luke 8:4–15.

31. This was one of the things that Charles Horton Cooley did not like about the Apostle. "The pure doctrine of Christ was and is for a few fine and pure minds," Cooley wrote in his journal. "Paul and the rest made it popular by tricking it out with superstition" (Charles Horton Cooley, Journals, July 30, 1903 [Vol. 17, 7], CHC Papers).

32. Schoeps, *Paul*, 220–21.

33. Dietary regimes made shopping in markets and eating at banquets difficult, while having one's penis cut as an adult (instead of an eight-day-old) was not a popular idea either. The relative lack of appeal of these rules helped create a category of God-fearers, Gentiles who had renounced polytheism, attended synagogues, and worshipped Israel's God, but who did not fully abide by laws about the cutting of the penis and the eating of the meats (Frend, *Rise of Christianity*, 91–93; Stark, *One True God*, 52–60). For a probing ethical discussion of Paul's position on meats, see Peters, *Courting the Abyss*, 36–45.

34. Meeks, *First Urban Christians*, 40–50; Hock, *Social Context*, 27–29; Rapske, "Christians and the Roman Empire"; Chilton, *Rabbi Paul*, 147–62. For a series of careful interpretations of Paul's travels cued by all available biblical texts (including Acts and the inauthentic Pauline letters), see Meinardus's three studies, *St. Paul in Greece*, *St. Paul in Ephesus*, and *St. Paul's Last Journey*. For a more recent and critical study of the same, see Dassmann, "Archaeological Traces."

35. Wallace and Williams, *Three Worlds*, 15–18; Meeks, *First Urban Christians*, 16–18; Murphy-O'Connor, *Paul*, 96–101; Riesner, *Paul's Early Period*, 307–17; Chilton, *Rabbi Paul*, 66–69. For a more extensive discussion of ancient travel, see Casson, *Travel in the Ancient World*.

36. Hock, *Social Context*, 20–25, 33–34.

37. Acts 18:1–3; Murphy-O'Connor, *Paul*, 85–89, 258–64. On the Isthmian Games held in Corinth, see Rothaus, *Corinth*, 84–92.

38. A living situation that may have been less than ideal for those who furnished the hospitality and perhaps motivated this useful rule of thumb recorded by the second century *Didache*: "Let every Apostle who comes to you be received as to the

Lord, but let him not stay more than one day, or if need be a second as well; but if he stay three days, he is a false prophet. And when an Apostle goes forth let him accept nothing but bread till he reach his night's lodging; but if he ask for money, he is a false prophet" (*Didache* 11:4–6, as excerpted in Harding, ed., *Christian Life and Thought*, 314).

39. Meeks, *First Urban Christians*, 29–32.

40. It is worth remembering that the same word, *pistis*, describes the end of both rhetoric, according to Aristotle, and religion according to Paul; on which see Kinneavy, *Greek Rhetorical Origins*.

41. Garland, *Daily Life*, 26.

42. This description of typical features of agoras is based on descriptions in the nine New Testament gospel passages that reference them (Matt. 11:16, 20:3, 23:7; Mark 7:4, 12:38; Luke 7:32, 11:43, 20:46; John 5:2), as well as Engels, *Roman* Corinth, 12–14; and Winter, *Philo and Paul*, 127–29. For a fine ideal-typical description of the sophistic performance of rhetoric, see Poulakos, *Sophistical Rhetoric*, 53–73.

43. Roetzel, *Paul*, 55.

44. Ibid., 64–68; see also Dodd, *Apostolic Preaching*.

45. See also Acts 16:19–22, where Paul and Silas are followed for "many days" by a slave woman who constantly shouted, "These men are the servants of the most high God." Paul apparently grew tired of it and commanded the spirit—which was also allowing her to divine the future—to leave her body. Her masters weren't happy about it (they had been making money out of the deal) and took the men to court at an agora where a mob joined in as well. This is I think a parable about fans who stalk celebrities, though a good friend thinks it's more about "Hollywood agents battening off the weird charisma of their talent."

46. The synagogue was nowhere explicitly referenced by Paul, but referring in the New Testament both to the building (Luke 7:5) and the group that worshipped there (Acts 6:9).

47. For a brief but insightful sociological analysis of the potential receptivity of the God-fearers, see Theissen, *Social Setting*, 102–06.

48. In addition to the conversions, healings, and mob frenzies brought about through his speech, Paul also has a narcotizing effect on at least one listener in Acts, though in the end the speaker saves the day. Gathering with fellow believers to break bread, Paul started talking and "continued speaking until midnight. . . . A young man named Eutychus [Lucky], who was sitting in the window, began to sink off into a deep sleep while Paul talked still longer. Overcome by sleep, he fell to the ground three floors below and was picked up dead." Paul went downstairs, found (or made) him to be alive, then returned to continue talking until dawn (Acts 20:7–12). This seems to me a cautionary tale to the long-winded, especially those with limited healing powers.

49. Fredriksen, *Jesus to Christ*, 154.

50. Stegemann and Stegemann, *Jesus Movement*, 51–73, 262–63, 274–77; Lang, *Sa-*

cred Games: A History of Christian Worship, 372–78; Frend, *Rise of Christianity*, 30–43; and Meeks, *First Urban Christians*, 29–31, 75.

51. Theissen, *Social Setting*, 70–96, 137–40; Meeks, *First Urban Christians*, 67–72. On membership of women in the early ekklesiae, see MacDonald, *Early Christian Women*; Stegemann and Stegemann, *Jesus Movement*, 389–407.

52. Murphy-O'Connor, "House-Churches," 134–36; Theissen, *Social Setting*, 145–74; Meeks, *First Urban Christians*, 157–62. Murphy-O'Connor suggests that there may have also been a shortage of space in the house-church, causing part of the group to be relegated to an outer courtyard while favored members dined and reclined inside (ibid., 129–34).

53. I am referring to 1 Cor. 13 (love is patient, kind, not arrogant or rude . . .) and not to two lesser-quoted passages that actually refer to marriage explicitly: "those who marry will experience distress in this life" (7:28); and "he who marries his fiancée does well; and he who refrains from marriage will do better" (7:38).

54. As Paul J. Achtemeier writes, "Dictation was recommended over writing in one's own hand by Dio Chrysostom (*Discourse 18* 18), and famous people, we are told, were regularly accompanied by a slave prepared at any time to take dictation, whether on horseback, in chariot or sedan chair (Pliny *Letters* 3.5), or at leisure in the baths (*Letters* 3.5)"("Omne," 13).

55. "See what large letters I make when I am writing in my own hand!" he told the Galatians (Gal. 6:11), apparently contrasting his scribal technique with his secretary's more practiced hand.

56. Richards, *Secretary*, esp. 189, 195.

57. On the concord speech, see Martin, *Corinthian Body*, 38–47, who draws partly from Mitchell, *Paul and the Rhetoric of Reconciliation*.

58. Poster, "Economy of Letter," 112–24; and Roetzel, *Paul*, 69–92.

59. Hughes, *Early Christian Rhetoric*, 19–50; and Kennedy, *New Testament*, 86–87.

60. On *grammatophoroi*, see Epp, "New Testament Papyrus"; and Bruce M. Metzger and Roland E. Murphy, "Letters/Epistles in the New Testament," *New Oxford Annotated Bible*, 204–207.

61. Dio Chrysostom, quoted in Engels, *Roman Corinth*, 231, fn. 78; and Aelius Aristiedes, *Orations* 46.24, quoted in Murphy-O'Connor, *Paul*, 109.

62. Chilton, *Rabbi Paul*, 175–76; Engels, *Roman Corinth*, 8–13, 43–48, 92–107; Meeks, *First Urban Christians*, 9–50; Theissen, *Social Setting*, 99–102; and Murphy-O'Connor, *Paul*, 108–9.

63. Working from Acts 15:30 ("When they gathered the congregation together, they delivered the letter") and following a point first made to me by Glenn Holland; see also Shiner, *Proclaiming the Gospel*.

64. For a stimulating discussion of Paul's letter and other New Testament rhetoric as a discourse of the opportune moment (*kairos*), with everything that implies, see Sullivan, "Kairos and the Rhetoric of Belief."

65. Using the Stephens 1550 Textus Receptus for the Greek, and Young's Literal Translation of 1 Cor. 10, as found on the online Parallel Greek New Testament (http://www.greeknewtestament.com/B46C001.htm; accessed June 4, 2008), which is part of the outstanding HTML Bible Web site (htmlbible.com).

66. Fredriksen, *Jesus to Christ*, 115. On the Nazarene banquet, see also see Feeley-Harnik, *Lord's Table*; and Stegemann and Stegemann, *Jesus Movement*, 268–71, 281–84.

67. On sectarian status: "God has appointed in the church [ekklesia] first Apostles, second prophets, third teachers; then deeds of power, then gifts of healing, forms of assistance, forms of leadership, various kinds of tongues" (12:28)—a hierarchy from which he arguably pulls back in Romans (12:3–8), a later letter. On patriarchy: "I want you to understand that Christ is the head of every man, and the husband is the head of his wife, and God is the head of Christ" (11:3), though the letter goes on to complicate that hierarchy in much the same way that it complicates the hierarchy of honor among parts of the body (11:11–12). On Paul's "rhetorical strategy of status reversal" in 1 Corinthians, see Martin, *Corinthian Body*, 69–103.

68. "Pauline blindness does not alter social hierarchies," John Durham Peters writes, "but it also does not reproduce them. It renders them momentarily irrelevant, putting them into a state of sabbatical cessation. This is the messianic option dwelling in any moment of social interaction" (*Courting the Abyss*, 261).

69. That the image had Stoic use is well known, but there was also a Jewish tradition, active in the first century, of understanding Diaspora Jews as far-flung members of Adam's body, with some peoples making up his hair, others his nose, ears, etc. Some rabbinic stories had Adam's body as originally traversing the universe but shrinking after the Fall to just 100 yards in size. Since Jesus was understood by believers as the second Adam, it would have been natural to apply these descriptions of his predecessor's body and its constitutive role with regard to its dispersed members (Davies, *Paul and Rabbinic Judaism*, 45).

70. Lang, *Sacred Games*, 372–83.

71. Cf. Rappaport, *Ritual and Religion*, 134–37, 151–52, 162–64.

72. "You yourselves are our letter, written on [y]our hearts, to be known and read by all; and you show that you are a letter of Christ, prepared by us, written not with ink but with the Spirit of the living God, not on tablets of stone but on tablets of human hearts" (2 Cor 3:2–3).

73. Haines-Etizen, *Guardians of Letters*.

74. Gamble, *Books and Readers*, 95–101; Collins, *Letters That Paul Did Not Write*, 69–75; Roetzel, *Paul*, 81–92; Richards, *Secretary*, 129–44.

75. Collins, *Letters that Paul Did Not Write*, esp. 82–87, 242–63. See also 69–82 for a lucid discussion of Jewish and Hellenistic precedents for writing letters and attributing them to earlier figures. The six letters are Ephesians, Colossians, 2 Thessalonians, 1–2 Timothy, and Titus. Hebrews is also traditionally attributed to Paul, but Collins sets it off because it does not explicitly lay claim to Pauline authorship.

76. An argument made in greater detail in Simonson, "Assembly, Rhetoric, and Widespread Community."

77. Kantorowicz, *King's Two Bodies.*

78. Badiou, *Saint Paul,* 98–106.

Chapter 3. Whitman's Polytheistic Mass

1. This would not always be the case, as Joli Jensen has shown in her critical study of Whitman's "Democratic Vistas" (1871), written by an older, crankier, and less idealistic man sobered by the Civil War. I disagree with her characterization of that rambling prose essay as "Whitman at his most Whitmanesque" and focus instead on the younger journalist and poet as a representative figure for democratic thinking and art (Jensen, *Is Art Good for Us?,* 31).

2. Merton's, ("Patterns of Influence").

3. I have been particularly influenced by Cmiel, "Whitman"; Reynolds, *Walt Whitman's America*; Kateb, "Whitman and the Culture of Democracy," in *The Inner Ocean,* 240–66; and Folsom, *Whitman's Native Representations,* and "What Do We Represent?"

4. Albion, "'Communication Revolution,'" which I discuss briefly in Ch. 1.

5. Loving, *Walt Whitman,* xi. Beyond Loving's wonderful study, biographies I have drawn upon include Reynolds, *Walt Whitman's America*; Rubin, *Historic Whitman*; Allen, *Solitary Singer*; Zweig, *Walt Whitman*; Krieg, *Whitman Chronology*; and Kaplan, *Whitman: A Life.*

6. See the notes from the trip he took with his father to West Hills on September 11, 1850, in Grier, ed., *Notebooks and Unpublished Prose Manuscripts* (NUPM) I, 4–7.

7. Reynolds, *Walt Whitman's America,* 8–15, 23–29; Rubin, *Historic Whitman,* 5–10; Kaplan, *Whitman: A Life,* 55–63; and Allen, *Solitary Singer,* 1–3.

8. Allen, *Solitary Singer,* 1–3.

9. Walt Whitman (hereafter WW), "Brooklyniana, No. 17" (1861), in Holloway, ed., *Uncollected Poetry and Prose* (UPP) II, 293.

10. WW in *PW 1892* II, 687–88. For Whitman's Brooklyn more generally, see Reynolds, *Walt Whitman's America,* 30–51, 107–10; Kaplan, *Whitman: A Life,* 95–113; Rubin, *Historic Whitman,* 13–23; and Allen, *Solitary Singer,* 4–29, 106–12.

11. UPP II, 256. "As good luck would have it," he wrote elsewhere, and perhaps with storyteller's license, "the writer of this series was one of those whom Lafayette took in his arms, and lifted down to be provided a standing place" (ibid., 284–85). On the episode, see Reynolds, *Walt Whitman's America,* 33–34; Rubin, *Historic Whitman,* 15–16; and Allen, *Solitary Singer,* 9.

12. UPP I, 293.

13. WW, "Democracy" (1867), quoted in Reynolds, *Walt Whitman's America,* 166–67.

14. Reynolds, *Walt Whitman's America,* 35–40, 166–75. Whitman portrayed Beecher in "Rev. Henry Ward Beecher," *Brooklyn Daily Advertiser* (1850), UPP I, 234–35. On

the transformation of language and oratory in the nineteenth century, see Cmiel, *Democratic Eloquence*; Antczak, *Thought and Character*; and Clark and Halloran, eds., *Oratorical Culture*.

15. Loving, *Walt Whitman*, 31–32; Reynolds, *Walt Whitman's America*, 34–35; Kaplan, *Whitman: A Life*, 57–63; Zweig, *Walt Whitman*, 144–46; and Allen, *Solitary Singer*, 9–11.

16. WW, "Specimen Days," 561; Reynolds, *Walt Whitman's America*, 40–44; Kaplan, *Whitman: A Life*, 71; and Loving, *Walt Whitman*, 32–33.

17. Rubin, *Historic Whitman*, 24–34 (quote at 24); and Loving, *Walt Whitman*, 33–36; Reynolds, *Walt Whitman's America*, 44–47; Greenspan, *Walt Whitman and the American Reader*, 39–44. For Whitman's own remembrances of working with the wooden press, see "Brooklyniana No. 6" (1861), in UPP II, 247–48.

18. Loving, *Walt Whitman*, 35.

19. WW, *Leaves of Grass: First Edition*, 95, 97. Subsequent references to this edition marked by parenthetical page numbers.

20. WW, "Specimen Days," 563.

21. Rubin, *Historic Whitman*, 29–31; Reynolds, *Walt Whitman's America*, 154–93; and Greenspan, *Walt Whitman and the American Reader*, 80.

22. Rubin, *Historic Whitman*, 34–36; and Loving, *Walt Whitman*, 36–39.

23. The literature on the development of American newspapers and journalism in the period is large. For a start, see Schudson, *Discovering the News*; Nerone, "Mythology of the Penny Press"; Baldasty, *Commercialization of News*; Nord, *Communities of Journalism*.

24. For a representative but admittedly incomplete list of critics who have written about Whitman's journalism, see the Preface to Bergman, Noverr, and Recchia, eds., *Collected Writings: The Journalism* (CWJ) I.

25. As Tom Lutz observes in his delightful history of loafers in America, the saunterer emerged as an Anglo-American figure in the mid-nineteenth century and appeared regularly from the 1860s on in a number of books and periodicals with titles like *A Saunter Through the West End* and *Saunterings in New England*. Like its French counterpart, the *flâneur*, the saunterer idled about city streets with "the time and sensitivity to make something quasi-artistic out of the purely mundane" (*Doing Nothing*, 155).

26. For an organized sampling of these sauntering-about stories, see Rubin and Brown, *Whitman and the New York Aurora*, Part I.

27. WW, "Life in New York," *Aurora*, March 14, 1842, CWJ I, 53–54.

28. A young printer for the *Aurora* remembered his editor arriving at the office between 11 and noon, looking briefly over the paper's exchanges, and then "strolling down Broadway to the Battery, spending an hour or two amid the trees and enjoying the water view" (William Cauldwell, in a 1901 letter on Whitman in the *New York Times*, reprinted in Rubin and Brown, *Whitman and the New York Aurora*, 140, fn. 28.

29. Ryan, *Civic Wars*, 27, 40.

30. WW, "Life in New York," *Aurora*, March 14, 1843, CWJ I, 53–54.

31. WW, "Our City," *Aurora*, March 8, 1842, CWJ I, 44–46.

32. WW, "An Hour in a Balcony," CWJ I, 66–67. The noise of the city led the journalist to write about its absence. "Silence?" he asked. "What can New York—noisy, roaring, rumbling, tumbling, bustling, stormy, turbulent New York—have to do with *silence*? . . . In our great metropolis, the only time that spirits of silence can properly call their own, is from about half past two until half past three o'clock in the morning. The whole city is then asleep" ("About Silence," *Aurora*, March 19, 1842, CWJ I, 61–62). On the concept of soundscape and a series of suggestive historical reconstructions of them, see Schaefer, *The Soundscape*.

33. WW, "Specimen Days," 564–65.

34. "We were both walkers," Whitman explained (quoted in Allen, *Solitary Singer*, 85).

35. WW, "City Intelligence: Fulton Street, Brooklyn" *Eagle*, June 4, 1846, CWJ I, 399–400.

36. WW, "An Hour Among Shipping," and "Stroll Along South Street," *Eagle*, March 9 and 16, 1846, CWJ I, 270–71, 285–86.

37. "We would that all the young fellows about Brooklyn were daily in the habit of spending an hour or two in some out-door game or recreation. The body and mind would both be benefited by it. There would be far fewer attenuated forms and shrunken limbs and pallid faces in our streets. The game of ball is glorious" (WW, "Brooklyn Young Men," *Eagle*, July 23, 1846, CWJ I, 477).

38. Loving, *Walt Whitman*, 103–4.

39. "A tolerably good German band, consisting of five persons, among whom is a female who plays the German flute, have recently commenced public business in our streets and discourse tolerably eloquent music. These peripatetic musicians manage to pick up (for a rarity) *less* 'kicks than coppers,' and are in a fair way to make money. The profession of street minstrelsy is getting somewhat overburdened, however" (WW, "City Intelligence: Public Serenades," *Eagle* July 24, 1846, CWJ I, 479–80).

40. A full-throated nationalist at the time, he approved of the war, glorified it with poetic prose, and supported annexation of Mexican territories. On the policy side of things, he favored annexation, particularly of the Yucatán, home to "the best and most industrious citizens in Mexico," for years on bad terms with the central government in Mexico City, and reportedly open to the idea ("Annexation," *Eagle*, June 6, 1846, CWJ I, 403–4). On the poetic side, he defended imperialism in terms of national superiority: "This republic—the richest nation on earth,—the fullest of means, of men, of *moral* power . . . the nation of nations" (May 19, 1846, "The Victory," ibid., 366–67); and with swashbuckling historic license: "The road to Mexico! We write the words with a thrill. . . . The road to Mexico! The phrase carries back our imagination more than three hundred years, to the time of the gallant but cruel Cortez. . . . We think of the Incas—of the earlier happiness and gentleness of their ill fated land. . . . The road to Mexico! how full of *wealth* is the sound" ("Vera Cruz—

and the Road to Mexico," June 8, 1846, ibid., 406). For brief discussions of Whitman and the Mexican War, see Allen, *Solitary Singer*, 82–87; Rubin, *Historic Whitman*, 142–49; and Kaplan, *Whitman: A Life*, 128–36.

41. The printer, William H. Sutton, is quoted in Bergman, Introduction, CWJ I, lxv.

42. Whitman read widely during his *Eagle* days and reviewed authors ranging from Milton to Thomas Carlyle and George Sand to American authors known and unknown, popular and higher-brow. "The number of lines the *Eagle* gave a book bore little relationship to its value in belles-lettres," Rubin observed three decades ago. "Acknowledged masters shared inches with farm manuals, treatises on the water cure, and advice for a happy life in a boarding house. Whitman remembered Rousseau for 'fascinating melancholy' and called Keats one of the pleasantest of poets, yet wrote at greater length about a cookbook in order to show Louisa Whitman's taste in pickling recipes" (*Historic Whitman*, 166).

43. WW, "The Oratorio of St. Paul," *Brooklyn Evening Star*, November 28, 1845, CWJ I 236–37.

44. See, e.g., the *Eagle* stories leading into the Fourth of 1846, in CWJ I, 426, 432, 453; see also "New York Amuses Itself—The Fourth of July" (1856), in Holloway and Adimari, eds., *New York Dissected*, 80–84.

45. Benjamin, "On Some Motifs in Baudelaire," in *Illuminations*, 174.

46. Poe, "The Man of the Crowd" (1840), in Levine and Levine, eds., *Short Fiction of Edgar Allen Poe*, 283–89; and Frank and Magistrale, *Poe Encyclopedia*, 218–19.

47. Benjamin, "Motifs in Baudelaire," in *Illuminations*, 172.

48. Baudelaire, "Crowds," in *Baudelaire in English*, 242–43.

49. See for instance Baudelaire, "Landscape," "To a Red-haired Beggar Girl," and "Dawn," in *Baudelaire in English*, 112–13, 114–16, 148–49. As Ross Chambers writes, "The alienation that most *flâneur* writing existed to exploit, to mitigate or to deny, is what [Baudelaire] persistently draws attention to, and he does so with an eye to pointing up what is pathological in the social reality it bespeaks" ("Baudelaire's Paris," in Lloyd, ed., *Cambridge Companion to Baudelaire*, 105).

50. Benjamin, "Motifs in Baudelaire," in *Illuminations*, 172; cf. Lutz's discussion of *flâneurs* and saunterers in *Doing Nothing*, 152–61.

51. He wrote stories for the *Aurora*, for instance, about Election Day hooliganism, intimidation, and violence by Irish gangs associated with Tammany Hall. "The indignation of large numbers of our citizens is roused to a pitch altogether ungovernable, against the insults and absolute trampling upon American citizenship, by the Catholics and the ignorant Irish," he wrote in a somewhat inflammatory tone for his nativist employers, just as mounted policemen and the army were being called in to quell disturbances ("Incidents of Last Night," *Aurora*, April 13, 1842, CWJ I, 114–15). For the most part, though, the crowds in his journalism and poetry are largely peaceable and celebrated, or at least portrayed in sympathetic light.

52. Whitman edited the paper from March 1846 to January 1848. For general discussions of Whitman and the *Eagle*, see Bergman's Introduction to CWJ I; Allen,

Solitary Singer, 73–91; Rubin, *Historic Whitman*, 139–80; Zweig, *Walt Whitman*, 25–57; and Reynolds, *Walt Whitman's America*, 113–27.

53. WW, "Ourselves and the 'Eagle,'" *Brooklyn Daily Eagle and Kings County Democrat*, June 1, 1846, CWJ I, 391–92.

54. E.g., "Without vanity, we can say that the *Aurora* is by far the best newspaper in the town" (WW, "The New York Press," *Aurora*, March 229, 1842, CWJ I, 81–82.

55. WW, "We," *Aurora*, April 9, 1842, CWJ I, 105–6.

56. WW, "[A Leisurely Day]," *Aurora*, April 6, 1842, CWJ I, 100–1; and "Snoring Made Music," *Aurora*, April 18, 1842, CWJ I, 125–26.

57. "The question whether or no there shall be slavery in the new territories which it seems conceded on all hands we are largely to get through this Mexican war, is a question between *the grand body of white workingmen, the millions of mechanics, farmers, and operatives of our country,* with their interests, on the one side—and the interests of the few thousand rich, 'polished,' and aristocratic owners of slaves at the south, on the other side" (WW, "American Workingmen *Versus* Slavery," *Eagle*, September 1, 1847, in UPP I, 171–74).

58. WW, "Starting Newspapers," *Specimen Days*, 749; Rubin, *Historic Whitman*, 181; and Loving, *Walt Whitman*, 114–16.

59. Loving, *Walt Whitman*, 114–40 (quote at 114). For other accounts of Whitman's time in New Orleans, see Allen, *Solitary Singer*, 91–100; Rubin, *Historic Whitman*, 181–205; Zweig, *Walt Whitman*, 58–78; and Kaplan, *Whitman: A Life*, 136–45.

60. Slavery had been outlawed in New York in 1828, when Whitman was nine.

61. WW, "The Worth of Liberty," *Eagle* December 10, 1847: 2, Brooklyn Daily Eagle Online, http://www.brooklynpubliclibrary.org/eagle.

62. Loving, *Walt Whitman*, 108–13 (quote at 112). Loving mistakenly identifies Giles's lecture as taking place on December 10, which was the day that Whitman's review of it was published. On Whitman, slavery, and the political crisis, see also Reynolds, *Walt Whitman's America*, 111–53; and Erkkila, *Political Poet*, 44–67.

63. WW, "Excerpts from a Traveller's Note Book [No.1]: Crossing the Alleghanies," *New Orleans Daily Crescent*, March 5, 1848, UPP I, 181–83.

64. WW, ibid., 183–86.

65. WW, "Excerpts from a Traveller's Note Book [No. 3]: Western Steamboats—The Ohio," *Daily Crescent*, March 10, 1848, UPP I, 186–89.

66. WW, "Western Steamboats," UPP I, 187–88.

67. WW, "Excerpts from a Traveller's Note Book [No. 2]: Cincinnati and Louisville," *Daily Crescent*, March 6, 1848, UPP I, 189–90; and Rubin, *Historic Whitman*, 184.

68. Rubin, *Historic Whitman*, 184–85; for a description of public space and culture in antebellum New Orleans, see Ryan, *Civic Wars*, 21–57.

69. Rubin, *Historic Whitman*, 185–201 (quote from Whitman at 200); Whitman, "New Orleans in 1848," *New Orleans Picayune*, January 25, 1887, *PW 1892*, II, 604–10; and Zweig, *Walt Whitman*, 68–71. Whitman published a poem about the revolutions in the *Crescent*, entitled "The Old World" (rpt. in Loving, *Walt Whitman*, 130–32).

70. Rubin, *Historic Whitman*, 190. In a post-1871 revision of an 1855 poem, Whit-

man would add the line, "For before the war I often go to the slave-mart and watch the sale." Whether this was an autobiographical statement or a poetic one is not clear ("I Sing the Body Electric" [1881], as reproduced in Bradley et al.) eds., *Leaves of Grass: A Textual Variorum of the Printed Poems* (hereafter *Variorum*) I.

71. Letter home from Jeff Whitman, March 14, 1848, quoted in Rubin, *Historic Whitman*, 193.

72. WW, "Wooding at Night," NUPM I, 84–85; "New Orleans in 1848," *New Orleans Picayune*, January 25, 1887, in *PW 1892*, II 607–10; Rubin, *Historic Whitman*, 204–205; Loving, *Walt Whitman*, 139–40.

73. Clark, *Rhetorical Landscapes*, 25.

74. Whitman's notebook writings are republished in Grier, NUPM, and WW, *Daybooks and Notebooks*. For dating of the notebooks, see NUPM I, 53–55, and White, "Earliest Known Notebook"; cf. Higgins, "Wage Slavery."

75. Grier, Introduction to NUPM I, xiii–xx (quote at xv). For Whitman's revisions of "Song of Myself," see Folsom's discussion and photographic reprints of the handwritten pages at http://bailiwick.lib.uiowa.edu/whitman/index.html (accessed August 21, 2006).

76. Hollis, *Language and Style*, 205.

77. See NUPM IV, 1436–44, 1554, and VI, 2221–44. For the contents of Whitman's Oratory sheath, see Finkel, "Whitman's Manuscript Notes on Oratory"; and Harned, "Walt Whitman and Oratory," in *Complete Writings* (CW) 8, 244–66 (inaccurate in some details). For a brief introduction to rhetorical commonplace books, see Moss, "Commonplaces and Commonplace Books," in Sloane, eds., *Encyclopedia of Rhetoric*, 119–24.

78. Bucke, CW 8, 254–55. For another variation on the image of the orator electrifying the audience, see Emerson, "Eloquence."

79. From an unnamed original source, in Bucke, CW 8, 251.

80. In Traubel, Bucke, and Harned, eds., *In Re*, 35.

81. "'Lectures' or 'Lessons,'" NUPM VI, 2234. See also "Walt Whitman's Lectures" [1858?], NUPM IV, 1436–39, which envisions his published poems and his lectures as "two co-expressions," "two athletic volumes, the first to speak for the Permanent Soul, . . . the second, temporary," both designed "to illustrate America—illustrate the whole, not merely sections, members—throbbing from the heart, inland, the West, around the great Lakes, the lowing Ohio, or Missouri, or Mississippi." Poetry addressed the permanent soul, oratory the temporary.

82. WW, "For Orations," NUPM VI, 2236.

83. Ibid., 2241–42. Punctuated as in original.

84. Hollis, *Language and Style*, 227; for a probing discussion of the oratorical elements in general, see idem, 36–64; in addition to Reynolds, *Walt Whitman's America*, 166–75.

85. Emerson, "Eloquence," 89.

86. Rubin, *Historic Whitman*, 305–10; Loving, *Walt Whitman*, 178–80; and Allen,

Solitary Singer, 147–51. Rubin links the "flesh is grass" verse from Isaiah to Whitman's prophecy in the prose preface, "Your very flesh shall be a poem" (306–7). Loving notes that when printers in Whitman's era had time on their hands, some would see how their handwritten creations "translated" to print layout. "Such casual amusement . . . produced what was known in the jargon of their trade as 'grass'—compositions of dubious value" (179).

87. WW, Preface, 1872, in Buell, ed., *Leaves of Grass and Select Prose*, 525–29 (quote at 527); and WW, "The Great Construction," June 1857, NUPM I, 353.

88. *Christian Spiritualist* (1856), rpt. in WW, *Leaves of Grass Imprints* (Boston: Thayer and Eldridge, 1860), 32–36, at Whitman Archive, http://www.whitmanarchive. org/criticism/reviews/index.html (accessed August 23, 2006).

89. *Boston Banner of Light 7* (June 2, 1860), 4, rpt. on the Whitman Archive, http:// www.whitmanarchive.org/criticism/reviews/leaves1860/anc.00037.html (accessed August 23, 2006).

90. *Christian Examiner 60* (1856), 471–73, at Whitman Archive, http://www.whit-manarchive.org/criticism/reviews/index.html (accessed August 23. 2006). The friend was Helen Price, who knew Whitman in Brooklyn; she is quoted in Reynolds, *Walt Whitman's America*, 252.

91. WW, "Proto-Leaf," *Leaves of Grass*, 1860 facsimile text, 11, 13. On Whitman's disciples, see Robertson, *Worshipping Walt*.

92. In a conversation with Horace Traubel, April 2, 1888, recounted in Traubel, *With Walt Whitman in Camden*, Vol. I (1906), 10, available at the Whitman Archives, through the Traubel link on "Whitman's Disciples," http://www.whitmanarchive.org/ disciples/ (accessed August 23, 2006).

93. Robertson, *Worshipping Walt*, 10.

94. For a magnificent reconstruction of the nineteenth-century cultural currents absorbed into Whitman's poetry, see Reynolds, *Walt Whitman's America*.

95. Rieff, "The Impossible Culture: Wilde as a Modern Prophet," in *The Feeling Intellect*, 286.

96. WW, "The New Theologies," n.d. [pre-1855], NUPM VI, 2043; cf. the revisions of this quote in the 1855 Preface (LG [1855] 2005, 14–15), and the 1856 "Poem of Many in One" (*Variorum* I, 191)—later renamed "Chants Democratic I" (1860), "As I Sat Alone by Blue Ontario's Shore" (1867–71), and from 1876 on "By Blue Ontario's Shore."

97. "Poem of Many in One" (1856), *Variorum* I, 191. Reynolds calls the poem, which arose from the 1855 Preface, "Whitman's definitive social statement" (Reynolds, *Walt Whitman's America*, 359). I discuss it at some length in "A Rhetoric for Polytheistic Democracy."

98. WW, "Religions—Gods," n.d. NUPM VI, 2024–26 (all punctuation and spelling as found in the original entry); cf. the list of gods in the poem that became "Song of Myself" (LG [1855] 2005, 80–81).

99. WW, LG [1855] 2005, 80–81, 84–85. Subsequent quotations followed by a number refer to pages in this edition. The quote appears in the poem that would become

"Poem of Walt Whitman, an American" (1856), "WALT WHITMAN" (1860–71), and from 1876 on "Song of Myself."

100. For stimulating accounts of the Protagorean concept of *dissoi logoi*, see Schiappa, *Protagoras and Logos*, 89–102; and Billig, *Arguing and Thinking*.

101. Preface, 1872, in *PW 1892*, II, 463.

102. WW, "Poem of Many in One" (1856), *Variorum* I, 194–95; cf. the 1855 Preface (LG [1855] 2005), 7–8, 24.

103. "Poem of Many in One" (1856), *Variorum* I, 194–95, 198 ("By Blue Ontario's Shore," Stanza 6).

104. "albot [*sic*] Wilson," n.d. [ca. 1847–54], NUPM I, 70.

105. "The Eighteenth Presidency" (1856), NUPM VI, 2126. For contexts of political disenchantment and cynicism in the era, see Altschuler and Blumin, *Rude Republic*.

106. "The Eighteenth Presidency," NUPM VI, 2120.

107. "Restrain Gesture," n.d, NUPM VI, 2234.

108. Erkkila, *Political Poet*.

109. "Democratic Vistas" (1871), in Buell, ed. *Leaves of Grass and Selected Prose*, 492.

110. Loving, *Walt Whitman*, 141.

111. WW, "To the Prevailing Bards" [1859?], NUPM I, 410; cf. Preface, LG [1855] 2005, 27.

112. "Walt Whitman and His Poems," *United States Review 5* (September 1855), 205–12; and "Walt Whitman, a Brooklyn Boy," *Brooklyn Daily Times*, September 29, 1855, 2, both reproduced on the Whitman Archive, http://www.whitmanarchive.org/criticism/reviews/index.html (accessed August 23, 2006).

113. Loving, *Walt Whitman*, 183–94, 209–14; WW, "Letter to Ralph Waldo Emerson," LG 1856, 346–58, reproduced on the Whitman Archive, http://www.whitmanarchive.org/works/leaves/index.html (accessed August 23, 2006).

114. Rpt. in Brasher, *Whitman as Editor*, 42.

115. *Boston Banner of Light 7* (June 2, 1860), reproduced on The Walt Whitman Archive, http://www.whitmanarchive.org/criticism/reviews/leaves1860/anc.00037.html.

116. Crowe, "Complacency and Concern," 76–77, 180.

117. James, "The Will to Believe," in *Writings, 1878–1899*, 505, 512.

118. James, "On a Certain Blindness in Human Beings," *Writings 1878–1899*, 851.

119. "Poem of Many in One" (1856), *Variorum* I, 194 ("By Blue Ontario's Shore," Stanza 5).

120. This mood, in the poem that became "Faces," was immediately preceded by one marked by something other than complacency, when the poet sees other faces he passes on the street as a dog sniffing for garbage, a home for snakes, and food for vermin and worms (138–39).

121. "Poem of the Last Explanation of Prudence" (1856), *Variorum* I, 244 ("Song of Prudence").

122. "Calamus 41" (1860), *Variorum* II, 405 ("Among the Multitude").

123. WW. "Letters from a Travelling Bachelor VII," *New York Sunday Dispatch*, November 11, 1849, in Rubin, *Historic Whitman*, 337.

124. Loving, "'Broadway, the Magnificent!'" 211.

125. "Poem of the Road" (1856), *Variorum* I, 227 ("Song of the Open Road," Stanza 3).

126. "Sun-Down Poem" (1856), *Variorum* I, 217–18).

127. *Christian Spiritualist* (1856), rpt. in WW, *Leaves of Grass Imprints* (Boston: Thayer and Eldridge, 1860), 32–36, at Whitman Archive, http://www.whitmanarchive.org/criticism/reviews/index.html (accessed August 23, 2006).

128. Sloane, *On the Contrary*, 57.

129. Hartnett, *Democratic Dissent*, 162.

130. Preface, 1872, in *PW 1892*, II, 463.

131. "Chants Democratic 16" (1860), *Variorum* II, 312 ("Mediums").

132. Huck Gutman, "Drum-Taps," in LeMaster and Kummings, eds., *Whitman: An Encyclopedia*.

133. Krieg, *Whitman Chronology*, 40–179; WW, NUPM III, 1028–49; and Eitner, *Whitman's Western Jaunt*.

134. Nelson, "Richard Maurice Bucke," in LeMaster and Kummings, eds., *Whitman: An Encyclopedia* (New York: Garland, 1998), and reproduced at the Whitman Archive, "Whitman's Disciples," http://www.whitmanarchive.org/disciples/ (accessed August 23, 2006).

135. James, "Varieties of Religious Experience," in *Writings 1902–1910*, 82–85, 452 fn. 6; idem, "On a Certain Blindness in Human Beings," in *Writings 1878–1899*, 851; and Ross, in a chapter on "social religion" in *Social Control*, 213. James also featured Whitman in "The Sentiment of Rationality" (1880) and "Is Life Worth Living?" (1895), both in *Writings 1878–1899*; and he opened the last of his *Pragmatism* lectures, "Pragmatism and Religion" (1907) with a long reading from Whitman's early poem, "To You" (pub. 1856), in which he found a vivid and congenial description of pluralism and the pragmatic temper (*Writings 1902–1910*, 606–9). On the Whitman cult, see Robertson, *Worshipping Walt*.

136. Loving, *Walt Whitman*, 414–17.

137. Cooley, *Social Organization*, 195. Cooley also called Whitman, along with Emerson and Thoreau, "men of signal distinction" (ibid., 176) and quoted a number of lines from his 1884 edition: "'All this I swallow, it tastes good, I like it well, it becomes mine; I am the man, I suffered, I was there.' 'Whoever degrades another degrades me.' 'By God! I will accept nothing which all cannot have their counterpart of on the same terms.' 'I believe the main purport of these states is to found a superb friendship, exalté, previously unknown'" (195–96). And, in a discussion of conflict among classes later in the book, Cooley writes, "'I do not call one greater and one smaller,' says Whitman, 'that which fills its period and place is equal to any'" (303).

138. Cooley, "Art and Social Idealism," in *Social Process*, 415.

139. Cooley, *Human Nature and Social Order*, 192.

140. A phrase found in Cooley, *Human Nature and Social Order*, 147.

141. For an illuminating discussion of poetry as "a creation which reveals, or as a revelation which at the same time defines and completes what it makes manifest," as that idea played out in the post-Romantic and modernist eras, see Taylor, *Sources of the Self*, 419–93.

142. Williams, *Culture and Society*, 300. Whitman is mostly absent in Schnapp and Tiews, eds., *Crowds*, which picks up its thread from Le Bon onward, save Michael Hardt's fine "Bathing in the Multitude" (35–40), which finds "the political feeling of love" that can occur at great demonstrations and links it to Whitman's stranger love (38).

143. "Sun-Down Poem" (1856), *Variorum* I, 225. For a stimulating contemporary essay on the subject, see Jackson, *Becoming Native to this Place*.

Chapter 4. Cooley's Transcendentalist Quest

1. Jandy, *Charles Horton Cooley*, 16.

2. The best short introductions to Cooley and his thought are Quandt, *Small Town to the Great Community*, 51–66; Coser, *Masters of Sociological Thought*, 305–30; Czitrom, *Media and the American Mind*, 91–112; and Schubert, "Introduction" to Cooley, *On Self and Social Organization*, 1–31. See also Schubert's fine "Foundations of Pragmatic Sociology," which among other things refutes Mead's influential early account; "Cooley's Contribution to American Social Thought" (on which, see also Jacobs, "Influence and Canonical Supremacy"); and Schubert, *Democratische Iden-titität*. The most complete English-language studies of Cooley's thought and life are Jacobs, *Charles Horton Cooley*, and Jandy, *Charles Horton Cooley*. For an index of Cooley's significance among leading American sociologists in the mid-1960s, see Reiss, ed., *Cooley and Sociological Analysis*, which includes articles by Talcott Parsons on internalization and Phillip Rieff on culture. Rieff wrote erudite introductions for republications of Cooley's *Social Organization* (1962) and *Human Nature and the Social Order* (1964), republished with the culture essay in *Feeling Intellect*, 294–320; see also the thoughtful chapter on Cooley and his father, Thomas McIntyre Cooley, in Sklansky, *Soul's Economy*, 205–24.

3. Czitrom, *Media and the American Mind*, 91; and Ross, *Origins of American Social Science*, 241, fn. 55.

4. Carey, "A Cultural Approach to Communication" (1975), in *Communication as Culture*, 13; see also Pooley, "Czitrom, Carey, and the Chicago School."

5. Schiller, *Theorizing Communication*, 60. Cooley actually wrote that "modern democracy as a historical current is apparently traceable back to the village community life of the Teutonic tribes of northern Europe, from which it descends through English constitutional liberty and the American and French revolutions to its broad and deep channels of the nineteenth and twentieth centuries" (*Social Organization*, 51).

6. Peters, *Speaking into the Air*, 184–88.

7. Cooley (hereafter, CHC), "On Autobiographies" and "The Plasticity of Human Nature," in *On Self and Social Organization*, quotes at 39 and 77.

8. Adorno, *Minima Moralia*, 156.

9. CHC, "Some Teachings of Emerson" (1887), in *On Self and Social Organization*, 35.

10. For the Emersonian Cooley, see Schubert, "Introduction," 3–7; Jacobs, *Charles Horton Cooley*, 153–59 et passim; Schwartz, "Emerson, Cooley, and the American Heroic Vision"; and Noble, "Transcendentalism of Social Science," in Noble, *The Paradox of Progressive Thought*, 103–24. Jacobs argues, "Emerson the man and Emerson's *writing*—its textual form and content—*both* definitively shaped Cooley's work on the self and other ideas; social psychologically via his internalization of Emerson as, to borrow Cooley's concept, a personal idea; and from the standpoint of the myriad ways in which style and the ideas embedded in these texts shaped Cooley's own texts" (*Charles Horton Cooley*, 154–55).

11. The earliest references to communication I have found in Dewey appear within pedagogical writings in an unpublished 1895 paper, "Plan of Organization of the University Primary School" (Dewey, *Early Works*, Vol. 5, 224–243); cf. Czitrom, *Media and the American Mind*, 112. The key Dewey books discussing communication are *Democracy and Education* (1916), *Experience and Nature* (1925), *Public and Its Problems* (1927), and *Art as Experience* (1934).

12. Quandt, "Charles Horton Cooley and the Communications Revolution," *Small Town to Great Community*, 51–66; see also her fine "Mary Parker Follett and Face-to-Face Communication," at 36–51; as well as Jacobs, *Charles Horton Cooley*, 106–29.

13. Thomas Macintyre Cooley (TMC), with John Greenleaf Whittier in mind in "The Next Generation" (1851), qtd. In Jones, *Constitutional Conservatism*, 45–46.

14. Jones, *Constitutional Conservatism*, 5–46, 122–40; Jacobs, *Law Writers and the Courts*, 209–15; Sklansky, *The Soul's Economy*, 209–15; and CHC, biographical sketch of his father, Journals, Vol. 6 (1895), 1–3. Thomas Cooley's work dictum comes from Thomas Carlyle's *Past and Present* (1843) and is quoted by Jones on p. 95. On the basis of a reputation established in *Constitutional Procedures*, James Bryce sent draft chapters of his *American Commonwealth* for Judge Cooley to comment upon.

15. TMC to CHC, January 4, 1872, Box 1, Charles Horton Cooley Papers (hereafter CHCP), Bentley Historical Library, University of Michigan.

16. TMC to CHC, February 16, 1873, Box 1, CHCP. See also travel letters to Charles from his father from Elmira, New York (May 3, 1877), Richmond, Virginia (May 18, 1879), Chattanooga, Tennessee (July 3, 5, and 6, 1885), and Jupiter and Ponce, Florida (February 13 and 19, 1894)—all Box 1, CHCP.

17. Dibble, "Young Charles Cooley," 7.

18. CHC Journals, Vol. 10, p. 4 (July 21, 1895), collected with the CHCP at the Bentley Historical Library [and available on microfilm]; subsequent references to the journals will be by volume, page, and date of writing.

19. Unnumbered Journals, 1, 2 (1882, n.d.).

20. "I have found that the best plan for getting up a subject for discussion is this. First of all consider all you already know about the question and all possible arguments on each side. Second, read until you feel yourself complete master of all pertinent facts. Third, still without taking up the pen, run over your speech in your head arranging the arguments and composing a forcible expression for each thought. 4th write it out polishing the language to the highest point you know how to. 5th, read over what you have written and then go over it with your mind introducing the connections you have made. 6th lay the subject aside until about 15 minutes before you speak; then run over the main points in your head. 7th get up and do the very best you can" (Unnumbered Journals [March 1, 1882], 50–51).

21. Unnumbered Journals (March 6, 1882), 53. See also Journals, Vol. 10 (July 21, 1895), 8.

22. For Cooley's American travels, see Jandy, *Charles Horton Cooley*, 19–21; Dibble, "Young Charles Horton Cooley," 8–15; and the letters between him and his parents (April 21 and 23, and May 20, 1882) and confession to his mother (July 1, 1882), Box 1, CHCP.

23. For the European travels, see Jandy, *Charles Horton Cooley*, 22–26; letters from CHC to his family, January 17 and 23, 1884, Box 1, CHCP.

24. Jandy, *Charles Horton Cooley*, 32–33; and Coser, *Masters of Sociological Thought*, 314–16.

25. Journals, 1887–18, n.d., 48–49. In addition to ten classes in engineering and drawing, Cooley also completed three classes in Greek, five in Latin, three in French, two in German, two in English, five in mathematics, five in history, and others in philosophy, political economy, physics, and chemistry (Jandy, *Charles Horton Cooley*, 27).

26. Journals, 1887–88, n.d., 62.

27. TMC to CHC, March 18, 1889, Box 1, CHCP. The judge's spelling of his son's name varied.

28. Using language that would be used for mass media like radio and television 50 years later, Judge Cooley wrote that railroads had "immense possibilities for evil as well as good," that the power of railroad managers was "certain to be more or less abused," and that railroad commissions should "be made the convenient and accommodating servant of the public, existing to do its will." (Jones, *Constitutional Conservatism*, 295–300). Railroad figures appear in John F. Stover, "Railroads," in Foner and Garraty, eds., *Reader's Companion*, 906–10.

29. CHC, "Social Significance of Street Railways," 71–73. Beyond that publication, Cooley also wrote a section of the ICC's Third Annual Report, "Federal Regulation of Safety Appliances," and a monograph published by the Census Bureau, "Statistics of Street Railways in the United States" (Jandy, *Charles Horton Cooley*, 31–32).

30. Ward had addressed communication as a social necessity that "contributed to the substantial benefit and true progress of man" in the earliest discussion of the subject I have found by an American sociologist (Ward, *Dynamic Sociology*, Vol. 2,

185]). *Dynamic Sociology* "had been virtually ignored until [Albion] Small, then president of Colby University, recognized its merit in 1890" (Stern, ed., *Letters of Small to Ward*, 163). Cooley later reported that when they met at the AEA meeting in 1890, "I knew hardly anything of his works" ("Development of Sociology at Michigan," in *Sociological Theory and Social Research*, 5).

31. Journals, Vol. 6 (May 7 and 27, 1890), n.p.

32. CHC, "Some Remarks on Emerson," *On Self and Social Organization*, 39. For a penetrating account of Cooley's journals as fieldnotes, method, and medium for spiritual integration, see Jacobs, *Charles Horton Cooley*, 196–215, 247–49.

33. Journals, Vol. 10, 23 (July 21, 1895).

34. Jacobs, *Charles Horton Cooley*, 131, 156–59.

35. Angell, "Introduction," *Sociological Theory and Social Research*, xiii.

36. Bain, "A Great Teacher," 162.

37. Angell, "Introduction," xiii; see also Jandy, *Charles Horton Cooley*, 32–34.

38. "Development of Sociology at Michigan," 6.

39. Small, Review of Schäffle, 310; and Ellwood, *History of Social Philosophy*, 473. Schäffle provided the unacknowledged basis for "The Psycho-Communicating Apparatus, or the Social Nervous System," a chapter in Small and George Vincent's 1894 *Introduction to the Study of Society* (215–34). Compare the indexed but less-focused entries on communication in Giddings *Principles of Sociology* (1896).

40. Hardt's valuable cross-national study of communication theories in Germany and the United States, *Social Theories of the Press*, usefully describes Schäffle's work, but overlooks Cooley's appropriation of him, which was far more consequential than Albion Small's, discussed there at length (41–74).

41. CHC, Notes on Schäffle, Papers Concerning Miscellaneous Subjects, Box 2, CHCP; Cooley also noted in his journals that he read Schäffle intensively in the fall of 1893 (Vol. 11, 64 [February 28, 1897]). An earlier generation of intellectual historians recognized Schäffle's influence on Cooley: Jandy, *Charles Horton Cooley*, 84–86; Noble, *Paradox of Progressive Thought*, 109–10.

42. "The Theory of Transportation" (1894), rpt. in *Sociological Theory and Social Research*, 17–118 (quote at 17).

43. CHC, Notes from John Dewey's Lectures in Political Philosophy, 1893, Box 7, CHCP.

44. "Development of Sociology at Michigan," 6.

45. Cooley reported that though he knew nothing of Ward's work when they met, he "read later, with profit, what [he] found to be the more readable of them, and had an interesting correspondence with him regarding Galton's views on genius." As part of his minor in sociology, Cooley set "to study the accredited authors. I read enough of Comte to give me a general idea of his system: Ward's *Psychic Factors of Civilization* and part of his *Dynamic Sociology*; Darwin's *Origins of Species* and *Descent of Man*; and more or less in Gumplowicz, Quetelet (statistics was my other minor), Maine, Morgan, McLennan and Westermack; and also in Jane Addams and other

philanthropic writers. But more time and labor than I put on any of these went to an arduous perusal of the first volume of Schäffle's *Bau und Leben des socialen Körpers*" ("Development of Sociology at Michigan," 5–6).

46. Dorothy Ross writes that "Cooley followed up [hearing Dewey's lectures] with an intensive study of Albert Schäffle's elaborate analyses of the organic functions of society" (*Origins of American Social Science*, 242); but Quandt (*From the Small Town to the Great Community*, 54–55) and Coser (*Masters of Sociological Thought*, 315) suggest the reverse order (i.e., read Schäffle before heard Dewey). There is good reason to believe Cooley read Schäffle for the doctoral exams he took in June of 1893, and followed with a more extensive study of the text in the fall (when he heard Dewey's lectures), before sitting down to write his 100–page thesis in earnest in November.

47. "Development of Sociology at Michigan," 7–8. He wrote that the class "had more of Schäffle in it than any one else" (Journals, Vol. 11, 64 [February 28, 1897]).

48. "Theory of Transportation," 17, fn. 1 (subsequent page references in parentheses). Details about the class content and graduate students in it are found in "Development of Sociology at Michigan," 7.

49. Anticipations of Innis's "space-binding media": "transportation bears very important relations to the political state. . . . Tribute and visits of ceremony are . . . the means by which the central organization is nourished and aggrandized, its function being the same as that of taxation" (49); of Foucault's theory of surveillance: like every institution "[t]he state tends continually to develop on the psychical rather than on the physical side. Legislatures, statistical bureaus, courts and the higher administrative officers have functions of observation, communication, decision and discussion as contrasted with the physical and directly coercive functions of armies, navies and police" (59); and Carey's argument about the telegraph (and Joshua's Meyrowitz's about television), space, and place: "In communication place relations, as such, are of diminishing importance, and since the introduction of the telegraph it may almost be said that there are no place relations" (61).

50. Peters, *Speaking Into the Air*, 184–88; cf. Sklansky's thoughtful critique of Cooley's position and its political consequences, based partly on the idea that "Cooley subtly shifted the focus of political economy from the sphere of production—that is, of labor and industrial capital—to the sphere of distribution and exchange" (*Soul's Economy*, 216).

51. TMC and CHC, "Transportation," 66. Subsequent page numbers referenced parenthetically.

52. "There are some analogies between the processes of the 'body politic,' or social organism, and those of the individual body which are more than analogies, which seem rather to approach a true identity of function, pointing to and illustrating that universal kinship of all forms of life which the newest philosophy teaches us. Such an analogy is that between the nervous system of the body and the means of transmitting intelligence from one part of a country to another" (ibid., 131).

53. About the missing journals Schubert writes, "The destruction and hiatus could

be seen to coincide with a strong crisis in orientation, caused by the excessive demands he made upon himself during this period," but one of Cooley's later journal entries suggests otherwise. In 1922 he wrote that his pre-1900 journals document "a strenuous attempt to grasp and control my life. What there was about falling in love was so painfully crude and priggish that I long ago destroyed it" (Schubert, "Introduction," 6; Journals, Vol. 22, p. 100 [June 15, 1922]).

54. Journals, Vol. 10, 2 (July 21, 1895), Vol. 14, 21 (October 15, 1900), Vol. 13, 1 (September 12, 1898); Vol. 15, 4 (January 2, 1902).

55. *Human Nature and Social Order*, 147.

56. Journals, Vol. 12, 1 (May 2, 1897).

57. Mead, "Cooley's Contribution to American Social Thought," 694. For a penetrating analysis of Mead's articles, see Jacobs, "Influence and Canonical Supremacy."

58. CHC, *Social Process*, 396–97; Schubert, "Foundations of Pragmatic Sociology," 58; Jacobs, *Charles Horton Cooley*, 130–84.

59. *Social Organization*, 7.

60. *Life and the Student*, 91; and Angell, "Introduction," xiii. Thousands of Cooley's cards, mostly undated, can be found in Boxes 3 and 4, CHCP, bundled together with titles like "Notes on Sociology," "Sociological Tradition," "References," "Botanical Notes," and "Life and the Student, First Draft." Each card has a title—"Art and Conscience" or "Transmission of ideas," for instance.

61. "Nothing is easy," Cooley wrote. "I go over and over my material. (1) I make scattered notes: these I have from 15 years old to those made yesterday. (2) I make a provisional outline, usually for lectures, costing much thought. (3) I sort over and roughly classify my notes with a view to this outline. (4) I go over this material one or several times meditating, arranging, and improving my outline. (5) I write a first draft, very laborious and trying, probably the hardest work of all. Frequently I totally change my previous ideas and outlines. I find how vague my ideas really were, how scant my illustrations. (6) I rewrite this *Stellenwiese*, looking up much new material, always pondering my previous work. (7) I rewrite the whole, working it into unity and clearness. (8) I copy it, reworking many passages and adding new material. After this comes (9) revision of the proofs" (Journals, Vol. 18, 17 [February 5, 1905]). See also Bain, "A Great Teacher," 162.

62. Journals, Vol. 18, 81 (July 21, 1906).

63. Journals, Vol. 12, 101 (July 31, 1898).

64. Journals, Vol. 13, 10 (October 2, 1898); and Jandy, *Charles Horton Cooley*, 41–46. On the craft ideal in the era, see Quandt, *Small Town to Great Community*, 79–101.

65. Journals Vol. 10, 39 (1895, n.d.). On Cooley's "literary reference group," see Jacobs, *Charles Horton Cooley*, 144–48.

66. *Charles Horton Cooley*, 64. Numbers in the introductory class grew to 450 in 1928, the last semester Cooley taught it (ibid., 63).

67. Ibid., 64–67; Hamilton, "Cooley"; and Wood, "Appreciation"; Journals, Vol. 20, 47 (December 29, 1910).

68. Journals, Vol. 18B, 34 (January 1, 1909).

69. "Process of Social Change," 73.

70. *Social Organization*, 66–97.

71. *Social Organization*, 61.

72. *Human Nature and the Social Order*, 54, 56.

73. *Social Organization*, 64.

74. Jandy, *Charles Horton Cooley*, 34.

75. Journals, Vol. 12, 23 (August 7, 1897); see also Vol. 11, 15 (May 7, 1896)

76. *Social Process*, 252.

77. Journals, Vol. 21, 30 (October 15, 1914).

78. Schubert, "Foundations of Pragmatic Sociology," 56.

79. Hughes, *News and the Human Interest Story* (1940), 285 (quoting Cooley, *Social Organization*, 177).

80. Tarde, "Opinion and Conversation" (1898) and "The Public and the Crowd" (1901), both rpt. in *On Communication and Social Influence*; Lippmann, *Public Opinion* (1922); and Dewey, *The Public and Its Problems* (1927).

81. Schubert, "Foundations of Pragmatic Sociology," 61–67.

82. Journals, Vol. 21, 4 (December 7, 1913).

83. Journals, Vol. 21, 1–2 (November 1, 1913).

84. Journals, Vol. 21, 7 (January 18, 1914).

85. Journals Vol. 21, 9 (February 20, 1914). Beyond the religious analogy, handwork of a sort also helped Cooley think about his teaching and higher education. "When I am raking and burning leaves, as I have to in the fall and spring, I often light one little pile, and, when it is well afire, I pick from it a burning leaf or two on my rake and carry them to the next pile, which thus catches their flame. It seems to me that this is what a university should do for the higher life of our people. It should be on fire, and each student who goes out should be a burning leaf to start the flame in the community where he goes" (*Social Process*, 392).

86. Journals Vol. 21, 9 (February 15, 1914).

87. For a statement of his method and Columbia research, see Tenney, "Scientific Analysis of the Press," 895–98.

88. The leading publication to emerge being Malcolm Willey's dissertation, revised and published as *The Country Newspaper* (1926).

89. Journals, Vol. 20, 46 (December 29, 1910).

90. Journals, Vol. 19, 50 (January 8, 1911).

91. Journals, Vol. 21, 113–14 (March 1917). For other comments he made on the war, including America's entry into it and the armistice, see ibid., 19–34, 58–82, 113–23, 149–52, 169–77.

92. Steel, *Walter Lippmann*, 4–15, 141–54; and Duke, "John Reed," in Foner and Garraty, eds., *Reader's Companion*, 925. On propaganda, see Sproule, *Propaganda and Democracy*.

93. Bruce Lannes Smith, "The Mystifying Intellectual History of Harold D. Lasswell," in Rogow, ed., *Politics, Personality*, 41.

94. "[A]uthor of some forty volumes of substantial works in such assorted areas as anthropology, international relations, political philosophy, empirical political science, economic policy, labor relations, psychiatry, quantitative semantics, and even such far-out fields as the law (if any) of outer space," Lasswell and his work—including that in propaganda and communications—is well represented in the 37–page bibliography in *Politics, Personality, and Social Science*, 407–43. (Quote is from Smith, "Mystifying Intellectual History," 41.)

95. Lippmann, *Public Opinion*, 3–20.

96. Journals, Vol. 22, 106 (September 13, 1923); for the trip more generally, see ibid., 104–11.

97. One seemingly unlikely admirer of the aphoristic book was Pitirim Sorokin, the Russian-born grand historical, theoretical, and quantitative sociologist who was soon to move from the University of Minnesota to Harvard and teach the subject of my next chapter, Robert K. Merton. Sorokin, whom Cooley had invited to Michigan before the forced émigré had found a job in the United States, compared *Life and the Student* to Schopenhauer's *Aphorisms* and Pascal's *Pensées*, calling it a welcome relief from the drier work he himself conducted and read (Sorokin to CHC, September 16, 1927, Box 1, CHCP; on Sorokin and Cooley's earlier visit, see Johnston, *Pitirim Sorokin*, 25.)

98. *Life and the Student*, 6.

99. On which, see the final four papers collected in *Sociological Theory and Social Research*: "The Roots of Social Knowledge" (1926), "Case Study of Small Institutions as a Method of Research" (1928), "Sumner and Methodology" (1928), and "The Life-Study Method as Applied to Rural Social Research" (1929). For a discussion of Cooley and method in the contexts of United States sociology, ca. 1940, see Jandy, *Charles Horton Cooley*, 230–61.

100. By 1925, Cooley had sold more than 33,000 copies of his books (Coser, *Masters of Sociological Thought*, 328). In 1927, sociologist Luther Bernard solicited autobiographical sketches from more than 250 sociologists, in which "Cooley was named more often than any other author in the field as having exerted a significant influence" (Schubert, "Introduction," 1, citing a study by Donald Levine).

101. Journals, Vol. 24, 17–18 (April 7, 1928).

102. Pooley, "Fifteen Pages."

Chapter 5. Merton's Skeptical Faith

1. Merton "was among the first sociologists whose reputation would rest more on articles than books," which is true if we include the three editions of *Social Theory and Social Structure* (1949/1957/1968; hereafter STSS), Merton's central work, which consisted mostly of previously published articles and newly written introductions (Calhoun and VanAntwerpen, "Orthodoxy, Heterodoxy, and Hierarchy," 390, fn. 36).

2. Letter-writing (or letter-typing) was an art Merton practiced with energy, wit, and high literate grace throughout his adult life, which is a topic for a paper in its

own right. Here I note in passing that some of those letters became inventional fodder for papers he wrote late in his life. See e.g., "Alvin W. Gouldner," "Texts, Contexts and Subtexts," "George Sarton"; "Sorokin-Merton Correspondence, 1933–34"; and "Epistolary Notes."

3. Dewey, *A Common Faith*; cf. Stout's discussion of the book in *Democracy and Tradition*, 31–35.

4. The best brief historically oriented general introduction to Merton remains Sica, "Robert K. Merton." Neither of the two main English-language books on Merton's sociology operates historically, though Sztompka comes closer, and his is the best comprehensive introduction to Merton's work (*Robert K. Merton*; see also Crothers, *Robert K. Merton*). The forthcoming Calhoun-edited volume promises to fill in the picture more.

5. Hollinger, "Defense of Democracy," in *Science, Jews, and Secular Culture*; "Knower and Artificer," and *Cosmopolitanism and Solidarity*, esp. Chs. 1, 7, 8.

6. Simonson and Weimann, "Critical Research at Columbia"; and Simonson, Introduction to RKM, *Mass Persuasion*, "Serendipity of Merton's Communications Research," "Public Image," and "Merton's Sociology of Rhetoric."

7. Merton described his mother as "a dedicated anarchist of the Kropotkin and Tolstoy persuasion, which, of course, the Bolsheviks vigorously attacked" (personal communication, June 12, 2002).

8. Personal communication with Merton's granddaughter, Kerstin Arusha, September 30, 2006. The best published accounts of Merton's childhood and life are his autobiographical "Life of Learning," and Hunt, "How Does It Come To Be So?"

9. Rubenstein et al., *Jews in the Modern World*, 64–67, 77–83.

10. Biale, "Journey between Worlds," 823–24; see also Rubenstein et al., *Jews in the Modern World*, 64–86.

11. Sarna, *American Judaism*, 151–271; Cohen, "Urban Visibility"; Rubenstein et al., *Jews in the Modern World*, 64–86; Biale,"Journey between Worlds"; and Slezkine, *Jewish Century*, 40–104.

12. Bechtel, "Lweberg/Lwów/Lvov/Lviv."

13. Rosenthal, Eisenstein, and Waldstein, "Lemberg."

14. "Life of Learning," 340–44; Sarna, *American Judaism*, 157, 169–70.

15. Kerstin Arusha, personal communication.

16. Interview with Merton (hereafter, RKM), September 20, 2002.

17. "Life of Learning," 340–41. For one tangible sign of that socialization, see the photograph of Merton at about five years old, outfitted in high-dress short pants and shirt, seated upon a stool where he studiously examines an open book, at 343.

18. He built first "a crystal radio set, followed by a peanut-tube set and ultimately by a grand heterodyne set" (ibid., 342).

19. "Life of Learning," 342.

20. On the modernist side, Merton developed an attraction for French writers like Baudelaire, Mallarmé, and Flaubert through the then well-known Philadelphia-born critic James Gibbons Huneker ("Life of Learning," 343–44).

21. Interview with Robert K. Merton's son, Robert C. Merton, November 19, 2005.

22. "Life of Learning," 345.

23. Merton described this in one of the countless digressions in *On the Shoulders of Giants* as a game he played in the streets, which involved striking "the cat (or tip-cat) with a stick in such a manner as to cause it to spring up preparatory to its being knocked a far distance" (*On the Shoulders of Giants*, 70–71).

24. Quoted in Hunt, "How Does It Come To Be So?" 56.

25. For the classic formulations about "typographic man," which I mean to echo but not strictly follow, see McLuhan, *Gutenberg Galaxy*.

26. "Life of Learning," 346.

27. Cynwyd Pennar, "Don't Look Now, but . . . Those Three-Card Monte Aces Ought to Picket Mr. Hopkins," *Philadelphia Bulletin*, December 14, 1939, E24; Hunt, "How Does It Come To Be So?" 56; interview with RKM, September 20, 2002.

28. RKM, "Harry Houdini (1874–1926)," whom Merton reported "[r]ose from an obscure nonentity to enduring fame" (RKM, personal files).

29. Interview with Robert C. Merton, November 19, 2005.

30. Erns, *Weakness Is a Crime*, 74.

31. In a letter to Granville Hicks, friend and author, Merton wrote, "I had no idea that you had absorbed so much of Freudism, and could put it to so much effective use. You may be amused to hear further that the eager Flora fully explains to me an experience I had at the age of fourteen, when I was hitchhiking through the West and had a farmer's daughter—her name was Nebraska, believe it or not—literally thrust on me by her father. He evidently felt it would happen sooner or later, so why not select a nice kid for the purpose" (RKM to GH, December 1, 1944; like all subsequent letters I will reference, this one is found in RKM, personal files).

32. RKM, "Life of Learning," 348; "20 Boys Cut Down S. Phila. High Terr.," newspaper clipping, n.d., RKM, personal files.

33. Hunt, "How Does It Come To Be So?" 56.

34. RKM, Class Notes, Principles of Sociology, Sept. 1928–Jan. 1929, Temple University, RKM, personal files.

35. Hunt, "How Does It Come To Be So?" 56.

36. RKM, Class Notes, Criminology and Penology, February 1929–June 1929, Temple University, RKM, personal files.

37. Simpson, *Negro in the Philadelphia Press*, i.

38. Tenney, "Scientific Analysis of the Press"; Willey, *Country Newspaper*; Simpson, *Negro in the Philadelphia Press*, 33–36.

39. RKM, "Life of Learning," 348.

40. Simpson, *Negro in the Philadelphia Press*, i, xiv, 1.

41. RKM, personal interview, September 20, 2002; "Suzanne Carhart Wins Exton Cup for Best Student," newspaper clipping, n.d. [June 1927], RKM, personal files; interview with Elizabeth Spragg and Charlotte Mae Weiler (RKM's former in-laws), June 19, 2006; and McMahon, *South Jersey Towns*, 300–303.

42. "Susanna Carhart Graduates from Temple University: Tuckerton Girl Attains Numerous Honors in College Career," newspaper clipping, n.d. [June 1931], RKM, personal files.

43. RKM, "Intermarriage and the Social Structure."

44. "Life of Learning," 348–49.

45. See the five letters between RKM and Locke, February 26, 1931–July 14, 1931. See also RKM to George E. Simpson (GES), April 21, 1940 (where Merton reports spending "a delightful evening" with Locke in New Orleans, in the girls dormitory of Dillard College where Locke was staying); and GES to RKM, April 29, 1987, all RKM, personal files. On Locke's Bahá'í faith, see Buck, "Alain Locke."

46. Letter from RKM to Barry V, Johnston, February 13, 1987, quoted in Johnston, *Pitirim A. Sorokin*, 86; RKM, "Some Thoughts on Sociological Autobiography," 20.

47. Karabel, "Status-Group Struggle," 7. On anti-Semitism in the social sciences in the interwar period, see Winton, "'As His Name Indicates.'"

48. Interview with RKM, September 20, 2002. On Jewish assimilation in the interwar years, see also Klingenstein, *Jews in the American Academy*.

49. Whitfield, "Declarations of Independence," 1100.

50. Hollinger, *Science, Jews, and Secular Culture*, 19; see also *Cosmopolitanism and Solidarity*, 135–53.

51. Sorokin, *Leaves from a Russian Diary*; Johnston, *Pitirim A. Sorokin*, 1–22.

52. One of Sorokin's genealogical lists included in his first lecture to Sociology A, "Sociology as Science," n.d., I-9, RKM, personal files.

53. RKM, "Recent French Sociology," "Durkheim's *Division of Labor in Society*" and "'Durkheim's *Division of Labor in Society*': A Sexagenarian Postscript"; see also Platt, "United States Reception."

54. Sorokin, "Outline and Readings for Sociology A: Principles of Sociology," n.d., 2, RKM, personal files.

55. Sorokin ran Merton's work virtually unchanged, with a footnoted, "In cooperation with R. K. Merton," as Chapters 3 and 12 of *Social and Cultural Dynamics*. Merton charted a panoramic array of greater and lesser scientific lights from Democritus, Anaximander, Plato, and Aristotle through Al-Baqilani, Abelard, and Albertus Magnus, to Descartes, Robert Boyle, Olaf Rudbeck, Augustin Fresnel, and Charles Darwin (among many, many others).

56. RKM to Sorokin, January 7, 1933, RKM, personal files.

57. RKM and Barber, "Sorokin's Formulations," 333. Barber was an undergraduate of Merton's at Harvard in the 1930s and returned for his Ph.D. in the 1940s.

58. "[T]heories of the middle range . . . lie between the minor but necessary working hypotheses that evolve in abundance during day-to-day research and the all-inclusive systematic efforts to develop a unified theory that will explain all the observed uniformities of social behavior, social organization and social change," Merton wrote, in his classic definition of the concept ("On Sociological Theories of the Middle Range," in STSS, 3rd ed., 39). The idea seems first to have appeared in print in STSS

(1949, 5–10), though parts of Merton's argument (absent the "middle-range" terminology) were developed in a criticism of Talcott Parsons's grand theory presented as a conference paper two years earlier ("Discussion of Talcott Parsons").

59. RKM, "Sorokin-Merton Correspondence," 297. Merton received two "A-" grades, the lowest he received at Harvard, both from Sorokin. For more clues about Sorokin's influence on Merton, see Johnston, *Pitirim A. Sorokin*, and in particular his brief characterization of the intellectual contours of the "Sociological School" represented by the partnership between Sorokin and his colleague at Minnesota and Harvard, Carle Zimmerman (44).

60. RKM, "George Sarton," x, xiii, xvii, xxxv, xxxv–xxxvi; see also Cohen, *Puritanism*, esp. 21–33; and Thackray and RKM, "On Discipline Building."

61. RKM, "Intermarriage and the Social Structure," 364. On modernist strategies of artifice, see Hollinger, "The Knower and the Artificer."

62. Over six years, Merton published some 65 reviews, perhaps half of them for *Isis*, along with another 20 or so entries in critical bibliographies as well as other notes about recent publications for the journal's readers. .

63. Florian Znaniecki to RKM, February 13, 1941. The 1941 review of Znaniecki's *The Social Role of the Man of Knowledge* (rpt. in *Sociology of Science*, 41–46) was instrumental in building Merton's "paradigm for the sociology of knowledge," as the editor of that volume points out (4–5). For a bibliography of Merton's book reviews, see Mary Wilson Miles, "The Writings of Robert K. Merton," in Coser, ed., *Idea of Social Structure*, 513–16. Merton remained an active book reviewer through the mid-1940s, but his production dropped off considerably in the postwar era. By five-year periods and counting from Miles's bibliography, the number of book reviews proceeded this way: 1935–39, 50; 1940–44, 31; 1945–49, 11; 1950–54, 8; 1955–59, 6; 1960–64, 3; 1965–69, 3. Merton's inventional media changed in his middle age.

64. Of John 8:31–32 ("Then said Jesus to those Jews which believed on him, If ye continue in my word, then are ye my disciples indeed; And ye shall know the truth, and the truth shall make ye free"), see RKM, "The Sociology of Knowledge," 496.

65. Derived from the Gospel of Matthew 25:29 ("For unto every one that hath shall be given, and he shall have abundance: but from him that hath not shall be taken away even that which he hath"), the Mertonian Matthew effect "consists of the accruing of greater increments of recognition for particular scientific contributions to scientists of considerable repute and the withholding of such recognition from scientists who have not yet made their mark," as he put it in admittedly "less stately language" ("Matthew Effect").

66. Cuddihy, *Ordeal of Civility*, xx.

67. RKM, "Oral Transmission," 22.

68. RKM, lecture notes for Sociology 5A, Sociological Method, September 30, 1937, RKM, personal files. For later amplifications, see "Three Fragments" and Afterword to RKM and Barber, *Travels and Adventures*, esp. 269–71.

69. RKM, "Race Relations and Culture Contact," Lectures 19–22, n.d. (1938?). That

class, taught in the fall of 1938 and developed in consultation with E. Franklin Frazier, among others, was one moment in Merton's longer attention to the sociology of race, which extended back to his work at Temple with George Simpson. In January 1940, he reported to a friend that his race relations bibliography had grown to a thousand or more sources, all filed in index cards (RKM to Henry Riecken, Jr., January 13, 1940, RKM, personal files).

70. For instance, the classic early essay that introduces the concept of "unanticipated consequences," a sociological analysis of an issue traditionally associated with "such heterogeneous subjects as the following: the problem of evil (theodicy); moral responsibility; free will; predestination; deism; teleology; fatalism; logical, illogical and nonlogical behavior; social prediction; planning and control; social cycles; the pleasure and reality principles; and historical 'accidents'" ("Unanticipated Consequences," 894).

71. RKM to Read Bain, July 16, 1938, RKM, personal files.

72. RKM, "Science and the Social Order," 332–33, 334. Four years later, skepticism was one part of a tetrapodal catechism that defined Merton's famous "ethos of science": *universalism, organized skepticism, disinterestedness,* and *communism* ("Note on Science and Democracy"). I discuss Merton's reading of Nazi propaganda as an inventional context for that paper in "Merton's Sociology of Rhetoric."

73. RKM to Kingsley Davis, May 8, 1939, RKM, personal files.

74. The Tulane University News Bureau, Faculty and Staff Biographical Record, filled out by RKM October 4, 1939; Tulane University Archives, Special Collections, Howard-Tilton Memorial Library, Tulane University.

75. RKM to Parsons, September 26, 1939; RKM to Nick Demerath, October 27, 1939; and RKM to Arthur and Ruth Miller, November 19, 1939. He told Simpson that "toward the end of the electioneering, 'the race issue' was deliberately and viciously introduced. I have some incredible dope on this, but it is too long and complex a story to detail in a letter" (RKM to George E. and Eleanor Simpson, November 20, 1940).

76. A story recounted in a letter from RKM to Janette LeBlanc, December 27, 1992. A month later, Merton gave an "opinionaire" on "the Negro" to his male students at Tulane, which appeared in his published "Fact and Factitiousness."

77. Hicks, Bulletin 3, "Marxism and Moralism," mimeographed circular document, n.d. [March/April 1940], 1, RKM, personal files.

78. Hicks, Bulletin 1, "What Are We To Do?" mimeographed circular document, n.d. [1939/40?], 1, RKM, personal files.

79. Hicks, "Marxism and Moralism," 1.

80. RKM to Hicks, February 15, 1940.

81. RKM to Hicks, May 4, 1940.

82. A sociological Neil Cassady (Dean Moriarity in Keroauc's *On the Road*), Merton left Sue and new baby behind, drove 1,600–plus miles from New Orleans to Coyoacán, the small town on the outskirts of Mexico City where the exiled Trotsky lived (and where future sociologist Si Goode rented an apartment), and went from

there to Teotitlan, a small Zapotecan village in Oaxaca. He observed the penetrance of social programs organized by the left-nationalist government of President Lázaro Cardenas. "The gap between the administration's plans and the local realities is very striking indeed," he wrote; the village "follows its ancient pursuits and seeks only to avoid the 'interference' of the government" (RKM to Simpson, October 24, 1940). On the trip to Mexico, see RKM to Arthur and Ruth Miller, August 7, 1940; RKM to Harlan Gilmore, August 9, 1940; William J. (Si) Goode to RKM, September 7, 1940; and Goode to RKM, n.d. [1946?].

83. RKM to Simpson, April 21, 1940. In late May, after France had surrendered and Britain was fighting Germany alone, the Mertons were glued to their radio receiver. "Listening to the short wave broadcasts, we have fought every battle several times over" (RKM to Parsons, May 20, 1940).

84. RKM and H.M. Johnson, Lectures in Social Psychology, 1940–41, unpublished course notes, Tulane University, RKM, personal files. On boomerangs, see Lazarsfeld and RKM, "Studies in Radio and Film Propaganda," 571–75; and RKM and Kendall, "Boomerang Response." On "manifest and latent," a Freudian conceptual pairing Merton adopted for sociology, see STSS (1968), 114–36 (originally published 1949). For Merton's writings on ambivalence, see Sociological Ambivalence; for his own dispositional ambivalence, see. Lazarsfeld, "Working with Merton," esp. 50–53.

85. See the correspondence between Merton and Robert MacIver, Chair of Columbia's Department of Political Economy (December 31, 1940, February 11. 1941, February 18, 1941).

86. RKM to Read Bain, July 31, 1941.

87. Parsons to RKM, July 21, 1941.

88. John Marshall to I. A. Richards, August 16, 1939; Marshall, "Detail of Information," April 1939. Box 223, Folder 2672, Rockefeller Archive Center, Sleepy Hollow, N.Y. For Marshall and Rockefeller's role in the development of mass communications research, see Gary, Nervous Liberals, 85–129; and Buxton, "Radio Research."

89. Gary, Nervous Liberals, 85–129.

90. On Lazarsfeld's institutional operating, see Barton, "Paul Lazarsfeld"; Morrison, "Opportunity Structures"; and RKM, "Working with Lazarsfeld."

91. For Merton's leave of absence and medically diagnosed exhaustion, see the note from Columbia President Nicholas Murray Butler to RKM, November 12, 1941; RKM to Parsons, December 2, 1941; and RKM to Bain, January 9, 1942. The dinner episode was first described in print by Hunt, "How Does It Come To Be So?" 60. Lazarsfeld picked it up and reflected upon it in "Working with Merton," 36; as did Merton in "Working with Lazarsfeld," 167–68. I discuss the run-up and consequences of the evening in some detail in "Serendipity of Merton's Communications Research."

92. Hunt, "How Does It Come To Be So?" 60; see also Levy, "Lazarsfeld-Stanton Program Analyzer."

93. Hicks, Part of the Truth, 204—photocopied and annotated in the margins by RKM ("Pearl Harbor, I remember it well—bright green"), RKM, personal files.

94. RKM to David Glueck, June 14, 1940.

95. RKM to Parsons, February 17, 1942.

96. "I realize this is not a very large sum to offer you," Lazarsfeld went on, "but I think you know about research budgets, and you might add morally the expenses for assistance we will give you as long as you need it. Don't hesitate to tell me if this seems to [sic] little to you and not worth the effort. In that case we would have to make some special arrangement for the work you have done so far, and hope that in the future, by some budget finagling, I might be able to satisfy you more adequately upon some other occasion. In any case, I am very impressed by your contribution, and I hope that it will keep on." Lazarsfeld suggested Merton's paper could be published as "'Morale Building Over Radio,' in our next volume, 'Radio Research 1942.'" (Lazarsfeld to RKM, February 24, 1942).

97. RKM to Hicks, March 8, 1942. The COI was the Coordinator of Information, a precursor agency to the Office of Strategic Services (OSS), which in turn birthed the Central Intelligence Agency (CIA).

98. Lazarsfeld, "Administrative and Critical Research" (1941), 169.

99. RKM to Arthur and Ruth Miller, May 26, 1942; RKM to Parsons, May 21, 1942. On the OWI, see Winkler, *Politics of Propaganda*.

100. "A representative of the New Masses approached me recently, asking that I contribute to their defense-fund. The libel suit of Cromwell has them worried. The N.M. man carried a 'letter of introduction' from a friend, who preferred to remain anonymous! As a 'liberal,' the story goes, I must see to it that all shades of political opinion be permitted expression. Ergo, my contribution is a moral obligation. The only surprise feature of the episode was the extreme diffidence of the solicitor; he was positively shy" (RKM to Hicks, August 9, 1942). For indications of Merton's research routine at army bases, see correspondence between him and Carl Hovland, head of the Research Branch of the War Department, and RKM to Hicks, July 2. 1943.

101. "Rumor has it that Hygeia—American style—had a hand in the making of the house, which is obviously built around tubs, showers, and associated unmentionables" (RKM to Simpson, June 20, 1942). Needless to say, he was a long way from living with a cold backyard crapper in Philly.

102. RKM to Hicks, December 8, 1942; see also Robert C. Tryon (Chief of Psychology Division, OSS) to RKM, Sept 25, 1942. On the wartime analysis of rumor, see Faye, "Governing the Grapevine."

103. RKM to Parsons, May 24, 1943; and RKM, "Tentative Outline for Interview Paper," unpublished memo, July 20, 1943. The outline was eventually written up and published with Patricia Kendall as "The Focused Interview."

104. "The Office of Radio Research may soon open a new division intended only to handle the fan mail elicited by the Life article," Merton wrote Hicks. "Crackpots from coast to coast beg us to admit that it is not so; that chicane and trickster's art have no place in Kemston's miracle mentalism. But now that Paul Lazarsfeld and I

have stepped down from the judge's hot seat, we hope to be returned to our previous state of obscure mediocrity" (RKM to Hicks, n.d.).

105. RKM to Richard Deninger, June 16, 1943; see also letters exchanged between Merton and Hicks, June 16 and 25. Merton had recently met Edward R. Murrow through Dr. Alfred Cohn, a physician and philosopher who also introduced Merton to Harold Laski, the socialist political theorist and British Labour Party official, about whom more below.

106. Lazarsfeld and RKM, "Mass Communication," 107. For the argument that this section of the paper was written by Merton, see Simonson and Weimann, "Critical Research at Columbia."

107. Lazarsfeld and RKM, "Studies in Radio and Film Propaganda," 564. Lazarsfeld, who was a member of the Writers Congress in 1943 (a fact that later got him into trouble with the Un-American Activities Committee, because the West Coast Writers Congress included a number of communists), may have delivered the paper in Los Angeles. Merton republished the article in all three editions of STSS, which suggests he may have been primary author—a hypothesis strengthened by my judgment, based on close reading of that piece, that it is written in Mertonian style.

108. Ibid., 572, 576.

109. For the longer history, see Morrison, *Search for a Method*. For an account of the development of the method within the gendered social contexts of research at the Office of Radio Research, see the documentary film *Out of the Question: Women, Media, and the Art of Inquiry*, produced and directed by Naomi McCormack.

110. "Studies in Radio and Film Propaganda," 578–82.

111. Ibid., 573, 576, 582.

112. Classically articulated in Katz and Lazarsfeld, *Personal Influence*; see also Simonson, ed., *Politics, Social Networks*.

113. RKM, "Institutional Ideologies and Propaganda," course notes, Columbia University, 1943, 1–2, 6, 11, RKM, personal files. About the relation between what Marxists call base and superstructure, Merton wrote that it was "not contended that [the] struggle of ideologies are simply epiphenomenal, but it is not sufficient to consider these as the determining factors in social change" (6).

114. The memo being "Mass Communication and Social Action" (RKM, personal files), which includes 11 enumerated headings, each followed by one or more single-spaced paragraphs of his thinking-in-process: The Role of Propaganda; Function of Mass Media of Making the Privately Known the Publicly Accepted; Relations between (local) Organized Groups and Centralized Media of Communication; "The Power of the Press" (or radio or film, etc.): Status-Conferring Functions; Analysis of the Newspaper or Radio Crusade: A Conspicuous Example of Influence on Mass Action through Communications; The Narcotizing Effect of Mass Communication; The Rise of Popular Education and the Decline of Popular Taste; The Superficialization of Experience; The Effect of Mass Communications in Creating and Preserving (civic,

intellectual, literary, musical, etc.) Interest; Mass Apathy and Mass Communication; A Flow of Opinion in the Social Structure; The Monopolization of Public Attention: The Effectiveness of Mass Communications in the Absence of Counter Propaganda (RKM, "Notes on Mass Communication and Social Action," unpublished memo, September 18, 1946; see also "Theses for the Annals Paper," unpublished memo, October 11, 1946.) The documents were composed with an eye toward a special issue of *The Annals of the American Academy of Political and Social Science* on social action, public discussion, and "the manufacture of consent" (as he termed it in the September 18 memo).

115. Quoting Gitlin, "Media Sociology," 207.

116. Simonson and Weimann, "Critical Research at Columbia," 23–24.

117. Lazarsfeld and RKM, "Mass Communication," 118.

118. Cooley, *Social Organization*, 84–85.

119. Lazarsfeld and RKM, "Mass Communication," 97, as underlined by Priscilla A. Marsden.

120. A revised version of his dissertation was published in George Sarton's journal *Osiris*, but it did not come out in book form until 1970 (*Science, Technology, and Society*).

121. RKM, "The Effectiveness of the Kate Smith Bond Drives," Office of Radio Research report, January 24, 1944 (46 pp.), RKM, personal files. See also McCormack, *Out of the Question*.

122. "The motive of pseudo-participation and goings-on seems to me to be very strong," Lowenthal offered. "Listening to a commentator is a vicarious attendance to world history. It is a welcome outlet if—as in the case of bond buying—you can change from fake activity to real action" (memo from Leo Lowenthal to RKM, n.d. [late 1943?], BASR Archives, Box 113, Folder B-0200, Rare Books and Manuscripts Library, Columbia University). Merton and Lowenthal admired one another's work, and together they forded some of the Frankfurt-Columbia divides symbolized by the difficult relation between Lazarsfeld and Theodor Adorno. Merton would call Lowenthal's classic "Biographies in Popular Magazines" (1944) "easily the most original effort at a sociologically sophisticated analysis of mass media that I know" (RKM to David Riesman, April 18, 1947), and he would single it out as a "hybrid" of Frankfurt-style Critical Theory and American mass communications research that was "distinctly superior to either of the two pure strains" (STSS [1968], 504).

123. Merton suggested that America of the 1940s was a society where people felt manipulated on all sides. "In place of a sense of *Gemeinschaft*—genuine community of values—there intrudes *pseudo-Gemeinschaft*—the feigning of personal concern for the other fellow in order to manipulate him the better. Best sellers provide popular instruction in the arts of pseudo-Gemeinschaft: 'how to influence people through the pretense of friendship'" (*Mass Persuasion*, 142; see also RKM, "On the Origins").

124. For lengthier discussions see Simonson, "Introduction," xi–xlv, and "Public Image."

125. Generalizing and depersonalizing feelings he probably had himself, Merton introduced a quote from a focused interview by observing that "many intellectuals and sophisticates of various kinds distrust her. She is not one of them. Her language is not their language and for them her sentimentality rings false, and her 'folksy' manner is rejected as 'lower class' and a little 'vulgar.'" RKM, "Swayed by Smith," n.d. [1945?], 109; BASR Archives, Box 113, Folder B-0200. See also Merton's annotated draft in B-0200-4, Kate Smith, and preliminary documents authored by Merton and Alberta Curtis (B-0200-1, B-0200-2, B-0200-3).

126. "Swayed by Smith," 126, 133.

127. Hicks to RKM, November 28, 1944.

128. RKM to Hicks, December 1. 1944.

129. Hicks to RKM, May 18, 1945. See their letters in December, where Hicks tells Merton his "writing is not bad in the sense that [Howard] Odum's is" (Hicks to RKM, December 4, 1944) and then proclaims Merton's chapter so "full of problems that I can't solve without discussing them with you" (Hicks to RKM, December 10, 1944).

130. "I have something which purports to be a manuscript, but I shall not do you the indignity of asking you to read it. In a week or so I plan to drop it on the desk of one or another publisher," Merton wrote (RKM to Hicks, May 8, 1945). Ten days later, Hicks replied, "I wish you could have heard Dorothy and me discussing (at midnight) my account of the discussion with you about writing for the general public. I think you'd have been amused" (Hicks to RKM, May 18, 1945).

131. RKM to Harold Laski, December 15, 1945.

132. *Mass Persuasion*, 2, 140–72. Subsequent page references noted parenthetically.

133. Morrison, "Influences."

134. For more on the body of Smith, see Peters, "Uncanniness."

135. The main informant, "an attendant to a 'half-woman, half-serpent freak' in a mid-Manhattan 'museum,'" offered the ORR interviewer this account of coming to phone in her pledge: "'Reptilina and I sat talking about it for a few minutes first. [At this point, the articulate Reptilina herself interrupted to explain: "*We thought about calling because we would be able to talk to Kate herself.*"] Then I said, well, I'll call up. I did, and found out that Kate was not talking to people. She really couldn't, now that I think of it, because so many people called up. But I couldn't back out then. I would have felt like a fool. Besides, I was going to buy one anyway'" (*Mass Persuasion*, 131–32).

136. On their repression from Katz and Lazarsfeld's *Personal Influence*, see Douglas, "*Personal Influence*."

137. "Mass Persuasion: A Technical Problem and a Moral Dilemma," *Mass Persuasion*, 174–89.

138. "You will see . . . how much we have profited from *Mass Persuasion*," Riesman wrote, sending Merton materials that would eventually become part of *The Lonely*

Crowd. Merton's book was "a model both in its use of general social theory to inform empirical work, and more specifically in its application of what seems to be Bureau technique in working with small samples. It encouraged us to believe we could find something out about our immense problems by means of a few dozen interviews" (Riesman to RKM, April 9, 1948). Riesman also made the book "required reading matter for all students who worked with me," as he reported four years later, triggering a note where Merton still called the project "Swayed by Smith" (Riesman to RKM, September 29, 1952; and RKM to Riesman, October 2, 1952).

139. Wyant, "Voting,"; and Wyant and Herzog, "Voting—Part II." Goldhamer, a graduate student and research associate at the Bureau since 1943, knew these mail studies when she learned of the Eisenhower letters and alerted Merton in 1948. See her excellent reconstruction of the stillborn study, "General Eisenhower."

140. RKM, "Mass Pressure," chapter draft ("The Material"), n.d. [Spring, 1949], 2. For the study, the research associates sampled 10% of the 8,450 letters of more than 50 words that Eisenhower received in that period, coding letters for geographical origin, sex of writer, single or multiple writer, occupation, veteran status, and—reasoning by sign from grammar and type of paper used (e.g., scrap paper, stationery)—the economic/educational status of the writer.

141. Sussmann, *Dear FDR*; see also Merton's Introduction to that book (xiii–xxv), and the recent analysis of the FDR letters in Hauser, *Vernacular Voices*, 232–67.

142. RKM, West, and Jahoda, *Patterns of Social Life*. For publications from the study, see RKM, "Selected Problems" and "Social Psychology of Housing," and Jahoda and West, "Race Relations."

143. RKM, "A Proposed Research in Housing Communities," November 15, 1944, RKM, personal files.

144. "Social Psychology of Housing," 179.

145. Ibid., 204.

146. Patricia Salter West and Marie Jahoda, "The Meaning of Hilltown for Negroes and Whites," unpublished ms, April 13, 1948, 134; see also West and Jahoda, "Social Fictions and Social Facts: The Dynamics of Race Relations in Hilltown," unpublished document, BASR, June 1949, both RKM, personal files.

147. Two exceptions were his Introduction to Dallas Smythe's *New York Television* and a study of books and reading that approached mass communication from its flank—McKeon, RKM, and Gellhorn, *Freedom to Read*.

148. RKM, "Self-Fulfilling Prophecy."

149. "That was a really impressive event for us," Kenneth Clark remembered. "It told us, really, that this was a decent community" (McCullough, "Kenneth Clark," 3).

150. RKM, personal interview, September 20, 2002; Vanessa Merton, personal interview, May 10, 2006.

151. "Social Science Statement Concerning Effects of Racial Segregation," n.d., RKM, personal files; interview with RKM, September 20, 2002. On the social scientific contribution to *Brown*, see Jackson *Social Scientists*, and "Blind Law."

152. For example, *On the Shoulders of Giants* (1965), "Matthew Effect," and "Oral

Transmission." For more on the shift, see Simonson, "Merton's Sociology of Rhetoric."

153. On the 1952 event, when Merton's signing of a published statement of criticism about Republican vice presidential candidate Richard Nixon prompted a dirty-tricks–like media smear campaign, see "Nixon Fund Vicious, Say 23 at Columbia," *New York Times*, October 6, 1952: 10; Jack Doherty, "9 Anti-Nixon Profs Tinted by Red Probe," *New York Daily News*, October 9, 1952: 3; "Link Nine Professors to Communist Fronts," *Columbia Spectator*, October 9, 1952: 1, 2, 4; "9 Nixon Fund Critics Listed in Red Probe," *Chicago Tribune*, October 9. 1952: n.p.; "Political Battle at Columbia Rages," *New York Times*, November 2, 1952: 59, all found in RKM, personal files. Perhaps sensitive about negative publicity, or finding himself more intellectually distant from the Marxissant vocabulary he occasionally deployed in his twenties and thirties, Merton purged the listed references to "ideology" for the second edition of STSS (1957). Whereas in the first edition, the indexed "ideology" referred one to passages in no less than five articles ("Social Structure and Anomie," "The Self-Fulfilling Prophecy," "Science and Democratic Social Structure" [the renamed "norms of science" essay], and two pieces on the sociology of knowledge), in 1957, the index suggested that only the sociology of knowledge pieces addressed "ideology." Notably, in both those essays Merton is trying to pull the sociology of knowledge away from its Marxian roots. The 1949 Merton announced that three of his later-classic essays addressed "ideology" in some way. The 1957 Merton did not.

154. RKM and Nisbet, eds., *Contemporary Social Problems* (1961); nor were mass media added in two subsequent editions of the book (1966, 1971).

155. RKM, notes for *Court of Reason*, n.d. In a response to a fan letter he received in December, Merton wrote, "There is a place in television, we believe, for the lively debate of public issues subject to the questions of a reasonably detached panel of reasonable men." It was a statement backed more by hope than evidence (RKM to Mrs. F. W. Saunderson, December 13, 1962, both RKM, personal files).

156. "A wild one for the kids. Beatnik Maynard Krebs turns into a hairy monster after swallowing a potion in a school lab. The scene in which Maynard takes a few sips of the potion and turns into an intellectual, is fine. When Maynard becomes greedy, swallows the bottle, and thinks like a gorilla, things begin to get silly." Afterward, psychiatrists examine Jed Clampett, "who manages to come up with some good, honest answers." "Tonight's Pick of the TV Best," *Yonkers Herald Statesman*, December 12, 1962: 79. Show titles are found in clippings of television listings included in RKM's file on *Court of Reason*.

157. "Non-Commercial Channels," *The New Republic*, April 13, 1963: 31–33.

158. "To have MacDonald publicly recant was a great achievement. And fun to see such an honest and thoughtful man. Bell's statement of what's wrong with MacDonald's kind of amateur or mass sociology was beautiful, and so neatly and firmly expressed" (excerpt of letter from Leonard Silk, in RKM to Joan Ganz, WNBT, March 29, 1963).

159. Robert S. Lynd to RKM, April 8, 1962.

160. David Boroff, "An Excess of Virtue," *The New Leader*, March 18, 1963: 29–30.

161. Chris Welles, "Educational TV: Is It Just 'Late, Late Lectures'?" *Life* (New York Extra Edition; clipping, n.d., RKM, personal files); Richard K. Dean, "New WNDT Dissent: A Moderator Bows Out," *New York Herald Tribune*, April 16, 1963: 19; Jack Gould, "NBC Donation to Channel 13 Will Be Investigated by F.C.C.," and "Texts of Letters on $100,000 Donation to Channel 13," *New York Times*, April 29, 1963: 1, 57; Gould, "Sarnoff Rebuts Report by WNDT," *New York Times*, May 18, 1963; and RKM to Samuel B. Gould, April 13, 1963.

162. Marchand, *Marshall McLuhan*, 132–33.

163. RKM, "McLuhanism: MM: The Entertainment Medium of Mass Media," undated notes in preparation WNDT-New York, "McLuhan on McLuhanism," broadcast May 7, 1966, RKM, personal files.

164. Harry Harris, "Screening TV," *Philadelphia Inquirer*, May 17, 1966: n.p. (clipping, RKM, personal files).

165. Bennett M. Berger to RKM, May 23, 1966; see also RKM to Berger, May 27, 1966.

166. Bain to RKM, December 13, 1938. He references Pitirim "Pete" Sorokin, Talcott Parsons, L. J. Henderson, and George Sarton, respectively.

Afterword: Assembling through a Fair

1. Latour, "From Realpolitik to Dingpolitik," in Latour and Weibel, eds., *Making Things Public*, 24.

2. Schaefer, *Soundscape*, 51–52, 67, 87, 114–15, and 179.

3. For a fertile discussion of rhetoric as *maieutic*, see Sloane, *On the Contrary*, esp. 1–27, 125–33. As Sloane observes, the idea of discourse as *maieutic* arises from Plato's Socrates, who identified himself as the son of a midwife and one who practiced midwifery by means of his dialogic process of question and answer (3–4).

4. Rappaport, *Ritual and Religion*, 21, 24, 37, 52; cf. Robbins, "Ritual Communication." For a fine introduction to communicative views on ritual, see Rothenbuhler, *Ritual Communication*.

5. Prosterman, *Ordinary Life*, 5, 191.

6. Hauser, *Vernacular Voices*.

7. In Flemish, they would be called *kirmiss*, or Church Mass (Benedict, *Anthropology of World's Fairs*).

8. Kniffen, "American Agricultural Fair"; Neely, *Agricultural Fair*; Prosterman, *Ordinary Life*, 42–56; and Anne Stewart, "One Hundred Forty-Three Years and Counting," in CCFHC, *History of Crawford County Fair*, 7–9.

9. Kniffen, "American Agricultural Fair"; and Jane Smith, "Through the Years," in CCFHC, *History of Crawford County Fair*, 11–25. For a look at state fairs and expositions across the country in this era, see Matthews, "America Goes to the Fair."

10. One year, George Jones is set to appear, and I join the line already formed half an hour before sales begin on a Monday morning. There are perhaps one hundred people there, a third of them white-haired ladies and nearly all of them over forty. "I heard on the radio they were camping out," one woman tells another standing in line in front of me. A gap-toothed woman in her sixties is first in line, and informs me she's been there since noon on Friday. "I'm a picture taker," she says. "If I can't get in the front row, it's no good." "We wanna be there," one of her companions chimes in. "We're country fans. We're hard core." They emerge with several handfuls of tickets, for themselves and their families. There's lots of sociable talk all around me in line. "How often do you go?" one woman asks another who looks to be sixty. "Oh, we come every day. We're fairgoers. I used to love to come on Sundays for the church service, and we would have breakfast after." "Are you a country singer too?" one woman asks me. I wish I could say that I am.

11. "[T]he vibratory effects of high-intensity, low-frequency noise, which have the power to 'touch' listeners, had first been experienced in thunder, then in the church, where the bombardon of the organ had made the pews wobble under the Christians, and finally had been transferred to the cacophonies of the eighteenth-century factory," Schafer writes. "Thus the 'good vibes' of the sixties, which had promised an alternative life style, traveled a well-known road, which finally led from Leeds to Liverpool; for what was happening was that the new counterculture, typified by Beatlemania, was actually stealing the Sacred Noise from the camp of the industrialists and setting it up in the hearts and communes of the hippies" (*Soundscape*, 115).

12. A survey asked "What do you like most about the fair?" The top three responses were the people (33%), the animals and related exhibits (24%), and the food (19%). Nothing else was close (T. L. Warburton, "Attendance Patterns and Promotional Effectiveness: A Report on the Crawford County Fair," Edinboro University of Pennsylvania, Department of Speech Communications, n.d.).

13. Durkheim, *Elementary Forms*, 217.

14. McLuhan, *Understanding Media*, 107.

15. Emerson, "Montaigne, or the Skeptic," in *Representative Men*, 99.

16. Arendt, *Lectures*, 43; see also Moynagh, "Politics of Enlarged Mentality."

17. "Stoking the mind with variety" is Thomas Sloane's take on rhetorical *copia* (*On the Contrary*, 56–79).

18. Putnam, *Bowling Alone*; for a review of understandings of social capital, see Kadushin, "Too Much Investment?"

19. Latour, "From Realpolitik to Dingpolitik," 21, 23, 31.

20. Alternately, as a censorious internalized voice suggested during darker moments of late stylistic revision, the book could be turd, which, as is well known, is not conducive to shining.

21. For further cues toward this project, see Jackson, *Becoming Native to this Place*.

Selected Bibliography

Abbott, Andrew. "The Historicality of Individuals." *Social Science History* 29 (2005): 1–13.

Achtemeier, Paul J. "*Omne Verbum Sonat*: The New Testament and the Oral Environment of Late Western Antiquity." *Journal of Biblical Literature*, 109 (1990): 3–27.

Adorno, Theodor. *Minima Moralia: Reflections from Damaged Life*. Trans. E. F. N. Jephcott, 1951. London: Verso, 1974.

Albion, Robert G. "The 'Communication Revolution.'" *The American Historical Review* 37 (1932): 718–20.

Allen, Gay Wilson. *The Solitary Singer: A Critical Biography of Walt Whitman*, rev. ed. New York: New York University Press, 1967.

Altschuler, Glenn, and Stuart Blumin. *Rude Republic: Americans and Their Politics in the Nineteenth Century*. Princeton: Princeton University Press, 2000.

Antczak, Frederick J. *Thought and Character: The Rhetoric of Democratic Education*. Ames, Iowa: Iowa State University Press, 1985.

Arendt, Hannah. *Lectures on Kant's Political Philosophy*. Ed. Ronald Beiner. Chicago: University of Chicago Press, 1982.

Badiou, Alain. *Saint Paul: The Foundation of Universalism*. Trans. Ray Brassier. Stanford, CA: Stanford University Press, 2003.

Bain, Read. "Cooley, A Great Teacher." *Social Forces* 9 (1930): 160–64.

Baldasty, Gerald. *The Commercialization of News in the Nineteenth Century*. Madison: University of Wisconsin Press, 1992.

Barnouw, Erik. *A Tower in Babel: A History of Broadcasting in the United States,* Vol. 1. New York: Oxford University Press, 1966.

Barton, Allen. "Paul Lazarsfeld and the Invention of the University Institute for Applied Social Research." In *Organizing for Social Research*. Eds. Burkart Holzner and Jiri Nehnevajsa, 17–83. Cambridge, Mass.: Schenkman, 1982.

Baudelaire, Charles. *Baudelaire in English*. Eds. Carol Clark and Robert Sykes. New York: Penguin, 1997.

Bechtel, Delphine. "Lweberg/Lwów/Lvov/Lviv: Identities of a 'City of Uncertain Boundaries.'" *Diogenes* 210 (2006): 62–71.

Benedict, Burton. *The Anthropology of World's Fairs*. London: Scholars Press, 1983.

Benjamin, Walter. *Illuminations: Essays and Reflections*. Ed. Hannah Arendt. New York: Schocken, 1968.

Bergman, Herbert, Douglas Noverr, and Edward Recchia, eds. *Collected Writings of Walt Whitman: The Journalism*. 2 vols. New York: Peter Lang, 1998.

Betz, Otto. "Apostle." In Metzger and Coogan, eds., *Oxford Companion*,41–42.

Biale, David. "A Journey between Worlds: East European Jewish Culture from the Partitions of Poland to the Holocaust." In *Cultures of the Jews*.

———, ed. *Cultures of the Jews: A New History*. New York: Schocken, 2002.

Billig, Michael. *Arguing and Thinking: A Rhetorical Approach to Social Psychology*. 2nd ed. Cambridge: Cambridge University Press, 1996.

Blair, Carole, Greg Dickinson, and Brian L. Ott, eds. *Places of Public Memory: The Rhetoric of Museums and Memorials*. Tuscaloosa: University of Alabama Press, 2009.

Bloomer, W. Martin. "Topics." In Sloane, ed, *Encyclopedia of Rhetoric*, 779–82.

Boyarin, Daniel. *A Radical Jew: Paul and the Politics of Identity*. Berkeley: University of California Press, 1994.

Bradley, Sculley, Harold W. Blodgett, Arthur Golden, and William White, eds. *Leaves of Grass: A Textual Variorum of the Printed Poems*. 3 vols. New York: New York University Press, 1980.

Brasher, Thomas L. *Whitman as Editor of the Brooklyn Daily Eagle*. Detroit: Wayne State University Press, 1970.

Buck, Christopher. "Alain Locke: Race Leader, Social Philosopher, Bahá'í Pluralist." *World Order* 36:3 (2005): 7–48.

Burke, Kenneth. *Attitudes toward History*. 3rd ed. Berkeley: University of California Press, 1984.

———. *Permanence and Change,* 3rd ed. Berkeley: University of California Press, 1984.

Buxton, William. "From Radio Research to Communications Intelligence: Rockefeller Philanthropy, Communications Specialists, and the American Policy Community." In *The Political Influence of Ideas: Policy Communities and the Social Sciences*. Eds. Stephen Brooks and Alain-G. Gagnon, 187–230. Westport, Conn.: Praeger, 1994.

Calhoun, Craig, ed. *Robert K. Merton: Sociological Theory and the Sociology of Science*. New York: Columbia University Press, 2010.

———, ed. *Sociology in America: A History*. Chicago: University of Chicago Press, 2007.

Calhoun, Craig, and Jonathan VanAntwerpen. "Orthodoxy, Heterodoxy, and Hierarchy: 'Mainstream' Sociology and Its Challengers." In Calhoun, *Sociology in America*.

Cantril, Hadley, and Gordon W. Allport. *The Psychology of Radio*. New York: Harper and Bros., 1935.

Cantril, Hadley, Hazel Gaudet, and Herta Herzog. *The Invasion from Mars: A Study in the Psychology of Panic*. Princeton, N.J.: Princeton University Press, 1940.

Carey, James W. *Communication as Culture: Essays on Media and Society*. Boston: Unwin Hyman, 1988.

Carey, John. *The Intellectuals and the Masses: Pride and Prejudice among the Literary Intelligentsia, 1880–1939*. London: Faber and Faber, 1992.

Casson, Lionel. *Travel in the Ancient World*. London: George Allen and Unwin, 1974.

Chaffee, Steven H., and Miriam J. Metzger. "The End of Mass Communication?" *Mass Communication and Society* 4 (2001): 365–79.

Chilton, Bruce. *Rabbi Paul: An Intellectual Biography*. New York: Doubleday, 2004.

Clark, Gregory. *Rhetorical Landscapes in America: Variations on a Theme from Kenneth Burke*. Columbia, SC: University of South Carolina Press, 2004.

Clark, Gregory, and S. Michael Halloran, eds. *Oratorical Culture in Nineteenth-Century America: Transformations in the Theory and Practice of Rhetoric*. Carbondale: Southern Illinois University Press, 1993.

Clark, Lynn Schofield. *From Angels to Aliens: Teenagers, the Media, and the Supernatural*. New York: Oxford University Press, 2003.

Cmiel, Kenneth. *Democratic Eloquence: The Fight over Popular Speech in Nineteenth-Century America*. New York: William Morrow, 1990.

———. "On Cynicism, Evil, and the Discovery of Communication in the 1940s." *Journal of Communication* 46.3 (1996): 88–107.

———. "Whitman the Democrat." In *A Historical Guide to Walt Whitman*. Ed. David S. Reynolds, 205–34. New York: Oxford University Press, 2000.

Cohen, I. Bernard, ed. *Puritanism and the Rise of Modern Science: The Merton Thesis*. New Brunswick, N.J.: Rutgers University Press, 1990.

Cohen, Richard I. "Urban Visibility and Biblical Visions: Jewish Culture in Western and Central Europe in the Modern Age." In Biale, *Cultures of the Jews*, 730–96.

Collins, Raymond F. *Letters That Paul Did Not Write*. Wilmington, Del.: Michael Glazier, 1988.

Cooley, Charles Horton. *Human Nature and the Social Order*. 1902. New Brunswick, N.J.: Transaction, 1992.

———. *Life and the Student: Roadside Notes on Human Nature, Society, and Letters*. New York: Alfred A. Knopf, 1927.

———. *On Self and Social Organization*. Ed. Hans-Joachim Schubert. Chicago: University of Chicago Press, 1998.

———. "The Process of Social Change." *Political Science Quarterly* 12 (1897): 63–81.

———. *Social Organization: A Study of the Larger Mind*. 1909. New Brunswick, N.J.: Transaction, 1985.

———. *Social Process*. 1918. Carbondale: Southern Illinois University Press, 1966.

———. "The Social Significance of Street Railways." *Publications of the American Economic Association* 6 (Jan–Mar 1891): 71–73.

———. *Sociological Theory and Social Research*. Ed. Robert Cooley Angell. New York: Henry Holt, 1930.

Cooley, Charles Horton, Robert Cooley Angell, and Lowell Juilliard Carr. *Introductory Sociology*. New York: Charles Scribner's Sons, 1933.

Cooley, Thomas McIntyre, and Charles Horton Cooley. "Transportation." In *The United States of America: A Study of the American Commonwealth, Its Natural Resources, People, Industries, Manufactures, Commerce, and Its Work in Literature, Science, Education, and Self-Government*, Vol. 2. Ed. Nathaniel Southgate Shaler, 65–133. New York: D. Appleton and Co., 1894.

Coser, Lewis A., ed. *The Idea of Social Structure: Papers in Honor of Robert K. Merton*. New York: Harcourt Brace, 1975.

———. *Masters of Sociological Thought: Ideas in Historical and Social Context*, 2nd ed. New York: Harcourt Brace, 1977.

Crawford County Fair Historical Committee (CCFHC). *A History of the Crawford County Fair—50 Years, A Harvest of History*. Meadville, Penn., 1996.

Crothers, Charles. *Robert K. Merton: A Key Sociologist*. London: Tavistock, 1987.

Crowe, Frederick E. "Complacency and Concern in the Thought of St. Thomas." In *Lonergan Workshop 16*, supplementary issue (2000): 71–203.

Cuddihy, John Murray. *The Ordeal of Civility: Freud, Marx, Lévi-Strauss, and the Jewish Struggle with Modernity*. 1974. Boston: Beacon Press, 1986.

Czitrom, Daniel J. *Media and the American Mind: From Morse to McLuhan*. Chapel Hill: University of North Carolina Press, 1983.

Dassmann, Ernst. "Archaeological Traces of Early Christian Veneration of Paul." In *Paul and the Legacies of Paul*. Ed. William S. Babcock, 281–306. Dallas: Southern Methodist University Press, 1990.

Davies, W. D. *Paul and Rabbinic Judaism*. London: SPCK, 1955.

Dewey, John. *Art as Experience*. 1934. New York: Perigree, 1980.

———. *A Common Faith*. New Haven: Yale University Press, 1934.

———. *Democracy and Education*. 1916. New York: Free Press, 1966.

———. *Experience and Nature*. 1925. New York: Dover, 1958.

———. "Plan of Organization of the University Primary School." In *Early Works*, Vol. 5. Ed. Jo Ann Boydston, 224–43. Carbondale: Southern Illinois University Press, 1972.

———. *The Public and Its Problems*. 1927. Athens, Ohio: Swallow Press: 1954.

Dibble, Vernon K. "The Young Charles Cooley and His Father: A Sceptical Note about Psychobiographies." *Journal of the History of Sociology* 4 (1982): 1–26.

Dodd, C.H. *The Apostolic Preaching and Its Developments*. New York: Harper and Row, 1964.

Donsbach, Wolfgang, ed. *The International Encyclopedia of Communication*. Malden, Mass. and Oxford: Blackwell, 2008.

Douglas, Susan J. *Listening In: Radio and the American Imagination*. New York: Times Books, 1999.

———. "*Personal Influence* and the Bracketing of Women's History." *Annals of the American Academy of Political and Social Science* 608 (2006): 41–50.

Durkheim, Emile. *The Elementary Forms of Religious Life*. Trans. Karen E. Fields. New York: Free Press, 1995.

Eberly, Rosa. *Citizen Critics: Literary Public Spheres*. Urbana: University of Illinois Press, 2000.

Eitner, Walter. *Walt Whitman's Western Jaunt*. Lawrence: Regents Press of Kansas, 1981.

Ellwood, Charles. *A History of Social Philosophy*. 1938. New York: Prentice Hall, 1969.

Emerson, Ralph Waldo. "Eloquence" (1847), rpt. in *Complete Works*, Vol. 7, 61–100. Boston: Houghton Mifflin, 1870.

———. *Representative Men: Seven Lectures*. Boston: Houghton Mifflin, 1876.

Engels, Donald. *Roman Corinth: An Alternative Model for the Classical City*. Chicago: University of Chicago Press, 1990.

Epp, Eldon Jay. "New Testament Papyrus Manuscripts and Letter Carrying in Greco-Roman Times." In *The Future of Early Christianity*. Ed. Birger A. Pearson, 35–56. Minneapolis, Minn.: Fortress Press, 1991.

Eriksson, Anders, Thomas H. Olbricht, and Walter Übelacker, eds. *Rhetorical Argumentation in Biblical Texts*. Harrisburg, Penn.: Trinity Press International, 2002.

Erkkila, Betsy. *Whitman: The Political Poet*. New York: Oxford University Press, 1989.

Erns, Robert. *Weakness Is a Crime: The Life of Bernarr Macfadden*. Syracuse: Syracuse University Press, 1991.

Faye, Cathy. "Governing the Grapevine: The Study of Rumor during World War II." *History of Psychology* 10 (2007): 1–21.

Feeley-Harnik, Gillian. *The Lord's Table: Eucharist and Passover in Early Christianity*. Philadelphia: University of Pennsylvania Press, 1981.

Finkel, William L. "Walt Whitman's Manuscript Notes on Oratory." *American Literature* 22 (1950): 29–53.

Fiorenza, Elisabeth Schüssler. "Rhetorical Situation and Historical Reconstruction in 1 Corinthians." *New Testament Studies* 33 (1987): 386–403.

Folsom, Ed. *Walt Whitman's Native Representations*. Cambridge: Cambridge University Press, 1994.

———. "What Do We Represent? Walt Whitman, Representative Democracy, and Democratic Representation." Presidential Lecture, the University of Iowa, Iowa City, February 15, 1998.

Foner, Eric, and John A. Garraty, eds. *The Reader's Companion to American History*. Boston: Houghton Mifflin, 1991.

Ford, Joseph B. "Is There Mass Communication?" *Sociology and Social Research* 37 (1953): 244–50.

Frank, Frederick S., and Anthony S. Magistrale. *The Poe Encyclopedia*. Westport, Conn.: Greenwood Press, 1997.

Fredriksen, Paula. *From Jesus to Christ: The Origins of the New Testament Images of Jesus*. New Haven: Yale University Press, 1988.

Freed, Edwin D. "Christian." In Metzger and Coogan, eds., *Oxford Companion*, 110–11.

Frend, W. H. C. *The Rise of Christianity*. Philadelphia: Fortress Press, 1984.

Gamble, Harry. *Books and Readers in the Early Church: A History of Early Christian Texts*. New Haven: Yale University Press, 1995.

Garland, Robert. *Daily Life of the Ancient Greeks*. Westport, Conn.: Greenwood, 1998.

Gary, Brett. *The Nervous Liberals: Propaganda Anxieties from World War I to the Cold War*. New York: Columbia University Press, 1999.

Gasque, W. Ward. "Tarsus." In *The Anchor Bible Dictionary*, Vol. 6, Ed. David Noel Freedman, 333–34. New York: Doubleday, 1992.

Giddings, Franklin. *The Principles of Sociology: An Analysis of the Phenomena of Association and of Social Organization*. New York: MacMillan, 1896.

Gitlin, Todd. *The Intellectuals and the Flag*. New York: Columbia University Press, 2006.

———. "Media Sociology: The Dominant Paradigm." *Theory and Society* 6 (1978): 205–53.

Given, Mark D. *Paul's True Rhetoric: Ambiguity, Cunning, and Deception in Greece and Rome*. Harrisburg, Penn.: Trinity Press, 2001.

Glander, Timothy. *Origins of Mass Communications Research during the American Cold War*. Mahwah, N.J.: Erlbaum, 2000.

Goldhamer, Joan D. "General Eisenhower in Academe: A Clash of Perspectives and a Study Suppressed." *Journal of the History of the Behavioral Sciences* 33 (1997): 241–59.

Greenspan, Ezra. *Walt Whitman and the American Reader*. Cambridge: Cambridge University Press, 1990.

Grier, Edward F., ed. *Walt Whitman: Notebooks and Unpublished Prose Manuscripts*, 6 vols. New York: New York University Press, 1984.

———. "Walt Whitman's Earliest Known Notebook." *Publication of the Modern Language Association* 83 (1968): 1453–56.

Grünzweig, Walter. "'For America—For All the Earth': Walt Whitman as an International(ist) Poet." In *Breaking Bounds: Whitman and American Cultural Studies*. Eds. Betsy Erkkila and Jay Grossman, 238–50. New York: Oxford University Press, 1996.

Haines-Etizen, Kim. *Guardians of Letters: Literacy, Power, and the Transmitters of Early Christian Literature*. New York: Oxford University Press, 2000.

Hamilton, Walton H. "Charles Horton Cooley." *Journal of Social Forces* 8 (1929–30): 183–87.

Harding, Mark, ed. *Early Christian Life and Thought in Social Context: A Reader*. London: T and T Clark, 2003.

Hardt, Hanno. *Critical Communication Studies: Communication, History and Theory in America*. New York: Routledge, 1992.

———. *Social Theories of the Press: Constituents of Communication Research, 1840s to 1920s*. 2nd ed. Lanham, Md.: Rowman and Littlefield, 2002.

Hartnett, Stephen J. *Democratic Dissent and the Cultural Fictions of Antebellum America*. Urbana: University of Illinois Press, 2002.

Hauser, Gerard A. *Vernacular Voices: The Rhetoric of Publics and Public Spheres*. Columbia: University of South Carolina Press, 1999.

Hays, Richard B. *Echoes of Scripture in the Letters of Paul*. New Haven: Yale University Press, 1989.

Hettinger, Herman. "Broadcasting in the United States." *Annals of the American Academy of Political and Social Science* 177 (1935): 1–14.

Hicks, Granville. *Part of the Truth*. New York: Harcourt Brace: 1965.

Higgins, Andrew C. "Wage Slavery and the Composition of *Leaves of Grass*: The 'Talbot Wilson' Notebook." *Walt Whitman Quarterly Review* 20.2 (2002): 53–77.

Hilmes, Michelle. *Radio Voices: American Broadcasting, 1922–1952*. Minneapolis: University of Minnesota Press, 1997.

Hock, Ronald F. "Paul and Greco-Roman Education." In *Paul in the Greco-Roman World*. Ed. J. Paul Sampley, 198–22. Harrisburg, Penn.: Trinity Press, 2003.

———. *The Social Context of Paul's Ministry: Tentmaking and Apostleship*. Philadelphia: Fortress Press, 1980.

Hollinger, David A. *Cosmopolitanism and Solidarity: Studies in Ethnoracial, Religious, and Professional Affiliation in the United States*. Madison: University of Wisconsin Press, 2006.

———. "The Knower and the Artificer, *with* Postscript 1993." In *Modernist Impulses in the Human Sciences, 1870–1930*. Ed. Dorothy Ross, 26–53. Baltimore: Johns Hopkins University Press, 1994.

———. *Science, Jews, and Secular Culture: Studies in Mid-Twentieth-Century American Intellectual History*. Princeton: Princeton University Press, 1996.

Hollis, C. Carroll. *Language and Style in Leaves of Grass*. Baton Rouge: Louisiana State University Press, 1982.

Holloway, Emory, and Ralph Adimari, eds. *New York Dissected*. New York: Rufus Rockwell Wilson, 1936.

Hoover, Stewart M. *Religion in the Media Age*. New York: Routledge, 2006.

Horsfield, Peter G., Mary E. Herr, and Adán M Medrano, eds. *Belief in Media: Cultural Perspectives on Media and Christianity*. Burlington, Vt.: Ashgate, 2004.

Hughes, Frank Witt. *Early Christian Rhetoric and 2 Thessalonians*, JSNT Supplement Series 30. Sheffield, England: Sheffield Academic Press, 1989.

Hughes, Helen MacGill. *News and the Human Interest Story 1940*. New York: Greenwood, 1968.

Hunt, Morton. "How Does It Come To Be So?" *New Yorker*, 36 (November 28, 1961): 36, 39–63.

Huxley, Julian. *UNESCO: Its Philosophy and Its Purpose*. Washington, D.C.: Public Affairs Press. 1947.

Jackson, John P., Jr. "Blind Law and Powerless Science: The American Jewish Congress, the NAACP, and the Scientific Case against Discrimination, 1945–1950." *Isis* 91 (2000): 89–116.

———. *Social Scientists for Social Justice*. New York: New York University Press, 2001.

Jackson, Wes. *Becoming Native to this Place*. New York: Counterpoint, 1996.

Jacobs, Clyde E. *Law Writers and the Courts: The Influence of Thomas M. Cooley, Christopher G. Tiedeman, and John F. Dillon upon American Constitutional Law*. Berkeley: University of California Press, 1954.

Jacobs, Glenn. *Charles Horton Cooley: Imagining Social Reality*. Amherst: University of Massachusetts Press, 2006.

———. "Influence and Canonical Supremacy: An Analysis of How George Herbert Mead Demoted Charles Horton Cooley in the Sociological Canon." *Journal of the History of the Behavioral Sciences* 45 (2009): 117–144.

Jahoda, Marie, and Patricia Salter West. "Race Relations in Public Housing." *Journal of Social Issues* 7 (1951): 132–39.

James, William. *Writings 1878–1899*. Ed. Gerald E. Myers. New York: Library of America, 1992.

———. *Writings 1902–1910*. Ed. Bruce Kuklick. New York: Library of America, 1987.

Jandy, Edward. *Charles Horton Cooley: His Life and His Social Theory*. New York: Dryden Press, 1942.

Jansen, Sue Curry, "Walter Lippmann: Straw Man of Communication Research." In Park and Pooley, eds., *History of Media*, 77–112.

Jasinski, James. *Sourcebook on Rhetoric: Key Concepts in Contemporary Rhetorical Studies*. Thousand Oaks, Calif.: Sage, 2001.

Jensen, Joli. *Is Art Good for Us? Beliefs about High Culture in American Life*. Lanham, Md: Rowman and Littlefield, 2002.

Johnston, Barry V. *Pitirim Sorokin: An Intellectual Biography*. Lawrence: University of Kansas Press, 1995.

Jones, Alan R. *The Constitutional Conservatism of Thomas McIntyre Cooley: A Study in the History of Ideas*. 1960. New York: Garland Publishing, 1987.

Judge, E. A. "Paul's Boasting in Relation to Contemporary Professional Practice," *Australian Biblical Review* (October 16, 1968): 37–50.

Kadushin, Charles. "Too Much Investment in Social Capital?" *Social Networks* 26 (2004): 75–90.

Kantorowicz, Ernst. *The King's Two Bodies: A Study in Mediaeval Political Theology*. Princeton, N.J.: Princeton University Press, 1957.

Kaplan, Justin. *Walt Whitman: A Life*. New York: Simon and Schuster, 1980.

Karabel, Jerome. "Status-Group Struggle, Organizational Interests, and the Limits of Institutional Autonomy: The Transformation of Harvard, Yale, and Princeton, 1918–1940." *Theory and Society* 13 (1984): 1–40.

Kateb, George. *The Inner Ocean: Individualism and Democratic Culture*. Ithaca: Cornell University Press, 1992.

Katz, Elihu, and Paul F. Lazarsfeld. *Personal Influence: The Part Played by People in the Flow of Mass Communication*. New Brunswick, N.J.: Transaction, 2006.

Katz, Elihu, John Durham Peters, Tamar Liebes, and Arvill Orloff, eds. *Canonic Texts in Media Research: Are There Any? Should There Be? How about These?* Cambridge: Polity, 2003.

Kennedy, George A. *New Testament Interpretation through Rhetorical Criticism*. Chapel Hill: University of North Carolina Press, 1984.

Kinneavy, James L. *Greek Rhetorical Origins of Christian Faith: An Inquiry*. New York: Oxford University Press, 1987.

Klingenstein, Susanne. *Jews in the American Academy, 1900–1940: The Dynamics of Intellectual Assimilation*. New Haven: Yale University Press, 1991.

Kniffen, Fred. "The American Agricultural Fair: The Pattern." *Annals of the Association of American Geographers* 39 (1949): 264–82.

Krieg, Joann. *A Whitman Chronology*. Iowa City: University of Iowa Press, 1998.

Lang, Bernhard. *Sacred Games: A History of Christian Worship*. New Haven: Yale University Press, 1997.

Lasswell, Harold D. *Propaganda Technique in the World War*. New York: A. A. Knopf, 1927.

Lasswell, Harold D., Ralph D. Casey, and Bruce Lannes Smith. *Propaganda and Promotional Activities: An Annotated Bibliography*. Minneapolis: University of Minnesota Press, 1935.

———, *Propaganda, Communication, and Public Opinion: A Comprehensive Research Guide*. Princeton, N.J.: Princeton University Press, 1946.

Latour, Bruno. "From Realpolitik to Dingpolitik or How to Make Things Public." In Latour and Weibel, eds., *Making Things Public*.

Latour, Bruno. and Peter Weibel, eds. *Making Things Public: Atmospheres of Democracy*. Cambridge, Mass.: MIT Press, 2005.

Lazarsfeld, Paul F. "Administrative and Critical Research." 1941. In Peters and Simonson, *Mass Communication and American Social Thought*, 166–73.

———. "Working with Merton." In Coser, *The Idea of Social Structure*, 35–66.

Lazarsfeld, Paul F., and Robert K. Merton. "Mass Communication, Popular Taste, and Organized Social Action." In *The Communication of Ideas*. Ed. Lyman Bryson, 95–118. New York: Harper, 1948.

———. "Studies in Radio and Film Propaganda." *Transactions of the New York Academy of Sciences* 2:6 (1943): 58–79. Reprinted in all editions of *Social Theory and Social Structure*.

Leff, Michael. "Hermeneutical Rhetoric." In *Rhetoric and Hermeneutics in Our Time*.

Eds. Walter Jost and Michael J. Hyde. 196–214. New Haven: Yale University Press, 1997.

LeMaster, J. R., and Donald D. Kummings, eds. *Walt Whitman: An Encyclopedia.* New York: Garland, 1998.

Levine, Stuart, and Susan F. Levine, eds. *The Short Fiction of Edgar Allen Poe.* Urbana: University of Illinois Press, 1989.

Levy, Mark R. "The Lazarsfeld-Stanton Program Analyzer: An Historical Note." *Journal of Communication* 32:4 (1982): 30–38.

Lewis, Tom. *Empire of the Air: The Men Who Made Radio.* New York: HarperCollins, 1991.

Lippmann, Walter. *Public Opinion.* 1925. New York: Free Press, 1997.

Lloyd, Rosemary, ed. *The Cambridge Companion to Baudelaire.* Cambridge: Cambridge University Press, 2005.

Loving, Jerome. "'Broadway, the Magnificent!' A Newly Discovered Whitman Essay." *Walt Whitman Quarterly Review* 12:4 (1995): 209–16.

———. *Walt Whitman: The Song of Himself.* Berkeley: University of California Press, 1999.

Lutz, Tom. *Doing Nothing: A History of Loafers, Loungers, Slackers, and Bums in America.* New York: Farrar, Straus and Giroux, 2006.

Lyons, Eugene. *David Sarnoff: A Biography.* New York: Harper and Row, 1966.

MacDonald, Margaret. *Early Christian Women and Pagan Opinion: The Power of the Hysterical Woman.* Cambridge: Cambridge University Press, 1996.

Mailloux, Steven. *Reception Histories: Rhetoric, Pragmatism, and American Cultural Politics.* Ithaca: Cornell University Press, 1998.

———. "Re-Marking Slave Bodies: Rhetoric as Production and Reception." *Philosophy and Rhetoric* 35 (2002): 96–119.

———, ed. *Rhetoric, Sophistry, Pragmatism.* Cambridge: Cambridge University Press, 1995.

Marchand, Phillip. *Marshall McLuhan: The Medium and the Messenger.* New York: Ticknor and Fields, 1989.

Marchand, Roland. *Creating the Corporate Soul: The Rise of Public Relations and Corporate Imagery in American Big Business.* Berkeley: University of California Press, 1998.

Martin, Dale. *The Corinthian Body.* New Haven: Yale University Press, 1995.

Marvin, Carolyn. "The Body of the Text: Literacy's Corporeal Constant." *Quarterly Journal of Speech* 80 (1994): 129–49.

Marx, Karl, and Friedrich Engels. "Manifesto of the Communist Party." In *The Marx-Engels Reader,* 2nd ed. Ed. Robert C. Tucker, 469–500. New York: Norton, 1978.

Mattelart, Armand. *The Invention of Communication.* Trans. Susan Emanuel. Minneapolis: University of Minnesota Press, 1996.

Matthews, Samuel W. "America Goes to the Fair." *National Geographic* 105:3 (September 1954): 293–333.

McChesney, Robert W. *Rich Media, Poor Democracy: Communication Politics in Dubious Times*. Urbana: University of Illinois Press, 1999.

——. *Telecommunications, Mass Media, and Democracy: The Battle for the Control of U.S. Broadcasting, 1928–1935*. New York: Oxford University Press, 1993.

McCormack, Naomi. *Out of the Question: Women, Media, and the Art of Inquiry*. Philadelphia: Annenberg School for Communication, 2009. Documentary film.

McCullough, David Willis. "Kenneth Clark: A Quiet Man Who Made a Difference." *Hastings Historian* 36 (Winter 2006): 1–5.

McKeon, Richard. *Rhetoric: Essays in Invention and Discovery*. Ed. Mark Backman. Woodbridge, Conn.: Ox Bow Press, 1987.

McKeon, Richard, Robert K. Merton, and Walter Gellhorn. *The Freedom to Read: Perspective and Program*. New York: R.R. Bowker Company, 1957.

McLuhan, Marshall. *The Gutenberg Galaxy: The Making of Typographic Man*. Toronto: University of Toronto Press, 1962.

——. *Understanding Media*. 1964. Cambridge, Mass.: MIT Press, 1994.

McMahon, William. *South Jersey Towns: History and Legend*. New Brunswick, N.J.: Rutgers University Press, 1973.

Mead, George Herbert. "Cooley's Contribution to American Social Thought." *American Journal of Sociology* 35 (1930): 693–706.

Meeks, Wayne A. *The First Urban Christians: The Social World of the Apostle Paul*. New Haven: Yale University Press, 1983.

Meinardus, Otto F. A. *St. Paul in Ephesus and the Cities of Galatia and Cyprus*. Athens, Greece: Lycabettus Press, 1973.

——. *St. Paul in Greece*. New Rochelle, NY: Caratzas Brothers, 1979.

——. *St. Paul's Last Journey*. New Rochelle, N.Y.: Caratzas Bros, 1978.

Merton, Robert K. "Alvin W. Gouldner: Genesis and Growth of a Friendship." *Theory and Society* 11 (1982): 915–38.

——. "Discussion of Talcott Parsons, 'The Position of Sociological Theory.'" *American Sociological Review* 13 (1947): 164–68.

——. "Durkheim's *Division of Labor in Society*." *American Journal of Sociology* 40 (1934): 319–28.

——. "'Durkheim's *Division of Labor in Society*': A Sexagenarian Postscript." *Sociological Forum* 9 (1994): 27–36.

——. "Epistolary Notes on the Making of a Sociological Dissertation Classic: *The Dynamics of Bureaucracy*." In *Structures of Power and Constraint: Papers in Honor of Peter M. Blau*. Eds. Craig Calhoun, Marshall W. Meyer, and W. Richard Scott, 37–66. Cambridge: Cambridge University Press, 1990.

——. "Fact and Factitiousness in Ethnic Opinionnaires." *American Sociological Review* 5 (1940): 13–28.

——. "George Sarton: Episodic Recollections by an Unruly Apprentice." In *The History of Science and the New Humanism*, by George Sarton, vii–xlvi. New Brunswick, N.J.: Transaction Books, 1988.

———. "Intermarriage and the Social Structure." *Psychiatry* 4 (1941): 361–74.

———. Introduction, *New York Television, January 4–10, 1951, 1952*, by Dallas W. Smythe. Urbana, Ill.: National Association of Educational Broadcasters, 1952.

———. "A Life of Learning," the Charles Homer Haskins Lecture, *American Council of Learned Societies Occasional Paper 25* (1994). Reprinted in *On Social Structure and Science*, 339–59.

———. "The Matthew Effect in Science: The Reward and Communications Systems of Science are Considered." *Science 199* (January 5, 1968): 55–63.

———. "A Note on Science and Democracy." *Journal of Legal and Political Sociology* 1 (1942): 115–26. Reprinted as "Science and Democratic Social Structure" in all editions of *Social Theory and Social Structure*.

———. "On the Oral Transmission of Knowledge." In *Sociological Traditions from Generation to Generation: Glimpses of the American Experience*. Eds. Merton and Matilda White Riley, 1–35. Norwood, N.J.: Ablex, 1980.

———. "On the Origins of the Term: *Pseudo-Gemeinschaft*." *Western Sociological Review* 6 (1975): 83.

———. *On the Shoulders of Giants: A Shandean Postscript*. Chicago: University of Chicago Press, 1993.

———. *On Social Structure and Science*. Ed. Piotr Sztompka. Chicago: University of Chicago Press, 1996.

———. "Patterns of Influence: A Study of Interpersonal Influence and Communications Behavior in a Local Community." In *Communications Research, 1948–49*. Eds. Paul F. Lazarsfeld and Frank Stanton, 180–219. New York: Harper and Brothers, 1949.

———. "Recent French Sociology." *Social Forces* 12 (1934): 537–45.

———. "Science and the Social Order." *Philosophy of Science* 5 (1938): 321–37.

———. *Science, Technology, and Society in Seventeenth-Century England*. 1938. New York: Howard Fertig Publishers, 1970/2001.

———. "Selected Problems of Field Work in the Planned Community." *American Sociological Review* 12 (1947): 304–12.

———. "The Social Psychology of Housing." In *Current Trends in Social Psychology*. Ed. Wayne Dennis, 163–217. Pittsburgh: University of Pittsburgh Press, 1948.

———. *Sociological Ambivalence*. New York: Free Press, 1976.

———. "The Sociology of Knowledge." *Isis* 28 (1937): 493–503.

———. *The Sociology of Science: Theoretical and Empirical Investigations*. Ed. Norman W. Storer. Chicago: University of Chicago Press, 1973.

———. "Some Thoughts on the Concept of Sociological Autobiography." In *Sociological Lives: Social Change and the Life Course*. Ed. Matilda White Riley, 17–21. Newbury Park, Calif.: Sage, 1988.

———. "The Sorokin-Merton Correspondence, 1933–34." *Science in Context* 3 (1989): 293–300.

———. "Texts, Contexts and Subtexts: An Epistolary Forward." In *The Grammar of*

Social Relations, by Louis Schneider, ix–xlv. New Brunswick, N.J.: Transaction Books, 1984.

———. "Three Fragments from a Sociologist's Notebooks: Establishing the Phenomenon, Specified Ignorance, and Strategic Research Materials." *Annual Review of Sociology* 13 (1987): 1–28.

———. "The Unanticipated Consequences of Purposive Social Action." *American Sociological Review* 1 (1936): 894–904.

———. "Working with Lazarsfeld: Notes and Contexts." In *Paul Lazarsfeld (1901–1976): La sociologie de Vienne à New York*. Eds. Jacque Lautman and Bernard-Pierre Lécuyer, 16–211. Paris: L'Harmattan: 1998.

Merton, Robert K., and Bernard Barber. "Sorokin's Formulations in the Sociology of Science." In *Pitirim A. Sorokin in Review*. Ed. Philip J. Allen. Durham, N.C.: Duke University Press, 1963.

Merton, Robert K., and Elinor Barber. *The Travels and Adventures of Serendipity*. Princeton, N.J.: Princeton University Press, 2004.

Merton, Robert K., with Marjorie Fiske, and Alberta Curtis. *Mass Persuasion: The Social Psychology of a War Bond Drive*. 1946. New York: Howard Fertig Publishers, 2004.

Merton, Robert K., and Patricia Kendall. "The Boomerang Response: The Audience Acts as Co-Author—Whether You Like It Or Not." *Channels* 21: 7 (1944): 1–4, 15–18.

———. "The Focused Interview." *American Journal of Sociology*, 51 (1946): 541–57.

Merton, Robert K., and Robert A. Nisbet, eds. *Contemporary Social Problems: An Introduction to the Sociology of Deviant Behavior and Social Disorganization*. New York: Harcourt, Brace and World, 1961.

Merton, Robert K., Patricia Salter West, and Marie Jahoda. *Patterns of Social Life: Explorations in the Sociology of Housing*. Unpublished manuscript, Bureau of Applied Social Research, Columbia University: 1951.

Metzger, Bruce M., and Michael D. Coogan, eds. *The Oxford Companion to the Bible*. New York: Oxford University Press, 1993.

Metzger, Bruce M., and Roland E. Murphy, eds. *The New Oxford Annotated Bible*. New York: Oxford University Press, 1994.

Mills, C. Wright. *The Sociological Imagination*. New York: Oxford University Press, 1959.

Mitchell, Margaret Mary. *Paul and the Rhetoric of Reconciliation: An Exegetical Investigation of the Language and Composition of 1 Corinthians*. Tübingen: Mohr, 1991.

Morgan, David, ed. *Keywords in Religion, Media, and Culture*. New York: Routledge, 2008.

Morgan, Teresa. *Literate Education in the Hellenistic and Roman Worlds*. Cambridge: Cambridge University Press, 1998.

Morris, Nathan. *The Jewish School*. New York: Jewish Education Committee Press, 1964.

Morrison, David E. "The Influences Influencing *Personal Influence*: Scholarship and Entrepeneurship." *Annals of the American Academy of Political and Social Science* 608 (2006): 51–75.

———. "Opportunity Structures and the Creation of Knowledge: Paul Lazarsfeld and the Politics of Research." In Park and Pooley, eds., *History of Media*, 179–203.

———. *The Search for a Method: Focus Groups and the Development of Mass Communication Research*. Luton, U.K.: University of Luton Press, 1998.

Moynagh, Patricia. "A Politics of Enlarged Mentality: Hannah Arendt, Citizenship Responsibility, and Feminism." Hypatia 12:4 (1997): 27–54.

Munson, Eve Stryker, and Catherine A. Warren, eds. *James Carey: A Critical Reader*. Minneapolis: University of Minnesota Press, 1997.

Murphy-O'Connor, Jerome. "House-Churches and the Eucharist." In *Christianity at Corinth: The Quest for the Pauline Church*, Eds. Edward Adams and David G. Horrell, 129–38. Louisville, Ky.: Westminster John Knox Press, 2004.

———. *Paul: A Critical Life*. Oxford: Clarendon Press, 1996.

Neely, Wayne Caldwell. *The Agricultural Fair*. New York: Columbia University Press, 1935.

Nerone, John. "The Future of Communication History." *Critical Studies in Media Communication* 23 (2006): 254–62.

———. "The Mythology of the Penny Press." *Critical Studies in Mass Communication* 4 (1987): 376–404.

Noble, David. *The Paradox of Progressive Thought*. St. Paul: University of Minnesota Press, 1958.

Nord, David Paul. *Communities of Journalism: A History of American Newspapers and Their Readers*. Urbana: University of Illinois Press, 2001.

Nordenstreng, Kaarle. "Institutional Networking: The Story of the International Association for Media and Communication Research (IAMCR)." In Park and Pooley, eds., *History of Media*, 225–48.

Ong, Walter. *Orality and Literacy: The Technologizing of the Word*. New York: Methuen, 1982.

Packer Jeremy, and Craig Robertson, eds. *Thinking with James Carey: Essays on Communications, Transportation, History*. New York: Peter Lang, 2006.

Park, David W., and Jefferson Pooley, eds. *The History of Media and Communication Research: Contested Memories*. New York: Peter Lang, 2008.

Perelman, Chaim, and Lucie Olbrechts-Tyteca. *The New Rhetoric: A Treatise on Argumentation*. Trans. John Wilkinson and Purcell Weaver. Notre Dame: University of Notre Dame Press, 1969.

Peters, John Durham. *Courting the Abyss: Free Speech and the Liberal Tradition*. Chicago: University of Chicago Press, 2005.

———. *Speaking into the Air: A History of the Idea of Communication*. Chicago: University of Chicago Press, 1999.

———. "The Uncanniness of Communication in Interwar Social Thought." *Journal of Communication* 46:3 (1996): 108–23.

———. "Witnessing." *Media, Culture and Society* 23 (2001): 707–24.

Peters, John Durham, and Peter Simonson, eds. *Mass Communication and American Social Thought: Key Texts, 1919–1968*. Lanham, Md.: Rowman and Littlefield, 2004.

Platt, Jennifer. "The United States Reception of Durkheim's *The Rules of Sociological Method*," *Sociological Perspectives* 38 (1995): 77–105.

Poe, Edgar Allen. *The Short Fiction of Edgar Allen Poe*. Eds. Stuart Levine and Susan F. Levine. Urbana: University of Illinois Press, 1989.

Pooley, Jefferson. "Daniel Czitrom, James W. Carey, and the Chicago School." *Critical Studies in Media Communication* 24 (2007): 469–72.

———. "Fifteen Pages That Shook the Field: *Personal Influence*, Edward Shils, and the Remembered History of Mass Communication Research." *Annals of the American Academy of Political and Social Science* 608 (2006): 130–56.

Poster, Carol. "The Economy of Letter Writing in Graeco-Roman Antiquity." In Eriksson et al., eds., *Rhetorical Argumentation*, 112–24.

Poulakos, John. *Sophistical Rhetoric in Classical Greece*. Columbia, S.C.: University of South Carolina Press, 1995.

Prosterman, Leslie. *Ordinary Life, Festival Days: Aesthetics in the Midwestern County Fair*. Washington, D.C.: Smithsonian Institution Press, 1995.

Putnam, Robert D. *Bowling Alone: The Collapse and Revival of American Community*. New York: Simon and Schuster, 2000.

Quandt, Jean. *From the Small Town to the Great Community: The Social Thought of Progressive Intellectuals*. New Brunswick, N.J.: Rutgers University Press, 1970.

Quintilian. *Institutio Oratoria*. 4 vols. Trans. H. E. Butler. Cambridge: Harvard University Press, 1920.

Ramsaran, Rollin A. *Liberating Words: Paul's Use of Rhetorical Maxims in 1 Corinthians 1–10*. Valley Forge, Penn.: Trinity Press, 1996.

Rappaport, Roy. *Ritual and Religion in the Making of Humanity*. Cambridge: Cambridge University Press, 1999.

Rapske, B. M. "Christians and the Roman Empire." In *Dictionary of the Later New Testament and Its Developments*. Eds. Ralph P. Martin and Peter H. Davids, 1059–63. Downers Grover, Ill.: InterVarsity Press, 1997.

Reiss, Albert J., ed. *Cooley and Sociological Analysis*. Ann Arbor: University of Michigan Press, 1968.

Reynolds, David S. *Walt Whitman's America: A Cultural Biography*. New York: Knopf, 1995.

Rice, Stuart A. "Quantitative Methods in Politics." *Journal of the American Statistical Association* 33 (1938): 126–30.

Richards, E. Randolph. *The Secretary in the Letters of Paul*. WUNT 42. Tübingen: Mohr, 1991.

Rieff, Philip. *The Feeling Intellect: Selected Writings*. Ed. Jonathan B. Imber. Chicago: University of Chicago Press, 1990.

Riegel, O. W. "Nationalism in Press, Radio and Cinema." *American Sociological Review* 3 (1938): 510–15.

Riesner, Rainer. *Paul's Early Period: Chronology, Mission, Strategy, Theology*. Grand Rapids, Mich.: Eerdmans, 1998.

Robbins, Joel. "Ritual Communication and Linguistic Ideology: A Reading and Partial Reformulation of Rappaport's Theory of Ritual." *Current Anthropology* 42 (2001): 591–614.

Robertson, Michael. *Worshipping Walt: The Whitman Disciples*. Princeton: Princeton University Press, 2008.

Roetzel, Calvin J. *Paul: The Man and the Myth*. Columbia, S.C.: University of South Carolina Press, 1998.

Rogers, Everett M. *A History of Communication Study: A Biographical Approach*. New York: Free Press, 1994.

Rogow, Arnold A., ed. *Politics, Personality, and Social Science in the Twentieth Century: Essays in Honor of Harold D. Lasswell*. Chicago: University of Chicago Press, 1969.

Rorty, Richard. *Achieving Our Country: Leftist Thought in Twentieth-Century America*. Cambridge: Harvard University Press, 1998.

———. "Inquiry as Recontextualization." In *Objectivism, Relativism, and Truth: Philosophical Papers* Vol. 1. Cambridge: Cambridge University Press 1991.

Rosenthal, Herman, Judah David Eisenstein, and A. S. Waldstein. "Lemberg." *The Jewish Encyclopedia* (1901–1906), rpt. at http://www.jewishencyclopedia.com/view .jsp?artid=175&letter=L&search=Lemberg (accessed October 2, 2006).

Ross, Dorothy. *The Origins of American Social Science*. Cambridge: Cambridge University Press, 1991.

Ross, Edward Aylsworth. *Social Control*. 1901. New York: Johnson Reprint Corporation, 1970.

Rothaus, Richard M. *Corinth: The First City of Greece: An Urban History of Late Antique Cult and Religion*. Leiden: Brill, 2000.

Rothenbuhler, Eric W. "Community and Pluralism in Wirth's 'Consensus and Mass Communication.'" In Katz et al., eds., *Canonic Texts in Media Research*, 106–20.

———. *Ritual Communication: From Everyday Conversation to Mediated Ceremony*. Thousand Oaks, Calif.: Sage, 1998.

Rubenstein, Hilary L., Dan Cohn-Sherbok, Abraham J. Edelheit, and William D. Rubinstein. *The Jews in the Modern World: A History since 1750*. London: Arnold, 2002.

Rubin, Joseph Jay. *The Historic Whitman*. University Park: Penn State University Press, 1973.

Rubin, Joseph Jay, and Charles H. Brown. *Walt Whitman and the New York Aurora: Editor at Twenty-Two*. State College, Penn.: Bald Eagle Press, 1950.

Ryan, Mary P. *Civic Wars: Democracy and Public Life in the American City during the Nineteenth Century*. Berkeley: University of California Press, 1997.

Saldarini, Anthony J. "Pharisees," In *The Anchor Bible Dictionary*, Vol. 5. Ed. David Noel Freedman, 294, 300–304. New York: Doubleday, 1992.

Sampley, J. Paul, ed. *Paul in the Greco-Roman World*. Harrisburg, Penn.: Trinity Press, 2003.

Sanders, E. P. *Paul: A Very Short Introduction*. New York: Oxford University Press, 1991.

Sarna, Jonathan D. *American Judaism: A History*. New Haven: Yale University Press, 2004.

Sarnoff, David. *Looking Ahead: The Papers of David Sarnoff*. New York: McGraw Hill, 1968.

———. "Possible Social Effects of Television." *Annals of the American Academy of Political and Social Science* 213 (1941): 145–52.

———. *The Voice of America and Freedom to Listen*. New York: Radio Corporation of America, 1947.

Scannell, Paddy. *Media and Communication*. Los Angeles: Sage, 2007.

———. "*Personal Influence* and the End of the Masses." In Simonson, ed., *Annals*. 115–29.

Schaefer, R. Murray. *The Soundscape: Our Sonic Environment and the Tuning of the World*. 1977. Rochester, Vt.: Destiny Books, 1994.

Schiappa, Edward. *Protagoras and Logos: A Study in Greek Philosophy and Rhetoric*, 2nd ed. Columbia, SC: University of South Carolina Press, 2003.

Schiller, Dan. *Theorizing Communication: A History*. New York: Oxford University Press, 1996.

Schnapp, Jeffrey T., and Matthew Tiews, eds. *Crowds*. Stanford: Stanford University Press, 2006.

Schoeps, H.J. *Paul: The Theology of the Apostle in the Light of Jewish Religious History*. Trans. Harold Knight. Philadelphia: Westminster Press, 1961.

Schramm, Wilbur, ed. *Mass Communications*. Urbana: University of Illinois Press, 1949.

Schubert, Hans-Joachim. *Democratische Identität: Der Soziologische Pragmatismus von Charles Horton Cooley*. Frankfurt am Main, Germany: Suhrkamp, 1995.

———. "The Foundations of Pragmatic Sociology: Charles Horton Cooley and George Herbert Mead." *Journal of Classical Sociology* 6 (2006): 51–74.

Schudson, Michael. *Discovering the News: A Social History of American Newspapers*. New York: Basic Books, 1978.

Schwartz, Barry. "Emerson, Cooley, and the American Heroic Vision." *Symbolic Interaction* 8 (1985): 103–19.

Schwock, James. *The American Radio and Its Latin American Activities, 1900–1939*. Urbana: University of Illinois Press, 1990.

Shiner, Whitney. *Proclaiming the Gospel: First-Century Performance of Mark*. Harrisburg, Penn.: Trinity Press International, 2003.

Sica, Alan. "Robert K. Merton." In *Key Sociological Thinkers*. Ed. Rob Stones, 111–23. New York: New York University Press, 1998.

Signorelli, Nancy, ed. *Women in Communication: A Biographical Sourcebook*. Westport, Conn.: Greenwood, 1996.

Simonson, Peter. "Assembly, Rhetoric, and Widespread Community: Mass Communication in Paul of Tarsus." *Journal of Media and Religion* 2 (2003): 165–82.

———. Introduction, *Mass Persuasion: The Social Psychology of a War Bond Drive*, by Robert K. Merton, xi–xlix. New York: Howard Fertig, 2004.

———. "Merton's Sociology of Rhetoric." in Calhoun, ed., *Robert K. Merton*.

———, ed. "Politics, Social Networks, and the History of Mass Communications Research: Rereading *Personal Influence.*" *Annals of the American Academy of Political and Social Science* 608 (2006).

———. "Public Image, Celebrity, and American Political Life: Re-reading Robert K. Merton's *Mass Persuasion.*" *Political Communication* (2006): 271–84.

———. "A Rhetoric for Polytheistic Democracy: Walt Whitman's 'Poem of Many in One.'" *Philosophy and Rhetoric* 36 (2003): 353–75.

———. "The Serendipity of Merton's Communications Research." *International Journal of Public Opinion Research* 17 (2005): 277–97.

———. "Writing Figures into the Field: The Parts Played by People in Our Histories of Media Research." In Park and Pooley, eds., *History of Media*, 291–320.

Simonson, Peter, and Gabriel Weimann. "Critical Research at Columbia: Lazarsfeld's and Merton's 'Mass Communication, Popular Taste, and Organized Social Action.'" In Katz et al., *Canonic Texts in Media Research*, 12–38.

Simpson, Christopher. *Science of Coercion: Communication Research and Psychological Warfare, 1945–1960*. New York: Oxford University Press, 1994.

Simpson, George E. *The Negro in the Philadelphia Press*. Philadelphia: University of Pennsylvania Press, 1936.

Sklansky, Jeffrey. *The Soul's Economy: Market Society and Selfhood in American Thought, 1820–1920*. Chapel Hill: University of North Carolina Press, 2002.

Slezkine, Yuri. *The Jewish Century*. Princeton, N.J.: Princeton University Press, 2004.

Sloane, Thomas O., ed. *The Encyclopedia of Rhetoric*. New York: Oxford University Press, 2001.

———. *On the Contrary: The Protocol of Traditional Rhetoric*. Washington, D.C.: Catholic University Press, 1997.

Sloterdijk, Peter. *Critique of Cynical Reason*, Trans. Michael Eldred. Minneapolis: University of Minnesota Press, 1987.

Small, Albion. Review of Albert Schäffle, *Bau und Leben des socialen Korpers*. *American Journal of Sociology* 2 (1896): 310–15.

Small, Albion, and George Vincent. *Introduction to the Study of Society*. New York: American Book Company, 1894.

Sorokin, Pitirim A. *Leaves from a Russian Diary—and Thirty Years After*. Boston: Beacon Press, 1950.

———. *Social and Cultural Dynamics: Fluctuation of Systems of Truth, Ethics, and Law*. 2 vols. New York: American Book Company, 1937.

Sproule, J. Michael. *Propaganda and Democracy: The American Experience of Media and Mass Persuasion*. Cambridge: Cambridge University Press, 1997.

Stanley, Christopher D. *Arguing With Scripture: The Rhetoric of Quotations in the Letters of Paul*. New York: T and T Clark, 2004.

Stark, Rodney. *One True God: Historical Consequences of Monotheism*. Princeton, N.J.: Princeton University Press, 2001.

Steel, Ronald. *Walter Lippmann and the American* Century. New York: Little Brown, 1980.

Stegemann, Ekkehard W., and Wolfgang Stegemann. *The Jesus Movement: A Social History of its First Century*. Minneapolis: Fortress Press, 1995.

Stern, Bernhard, ed. *The Letters of Albion W. Small to Lester F. Ward*. Baltimore: Waverly Press, 1937.

Stout, Jeffrey. *Democracy and Tradition*. Princeton, N.J.: Princeton University Press, 2004.

Sullivan, Dale L. "Kairos and the Rhetoric of Belief." *Quarterly Journal of Speech* 78 (1992): 317–32.

Sussmann, Leila A. *Dear FDR: A Study of Political Letter-Writing*. Totowa, N.J.: Bedminster Press, 1963.

Sztompka, Piotr. *Robert K. Merton: An Intellectual Profile*. New York: St. Martin's, 1988.

Tarde, Gabriel. *On Communication and Social Influence*. Ed. Terry N. Clark. Chicago: University of Chicago Press, 1969.

Taylor, Charles. *Sources of the Self: The Making of the Modern Identity*. Cambridge: Harvard University Press, 1989.

Tenney, Alvan A. "The Scientific Analysis of the Press." *The Independent* 73 (October, 17, 1912): 895–98.

Thackray, Arnold, and Robert K. Merton. "On Discipline Building: The Paradoxes of George Sarton." *Isis* 63 (1972): 473–95.

Theissen, Gerd. *The Social Setting of Pauline Christianity: Essays on Corinth*. Philadelphia: Fortress Press, 1982.

Traubel, Horace L., Richard Maurice Bucke, and Thomas B. Harned, eds. *In Re Walt Whitman*. Philadelphia: David McKay, 1893.

Vos, Johan S. "'To Make the Weaker Argument Defeat the Stronger': Sophistical Argumentation in Paul's letter to the Romans." In Eriksson, et al., eds., *Rhetorical Argumentation*, 217–31.

Wallace, Richard, and Wynne Williams. *The Three Worlds of Paul of Tarsus*. London: Routledge, 1998.

Ward, Lester. *Dynamic Sociology*. 2 vols. New York: D. Appleton, 1883.

Weber, Max. *Economy and Society*. 2 vols. Eds. Guenther Roth and Claus Wittich. Berkeley: University of California Press, 1978.

Welch, Kathleen. *Electric Rhetoric: Classical Rhetoric, Oralism, and a New Literacy*. Cambridge, Mass.: MIT Press, 1999.

White, William. "Walt Whitman's Earliest Known Notebook." *Publication of the Modern Language Association* 83 (1968): 1453–56.

Whitfield, Stephen. "Declarations of Independence: American Jewish Culture in the Twentieth Century." In Biale, *Cultures of the Jews*, 1099–46.

Whitman, Walt. *Complete Writings*. Ed. Richard Maurice Bucke, Thomas Biggs

Harned, Horace Traubel, Oscar Lovell Triggs. New York: G. P. Putnam's Sons, 1902.

———. *Daybooks and Notebooks*. 3 vols. Ed. William White. New York: New York University Press, 1977.

———. *Leaves of Grass: The First (1855) Edition*. New York: Penguin, 2005.

———. *Leaves of Grass*. Facsimile edition of the 1860 text. Ithaca: Cornell University Press, 1961

———. *Leaves of Grass and Selected Prose*. Ed. Lawrence Buell. New York: Modern Library, 1981.

———. *Prose Works 1892*. 2 vols. Ed. Floyd Stovall. New York: New York University Press, 1964.

———. "Specimen Days." In *Leaves of Grass and Selected Prose*. Ed. Lawrence Buell. New York: Modern Library, 1981.

———. *The Uncollected Poetry and Prose of Walt Whitman*. 2 vols. Ed. Emory Holloway. New York: Peter Smith, 1932.

Willey, Malcolm M. "Communication Agencies and the Volume of Propaganda." *Annals of the American Academy of Political and Social Science* 179 (1935): 194–200.

———. *The Country Newspaper: A Study of Socialization and Newspaper Content*. Chapel Hill: University of North Carolina Press, 1926.

Willey, Malcolm M., and Stuart A. Rice. *Communication Agencies and Social Life*. New York: McGraw Hill, 1933.

Williams, Raymond. *Culture and Society, 1780–1950*. London: Chatto and Windus, 1958.

Winkler, Allan M. *The Politics of Propaganda: The Office of War Information*. New Haven: Yale University Press, 1978.

Winter, Bruce W. *Philo and Paul Among the Sophists*, 2nd ed. Grand Rapids, Mich.: Eerdmans, 2002.

Winton, Andrew S. "'As His Name Indicates': R. S. Woodworth's Letters of Reference and Employment for Jewish Psychologists in the 1930s." *Journal of the History of the Behavioral Sciences* 32 (1996): 30–43.

Wirth, Louis. "Consensus and Mass Communication." *American Sociological Review* 13 (1948): 1–15.

Wood, Arthur Evans. "Charles Horton Cooley: An Appreciation." *American Journal of Sociology* 35 (1930): 707–17.

Wyant, Rowena. "Voting Via the Senate Mailbag." *Public Opinion Quarterly* 5 (1941): 359–82.

Wyant, Rowena, and Herta Herzog. "Voting Via the Senate Mailbag—Part II." *Public Opinion Quarterly* 5 (1941): 590–624.

Yates, Frances. *The Art of Memory*. 1966. London: Routledge, 1999.

Žižek, Slavoj. *The Puppet and the Dwarf: The Perverse Core of Christianity*. Cambridge, Mass.: MIT Press, 2003.

Zweig, Paul. *Walt Whitman: The Making of the Poet*. New York: Basic Books, 1984.

Index

PETER SIMONSON is an assistant professor
of communication at the University of Colorado
at Boulder.

THE HISTORY OF COMMUNICATION

Selling Free Enterprise: The Business Assault on Labor and Liberalism, 1945–60
Elizabeth A. Fones-Wolf

Last Rights: Revisiting *Four Theories of the Press*   Edited by John C. Nerone

"We Called Each Other Comrade": Charles H. Kerr & Company, Radical Publishers
Allen Ruff

WCFL, Chicago's Voice of Labor, 1926–78   Nathan Godfried

Taking the Risk Out of Democracy: Corporate Propaganda versus Freedom and
Liberty   Alex Carey; edited by Andrew Lohrey

Media, Market, and Democracy in China: Between the Party Line and the Bottom
Line   Yuezhi Zhao

Print Culture in a Diverse America   Edited by James P. Danky and Wayne A. Wiegand

The Newspaper Indian: Native American Identity in the Press, 1820–90
John M. Coward

E. W. Scripps and the Business of Newspapers   Gerald J. Baldasty

Picturing the Past: Media, History, and Photography   Edited by Bonnie Brennen and
Hanno Hardt

Rich Media, Poor Democracy: Communication Politics in Dubious Times
Robert W. McChesney

Silencing the Opposition: Antinuclear Movements and the Media in the Cold War
Andrew Rojecki

Citizen Critics: Literary Public Spheres   Rosa A. Eberly

Communities of Journalism: A History of American Newspapers and Their Readers
David Paul Nord

From Yahweh to Yahoo!: The Religious Roots of the Secular Press   Doug Underwood

The Struggle for Control of Global Communication: The Formative Century   Jill Hills

Fanatics and Fire-eaters: Newspapers and the Coming of the Civil War
Lorman A. Ratner and Dwight L. Teeter Jr.

Media Power in Central America   Rick Rockwell and Noreene Janus

The Consumer Trap: Big Business Marketing in American Life   Michael Dawson

How Free Can the Press Be?   Randall P. Bezanson

Cultural Politics and the Mass Media: Alaska Native Voices   Patrick J. Daley and
Beverly A. James

Journalism in the Movies   Matthew C. Ehrlich

Democracy, Inc.: The Press and Law in the Corporate Rationalization of the Public
Sphere   David S. Allen

Investigated Reporting: Muckrakers, Regulators, and the Struggle over Television
Documentary   Chad Raphael

Women Making News: Gender and the Women's Periodical Press in Britain
Michelle Tusan

Advertising on Trial: Consumer Activism and Corporate Public Relations in the 1930s
Inger Stole

The University of Illinois Press
is a founding member of the
Association of American University Presses.

———————————————————————

University of Illinois Press
1325 South Oak Street
Champaign, IL 61820-6903
www.press.uillinois.edu